VALLEY OF THE GUNS

Top row: Ed Tewksbury, George Wilson, Charlie Meadows, Tom Horn,
Jim Tewksbury. *Bottom row:* John Rhodes, Carter Hazelton, Jim Roberts,
J. D. Houck, ca. 1886. *Courtesy Chris Slosser.*

VALLEY
OF THE
GUNS

THE PLEASANT VALLEY WAR
AND THE TRAUMA OF VIOLENCE

EDUARDO OBREGÓN PAGÁN

UNIVERSITY OF OKLAHOMA PRESS : NORMAN

Library of Congress Cataloging-in-Publication Data

Name: Pagán, Eduardo Obregón, 1960– author.
Title: Valley of the guns : the Pleasant Valley War, and the trauma of violence /
    Eduardo Obregón Pagán.
Description: Norman, OK : University of Oklahoma Press, [2018] | Includes
    bibliographical references and index.
Identifiers: LCCN 2018003951 | ISBN 978-0-8061-6154-9 (hardcover : alk. paper)
Subjects: LCSH: Graham-Tewksbury Feud—Psychological aspects. | Graham-
    Tewksbury Feud—Economic aspects. | Vendetta—Arizona—History. | Frontier
    and pioneer life—Arizona—Pleasant Valley. | Pleasant Valley (Ariz.)—History.
Classification: LCC HV6452.A7 P44 2018 | DDC 979.1/55—dc23
LC record available at https://lccn.loc.gov/2018003951

Copyright © 2018 by the University of Oklahoma Press, Norman, Publishing Division
of the University. Manufactured in the U.S.A.

1 2 3 4 5 6 7 8 9 10

To dedicated and patient teachers who still guide my understanding:

MARÍA MARGARITA OBREGÓN PAGÁN

INEZ UDALL TURLEY

NELL IRVIN PAINTER

CONTENTS

ILLUSTRATIONS

Figures

Maps

Chart, Tables, and Graph

ACKNOWLEDGMENTS

I don't quite remember when I first learned of the Pleasant Valley War. Like many residents of the Salt River Valley, the Mogollon Rim was like a second home in the summertime. As a child, I played in Christopher Creek in the Tonto National Forest, and as a teen, I worked a ranch in the Arizona high country, riding horses with my best friend, Eric Tenney, along the winding trails of the Mogollon Rim. Eric was a descendant of Ammon Tenney, the famed settler of the Mormon colonies along the Little Colorado River. My own family was from a different chapter in Arizona's history, with the Yaqui and the Spanish settlers of southern Arizona. Together, we grew up alongside children from the Salt River, Tohono O'odham, and Navajo reservations. Somehow, somewhere, of the many tales we listened to about Arizona's past, the story of the Pleasant Valley War stood out. It was a curious tale that has long stayed with me, because I never quite understood what the fighting was about, and the story seemed to change with each storyteller. What follows is my attempt to piece together what drove that settlement into a long night of mayhem.

My parents instilled in me a fascination with the deep history of the American Southwest, and some of my earliest memories are of exploring the ancient ruins of Arizona with them. I hope I've passed on some of that to my own children. Stephen Marcus Pagán and Jordan Catherine Pagán were a great help in research-ing, editing, and indexing this manuscript. Ruth Liljenquist generously read, critiqued, and edited the entire manuscript. Marlene Tromp deserves special thanks for her generous support and encouragement all throughout this project, as a friend and as the Dean of the New College at Arizona State University. My New College colleagues Siân Mooney, Tess Neal, Lara Ferry, and Monica Caspar were wonderfully generous with their time in helping me sort through scholarship in economics, psychology, physiology, and trauma studies, respectively. Further, I am especially indebted to Shari Collins, Gloria Cuádraz, Marlene Tromp, Melissa Fitch, and Cameron Trejo for reading and commenting on earlier drafts. I am particularly grateful to Philip VanderMeer and Heidi Osselear for their generous insights and counsel. Of course, I am indebted to Kent Calder, who early on expressed interest in this project, and Daniel Herman, Bryan Cannon, and the anonymous reader, who read and commented on this manuscript for the University of Oklahoma Press with care and attention. And Nancy Warrington deserves particular priase for her patience, humor, and diligence in copyediting this project.

The archivists who provided critical support for this project warrant special recognition: Laura Palma-Blandford, Sara Guzmán, and Wendi Goen at the Arizona State Library, Archives, and Records Management; Renee James at Hayden Library, Arizona State University; Joshua Roffler and Jared Smith of the Tempe History Museum; Mara MacKay, executive director of the Boone History Center; Linda Lopez, director of the Gila County Historical Society Museum; Lynn Lourenco at the Ferndale Museum; and the all-volunteer staff at the Pleasant Valley Historical Society. I am also grateful to Frank Chapman for sharing his collection of historic firearms, and to Robin and Karla Alborn of the Dead Broke Inn for their wonderful hospitality. Thanks also go to Michael and Sheri Lechter for allowing me to explore the historic sites on their property, and to the wranglers at the Cherry Creek Inn for riding with me. Lastly, I thank the good people of Young, Arizona, for their patience and humor as I wandered about their home.

This project could not have been completed without the support from the Center for Critical Inquiry and Cultural Studies, and the Bob Stump Endowment, both at Arizona State University.

VALLEY OF THE GUNS

PROLOGUE

For a moment, their eyes met.

Cicadas in the surrounding mesquite trees, which had obliviously been buzzing their mating songs, were now startled silent by the gunfire. The acrid smell of spent gunpowder hung in the morning air. It was already beginning to grow warm in the Arizona Territory.

What was the dark horseman thinking at that very instant when he had Tom Graham squarely in his rifle sights? What was he waiting for? Why didn't he take the kill shot? His black eyes were generally inscrutable, especially now as he looked down the barrel of his Winchester rifle, held tight against his shoulder, his cheek resting on its smooth wooden stock.

Was the horseman satisfied that Graham's neck wound was mortal? Did he take bitter comfort in knowing that the man splayed out before him on the wagon, gasping for air, would die a slow death as spurts of blood stained his face and blond hair? Or did that dark rider, for the briefest of moments, feel even a fleeting degree of compassion for his old friend looking up at him, now lying helpless on his sacks of grain? Whatever his thoughts, the horseman never spoke of that moment to anyone.

He simply lowered his weapon, spurred his horse, and galloped down the dusty road that led to Pleasant Valley.

INTRODUCTION
AT THE CROSSROADS OF FEAR
AND DEATH

This is the story of a community of homesteaders in territorial Arizona that cracked under the strain of chronic fear. The source of some of their fears they could easily see, but what they could not see drove them to suspicion, accusations, threats, and murder. The line between right and wrong disappeared in a fog of ambiguity as settlers found themselves left with only desperate choices. No "Code of the West" or "Cowboy code of honor" guided them. As their small community descended into madness, and as life hung in the balance, the actions they took to survive a hostile and deadly environment brought out as much ignominy as nobility. Justice was whatever the settlers could impose with underfunded lawmen of limited manpower three days distant by horseback.[1] And when the law arrived, death often rode with these untrained men who charged into situations with weapons cocked and fingers on the trigger. By the time the Pleasant Valley War was over, nineteen men were dead. The four who survived their wounds fled the territory, never to be seen again.[2]

"Anyone attempting at this late date to write the outstanding incidents of this unfortunate chapter in Arizona's history faces a perplexing task," lay historian Will C. Barnes wisely observed in 1931. Forty years had passed since the settlers of Pleasant Valley had taken up arms against each other. At the time of the Pleasant Valley War, Barnes had worked as a range detective in Arizona's north country, tracking lost or stolen livestock. In time, he turned his attention to writing histories of the territory, so when State Historian Effie Keen, who was also the editor of the *Arizona Historical Review,* was looking for some perspective on the conflict, Barnes was a natural choice.[3] But finding that perspective proved to be no easy task. "In the first place," Barnes lamented, "what little written history there is on the subject is mostly a mass of conjectures, romance and glorified moving picture scenarios."[4]

The Pleasant Valley War is indeed a much-storied moment in the history of the Old West. Despite its having been overshadowed by the shootout at the O.K. Corral, legends abound about that conflict that are full of the stuff that frustrated Barnes. Legends about the Pleasant Valley War began to form at the very time that the conflict was raging in the Arizona Territory, from 1881 to 1887, until it finally ended in 1892. Both visitors to the valley and residents themselves regularly gave or sent reports to Prescott newspapers, which were then published verbatim with little analysis, corroboration, or research (the ethos of journalism was very different in that day). The popular perceptions of the events—and perhaps more importantly, misperceptions—framed the growing narratives reported in newspapers from San Francisco to New York City. These perceptions continue to shape how the Pleasant Valley War is understood today.

When Barnes complained of the "romance and glorified . . . scenarios," no doubt he had in mind Zane Grey's 1921 novel *To the Last Man*. As a popular western writer, Grey was perhaps the first to craft a story for a national audience already hungry for such tales about the Old West. Grey reimagined the story of the Pleasant Valley War as a frontier version of Romeo and Juliet, placed within a fictional family feud in the Pleasant Valley settlement. In fairness to Grey, he never set out to write the definitive history of the conflict, although he insisted that "this romance is true to my conception of the war, and I base it upon the setting I learned to know and love so well, upon the strange passions of primitive people."[5] However true his novel may have been to *his* conception of the conflict, it bore no relationship to the actual families or events. Barnes thus followed up on his *Arizona Historical Review* article a decade later with a memoir that expanded on his initial study of the Pleasant Valley War. *Apaches and Longhorns* became the first nonfiction account of the conflict.

These two works—one fiction and the other nonfiction—frame the field of lay histories of the Pleasant Valley War. Most subsequent studies tend either to mirror the ways in which Grey and Barnes viewed the conflict or to respond to those views with their own theories.

Both authors, despite their different purposes and audiences, saw the violence as the product of a blood feud between two families, one that was not that different from the storied Hatfields and McCoys. That interpretation stood until

1936, when cattleman-turned-author Earle R. Forrest published *Arizona's Dark and Bloody Ground*. Forrest took the blood feud thesis and pushed it further. He proposed that what started out as a fight between families transformed into a range war as cattlemen and sheepherders were drawn into the conflict. In 1988, journalist Don Dedera expanded that interpretation even further in *A Little War of Our Own: The Pleasant Valley Feud Revisited*. Dedera championed the view, first proposed by territorial newspapers, that what lay at the heart of the conflict was not really a feud at all, but in fact, entirely a range war. A variety of local authors since then, such as Barbara Zachariae, Jinx Pyle, and Jayne Peace Pyle, have attempted to return to the middle ground first established by Forrest in seeing the violence as both a blood feud and a range war.

The problem with the commonly employed blood-feud thesis is that although revenge killings became one part of the Pleasant Valley War, that thesis does not fully capture the multiple points of contention that drove settlers to turn on each other. The settlement was plagued by violence and murder long before the Grahams accused the Tewksburys of killing one of their own. Indeed, the Graham and Tewksbury brothers were on the same side of an early gun battle in the settlement, and even after these two families fell out with one another, neither side engaged in any hostility toward the other for three more years while gun battles continued to flare within the settlement. To be sure, stories are told that the Tewksbury brothers or the Grahams were manipulating events all along to hasten the deaths of one another. While such stories simplify the complicated set of dynamics at work and make for a good tale, they are based on hearsay and speculation. The historical evidence simply does not support these claims.[6] The Pleasant Valley War was larger than both sets of brothers, and something that lay beyond the Grahams or the Tewksburys compelled the settlers to turn on one another.

If the violence was not the result of a blood feud, was it then a range war? The key problem with this interpretation is that though the Grahams were cattlemen, the Tewksburys were not sheepherders. Their primary economic activity was instead raising horses, and this was well known even among those who quarreled with them. The only documented time that sheep were on Tewksbury property was between 1886 and 1887, when John Tewksbury, the eldest brother, entered into a business arrangement with a Flagstaff businessman who had earlier helped the Tewksbury family when they were in financial need.[7] If John Tewksbury did this to rile the Grahams, as some writers have theorized, it is not clear why this action would do it. His property was over two miles from the Graham property, the traditional buffer zone observed in the territory for keeping sheep separated from cattle.[8] Furthermore, several cattlemen in Pleasant Valley regularly came to the aid of the Tewksburys during the conflict, and at least one sheepherder, Charlie Duchet, was a steadfast defender of the Grahams. Perhaps more significant is that none of the cattle ranchers whose property lay between the Grahams' and the Tewksburys' expressed any known opinion about John Tewksbury allowing sheep on the Tewksburys' property, or took any hand in the shootings that broke out in the valley. Neither did sheepherding families in Pleasant Valley take any role in the conflict, as violence rolled from one end of the valley to the other like a summer lightning storm.

If the conflict in Pleasant Valley was neither a blood feud nor a range war, then what was it? Leland J. Hanchett deserves mention among the lay historians.[9] He has devoted four works to the conflict: *The Crooked Trail to Holbrook, Arizona's Graham-Tewksbury Feud, Black Mesa: The Hanging of Jamie Stott*, and *They Shot Billy Today*. Collectively through these studies, he developed an interpretation first offered by Tom Graham: a high-level conspiracy to murder the Grahams was at work to acquire their land. The plot, according to Hanchett, was "born in greed and nourished by power politics" and involved the Tewksbury family, "all of the county sheriffs, most of the local media, the best legal minds of the Southwest, and the Governor."[10] Yet significant questions remain unanswered from this body of work: the Grahams were relative latecomers to Pleasant Valley. Why would their land merit such singular attention from so many in the territory, particularly over other parcels deemed of greater value and utility in the valley? Why did none of the conspirators that Hanchett accused make any effort to acquire that land after the Grahams left the valley?

Daniel Herman's *Hell on the Range* stands at the pinnacle of the studies of the Pleasant Valley War, and Herman is the only academically trained historian thus far to devote attention to the conflict. He sees the gun battles in Pleasant Valley as part of a larger context of cultural tension and social violence throughout the region, and he describes the battle in Pleasant Valley as only one theater in what he sees as a Rim Country War. In recasting the Pleasant Valley War, he offers an intriguing conceptualization of the values and tensions that underwrote the settlement of the region, if not much of the American West. "Conscience," which Herman refers to as the social and cultural forces of moderation and self-control—what one in the nineteenth century might call "civilization"—clashed with the social and cultural forces of "honor," which Herman defines as "aggressive self-assertion." While he concedes that the battles in Pleasant Valley were not driven by honor, he nonetheless holds that the imperative to resolve differences "through grim assertion" shaped the actions of settlers in that conflict.[11] As cowboys hired from Texas came "deeply imbued with honor" to oversee the herds of the Aztec Land and Cattle Company in the territory, according to Herman, the "conflict yielded to cruelty."[12]

Herman and I consider the historic moment of the Pleasant Valley War through different lenses and from different vantage points, which leads us to different conclusions about that conflict. *Hell on the Range* explores the nature of violence in the American Southwest from a regional perspective by looking at settlements from the central Arizona highlands east to New Mexico as a whole. His honor/conscience paradigm thus helps connect these different communities within the historic moment. My study is motivated by a different kind of question, one that seeks to understand why this particular settlement in a remote part of northern Arizona ultimately turned on itself with murderous violence. The people of the small settlement knew one another reasonably well; they were neighbors, they labored together, helped one another, and had shared meals together. What, then, prevented them from amicably settling their disagreements? How did disagreements deepen? And when they appealed to the courts to settle their differences—repeatedly—why did they end up becoming their own judges and executioners?

In seeking to understand how dynamics within this community led to such a harrowing outcome, I am influenced by microhistory, which employs a Geertzian method of thick description borrowed from anthropology. I also draw from studies of human geography and, to some degree, social network analysis. Herman's honor/conscience paradigm is indeed useful in understanding the larger tensions generally at work in the settlement of the West, but for my purposes, a closer look at the nuances of social interaction *within* this particular settlement, at this particular time, is necessary to fully understand why it collapsed into a state of war.

I do agree with Herman on the importance of understanding the conflict within a larger perspective, but I look to a different social matrix to do so. I believe that one must consider the complex interplay of geography, economics, and social dynamics to more fully understand what happened in that settlement and why. Herman would not disagree, I believe, but again we stand at different vantage points and see different kinds of geographies and economies. Considering the location of Pleasant Valley becomes a significant piece of the puzzle, because this settlement sat at the crossroads of violent economies.

Ned Blackhawk's observation in *Violence over the Land* that "violence weds the history of . . . Native groups to larger, imperial histories" grounds this study of Pleasant Valley. This settlement lay within the geographical boundaries of a dynamic international market that had been in place long before the arrival of white settlers.[13] Blackhawk's work is part of a body of important studies that have explored the reach of a complex economy that moved raided goods, livestock, and people among American Indian nations in the West, and with trading partners in Mexico; among these are James Brooks's *Captives and Cousins,* Pekka Håmålåinen's *Comanche Empire,* Natalie Zappia's *Raiders and Traders,* Anne Hyde's *Empires, Nations, and Families,* Karl Jacoby's *Shadows at Dawn,* and Katherine Benton-Cohen's *Borderline Americans.* In the Arizona Territory, as white settlers moved onto Indian lands, that market proved resilient enough to endure after the American military restricted the movements of southwestern Indian nations to reservations. White settlers simply moved in as principal suppliers and buyers, while Indians continued to remain an active link in that supply chain, even with the limitations imposed by reservations. For ranchers in Pleasant Valley and in the surrounding communities, that meant that their livelihoods were under constant assault—sometimes from their own neighbors.

Thus, physical location is an important factor in the Pleasant Valley War.[14] Because the Pleasant Valley settlement lay within ten miles of the Fort Apache Reservation, the activities of the Apaches were of paramount concern to the settlers there, much more than were neighboring settlements some 80–120 miles away.[15] Apaches had long been proficient hunters and raiders who ranged over great distances in the American Southwest, and although they began moving onto reservations beginning in the 1870s, such a dramatic change for the generation that did so was still an exceedingly difficult adjustment.[16] Such changes were even more difficult to accept when promised rations were in short supply, or when military leaders proved indifferent to Apache concerns. For a variety of reasons, outbreaks were common enough until the turn of the century, and raiders frequently slashed through the lands they knew well—among them Pleasant Valley.[17]

Settlers responded to homesteading an area vulnerable to sudden attack by keeping themselves prepared for deadly clashes that could come at any moment. They built their homes as fortresses, carried arms and ammunition at all times, and maintained constant vigilance about activities to their east. Territorial newspapers devoted significant attention to developments on the Apache reservation, but this form of information was often a week late, and there simply was no formal warning system in real time for settlers. So, they devised their own system that depended largely on word of mouth, with settlers setting out on horseback (if they were lucky enough to outrace renegades) to warn others of imminent attack. Although it was a deeply flawed system, and prone to misreadings and exaggerations of Apache activities, it was better to be ready for an attack by a false report than to be caught unaware. Still, even with this informal warning system, settlers were just as likely to never know about an outbreak until an attack was already upon them. Their firearms and their constant vigilance were their surest means of security.

Revising the story of the Pleasant Valley War to include the role that geography and the Apaches played in the conflict recasts the periodization and indeed the very nature of the Pleasant Valley War. In most accounts, this conflict is defined as a war between the homesteaders of Pleasant Valley, but the settlers had *already* been living in a war zone for several years before their defensive postures toward external threat became internal battles with one another. For my purposes, the Pleasant Valley War began with the first Apache outbreak in 1881, and it was a war fought between neighbors with words and in the courts long before the settlers turned on one another with murderous intent.

In exploring this borderlands tragedy, I cannot simply stop at describing the acts of violence that came to characterize this conflict. To do so, I believe, would deny a more fully human experience to historical actors, especially those who have been reduced to caricature by legend. Like Brooks, Jacoby, and Blackhawk, I seek to understand what violence meant to those settlers. As they constantly scrutinized their surroundings for signs of Apaches, how did the relentless anticipation of surprise attack wear on them day after day, year after year? As they watched their livelihoods strangled from unremitting livestock theft, who did they blame, and what did they believe they had to do to remedy the situation?

When the violence turned internecine, how did the grief of loss and betrayal shape their perceptions of what was happening, of each other, and of what they would do next as they tried to nurse their wounded and bury their dead?

Admittedly, pursuing these questions requires a degree of resourcefulness with source material. In quoting literary critic Elaine Scarry, Jacoby wisely observed that "the psychological horror and physical pain inherent to violence can . . . lead to a 'shattering of language,' as lived experience comes to exceed the limits of human description. Intimidation can render storytellers mute or confine their narratives to the margins of society. The denial of materials can inhibit the creation of the records so essential to the historical enterprise."[18] Scholars in trauma studies have become more attuned to how survivors of chronic violence and the fear of violence—be they aggressors or victims—continue to live with the effects, often long after the moment. Here is where the historical record often falls silent, partly because the survivors of the conflict did not fully comprehend the repercussions of what modern researchers would see as continuous traumatic stress, and partly because working people unaccustomed to recording their thoughts and feelings in print left behind few records that constitute proper evidence.[19]

In turning to trauma studies, my aim is not to diagnose the settlers but to gain insight into why these historical actors acted in critical moments contrary to the shared norms of social cohesion that defined them as a community, norms that they had previously maintained. If the settlers relied upon a degree of mutual dependency and cooperation necessary to survive in the frontier—sharing meals, resources, and workloads; coming to one another's aid in times of distress; joining in business arrangements; and even uniting to defend the settlement from outside attack—why were they unable to reconcile disagreements, even when it became clear that their disagreements were driving the settlement toward bedlam? What prevented them from appealing to what Abraham Lincoln described as "the better angels of our nature"?[20]

While drawing from research in human physiology to approach a better understanding of these questions, I am mindful of the deep challenges that come with interdisciplinarity. I readily admit that engaging these fields of inquiry requires a fair degree of care and dexterity, particularly in handling some important methodological differences in how historians, biologists, and psychologists approach the study of the human experience. For historians, having direct evidence that the settlers in fact experienced such reactions is key. For biologists and psychologists, however, understanding how human physiology works is the key. While I concede that there is little direct evidence in the form of first-person narrative, I believe there exists enough circumstantial evidence, when taken together, to provide a compelling interpretation of the settlement of the West worthy of further exploration.

It was no accident of timing that during the period when settlers labored to protect their lives from Apaches and their livelihood from rustlers, the settlement of Pleasant Valley transformed into an astonishingly litigious community. Between 1883 and 1888, there were perhaps some two dozen households in Pleasant Valley, yet during this five-year period, they were participants in as many as thirty court hearings as either complainants, defendants, or material witnesses against one another.[21] The courtroom proved to be no place to bridge deepening fissures within the community, however. To the contrary, failed convictions merely seemed to deepen the desire to succeed with the next grievance.

Territorial law enforcement practices, therefore, became another critical factor in these deepening social tensions. The men who were authorized to serve warrants and to make arrests—the sheriffs and deputy sheriffs—were outsiders to the community who rode into the settlement with the fundamental objective of not getting killed. Their means of surviving such a dangerous line of work was to approach every suspect fully armed and ready to shoot before the other man did. More often than not, this is exactly how an arrest played out, and it was the death of a particular settler during an attempted arrest that turned the Pleasant Valley community on itself. After years of fighting Apaches and battling one another in court, the killing of this settler in a case of mistaken identities pitched the settlement headlong into a nightmare of accusations, judgments, and executions.

What emerges from my reading of this historical moment, I believe, is a very human story in the Arizona Territory, of hope sown in the dreams of youth and the despair reaped from unforgiving circumstances; of friendships forged in necessity and lost amid misunderstanding and tragedy; of enmity spawned by conflict, and the humanity that some were willing to sacrifice to survive just one more day.

1

TERROR ON THE RANGE

Humans have forged a complicated relationship with their natural surroundings since recorded time. Some cultures embraced their physical world and wove its features into the fabric of their narratives, while others rejected their natural surroundings and imbued it with frightening power. Among the cultures of Western Europe, ancient legends, often told as mere children's tales, described the wilderness as a foreboding place, full of evils and dangers to be conquered and tamed.

The immigrants who sought to settle the American West carried with them such legends, embedded within the framework of their thoughts as they gazed upon the land. They surely did not believe that witches fattened little children for consumption or that wolves could dress up as grandmothers. Yet they no doubt accepted the fundamental premise that nature could appear deceptively tranquil when danger lurked in the shadows, and that the wilderness was a dangerous place. For those who dared push out into contested Indian lands, whether European immigrants or descendants of immigrants, that underlying belief that danger lurks in the wilderness took on an entirely new meaning.

Such was the setting in territorial Arizona as whites laid claim to lands long controlled by the Ndee, or Apache.[1] Although the Western Apache had accepted confinement to the reservation just east of Pleasant Valley, that acceptance was reluctant at best, and entirely rejected at worst. The problem for those early settlers was that they never knew which it would be. If the Apaches stayed on their land, then settlers could go about their daily struggles to survive in the Arizona wilderness. If the Apaches did not stay on their land, then the consequences for the settlers could be swift and deadly.

Apaches were skilled warriors who excelled in the art of stealth. Even for neighboring Indian tribes, Apaches were often unseen until the attack was upon them.[2] The only protection the settlers had on lands still contested was to remain heavily armed at all times, vigilant of every shadow and brush movement—almost to the point of paranoia—and to build their small cabins as fortresses in the hope that they could wait out an ambush until nightfall, as it was known that Apaches would attack only until twilight.[3]

When night fell, however, settlers still found no rest. Darkness called out the rustlers. They rarely attacked settlers, but they actively preyed upon their means of supporting themselves. So, living in the crossroads of Apache discontent and an active theft economy meant that the threat to life by day and the loss of livelihood by night were unrelenting. Unyielding vigilance was the price of settling within this hostile environment.

These two factors were critical in shaping the events known as the Pleasant Valley War: the social geography and the Apache presence. Even though Apaches agreed to live on reservations, the fear of Apaches loomed large enough to shape the lives and actions of the settlers who tried to claim that land. For any true appreciation of what happened in Pleasant Valley and why, both the environment and the people who dominated it for centuries must be written back into the story.

THE ARIZONA HIGHLANDS

The landscape of this story unfolds from the southern repose of the Colorado Plateau. That plateau is a truly unique geographic formation in the American West, and its elevation is one of the dominant features of the northern Arizona landscape. This expanse of compressed sediment, reaching 11,000 feet above sea level at its highest point, first began to arise from an ancient seabed some 80 million years ago, during a period that shaped much of the topography of the American West, including an enormous fold of the earth's crust known today as the Rocky Mountains.[4] Today the plateau covers about 130,000 square miles of northern Arizona, southern Utah, and parts of western Colorado and New Mexico.

It is a dramatic landscape.

Canyons carved by primordial rivers have exposed vibrant colors in the cliff walls that tower like ancient temples. The vivid names given to the cliffs of the Grand Staircase in southern Utah could easily apply to the many canyon walls found throughout the plateau: the Chocolate Cliffs, the Vermillion Cliffs, the White Cliffs, the Gray Cliffs, and so on. The land is peppered with creosote bushes, sagebrush, shadscale scrub, and prickly pear cactus.[5] Dark brown remains of ancient lava flows, which have not been active for at least a thousand years, also break through the soil across this terrain.

In the summer months, billowing clouds hang low over the jagged southern rim of the plateau, just as they have for millennia, dark and pregnant, ready to birth another squall. Warm oceanic air from the southwest meets the higher, cooler air on top of the plateau, creating a condition that meteorologists refer to as a "rain shadow."[6] Rain falls heavily at the rim, leaving only dry air to move northward across the plateau. When the afternoon rains begin, sometimes with a clap of thunder, sometimes only with a gentle rush of wind, water droplets fall to the earth, pulling trails of cloud downward. From a distance, the rain appears like a long misty veil let down from the heavens. It is easy to see why tribes of the Athabaskan speakers often represented sky deities as elongated beings.

In these higher elevations, the precipitation is great enough to support forests.[7] Tall, broad-leafed trees such as alder, white oak, walnut, sycamore, and single-leaf ash have made their homes amid deep vertical crags cut into slate-brown rock faces. Dense thickets of smaller shrubs such as the birchleaf buckthorn, Utah serviceberry, western hackberry, and buttonbush can be nearly impenetrable at times, but the vegetation is rich enough to support a variety of large woodland mammals such as black bear, mountain lions, white-tailed deer, Rocky Mountain elk, bighorn sheep, javelina, pronghorn antelope, wild turkey, and all manner of small game and reptiles.[8]

At the southern edge of the plateau is a richly forested ridge that runs almost the entire width of northern Arizona. From that ridge, the elevation drops steeply more than three thousand feet down to the large geological shallow known as Tonto Basin. Since the time of Spanish exploration, that ridge has been called the Mogollon Rim, named after an early Spanish governor of New Mexico, Juan Ignacio Flores Mogollón. But its naming was nothing more than an act of colonial hubris; the Spaniards who laid claim to the land never controlled it. Instead, it remained firmly in the hands of Apaches, Navajos, Utes, and Southern Paiutes for centuries.

At the base of the Mogollon Rim, within the Tonto Basin, lies a particular valley that was once known as Pleasant Valley. No one knows why that valley was first named "pleasant," but most guess that it was because of the meadows fed by streams of melting snow and rainwater from the Rim. One of the earliest published reports about the valley, in 1875, described it as an Eden: "They found the grass in Tonto Basin from six to ten inches high, and the aroma of flowers assailed their nostrils before they were half-way down the mountain."[9]

Before the coming of American settlers, this had been Apache land, prized for its lush fields and game. But even after the Americans laid claim to the land, the Apache presence was never very far away. The fear of their return loomed very large in the lives of the settlers who tried to make Pleasant Valley their own.

SETTLING THE RIM COUNTRY

Apache encampments kept all but the daring, the desperate, and the foolhardy away from much of the Arizona Territory. Captain Joseph R. Walker led the first military foray into the territory in 1862, which included native Georgian Jack Swilling, who is credited with later founding Phoenix. Although ostensibly on a mission to survey the territory, they were gold seekers, really, who came with the expectation of exploring Arizona's north country, where Walker had discovered gold as a trapper some twenty years earlier. The party followed the Gila River to the Akimel O'otham (Pima) villages where they resupplied, and from there they ascended the Hassayampa River. Although they were harassed by Apaches almost every step of the way, they took possession the following year of an area named the Walker Diggings, about ten miles east of Prescott. They pressed on farther to the east to Lynx Creek and then into the Tonto Basin.[10]

In 1877, Latter-day Saint colonizer Brigham Young sent Mormon families to settle in Navajo and Apache country up on the Rim. William Jordan Flake led a colonizing party south from Utah through imposing desert terrain until they found more hospitable lands fed by the Little Colorado River. Along one of its tributaries, Silver Creek, lived James Stinson from Massachusetts, who claimed the land by squatter's rights. Stinson originally asked Flake for $12,000 for his land, but he eventually reduced the price and agreed to accept in payment a substantial herd of Midwestern cattle that the Mormons had driven out with them. The cattle were considered far superior to the Mexican range cattle common in the territory. So, on 21 July 1878, Stinson became a wealthy cattleman, perhaps the wealthiest in the region, and Flake's colony took possession of what was known as Stinson Valley. The settlers renamed their new home Snowflake, in honor of Flake, and Mormon apostle Erastus Snow.[11]

Brigham Young also sent missionaries to survey the Four Corners area. Two years after the founding of Snowflake, the Mormon apostle Wilford Woodruff authorized the purchase of 1,200 acres of land near the small Mexican pueblo of Doña María de San Juan (later anglicized as St. Johns). It was a good day's walk directly east of Snowflake, along the southern border of the Navajo Reservation.[12] Although they faced rigorous and often violent opposition from the Mexican and Indian inhabitants of the area, Mormon settlers began to seek public office once they established themselves as a commercial power to be reckoned with in the region.[13]

Around that same time, a widower and his children by the name of Tewksbury moved into the territory. James Dunning Tewksbury—Jim, as he was more commonly known—left his native state of Maine twenty years earlier to seek his fortune in the goldfields of northern California. In Pacific Township, Humboldt County, he met his first wife, an Indian woman from the Bear River Clan. What she called herself has been lost to time; as was so often the case in the early ter- ritorial records, an Indian spouse was often only designated by race. Tewksbury homesteaded a spread on Eagle Prairie, along the Eel River, which was close to several villages of the Bear River Clan. He could have lived in complete apathy to the fate of the Indians, as so many did, but he was different. Something compelled him to learn the language of the Bear River Clan, and in time he became fluent enough to be called upon to interpret in times of crisis. He earned the respect of both communities, so much so that he married the daughter of a large warrior whom the settlers called "Goliath" (others called him a chief). However she was known to those who loved her, this woman of the Bear River Clan bore Tewksbury five children: John, Edwin, Frank, James, and Elvira.[14]

But by the time the Tewksburys left California, Jim was a single father. Tewksbury family tradition has it that the mother of those five children died of tuberculosis.[15] But it was also a time of unspeakable violence toward California Indians. Settlers wantonly attacked villages for reasons great and small—the death of a white man, the loss of a cow, or simply because they were Indian. In their bloodlust, settlers killed with impunity, attacking even peaceful villages that sought alliance with Americans. One of the massacres of 1860 occurred at Eagle Prairie, where Tewksbury lived, killing thirty-five California Indians.[16] Were the Tewksburys caught in the crossfire? Whatever the reason for her death, by 1875, Tewksbury had left the state, never to return.[17]

In the fall of 1879, James Dunning Tewksbury married Lydia Marston Crigler Shultes in the small settlement of Tempe, Arizona.[18] Lydia's family came from Wales as Mormon converts who wished to help build Zion in Utah. They came with the help of the Perpetual Emigration Fund, a program established by the LDS church to support European immigrants. By the time the Marstons arrived in 1851, the wagon trails west were well established, but curiously they did not settle in the Utah Territory. They may have been part of the smaller groups of Mormons who set out to colonize California, or they may simply have left the faith altogether. Either way, they settled in Salinas, California. Once there, Lydia met Rufus Crigler, who also journeyed on foot with the Mormons to the Utah Territory, and also elected to continue on to California. At the age of thirteen, Lydia bore Crigler their first child. What became of Crigler is unclear, but within three years Lydia married German immigrant David Shultes. After ten years, the Shulteses moved to Sunflower in the Arizona Territory, where David contracted typhoid fever and died. At thirty years old, Lydia was now a widow with multiple children.[19] She was in the same difficult position as James Tewksbury, who also lived in Sunflower, and within a year, they joined families.

Shortly after that marriage, the four Tewksbury boys moved out of the house. There may simply have been too little room for all of them with their new family. That same year, their sister Elvira also moved out and married Henry Earnst Albert Slosser of Prussia.[20] Such changes at home probably meant that it was simply time for them to strike out on their own, and they looked northward to the newly opened Apache land below the Mogollon Rim, which some were still referring to as "Apacheria."[21]

The four Tewksbury boys were among the earliest to break land in Pleasant Valley, although they were not the first to do so.[22] That honor likely went to Albus Roos (better known as Al Rose), a Swedish immigrant who still bore the wounds from his service as an infantryman in the Civil War.[23] Why the Tewksbury brothers chose this remote location, so close to the Apache Reservation, is a bit of a curiosity, but circumstantial evidence allows for some reasonable guesses.[24] The site they chose to homestead bore a striking similarity to their California home on Eagle Prairie. And its very remoteness, far from other whites and close to other Indians, may have provided a sense of refuge to the brothers who, while still children, had been exposed to white brutality toward Indians.

Twenty-four-year-old John was the eldest, and he did his best to keep his brothers in line, but it was not always easy. Twenty-two-year-old Edwin tended to be quiet and observant but would never back down from a fight. Nineteen-year-old Frank was frail and in poor health, and seventeen-year-old James—better

John Tewksbury, ca. 1880s. *Courtesy Arizona Historical Society Library and Archives, Tucson.*

known as Jim—was impetuous but likeable. Few others were living in the valley and the brothers almost had their pick of land. Although flatter areas were available, they chose the well-watered area along Cherry Creek for their horse and hog ranch. The rocky foothills provided some protection from the winter winds and helped keep the livestock reasonably close.[25]

Others followed within time. They were mostly small-time farmers and ranchers, although a few hoped to find gold in the rivers and streams of the valley. But the number of settlers was by no means great. Less than half a dozen small ranches dotted the roughly 7,600 acres in Pleasant Valley in 1880.[26] Some settlers clustered close together, while others chose places a good distance away. Perhaps no more than 250 people were settled in the entire expanse of the Tonto Basin.[27]

Pleasant Valley was differently situated from other communities in the territory. Unlike the nearest Mormon settlements of Snowflake, some eighty miles

Edwin Tewksbury, ca. 1890. *Courtesy Arizona Historical Society Library and Archives, Tucson.*

away along the Little Colorado, the settlers of Pleasant Valley were not bound by a common migration experience, a common faith, and a singular religious organization. The people drawn to that small settlement were a curious mix of nationalities and races that, in some ways, reflected the nation's diversity. When they came together, typically at barn raisings or at roundup time, one could hear the settlers of Pleasant Valley speaking to one another with a cacophony of pronunciations. Some accents were international, from Sweden, England, French Canada, Mexico, and Poland. Even the native-born settlers spoke with regional accents from New York City, the upper Midwest, or the varieties of southern drawls from Texas to Tennessee.

Most were single males, who ranged in age from their early twenties to their early fifties.[28] The younger men tended to have come out west seeking fortune and adventure. While some of the older settlers were still chasing fortune, after decades of trying, they tended to have come to the territory seeking what treasure would never provide: a measure of peace from the buffetings that life had already given them. "I would rather enjoy myself a little than be a slave for someone else for all of my life," Garrat "Bob" Sixby wrote to his sister in Canada about his meager ranch in the valley.[29] Some came as survivors of Indian wars, and some as veterans of the Civil War, with bodies that had been irreparably altered by conflict, or whose wounds were unseen and buried deep. In this regard, the Tewksbury brothers were unusual: they were not unlike other young men their age, but prosperity never seemed to be their aim in life. Instead, the solitude and sanctuary that the Arizona wilderness offered seemed to be of greater importance.

Because Pleasant Valley was a small community, the settlers knew each other, and of each other, and they shared an unspoken expectation of mutual cooperation. Half of the initial settlers were joined by blood: forty-four-year-old Charles Sixby moved to the settlement with his older brother Garrat (more commonly known as Bob), and forty-nine-year-old Edvard Roos (also known as Ed Rose), came from Sweden to join his brother Albus.[30] Other settlers bunked together: twenty-three-year-old Joseph Boyer shared a small, one-room cabin with forty-one-year-old Louis O. Houdon and twenty-three-year-old Jacob "Jake" Lauffer.[31] Only George Church, the eldest of the group at fifty-two, lived alone.

When James and Lydia Tewksbury moved their family to Pleasant Valley, they occupied a distinctive social space within the settlement. They were the only multigenerational family there, and of the perhaps thirteen children who lived in the settlement, half were Tewksburys.[32] That put the older Tewksburys in a unique frame of mind, especially after Lydia's seven-year-old daughter Anna Shultes drowned in a flashflood while playing in Cherry Creek.[33] The adult children of James Dunning Tewksbury took on a more watchful and protective role over their younger siblings. With mountain lions and bears in the hills, Apache outbreaks, and violent rainstorms, the valley was still a dangerous place to call home, even for adults. Protection was the key to their survival.

For a time, Lizzie Koehn Rose (wife of Al Rose), Lydia Tewksbury, and her daughter Mary Ann, who married Jim's oldest son, John, were perhaps the only women who lived permanently in Pleasant Valley.[34] Some of the other ranches were owned by families that lived in Globe City, as it was originally called, so there may have been other women who periodically visited the settlement when their husbands came to tend their holdings. As frontier women, Lizzie, Lydia, and

PLEASANT VALLEY GENEALOGIES

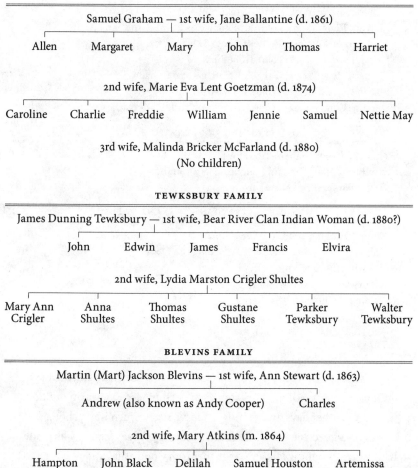

GRAHAM FAMILY

Samuel Graham — 1st wife, Jane Ballantine (d. 1861)

| Allen | Margaret | Mary | John | Thomas | Harriet |

2nd wife, Marie Eva Lent Goetzman (d. 1874)

| Caroline | Charlie | Freddie | William | Jennie | Samuel | Nettie May |

3rd wife, Malinda Bricker McFarland (d. 1880)
(No children)

TEWKSBURY FAMILY

James Dunning Tewksbury — 1st wife, Bear River Clan Indian Woman (d. 1880?)

| John | Edwin | James | Francis | Elvira |

2nd wife, Lydia Marston Crigler Shultes

| Mary Ann Crigler | Anna Shultes | Thomas Shultes | Gustane Shultes | Parker Tewksbury | Walter Tewksbury |

BLEVINS FAMILY

Martin (Mart) Jackson Blevins — 1st wife, Ann Stewart (d. 1863)

Andrew (also known as Andy Cooper)   Charles

2nd wife, Mary Atkins (m. 1864)

| Hampton | John Black | Delilah | Samuel Houston | Artemissa |

Mary Ann would have had their days filled with numerous demands. There were gardens to tend, meals to prepare, food to preserve and store, children to tend, and clothes to mend. "They kept close eyes on their little ones as they played outside," Jayne Peace Pyle surmised, "[as] the men were away for many hours at a time."

Lydia told the children stories as they gathered around the stove in her cabin. As she told the stories, Mary Ann worked on quilts. Pieces of material were cut from worn-out clothing, then sewn together to make blocks,

1887 RESIDENTS OF PLEASANT VALLEY AND SURROUNDING AREAS

PLEASANT VALLEY

Charles (44 years old) and Garrat (Bob) Sixby, from lower Canada
Edvard Roos (49 years old), also known as Edward Rose, and Albus
    (also known as Al Rose), from Sweden
Joseph Boyer (23 years old), from England
Louis O. Houdon (41 years old), from eastern Canada
Jacob Lauffer* (23 years old), from Michigan
George Church (52 years old), from New York

GRAHAMS LIVING IN PLEASANT VALLEY

John and Tom Graham, from Iowa
William "Billy" Graham (half brother), from Iowa
Louis Parker (first cousin), from Iowa

TEWKSBURYS LIVING IN PLEASANT VALLEY

James Dunning and Lydia Tewksbury
John and Mary Ann Crigler Tewksbury
Ed(win), Jim, and Francis Tewksbury
Henry and Elvira Tewksbury Slosser
Thomas Shultes (stepbrother)

* Also spelled Lawford in territorial records.

which were sewn together to make rows, which were sewn together to make quilt tops. It was tedious work, but each person needed a warm quilt for winter. On other days, the women made lye soap, which was a chore. The soap, considered the pioneer woman's multi-purpose cleaner, was made with leftover cooking fats and lye made from wood ashes and was used to clean clothing, dishes, and floors. Wash days were hard work and all of the kids helped. Wood had to be chopped, so fires could be built to heat water in two big pots. The water was heated close to Cherry Creek, so it wouldn't have to [be] carried far. The laundry was done down by the creek and hung on bushes to dry. Lydia and Mary Ann had their hands full with wet clothing, plus they had to keep their eyes on the little ones. In warm weather, the kids played in the creek on wash days.[35]

Lizzie Rose and Mary Ann Tewksbury were only two years apart in age, and although Lydia was the oldest, and mother to Mary Ann, babies came to all three

1887 RESIDENTS IN THE TONTO BASIN NEAR PLEASANT VALLEY

CANYON CREEK

Martin "Mart" Jackson Blevins and Mary Atkins Blevins (1864)
Andrew (aka Andy Cooper)
John Black and Eva Blevins, and baby
Charles "Charlie"
Hampton "Hamp" Blevins
Artemissa Blevins
Samuel Houston Blevins

MARSH VALLEY

John Gilleland

1887 LAW ENFORCEMENT PERSONNEL IN TONTO BASIN

YAVAPAI COUNTY

William J. "Billy" Mulvenon, Sheriff, Yavapai County

APACHE COUNTY

Commodore Perry Owens, Sheriff (Holbrook)
James D. "Denny" Houck, Deputy Sheriff (Houk's Tank)
Joseph Thomas "Joe" McKinney, Constable of Winslow
Osmer "Oz" Flake, deputized citizen (Snowflake)

women while they lived in Pleasant Valley. Their ranches were only a few miles from one another along Cherry Creek, so it is likely that these three developed a particular bond as they socialized, midwifed one another, looked after one another's children, and shared meals.

In 1886, Olive "Ollie" Crouch moved to Pleasant Valley with her husband and children, and they chose to homestead a place on Crouch Creek, about five miles north of the Tewksburys.[36] Other women began moving to the area with their families around that same time, but the total number of women in the settlement always remained small in relation to the men, and most of the later arrivals homesteaded areas that were even farther removed from the settlement. Thus, the women of these newer families may have only had periodic contact with the women of the settlement.[37] For most of the 1880s, Lizzie, Ollie, Mary Ann, and Lydia likely constituted the core of frontier domesticity in Pleasant Valley.[38]

"OH, GIVE ME A HOME"

Those who broke this remote land were not people of letters. They left behind little that could reveal something about their inner lives during this terribly precarious time. But some of their handiwork remains. Some of the homes that these settlers erected have endured. The Perkins "rock house" store, made with stone and adobe, and the Graham cabin, though dilapidated, still stand.[39] The "Flying V" cabin, believed to have been built by John Tewksbury, has been preserved by the Pioneer Living History Museum outside of Phoenix.[40] These dwellings prompt a question: Is it possible to read these structures to begin to discern the thoughts and intentions of their builders?

The cuts from a broad axe are dug deep into the wood of the Flying V cabin, and they still speak of purpose and to the preoccupations of its builders. Were those cuts deep because of the sinew and muscle of the wood chopper, or were those cuts deep because the axe was swung with a particular urgency? Either way, the regular spacing of the cuts suggests that the wood chopper knew how to handle an adz and a broad axe, and no time was wasted in finishing the logs with a smooth surface.

These were no ordinary log cabins, though they looked like others in the area. With every swing of the axe and pull of the saw, these men knew exactly just what kind of structure they needed to erect in this dangerous land. Just as the logs were carefully chosen for their thickness and durability, the gun ports sawed into the logs were not created as afterthoughts, and certainly not for decoration. They were integral parts of the cabin's carefully planned design.[41]

It is well worth pondering why. The settlers to this valley knew what kind of land they were entering, and what price they might have to pay for daring to do so. The western boundary of the Apache reservation lay just eight miles away. No barrier sealed that porous border, and the Apaches knew the route to Pleasant Valley well. Skilled warriors could reach the fledgling settlement in just a few hours, which made Pleasant Valley, for much of the 1800s, a deadly place to make a home.

So, as the men shaped the timber, they cut special V-shaped gun ports into those logs that would allow maximum lateral mobility with a firearm from a fixed position. In all, there were eight gun ports cut into the cabin, two per wall. Over by the bed, just above where a man would lay his head, a gun port was cut into the wall, and another was cut just beyond the foot of the bed. On another

"Flying V" cabin built by John Tewksbury. *Photograph by the author.*

Gun ports in cabin wall. *Photograph by the author.*

wall, the gun port was cut just above the kitchen table, next to where a meal might be set. Still another two gun ports were cut on either side of the fireplace, at about the eye line of a person sitting in a chair by the fire.

These gun ports tell an important story. There was no place within that cabin that was more than a few strides away from a gun port, where you would be able to fire your weapon if attacked. Just as important, those gun ports allowed the occupants to keep a watchful eye on their livestock.

The gun ports speak of vulnerability. Staying alert and on guard was an absolute necessity. There was no meal to eat or place to lie down without a gun port in front of you, reminding you of the danger that lurked just beyond your cabin wall. There was no place within that cabin where you were not constantly reminded that Apache attacks came swiftly and without warning.

Your home, if it came to it, was built to be your last stand.

THE THEFT CORRIDOR

When American settlers began moving onto Indian lands in the Arizona Territory, they were entering into a well-established economy that Natalie Zappia described as "traders and raiders."[42] Archaeological evidence has long suggested that extensive trade networks existed among tribal nations of the American West.[43] James Brooks was the first ethnohistorian to probe what that "exchange economy" meant for native nations in his award-winning *Captives and Cousins.*[44] People, in the form of slaves, spouses, or adopted kin, were among the main commodities that moved from suppliers to consumers. At times, such exchanges were made simply for cultural reasons, and at other times for economic reasons. Either way, regional markets developed from these exchanges, with their own dynamics of supply chains, competition, takeovers, and even monopolies.[45] So enduring was that market that even with the coming of the Spaniards, and the imposition of Spanish legal and religious institutions, that economy altered little. Spanish colonists, instead, became among the major consumers of that market.[46]

The introduction of horses to the American landscape fundamentally transformed the nature of what Pekka Håmålåinen termed "the ancient Rocky Mountain trade corridor."[47] Horses were simply easier than people to procure and to move in greater numbers. And this new commodity proved to be a greater economic and military asset than slaves for those who mastered the art of horsemanship. Lands that took weeks to access on foot could be reached in a matter of days, and the extent of raiding trips in search of new encampments to exploit expanded exponentially. At the same time, the horse provided mobility to vulnerable tribes and facilitated the shifting demographics of the West as the reach of predatory tribes grew longer, and those preyed upon sought more defensible land.[48]

These Athabaskan speakers, whom the early Spanish explorers called "Apachus de Nabajo," transformed from nomadic followers of buffalo to fearsome regional warriors.[49] With the Utes and Navajos dominating the regions to the north, and Comanches dominating the lands to the east, the Apaches gained control of the regions to the south.[50] Their raiding and trading ventures struck deep into the heart of Nueva Vizcaya (present-day Sonora and Chihuahua),

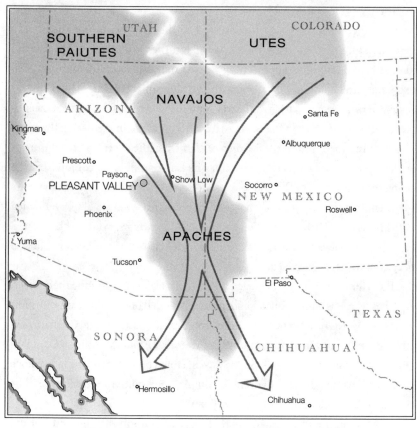

Theft Corridor of the American Southwest before 1870.
Map by Tom Jonas.

moving goods and people up to Arizona for trade and back again.[51] In 1757, for example, a group of Apache women arrived at a Spanish outpost and told officials there that "their chief wanted to trade Spanish captives for cows, horses, and clothing." The officials dispatched a patrol of cavalrymen to find the captives, but they failed to locate the Apaches. A week and a half later, a raiding party struck a large hacienda with devastating impact.[52]

This was not, by any means, the first time that Apaches plundered Spanish outposts. The Marqués de Rubí set out to tour New Spain's northern provinces to witness firsthand the impact of Indian raids on the missions and settlements of Nueva Vizcaya. His tour included the settlement of Tubac and the nearby mission of Guevavi in southern Arizona. From accounts given by colonial officials and survivors, he was convinced that the destruction to life and property was exclusively from Apaches.[53]

Convinced that New Spain possessed neither the means nor the men to prevent raiding through arms, colonial officials turned to diplomacy. Apaches had already begun cautiously approaching Spanish outposts seeking a more peaceful exchange, and colonial officials saw the wisdom in accepting the overture.[54] Spaniards and Apaches thus initiated a tenuous network of trading alliances to buy a measure of security that worked for a time, at least in mediating the worst effects of incessant raiding of Spanish settlements. The decentralized nature of Apache political organization, as well as its inherent fluidity, complicated the best intentions of peace through trade, and some enterprising clans found ways to benefit handsomely from the peace. "Caravans from Mexico City, overloaded with provisions," Henrietta Stockel wryly noted, "were highly vulnerable to attack from hostile tribes so the largesse from which bribes were frequently allotted occasionally never arrived at all."[55]

The tribes to the north, however, had no such agreement among themselves. Apaches, Navajos, and Comanches continually raided one another, as well as targeting the agricultural settlements in central Arizona of the Akimel O'otham (Salt River People) and Xalychidom Piipaash (Maricopa), and the Tohono O'odham (Papago) in southern Arizona. So the flow of stolen people, goods, and livestock continued to move along the corridor from Arizona south to Mexico, as mobile parties traded stolen livestock and property.[56]

To be sure, the Indian nations that depended upon raiding and trading were not the only people who supplied this economy. Mexican settlers fled to the remote region of present-day Arizona precisely to avoid capture for crimes committed elsewhere. "Many of the first settlers of Apache County were made up of this class," lamented Joseph Fish, who, in 1879, began recording the history of Mormon settlement in northern Arizona. "Consequently, they were not the class to respect the rights or property of others, and they were not willing to be governed by any law except that of their own make which smacked strongly of the freebooter's system."[57]

When Americans gained possession of Mexico's northern provinces, the supply chain of stolen goods and livestock moving south was well established. It is telling that Article XI of the Treaty of Guadalupe Hidalgo, which ended the U.S. war with Mexico, assured the Mexican Republic that the United States would put an end to "incursions of savage tribes . . . whose incursions with the territory of Mexico would be prejudicial in the extreme." To finally break the trade in raided goods, the treaty made illegal the purchase of goods and livestock stolen by Indians from Mexican territory, obligating the U.S. government "in the most solemn manner . . . in the faithful exercise of its influence and power" to rescue Mexican citizens captured by Indians and transported to U.S. soil.[58] The implementation of that clause, however, proved to be exceedingly difficult.[59]

Despite these efforts to end the trade in stolen livestock, the theft economy proved resilient when American settlers not only brought fresh supplies of horses but also quickly replaced Spanish colonists as its main consumers. In 1849, Indian Agent James Calhoun wrote from Santa Fe, New Mexico, to complain to the Commissioner of Indian Affairs in Washington, D.C., about what he termed "the indiscriminate and vicious commerce." Navajos, Utes, Apaches, and Comanches continued to supply livestock to American horse traders, "against which there seems to be at this time not the slighted impediment. . . . It is through the medium of these trades that arms and ammunition are supplied to the Indians who refuse submission to our authority. These traders go where they please, without being subjected to the slightest risk . . . the question cannot be answered in such a way as to justify a further toleration of these travelling merchants."[60]

That same year, Indian Agent John Wilson also complained to the Secretary of the Interior from California that Americans were encouraging the flow of stolen livestock by purchasing horses from Indians. "Heretofore the [Utes] have driven a large trade in horses, the larger number of which they have stolen from the Mexicans. Some check should be placed on this traffic, which now forms much the larger item of trade between them and the traders, who have heretofore enjoyed a monopoly of this traffic."[61] Unless some means were implemented to guarantee that livestock was legally acquired, he continued, "it will be exceedingly hard to induce them to quit stealing horses, as long as traders are at liberty to purchase from them."[62] That market proved flexible enough to include the traffic in cattle and sheep.[63]

Restricting Indians to reservations should have brought an end to the trading and raiding economy, but the military's success also created an economic vacuum. The sounds of herds on the move sang like the siren call for American settlers looking for a quick profit, as livestock poured onto former Indian lands by the thousands. Americans moved into the vacuum created by restricting

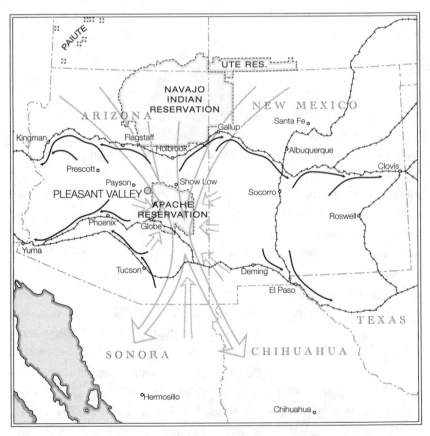

Theft Corridor of the American Southwest after 1870.

Map by Tom Jonas.

Indians to reservations to entirely transform what was a raiding and trading economy into a lucrative theft market. Some cowboys specialized in stealing livestock, others in altered brands, and still others specialized in transporting that livestock along the supply chain. An 1883 edition of the *Arizona Silver Belt,* published in Globe City, complained about herds stolen from American ranchers and sold to Mexican ranchers.[64] That same year, the Spanish-language newspaper *Fronterizo* also complained that American ranchers were far too willing to purchase livestock stolen from Mexico. "Arizona [is] an open market for whatever stock they succeed in getting from across the line. Within recent date two band[s] of cattle known to be stolen, have been marketed in Arizona without claim for them in Sonora having been made. A like thing happened with three other herds previously brought in. . . . The owners of cattle in Sonora are advised to watch strictly, pursue the robbers, and should they escape to the Territory then at once call in official aid and by that means debar them from the immunity they now enjoy for want of prompt and effective action in the matter."[65] *The Prescott Journal* in 1885 warned of "respectable thieves" operating in their midst—local ranchers who surreptitiously aided and abetted that market. The "line shall be very tightly drawn between those in the cattle business who act upon honor under all circumstances," the editors warned, "and those in the same line of business, who . . . appropriate to themselves the property of their neighbors. The live stock [*sic*] interest of our county should be fostered and protected to the full extent of the law."[66]

Pleasant Valley was singled out as a particular problem. "Parties from the Tonto Basin complain of the prevalence of horse stealing in the extreme eastern portion of the county," Prescott editor Bucky O'Neill observed in his livestock journal *Hoof and Horn.* "It is believed that the parties operating have confederates in Apache County who assist them in escaping to New Mexico with their plunder. We do not doubt that they have confederates in this county. From all we can learn there is a chain of them and they pass horses both ways. We suspect if they were followed up closely from Tonto Basin, it would be found they were driven to New Mexico by the way of Canyon Creek, and if the trails of those stolen from the western portion of this county were followed, it would be found they were driven south by way of Tonto Basin." O'Neill concluded his editorial with a call not for better law enforcement, but for the citizens to take action. "When will the people have energy, vim, and determination sufficient to break up this gang?" he implored. "The existence of such a gang for such a length of time, when their rendezvous is so well known, is a burning shame and a disgrace to our people."[67]

--- · ---

Just a few miles to the east of Pleasant Valley, White Mountain Apache shaman Nakaaidoklini[68] began to spread the news that dramatic changes lay ahead if the Apaches would unite and purify themselves. If they would throw off their dependence on American goods and return to their traditional ways, their dead would return to avenge their losses to the whites. This promise of redemption had a powerful effect on the Apaches.[69]

While Wovoka is largely credited with founding the so-called "Ghost Dance" religion in 1890, which carried a similar message, the roots of Nakaaidoklini's apocalyptic vision stretched far back into American Indian history. Nearly a century earlier, a disfigured Shawnee named Lalawethika emerged from an ecstatic state with a new name, Tenskwatawa, and with a powerful message that called for a purification from dependence upon American goods and the unification of native communities to oppose the assault on Indian cultures and lands. His message was not new, either, having first been preached by the Lenape prophets Scattamek and Neolin in the mid-1700s. Although Tenskwatawa's movement, led by his brother Tecumseh, was crushed at the Battle of Tippecanoe and the Battle of the Thames, that core message of returning to native lifeways and embracing intertribal unity found new life in the West.

By the end of August 1881, Fort Apache commander Colonel Eugene Asa Carr had become sufficiently alarmed by the growing movement among the White Mountain Apaches and concluded that Nakaaidoklini had to be stopped. He led a detachment of Apache scouts to Nakaaidoklini's encampment at Cibecue Creek to arrest the prophet, but rather than carry out their orders, the scouts revolted and drew their weapons on Carr. A ferocious gun battle ensued, and in the end, Captain Edmund C. Hentig, six privates, and Nakaaidoklini were killed.[70]

Upon hearing the news that their prophet had been murdered, Natiotish, from the neighboring San Carlos Reservation to the south, led a revolt with about fifty warriors. They swept straight through Pleasant Valley, stealing horses, cattle, and ammunition, and burning all property in their path.[71]

After soldiers returned from Cibecue Creek to Fort Apache to bury their fallen comrades, Natiotish's followers invaded the Fort Apache Reservation and laid siege to the fort.[72] The following day, on 2 September, a small detachment of Apache warriors appeared at the ranch of blacksmith William Middleton, who lived just south of Pleasant Valley, some thirty miles from the fort, with his wife and children.[73] Moments before the Apaches arrived at the ranch, two neighbors, Henry Moody and George L. Turner Jr., came racing up on horses to warn the Middletons of the uprising.[74] Although the Apaches who appeared at Middleton's cabin were well armed, they appeared to be friendly, and the Middletons took them to be army scouts. Middleton inquired whether the news was true. The Apaches assured them that the rumor was false. The warriors then stunned their hosts by firing upon the Middletons.[75] What happened next became the stuff of legend.

Although mortally wounded with a shot to the bowels, so the story goes, teenager Henry "Harry" Middleton calmly asked for a pair of scissors from his mother after they fled to the safety of their cabin. Upon receiving them, he deftly trimmed off his protruding bowels and then resolutely defended his family for another three hours before the Apaches relented. He then died in the arms of his grateful family.[76] It is an awe-inspiring and oft-repeated story of pioneer grit and self-sacrifice. The problem is, though, that none of it happened. The truth is far more interesting.[77]

Deputy Sheriff George Turner was in the new telegraph office in Globe City when news of Captain Hentig's murder came through the wire.[78] Knowing that the Middletons were in an isolated area close to the reservation, Turner immediately set out on the day-and-a-half journey to warn them. After spending the night at the Moody ranch, he convinced his friend Henry Moody to join him for the rest of the journey.

It was late on a Sunday morning when Turner and Moody arrived at the Middletons' ranch, bearing news of the outbreak. The Middletons had not seen or heard any sign of Apaches, and they were on good terms with those they had met. While grateful for the effort that Turner and Moody had made on their behalf, they felt that they were safe.

After lunch, the family set about finishing their Sunday chores. Miriam Middleton took her young children into the milk house, directly behind the cabin, to make butter. George Turner followed to get a cup of buttermilk. William Middleton and thirteen-year-old Willis set about to make butter boxes in the yard. Sixteen-year-old Hattie moved a box near the front door to sit on while she sewed. Henry Moody sat down on the porch, in front of her, to chat. Older brother Henry Middleton was busy in the cabin.

A small contingent of Apaches suddenly appeared near the porch. One of the Apaches, possibly Nantangotayz, climbed on top of a pile of wood outside the fence that ringed the house, giving him a good view of the compound.[79] One of the Apaches standing by the porch asked for a kettle to cook with. The Middletons were used to sharing food and supplies with Apaches, being so close to the reservation, so Hattie got up and handed him a kettle. She asked about the violence at Cibecue, but the men replied that they had been out hunting and knew nothing about it. Hattie sat back down, and the Apaches moved closer to the milk house, where Miriam was working. Another asked for a loaf of bread, and Miriam sent ten-year-old Della to fetch a loaf. When Della handed them the bread, the Apaches turned to leave. At that moment, the Apache standing on the wood pile said: "Now!" Shots rained down on the Middletons from all directions.

A bullet sailed through the open cabin door from behind Hattie, clipping off a lock of her hair, and piercing Henry Moody's eye. The explosion out of the back of his head pitched his body forward, hitting the box where Hattie was sitting, and sent her stumbling backward into the cabin.[80] George Turner, who had been standing outside with his cup of buttermilk, took a bullet in the first volley and fell backward.[81] William Middleton was luckier: with one bullet passing through his hat and another through his shirt, he escaped death twice.

Henry Middleton grabbed the only weapon the family had and returned fire on the scrambling Apaches, wounding one who started sprinting toward the milk house. Miriam immediately shuttered the open window of the milk house and barred the door. Henry then ran to the other side of the cabin to fire on another group of Apaches who were shooting from behind an embankment, as William dashed into the cabin, with Willis on his heels. One warrior who had been stationed farther up the hill drew a bead on Henry and winged him in the shoulder.

Hattie screamed in terror. Miriam, who was safely barricaded in the milk house with the little ones, heard the anguished cry of her daughter and thought that she had been shot. She gathered up the children, flung the door open, and bolted back toward the cabin as another volley of bullets whizzed by them.

By now, the entire family was in the cabin, miraculously safe for the moment.

They threw the chairs and tables up against the doors, and then lay on the floor. Bullets tore through the cabin, lodging deeply into the walls.[82] From the Apache voices outside, they knew that they were surrounded. Huddled together, they expected the Apaches to charge the cabin at any moment and slaughter them. In desperation, Miriam raised herself up on her knees. "I shall never forget my mother," Hattie recalled sixty years later, "as she knelt in prayer and prayed that all would be spared."[83]

For three more hours, the Apaches continued to fire upon the cabin—until sunset. Then, as suddenly as the attack began, all fell silent. The Apaches took the Middletons' horse herd, leaving only one wounded horse behind.

The Middletons dared not move for fear of giving any sign of life. For several hours longer, they lay still in the cabin, straining to understand the source of every sound outside their cabin walls. Finally, after 1:00 A.M., when the moon went down, they slowly began to move. First, they slightly cracked the door open, and they studied the blackness for any movement. Then, slowly, silently, they stole away into the darkness and climbed up to a rocky outcropping, high up in the hills. They had to leave Turner and Moody where they lay. Once the family was hidden, William took the wounded horse and rode through the night to Pleasant Valley for help, leaving the family in Miriam's care. It would be a desperate ride with armed Apaches swarming the area. William warned Miriam not to look for him if he failed to return by daylight.

The sun rose the next morning, and the Middletons anxiously watched and waited. The hours slowly passed, and William still did not return. When they finally accepted that they would not see him again, they heard his voice calling out from below. He had returned from Pleasant Valley with George Church, who had only one rifle and one cartridge left.

William's news was not good. Pleasant Valley had been sacked by raiding Apaches, who drove off horses and burned cabins. Al Rose and George Church had agreed to help, but Rose was attacked before he could ride out, and Middleton and Church fled from the settlement.[84] All along Cherry Creek, Apaches harassed Middleton and Church, forcing them to take a longer, winding route back to the Middleton ranch.

Although they were together again, their circumstance was still dire. "I don't think we will ever get out of here alive," William confided to Miriam, "the hills are full of Indians."[85] They now faced a desperate choice. They dared not go back to the ranch house, nor could they stay where they were, with no provisions and little shelter. They finally decided that their only course was to make their way to Globe City following a little-traveled route, twenty miles out of the way, to avoid any renegades watching the main roads. Once they finally reached the main trail heading toward Globe City, they were overwhelmed with relief to be greeted on the road by Eugene, an older son, who brought a rescue party with him.

On their way to Globe City, they still had an obligation to perform: bearing the news of his son's death to Henry Moody's father. "The most heart rendering thing," Hattie recalled, "was to break the news to Mr. Moody of the death of his only son who had so nobly sacrificed his life for his friends. The old man was alone now, his wife was dead too."[86]

After the Middletons found shelter in Globe City, Miriam refused to return to the ranch. William sold his stock and ranch to two town businessmen, George A. Newton and J. J. Vosberg.[87]

The renegades led by Nantangotayz continued their rampage. About ten days after the attack on the Middleton ranch, Apache warriors attacked soldiers stationed at Fort Apache.[88] The renegade attacks finally died down over the fall and winter months of 1881, most likely because Natiotish took his warriors south into Mexico.

When 1882 came, Navajos, along with Mexican, Mormon, and "gentile" settlers, gathered for miles around to celebrate the railroad line reaching Holbrook.[89] That summer, however, Nantangotayz's renegades boldly returned from Mexico and struck directly at the San Carlos Reservation. Four Apache policemen, including Chief of Police John "Cibecue Charley" Colvig, were killed, and a dozen Apache women—who were most likely the wives of several warriors—were "kidnapped."[90] The renegades raided more ranches and killed eight more Apaches who had served as scouts for the military. They then turned westward and again swept through the Tonto Basin, killing six more ranchers. The only resistance they received was at McMillenville, a small settlement built around a silver mine. The miners quickly organized and successfully repulsed the Apaches.

Despite their setback at McMillenville, Natiotish's forces seemed to grow with each attack. By the middle of July 1882, about 250 mounted warriors again swept through Pleasant Valley, stealing horses from the Tewksburys and from their neighbor, Ed Rose.[91] Farther to the north of the settlement, two Québécois residents, Charles Sixby and Louis Houdon, were not so lucky. When their bodies were found near Haigler Creek, "they had been dead for several days," the official report read. "Both men were naked, lying face up, and bore many marks of the torture inflicted on them before they died. Their feet and hands had been burned. One had a large rock on his stomach. The other had been hacked wide open and his entrails pulled out on the ground."[92] Bob Sixby was also gravely wounded in the attack, but he survived.[93] Soldiers from H Troop—the Buffalo Soldiers— quickly mobilized and chased the Apaches out of Pleasant Valley, but within a few days the warriors struck again at the Meadows ranch near Diamond Point, about fifteen miles northeast of Payson.[94] According to newspaper accounts, "a dozen or more whites, including a number of the Meadows family, were killed before the Indians were penned up by Major Chafee near Baker's Butte."[95]

U.S. Cavalry Captain Adna Chaffee pursued Natiotish, and the Battle of Big Dry Wash in July 1882 was a major defeat for the Apache revolt. Natiotish and dozens of warriors were killed, and the captured warriors were returned to the reservation without further resistance.[96] But that would not last long. Frustration and hunger would continue to breed discontent, and with discontent came militancy.

For the settlers of Arizona's north country, where these attacks occurred, the price of homesteading a land so continuously stalked by theft and death was an unrelenting vigilance and a reliance on loaded weapons close at hand. Yet heightened vigilance, over time, can easily turn into a foreboding about the next outbreak that lingers in the back of the mind and underlies every conversation. The strain of vigilance would begin to take its toll on that small community.

FRIENDSHIPS BORN IN STRIFE

Apache raids often sent settlers fleeing to the safety of towns, and the recent Apache assaults on Pleasant Valley may have been the reason why Ed Tewksbury was in Globe City, Arizona. The high cliffs of the Colorado Plateau made travel to the towns up on the Mogollon Rim a bit of a challenge from Pleasant Valley. It was not impossible, and well-traveled trails connected Pleasant Valley to towns on the Rim like Heber and Holbrook, and to Payson in the west, but the path south to Globe City was a relatively flatter ride. It also had the benefit of being out of the path of Natiotish's forces.[97] It was there while in Globe City that Ed struck up a conversation with an Ireland-born miner.[98]

The day that Ed Tewksbury met John Graham was an inauspicious one.[99] It was just a couple of men conversing in a bar, perhaps over a beer.[100] Johnny, as he was known to his friends, was interested in a new venture, and cattle could command as much as $40 a head at market. Cowpunchers had opened trails to bring thousands of cattle to eager eastern markets as the meatpacking industry rapidly expanded to meet consumer demand. Eastern investors were soon looking to the open ranges of the unsettled West as profitable investment opportunities for raising beef. There was work to be had in the changing economy, and for the enterprising, profits to reap.[101]

The two men chatting in the saloon that afternoon liked each other, enough for Ed to extend an invitation to Johnny to bring his brother Tom to look at Pleasant Valley. Although they were of very different backgrounds, both Tewksbury and Graham shared enough in common: both had lost their mothers at a young age, both had lived for a time in northern California (not too far from each other, actually), both were young and eager for adventure, and both needed work.[102]

The Graham brothers came from a respectable family. Samuel Graham was a tall, stately Scotsman who married Jane Ballantine from Ireland, and they both immigrated to the United States after the birth of Johnny, their fourth child.[103] The Grahams settled down to a life of modest comfort in Boone, Iowa, raising their growing family in a two-story white clapboard house.

Sixteen years after the Grahams established themselves in Boone, however, the three oldest boys, Allen, Johnny, and Tom, left the Graham household for good.[104] Their mother died in 1861 giving birth to her sixth child, Harriet, and not quite two years later Samuel married French-born Marie Eva Lent Goetzman.[105] By the time the Graham brothers decided to leave, three more children, William, Jennie, and Samuel, had been born. Their home was getting crowded, and the boys had difficulty getting along with their new stepmother. So, with wanderlust in their eyes and dreams of striking it rich in the western gold mines in their heads, they left the farm.[106]

For a time, they worked in Alaska and then tried their hand in California.[107] But they were relatively late to the great gold rush, and their timing played a part in shaping their experience in California and their view of the world. Although new lodes were still being discovered during the years that they were picking their way through the mining regions of northern California, several of the prosperous mines were already played out, and large swaths of land had already been claimed. Often those claims were unmarked, which resulted in many latecomers devoting hard labor to working a site before discovering that the land belonged to someone else. Many latecomers resented the network of rules and relationships that were already in place before their arrival, which then became codified into law.[108] Those laws, which seemed like a web that prosperous men had woven to deny them access to prosperity, frustrated the dreams of many latecomers. Such was the view that the Grahams brought to Pleasant Valley as they grappled to articulate the economic and social struggles of their times. They were convinced that wealthy men were colluding to deprive them of prosperity.

Their years in California were disappointing, to say the least. They started out working a claim on the Sacramento River, near Redding. It was hard labor, and after a few years, Allen, the oldest brother, had had enough. He chose a different life, moving on to the Washington Territory and settling down as a farmer with a sixteen-year-old bride.[109] Johnny and Tom stayed behind in California for another decade, at times logging and at other times working their claim, until news of richer yields in the Arizona Territory moved them to finally give up on their California dream.[110] Sometime after 1880, they put that state behind them to try their luck in the Arizona Territory.

Johnny and Tom immediately staked out three claims upon their arrival in Arizona, but mining was still backbreaking work, even though they were, by now, seasoned hands.[111] They seemed to leap at Ed Tewksbury's invitation to join him and his brothers in Pleasant Valley. Work was readily available tending Stinson's herd.[112] Although moving to Pleasant Valley was a risk for the Grahams, given the ongoing Apache outbreaks, they found the grasslands and flowing creeks a perfect place to try their hand at cattle ranching—as long as the army could keep the Apaches on the reservation.[113]

There is only one picture known to exist of Johnny and Tom Graham. Their portraits were taken just a few years before coming to the Arizona Territory. Johnny was thirty-one years old when his portrait was taken in San Francisco. He was a handsome man, who still looked young for his age. He was a bit on the smaller side, but he had a look of steely determination in his clear blue eyes that suggested that he was not one to back down easily. He had his father's high cheekbones and high forehead and wore his sandy-brown hair short. He grew a respectable mustache, a fashion that was common to many men in his day.[114] Tom was twenty-eight years old when his portrait was taken farther inland, in Red Bluff, the seat of Tehama County. It was also a major staging area for mining in northern California. Tom favored his mother more, with wavy blond hair and deep-set blue eyes. He was a bit fuller in the face than Johnny, with smooth

Johnny Graham, ca. 1882.
Courtesy Arizona Historical Society Library
and Archives, Tucson.

Thomas Graham, ca. 1882.
Courtesy Arizona Historical Society Library
and Archives, Tucson.

cheeks and a prominent jaw. If still pictures can speak, he had the appearance of a thoughtful and pensive man.[115]

Within a few months of meeting Tewksbury, the Graham brothers pulled up stakes and moved north to Pleasant Valley.[116] The two sets of brothers made a curious sight as they roamed about the valley. One set was a little older, in their thirties, and the other set was a little younger, still in their twenties. One set was fair-haired, blue-eyed, and fair-skinned, and the other set was black-haired, dark-eyed, and dark-skinned. They certainly made an impression on Joseph Pearce, who, as a boy, remembered being awed by the sight of the weapons that the Grahams carried. "Each lugged a .45 strapped to his hip and packed a .45–60 Winchester in a saddle holster. Their belts carried full rounds of pistol and rifle cartridges. Each wore stogie boots and clanked heavy spurs." Pearce and his friends were equally impressed by the exotic look of the Tewksburys, who carried, instead of weapons, rawhide ropes and hobbles. "They had Indian blood in them, it was said; their skins were smooth, their eyes black and glittery,

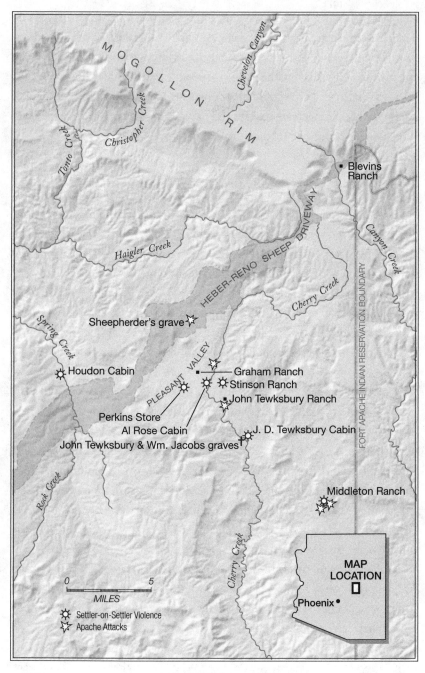

Pleasant Valley War Sites.

Map by Tom Jonas.

and their noses hooked. They were slow moving, slow talking [and] sort of took panther steps. Their outfits popped our eyes out: chaperajos [*sic*] chaps made of cowhide with the hair out; shoes, not boots, with long work socks pulled up high and their pants tucked into the socks. Their hats carried leather chin straps that fitted almost to the point of the chin, the hats sitting straight on their heads and not tipped back . . . we were bashful and half afraid of them," he recalled. "But we couldn't take our eyes off of them."[117]

———•◦•———

The first months in their new home went smoothly for the Graham brothers. Fortune appeared to be on their side. Together with the Tewksbury brothers, the Grahams erected a one-room, split-log cabin amid the open range of Pleasant Valley, about five miles up the road from the Tewksburys.[118] The Graham brothers were a welcome addition for the Tewksbury boys.[119] Their nearest neighbors were still miles away, and they were practically the only men around their ages. Even with the arrival of the Grahams, though, Pleasant Valley remained sparsely settled. Only a dozen souls lived in about 2,600 acres of land, spread out along the creeks.[120]

The Grahams had saved enough money to invest in Mormon cattle.[121] Eager to begin their new venture, the Graham brothers hired Jim Tewksbury to help them move their new herd down from Snowflake.[122] The journey there and back was no more than a couple of nights sleeping under the stars.

Surely these were heady days for the Grahams in the fall of 1882, driving their first herd from the high desert of Snowflake down into the pines of the Mogollon Rim, and then farther down into the lush grasslands of Pleasant Valley. "Tom Graham had fantastic dreams and schemes of getting rich quick in Arizona and of becoming a cattle baron . . . with what mavericks they were finding," recalled Drusilla Hazelton, who knew the Grahams.[123] The land was untamed and still contested, but there was profit to be made by the daring. And indeed, the newly established railroads that could export Arizona cattle to hungry markets promised opportunities, even for smalltime ranchers.[124] They were no doubt buoyed by the presence of the Tewksburys and by confidence in their own abilities to handle themselves on the frontier.

In the days that followed that seemingly ordinary cattle drive, however, and early in the Tewksburys' friendship with the Grahams, the seeds of strife were sown that reaped the terrible whirlwind that tore through the community.

2

FRONTIER ENTREPRENEURS

The work of Patricia Nelson Limerick, William G. Robbins, and other scholars of the New Western History offers a clearer-eyed story of the settling of the West than what our popular narratives often allow.[1] Americans of the nineteenth century looked upon the West, as indeed did generations before them, as a vast resource to exploit in the pursuit of profit. The West was transformed by eastern industrialists and investors who financed and controlled the emerging markets that in turn shaped the history of the region, from the fur trade to farming, cattle ranching, and mining. It is a decidedly unromantic view of how the singular, headlong quest for profit underwrote why Americans drove onto lands already occupied by Indians, and what they did once they got there.

It was no coincidence, therefore, that the information that territorial settlers produced and consumed centered on business. Territorial newspapers devoted much space to advertising for businesses, and most of the news printed centered on national and local markets or on legislative and technological developments that could affect the economic growth of the community. Occasionally, news of social and cultural developments peeked out between business reports, but newspapers existed to make money reporting about money, and they gave their subscribers what they wanted to read.

Thus Arizona's earliest settlers—the miners, the stock herders, and the farmers—came to the territory to make a profit, and they were willing to take great risks to do so. For territorial farmers and stock herders, their principal customer was the United States government in the form of the military outposts that dotted the land. Internal community markets—settlers selling to settlers—were just developing. But regional markets, national markets, and even illicit markets were well established, and transportation technology greatly facilitated the ability of many residents to orient their activities around those markets.

Railroads transformed the territory. While they allowed settlers to more easily move goods to market, the railroads also made the raw resources of Arizona accessible to corporate interests. As eastern corporations moved assets to the territory—primarily cattle but also workers—those resources began to dominate the local economies. Within a short period, small ranchers in Pleasant Valley found themselves in hard competition for the same natural resources that attracted outside corporate interests. What had once been a shared economy based on cooperation became an aggressively competitive environment that threatened the livelihoods of local ranchers. Some of those threats came in the form of competition for land and water, and others came in the form of corporate cowboys hired to enforce their company's interests.

The influx of cattle by the thousands also transformed the trade in stolen livestock. As Americans increasingly moved onto contested lands, American goods and livestock began to move through that supply chain. Some enterprising Indians would also take horses from neighboring American settlers and require the owners to pay a trespass fee guaranteed them by treaty rights.[2] But it would be a mistake to credit Indians as the principal suppliers of illicit goods. The temptation to turn a quick profit by theft was great for some of the settlers, even for some of the hired hands who were brought into the territory to control the corporate herds. Stealing livestock from an unsuspecting neighbor or an employer was perhaps as profitable an enterprise as the legitimate ones. Over time, settlers in Pleasant Valley began to suspect one another of betraying the common trust that they had once shared.

THE LONG REACH OF NATIONAL MARKETS

One of the concessions made to the railroad companies had a particularly unsavory impact on the settlers living near the railroads. To allow railroad companies to raise sufficient capital to complete the railroad, Congress deeded ten square miles of federal land to these corporations for every mile of track they built. To prevent the railroads from monopolizing good land, the land was deeded in a checkerboard pattern that left federal land in between the land granted to railroads. That federal land could then be purchased by private citizens, businesses, or even by the railroads. One eastern corporation, the Aztec Land and Cattle Company, took particular advantage of huge swaths of land for sale in Arizona.[3]

By the mid-1880s, the heyday of the cattle industry was already beginning to decline, but the market was still dynamic. The iconic cattle drives over the open ranges of the West were rapidly becoming difficult to continue. Railroads hastened settlement in places that were once open land, and settlers wanting to protect their crops from roaming cattle, as well as cattlemen wanting to protect their grazing land from competition, put up ribbons of barbed wire. Further, overgrazing and a devastating drought followed by an exceptionally severe winter in 1886 and 1887 distressed the grasslands of the Great Plains, prompting cattlemen to turn their gaze toward the grasslands of northern Arizona. Early visitors to the region reported oceans of Blackfoot and Crowfoot gamma grass in the Arizona highlands, waist deep and as far as the eye could see.[4] The absence of large herds of herbivores and almost four centuries of a wetter and colder climate known as the Little Ice Age produced an overabundance of vegetation. It was in these forest meadows that an enterprising Bostonian saw an opportunity.

Edward Wilkinson Kinsley was an abolitionist who raised a "colored" regiment in North Carolina (later reassigned as the 35th United States Colored Troops) during the Civil War. He enjoyed personal audiences with the president, and he energetically lobbied Lincoln to emancipate the slaves.[5] After the war, as the commissioner for the Atlantic and Pacific (A&P) Railroad Company, Kinsley devised a plan to merge the assets of two companies that were in distress.[6] The A&P Railroad was still deeply in debt after two years of operation, and it was eager to sell off its western land.[7] Around the same time, the Continental Cattle Company in Texas was anxious to liquidate much of its livestock before it succumbed to the crippling drought.[8] Seeing opportunity, Kinsley arranged for the purchase of one million acres in northern Arizona from the A&P Railroad at fifty cents an acre, and 33,000 longhorn cattle and about 2,000 horses from the Continental Cattle Company, along with its distinctive hashknife brand. From these acquisitions, the Aztec Land and Cattle Company was born.

The "Hashknife outfit," as it became known, located its headquarters in Holbrook, Arizona, one of the stops along the A&P line. Texas cowboys, drifters, and some of the local Arizona boys—about eighty in all—signed on to ride with the new company. Once the employees were in place in Arizona, all that was needed was the livestock, so in a move that signaled the beginning of the end of the long cattle drive, the Aztec Land and Cattle Company shipped its livestock to Arizona by railroad. Although long drives were still made on occasion until the 1890s, by that time railroads covered most of the land, and long cattle drives were no longer necessary. Once the cattle arrived in the Arizona Territory, Hashknife cowboys began raiding the range of the Rim country, much to the dismay of its settlers.

While the American cowboy has become such an iconic image of the Old West, if not of America itself, many contemporaries of real cowboys held a starkly different view—especially in Arizona. Cowboys, according to the *Arizona Champion,* were little more than "white Indians," rootless, vice-ridden thieves on horseback who lived fast and died young. There were indeed good cowboys, the editors acknowledged, and some even had a modicum of education and refinement, but not in Arizona. "Here in Arizona we certainly have the bad ones. . . . The cowboys make their headquarters in some out-of-the-way place where their actions are not apt to be observed. They will start out on mysterious journeys and return with strange cattle and horses. Quick, alert, and cautious in their movements, depredations can seldom be traced directly to them and their pals generally dispose of their cattle in the same mysterious manner as they were acquired. . . . Civilization and cowboys do not assimilate. . . . While alive they add nothing to the advancement and happiness of the world and no one mourns their death."[9]

This unforgiving editorial expressed the view held by many in northern Arizona as confrontations between Hashknife cowboys and local settlers mounted.[10] Many settlers believed that these cowboys from Texas, with their six guns conspicuously displayed, were really desperados who had been driven out of state by the law.[11] Joseph Harrison Pearce was an inquisitive Mormon lad who walked up to a group of newly arrived Texan cowboys.

"What you boys wearing your six-shooters for? Why did you all leave Texas?" he asked.

"Reckon it was because folks back in Texas wanted us to build a church," one said with a sly grin, "an' we wouldn't build it."[12]

Trouble for local settlers began quickly as the Aztec Land and Cattle Company aggressively asserted ownership of its newly acquired land, prosecuting squatters through the courts or driving them off the range with cocked pistols. Even for those who were living legitimately on parcels adjacent to Hashknife land, the Aztec Land and Cattle Company showed little sympathy for damage caused by Hashknife cattle, or when cattle from local ranchers got mixed up with the larger herds. To be sure, not all settlers had difficulty with the Hashknife cowboys, but many did, and some fought back.[13]

Some lay histories have argued that the coming of the Aztec Land and Cattle Company was the trigger for tensions between cattlemen and sheep men in the territory, but that is only partially true, and certainly not the entire story. In 1885, sheep men and cattlemen came together to form the Mogollon Live Stock Protective Association to publish notices of missing livestock and offer rewards for the arrest and conviction of anyone stealing or selling livestock belonging to association members. The organization also coordinated spring "rondeos"—roundups and sporting competitions—as well as social gatherings for members and their families.[14] In the spring of 1887, the territorial legislature also eased restrictions prohibiting sheep owners from coming within two miles of established stock ranges, lobbied for primarily by prominent Flagstaff businessman P. P. Daggs.[15]

As amicable as sheep and cattle owners could be, confrontations between herders on the range did arise, and some were bloody. In early 1887, four Mexican vaqueros murdered two American sheepherders and set fire to their encampment near Buffalo Springs, New Mexico, about 160 miles northeast of Pleasant Valley on the Navajo Reservation.[16] Within a few weeks of that incident, four American cowboys rode up to where some Mexican sheepherders were watering their flocks near Grants, New Mexico, and ordered them away. The sheepherders refused to leave until their flocks were finished, and threats quickly escalated into gunfire. Justus Montaño, the lead herder, was fatally wounded but not before he returned fire and killed his murderer. Three other herders were wounded in the gun battle before the cowboys hastily rode off for Arizona at top speed. A posse of cattle ranchers and sheepherders quickly organized to pursue the cowboys.[17]

At times, conflicts arose between sheepherders themselves. In mid-December 1885, sheep man Ralph Cameron attempted to chase off a group of Mexican sheepherders who were heading toward his land along the Little Colorado River near Winslow. The lead sheepherder replied that it was a free country and free grass and that they were not leaving. A gun battle broke out, lasting until dark, and three were wounded. Cameron left for Flagstaff early the next morning for reinforcements and returned with two deputy sheriffs with warrants for the arrest of the Mexican sheepherders. In the meantime, other ranchers came to the aid of the Mexican sheepherders and protected their herds. When Cameron and the deputies arrived, they considered it the better part of valor to suspend their quest to arrest the other sheepherders.[18]

Each incident illustrates the complicated nature of violence on the Arizona frontier. While extremists can be found in every group, most of the time, Arizona sheep men and cattlemen respected each other. Conflicts were relatively infrequent, but at times hired hands on the range quarreled over rights of way and access to resources. Cattlemen also fought cattlemen and shepherds fought shepherds over the same issues, with the same intensity. Economic competition, coupled with long workdays and extreme temperatures, could lead to short tempers.

At the same time, one cannot dismiss the role of race and nationality in these confrontations. While it is doubtful that Cameron would have welcomed onto his land a herd of sheep driven by white Americans, or that the Mexican sheepherders would have turned away from Cameron's land had he been a fellow countryman, codified racism was on the rise. The end of Radical Reconstruction in the fateful Compromise of 1877 ushered in a long night of legally sanctioned racial hostility in the United States. Rudyard Kipling's "The White Man's Burden" would not be published for another decade, but the Arizona territory was already being eyed as a place for a new school to educate Indian children out of their traditional ways.[19]

THE LIVESTOCK BLACK MARKET

With the threat of Apache outbreaks constantly looming like ominous storm clouds on the Rim, the small settlement of Pleasant Valley might have turned to mutual cooperation in response to external threat. But the increase in horses and cattle by the thousands in northern Arizona also increased the temptation to profit by theft. The Tonto Basin—and Pleasant Valley in particular—already had a reputation for being an unsafe place to keep livestock. What with the frequent Apache outbreaks, as well as Mexican vaqueros, American outlaws, and at times unethical settlers all operating in a remote area three-days' ride from the law, complaints of stolen livestock were common.[20] Virtually every issue of the *Arizona Champion* dedicated a full page to notices of missing sheep, cattle, horses, and mules.

There was, at the same time, no lack of buyers for stolen livestock. Some of the cattle, sheep, and horses were sold off in Mexico. Some livestock were sold to residents of the Salt River Valley who were not terribly inquisitive about why they were able to purchase livestock so cheaply.[21] And some neighbors in the Tonto Basin were simply brazen.

William Jordan Flake, who lived on the Rim in the Mormon settlement of Snowflake, rode out one day to track his stolen horses. Eventually he came across three heavily armed white men on horseback. He recognized one of them, Louis Parker. Parker was a nephew of the Graham brothers and had recently moved out from Iowa to stay with them.[22] Flake did not recognize the other two, but he certainly recognized the horse that Parker was riding. It was one of his missing horses. The three asked Flake what he was doing.

"I am looking for more of my horses that were stolen," Flake replied. Parker asked if he had found them.

"Yes, you are riding one of them." The three laughed. "Do you think you will take him?" Parker asked.

"I guess not," Flake cautiously replied. "You are well armed, and I am not." Then he looked directly at Parker and said, "But we may meet again."[23]

Why would the Grahams gravitate toward the illicit livestock trade, as many in the area suspected of them? To be sure, some small-time ranchers looked upon the rustling of corporate-owned cattle as a kind of leveling of the imbalance created by corporate cattle ranching—their strong-armed tactics, their domination of grassland and watering holes, and their price gouging.[24] At the same time, however, when Johnny and Tom came to the Arizona Territory, they were no longer the young men who left the farm with adventure in their eyes. In the harsh reality of the hardscrabble life of mining and lumberjacking, their youthful dreams of finding ready riches faded quickly. The nine years they spent in California cutting timber or scraping the earth for riches—finding rude entertainments in the rough-and-tumble camps along the Sacramento River, or perhaps searching for a measure of solace in cheap whiskey and makeshift whorehouses—had changed them. They had, in those years, transformed from carefree, adventurous boys to hardened men. They had grown leaner, tougher, and more dogged in their quest to find wealth.[25]

Though not wealthy in the ways they expected, they emerged from their years in California more strongly bound by brotherhood and wiser for the experience, having learned to live by their wits and to hold their own in the unforgiving frontier. In becoming survivors, they learned to play off their strengths. Johnny was more inclined toward risk-taking, calculating the angles while looking for the big score, while Tom was more cautious and reflective. Though they never earned enough to return home wealthy men, they also never returned home. Their resolve to find a profitable venture only seemed to deepen and strengthen with time, and this is what led them to the Arizona Territory.

Upon moving to Pleasant Valley, the Grahams soon discovered a well-established black market in stolen livestock that ran straight through the valley. All around them, their neighbors took great precautions to protect their investments, but the Grahams may have looked upon the situation differently. Rather than fight against that market, they may have seen it as just another profit-making opportunity for those who were quick and daring enough.[26]

It does not appear that Johnny and Tom were involved in the direct procurement of stolen livestock—at least not at first. Rather, with their spread bordering the main trail used for moving livestock through the area, they may have simply agreed to allow livestock to water and feed on their land with no questions asked, for a price. Tom's daughter Estella recalled that it was young Louis Parker who first joined the rustlers, recruited by a friend of Tom Graham's named "Gurell," probably Ross Gruwell, who was later arrested in Phoenix for rustling.[27]

The theft economy prompted the rapid creation of livestock protective associations throughout the territory between 1884 and 1885. From the Mogollon Live Stock Protective Association in the north to the Pinal County Live Stock Association in the south, cattlemen and sheep owners banded together to protect their respective livelihoods.[28] The constitution of the Pinal County Live Stock Association, which utilized prose common to territorial livestock association charters, cites the conditions that necessitated their formation: "The members of this Association agree to unite themselves together for mutual protection . . . against the lawless bad men found disturbing the country. It shall be the duty of members, in a lawful manner to procure all evidence that will aid in the conviction of the offenders against the laws of the Territory, and whenever any member of this Association is required to give any evidence against criminals in the courts, we pledge ourselves to protect the same in a lawful manner in the discharge of such duty."[29] One of the principal ways in which these associations sought to protect one another was to post notifications in local newspapers, which often ran several pages long, about stolen livestock and to offer rewards up to $1,500 for the successful prosecution of rustlers.

While most of these early associations tended to be small collectives of neighboring stockmen, many recognized the value of creating larger, regional coordination. The Arizona Live Stock Association met in Tucson in April 1885 with representatives from the Southeastern Stock Growers Association, Stock Growers Association of Tombstone, and the Stock Growers Association of Gila County present.[30] Two years later, the Territorial Live Stock Association of Arizona formed to organize the northern associations. Their mission statement cites the ongoing concern about theft in 1887: "The object for which this Association is formed is not to do the work of the local associations, but to bring such associations into a closer union and to assist them in securing legislation, *to be the means of their co-operating in bringing criminals to justice*, and to have a general supervision of the stock interests of the Territory as a whole" (italics added).[31]

Thus, from the local to the regional levels, mutual protection was the primary aim. But how were they to do that? Again, the language of the Pinal County Live Stock Association is instructive: members were to remain especially vigilant about the livestock moving along trail routes and about who was moving them. "On all routes where cattle are being driven from the country, strict watch must be kept in the interest of all . . . and should assistance be needed, in stopping herds, or arresting parties driving cattle from their accustomed range, it shall be the duty of each and every member of the Association to render all necessary aid in his power."[32]

Self-policing on the trail made sense, given Arizona's expansive rangeland and the limited reach of the law in the counties. But the danger in self-policing is that the thin line between vigilance of the trails and vigilantism could easily be crossed in the heat of the moment. And when that line was crossed, tragedy often ensued.

———•◦•———

James Stinson's effort to find relief from relentless cattle rustling set off the chain of events that tore the small community of Pleasant Valley apart. After continued losses to his prized herd of "Mormon beef" that he kept up on the Rim, he decided in 1883 to move his cattle down into Pleasant Valley and hire local men to watch his herd.[33] Among those hired were the Tewksbury and Graham brothers.[34] That move brought welcomed employment and income for the men employed, but for some, the temptation to boost their fortunes a bit more by poaching Stinson's cattle was just too great to pass up.

In the valley, cattle roamed free, grazing where they would, until roundup. Cattle generally stayed together in herds, but there was always some risk in open range grazing. Some cattle would wander off and never be found again, perhaps lost to wolves or mountain lions. Others simply died of natural causes. A good crew could minimize such losses, but not every loss every time.

For the less than scrupulous, opportunity could be found in this unpredictability. Sometimes newborn calves could be branded with the wrong herd. Sometimes cattle would wander off to another herd and could also wind up being sold with the wrong herds. In such conditions, honest mistakes could occur. So could intentional deception.

3

BLOOD OF THE COVENANT

Pressures compounded for the settlers of Pleasant Valley as the 1880s progressed. Already apprehensive about Apaches to the east and the active theft economy that cut through the region, they began to fear that the Aztec Land and Cattle Company was going to drive them out of the valley.[1] Settlers chafed at the power and influence that the large cattle operations wielded, and at the constant run-ins with aggressive Hashknife cowboys. They worried that they could not compete against such large operations or that their property would be swamped in the flood of corporate cattle washing over the land.

Within this already strained environment, the beat of Apache war drums arose once again as promised provisions failed to materialize and clans clashed with each other on the reservation. Their unrest prompted warnings to fly among the settlers that outbreaks were imminent, and their watchfulness moved into high alert. Fear of surprise attack loomed over the valley as settlers looked over their shoulders and scrutinized every shadow or flutter of movement behind the trees and rocks surrounding them.

Pleasant Valley settlers began banding together in loose confederations created by friendship and economic ties. Some of the settlers chose to ally with the large cattle operations that employed them. Others came together as small-time ranchers to defend their rights to open land and water. But the circumstances of the frontier tested these loose alliances. Because they lived close to one another and at one time shared meals and helped one another build their homes together, their different needs and affiliations became personalized over time, especially as confrontations over missing livestock led to deeper rifts. Amid the pressures of a rapidly changing economy and the constant threat of Indian attacks, unresolved differences that had been simmering between the settlers began to boil.

Their divisions did not at first lead to open assaults. Pleasant Valley settlers turned instead to the courts, and Johnny Graham initiated a pattern within the settlement of using the courts to pursue personal objectives. He accused neighbors of stealing James Stinson's cattle, but not before he secured a contract from Stinson rewarding him for his testimony. Stinson turned to the court in the belief that the law could settle disagreements over the ownership of cattle. In time, however, what may have started as an appeal to civility turned into harassment by lawsuit. Settler complaints against one another compounded as they sought to litigate their way out of their quarrels. A five-year pattern of repeated lawsuits suggests that at least some of the settlers tried to use the court to drive their neighbors out.

Amid these implacable threats to life and livelihood, settlers could not help but begin to experience a new reality of emotional and mental strain, one that they were likely unable to entirely name or understand, but surely felt—the insidious effects of chronic fear and stress that silently and relentlessly wove into their lives over time.[2] Given the state of medical knowledge of the period, they could not have fully articulated what was happening to them because the closest that medical research came to understanding continuous traumatic stress was "neurasthenia."[3] By 1881, George Miller Beard had established himself as the foremost authority on "Americanitis" (as it was more popularly known), in *American Nervousness: Its Causes and Consequences; A Supplement to Nervous Exhaustion (Neurasthenia).*[4] Beard distinguished between simple "nervousness" and "nervous exhaustion," which he termed "neurasthenia" and described as: "Insomnia . . . bad dreams, cerebral irritation, dilated pupils, pain, pressure and heaviness in the head . . . nervous dyspepsia, desire for stimulants and narcotics . . . deficient mental control, lack of decision in trifling matters, hopelessness."[5]

While these symptoms today would be more readily associated with chronic stress and anxiety, Beard believed that the condition was brought on by the fast-paced demands of modern urban life.[6] Even if someone in the rural settlements of the Arizona Territory had state-of-the-art medical training, medical research in the 1880s had not yet developed a full understanding of how the mind responds to long-term physiological threat and provocation. Settlers who endured these chronic conditions could only draw upon rudimentary cures—often alcohol, tobacco, or opiates—to treat the results of unrelenting tension.

TO BE AN INDIAN IN THE ARIZONA TERRITORY

It was a difficult time to be the product of a white-Indian relationship in the decades following the Civil War. While such unions were not uncommon for that first generation of white Americans who moved onto Indian territory in the West, it did not ease the acceptance of their children. Many whites tended to scorn such relationships and attribute to "half breed" children all the negative qualities of both races. It was a burden the Tewksbury children would bear all their lives.

Territorial settlers in Arizona tended to hold more mixed views toward Mexicans.[7] The cattle industry was still highly dependent on Mexican practices and customs, and Mexican vaqueros working the range for white ranch owners were a common sight. In fact, Spanish continued to serve as the lingua franca of the territory, as it had in the region for centuries, allowing Indians, Mexicans, and whites to communicate with one another. At least one Spanish-surnamed individual, Alfred Ruiz, served as a county clerk in northern Arizona, and then as a judge in Apache County in 1894. Spanish-surnamed citizens were also elected or appointed as lawmen in parts of the territory, and white settlers often married Mexican women. Still, if the editorials of territorial newspapers were representative of the majority views of white Arizonans, they did not look upon Mexicans as equals, and in most cases held that American practices and customs were superior to those of Mexicans.[8]

When it came to the Indian nations of the Arizona Territory, however, white settlers held a near consensus on what to do: either remove them or kill them, for they would not tolerate Indians living in the territory. In northwestern Arizona, the editors of *The Arizona Champion* reflected on the murder of white settlers during a recent Apache outbreak. "The recent escape of a number of Indians from the San Carlos reservation and the subsequent murders . . . show what a treacherous set of red devils they are and how impossible it is to prevent them from committing such crimes. The whole crew must be fired out of the territory before human life will be secure. If the Indian Friendly Bureau object to their imprisonment, ship the whole gang out to their care when they can place them in a New England dime museum and pet them to their hearts content."[9] In another section, the editors wrote: "If there are any good Indians outside of graveyards, they do not live in Arizona."[10] In central Arizona, in the territorial capital of Prescott, the *Arizona Journal-Miner* lamented that Indians and the newly freed African Americans were not dying off as quickly as hoped. Whites would be forced to compete with "colored people," the editorial warned: "Rip! Goes another dream! It was confidentially believed that the colored people will gradually die out in freedom. But their percentage outruns the whites. Then it was thought that death was a silent partner of civilization exterminating the Indians, but statistics show that they are increasing too. It will not be long before the whites will have to dicker with these two races for foothold."[11] In the south, on the U.S.-Mexican border, the editors of the *Tucson Star* were not any more forgiving. They differed only in how Indians should be shipped out of the territory. "The people of Arizona demand the removal of all of the Apache Indians from Arizona and the government sooner or later will learn that this is the cheapest policy for the government, the most humane for the Indians, and the most just for the people of the territory. But until that can be accomplished let the Indians be weakened in Arizona by division, and the smaller the number that can be located in one place, the less danger to the people."[12]

This was the world the Tewksbury brothers inhabited.

The Tewksbury brothers were by no means "blanket Indians." They spoke English as well as anyone else, and they looked and dressed and acted as other young men in the territory who were at home on a horse and good with a gun. Indeed, some called Ed Tewksbury a dandy behind his back because he dressed better than most.[13] The only real difference between the Tewksbury brothers and their peers was that their hair was black, their eyes dark brown, and their skin dark. Strangers often mistook them for Mexicans.

One might assume, based on the rhetoric of removal, that once the "red devils" were turned from their "savage" ways and became Christian gentlemen and women, they would be welcomed by Arizona settlers. Ed Tewksbury had an encounter in Payson that revealed otherwise. He was present in Payson when a man named Gladden—most likely ex-convict George Gladden from Texas—rode into town one afternoon and boasted that he had just killed two men in self-defense.[14] For that, he wished to treat the crowd to a drink at the saloon. As men cheerfully stepped up to the bar, Gladden looked down the line at his newfound friends. His eyes stopped at Tewksbury.

"Here is where I draw the line!" he roared. "I'll not drink with a black man!"

Ed Tewksbury turned to look at Gladden, then stepped back from the bar and walked past the line of men to where Gladden was standing. With an open hand he smacked Gladden on both sides of his face hard enough to stun Gladden, who was motionless and wide-eyed. There the two men stood, staring down one other, both waiting to see what the other would do. Tewksbury again slapped Gladden hard on both sides of his face.

"If you can't use both guns, draw one!" he snarled.

Gladden stumbled backward and ran out of the saloon. "Give me my rifle!" he shouted, "Give me my rifle!"

Ed walked out after him. "Walk down the road to the right distance and place, and we will shoot it out!" he yelled to the fleeing man.

Gladden continued running, and he was not seen in town again.[15]

Many settlers to the territory were refugees from the former Confederate states who imported definitions of color shaped by the southern experience. Yet Gladden's invoking the term "black" to describe Tewksbury was articulating a view that many Americans shared in that era, not just southerners. This was the time in American history when a host of segregation laws were recognized as constitutionally valid. The lynchings of blacks and Mexicans who defied the increasingly stringent racial order were on the rise, and many Americans commonly shared the belief that nonwhite people were socially, if not biologically, inferior to whites, whether they were African, Asian, Indian, or even half-white.

At the same time, Tewksbury's response reveals something about his state of mind and character. Rather than laughing it off or perhaps insisting on his white parentage, he was simply not going to be pushed around. He could easily match social violence with physical violence, and this may not have been the first time for him. He seemed hardly surprised by Gladden's objection to sharing a drink with him, and very accustomed to physically asserting his social presence.[16]

THE FIRST SHOOTOUT IN PLEASANT VALLEY

In early January 1883, three men rode through the snow to John Tewksbury's ranch.[17] John's ranch was really nothing more than a small, half-built, one-room log cabin; a barn still under construction and not much larger than the house; and some rudimentary pens. The oldest of the three men, forty-eight-year-old Epitacio Ruiz, was a native New Mexican who had been with Stinson for years, serving as his cook. Twenty-five-year-old John Cullen Gilleland was too young to remember his father, who died fighting for the Confederacy at the Battle of Val Verde (sometimes anglicized to Valverde) in New Mexico.[18] His mother, Emily, remarried a few years later to Oscar Felton, a stock raiser, and Gilleland lived with his mother, stepfather, and half siblings seven miles to the north of Pleasant Valley, along Marsh Creek. Gilleland was employed as Stinson's range foreman.[19] The third was fourteen-year-old Elisha Gilleland, newly arrived from Texas and staying with his aunt and cousin. The three men rode to the Tewksbury ranch at James Stinson's request, to allow the Tewksburys to "vent" the Stinson cattle mistakenly branded as theirs at the last rodeo.[20]

The Tewksbury brothers originally offered to return and rebrand the cattle, but Stinson refused and promised to prosecute them. He eventually relented and sent his men to inform the Tewksburys of his change of heart. What happened next was highly contested, but the results were not.

About 10:00 A.M., the Tewksbury brothers were working on their cabin, with the help of Johnny and Tom Graham. It was cold outside, and their breath hung in the air, but there was still work to be done. Young Francis Tewksbury was about a half mile away, coming back on a wagon with supplies. Johnny Graham was about two hundred yards away looking for stones in the creek bed to help construct a hearth. Tom Graham was busy splitting a log to make a cupboard, and Ed was working on a fuse to blast a hole in the cold ground to erect posts. Jim was working a small foundry.

John Gilleland rode up first, followed by Elisha and Epitacio.[21] All were armed: John with a six-shooter, Elisha with a six-shooter and a Winchester rifle, and Epitacio with a holstered pistol. Their cartridge belts were well stocked. Of the Tewksburys and Grahams, only Ed was armed with a small "bull dog" pistol shoved in his pants pocket.

Gilleland steered his horse around Jim, looking him over, and stopped in front of Ed.[22]

"Good morning," said Ed. "Who are you looking for?"

"You, you son of a bitch," John Gilleland snapped as he drew his pistol. Whether he intended to shoot Tewksbury, or unintentionally pulled the trigger in the ferment of the moment, is unclear. It probably did not help that he had been warming himself with whiskey.[23] Either way, his pistol discharged and the shot went over Tewksbury's head.[24]

Ed Tewksbury's reaction was quick, almost instinctive. He pulled out his pistol and fired at John Gilleland as Gilleland returned a second shot, missing Ed Tewksbury but going through Johnny Graham's hat and splattering close to Jim Tewksbury's head.

Tom Graham and Jim Tewksbury scrambled to arm themselves with their revolvers that were hanging inside the half-built cabin.[25]

Epitacio struggled to pull his pistol from its holster, but in his panic he forgot that it was tied down. His horse began to jump wildly at the gunfire as he continued yanking his pistol. Elisha froze still.

Tewksbury stood his ground and fired twice more. The slug from the second shot tore through John Gilleland's elbows.[26] At the third shot, Elisha, who was behind his cousin, jolted in his saddle.

John Gilleland fired a third time, but again his shot went wild as his horse jerked to the left and his arms gave out.

Elisha spurred his horse around and charged back up the creek, followed quickly by Epitacio. John Gilleland, now bleeding from both arms, clamped his reins with his teeth and raced away.[27] Elisha Gilleland did not get very far, however. After a short distance, he slid off his horse and fell to the ground.

"I am killed!" he shouted.

John Gilleland and Epitacio continued their escape up the creek at full gallop. With the clamor of hooves on wet stones and their hearts racing in their throats, they may not have heard his shout.

Jim Tewksbury had already mounted his horse and started off after Gilleland. Tom Graham fled the scene on horseback as his brother Johnny ran over to where Elisha had fallen. Together, Jim and Johnny Graham carried Elisha to the cabin, and then took him over to Stinson's ranch. They found Elisha's Winchester cocked, but unfired.[28]

The teenager was wounded in the hip, but he would survive.

How people behaved in such moments of violent confrontation was frequently understood during the period as either bravery or cowardice, but advances in understanding human physiology provide for a more nuanced perspective of what happened and why. The acute stress response, or, as it is more commonly known, the fight-or-flight response, is an evolutionary advantage to ensure survival, be it through freezing still, running away, or fighting back.[29] All these responses were manifested by the different men during the gunfight.

In such moments, a powerful cocktail of neurochemicals floods the brain to ramp up the nervous and hormonal systems, which in turn sharpens the senses and increases blood flow to the muscles. All of this allows for rapid, almost instinctive responses to danger that are much quicker than what the cognitive process of thinking would allow. So, in high-stress situations, when the brain perceives an existential threat, action frequently occurs much more quickly than thought. Such response is so rapid and unconscious that people often are unable to recall reacting at all (whatever the reaction may be) during such moments.[30]

But the acute stress response can also lead the brain to read circumstances and process information differently than it would in more tranquil conditions.[31] That powerful cocktail of neurochemicals can also alter one's perception of control in a perilous situation, which can result in an overestimation or an underestimation of circumstances. This, in turn, can lead to increased anxiety or aggression, depending on perception. One's ability to read the nuances of social interaction is also affected, causing a person to perceive hostility, especially in ambiguous situations, when it may not actually exist.[32]

———————

Unlike classic scenes in western movies where cowboys simply walked away after a gunfight, the real West was quite different. Investigations were made and inquests were held. Depositions were taken, and, if the evidence so indicated, warrants for arrest were handed out, and defendants were given their day in court. A neighbor of the Gillelands, expecting Elisha to die, swore out a murder complaint against Ed Tewksbury. When it became clear than neither John's nor Elisha's wounds were life-threatening, the state nonetheless pressed charges against both John Gilleland and Ed Tewksbury for assault with intent to kill.

At the end of January 1883, Constable William Bunch and a posse of eighteen men rode out to Pleasant Valley and arrested John, Jim, and Frank Tewksbury, along with Tom Graham. Ed Tewksbury and Johnny Graham had already left for Prescott to file their own complaint against John Gilleland. Within a few days, John Gilleland and Epitacio Ruiz were also in custody in Prescott; Elisha Gilleland was too wounded to travel.[33]

The *Territory of Arizona vs. Ed Tewksbury and John Gilleland* commenced four months later, in May. The territory was not so much interested in who was the more belligerent, only in who was the first to discharge his weapon. After that, any actions taken in self-defense were considered legal and appropriate. The problem for the jury was that both sides insisted that *they* were the ones acting in self-defense, while the other was the aggressor. After two days of testimony, without any further evidence to sway the jury toward one side or the other, the jurors simply could not support either charge against Gilleland and Tewksbury. They found both not guilty. Within the ethos of the day, since no one was killed or seriously wounded, the confrontation may have appeared to the jurors as simply a disagreement gone bad.

So the trial was a relatively short one, and a seemingly minor inconvenience for all involved. But it was also the first in what would become a series of vexing trials that ensnarled the lives of the settlers of Pleasant Valley.

Despite the jury's ruling, local historians since that time have long debated who provoked the fight. Their positions depended on whether their sympathies ultimately lay with the Grahams or the Tewksburys. Clearly the Grahams and the Tewksburys worked together at this period in their relationship and uniformly acted as an attacked group during the shooting. Yet it was not too long after this event that Johnny Graham turned against the Tewksbury brothers and charged them with cattle rustling. Their relationship soured from that moment, never reconciling, and this fact is critical in testing the reliability of their statements about what happened at John Tewksbury's ranch.

One might expect that none of the Tewksburys would testify against their brother, yet even at the darkest point when both the Grahams and the Tewksburys accused each other of murdering family members, and both sides eagerly pressed their case to anyone who would listen, neither Tom nor Johnny Graham ever recanted their version of what happened in January 1883, even though they had every reason to do so afterward. In rehearsing their story of injustices perpetrated by the Tewksburys, the Grahams never told a different version of when the Gilleland cousins were shot. Thus, their version, which confirms the Tewksburys' version, seems the most credible.

Despite the disagreement between the Gillelands and the Tewksburys about who was the most aggressive, there is a surprising amount of agreement in their testimonies about what happened. Both agree that Stinson's cowboys left for the Tewksburys' ranch fully armed. Both agree that the verbal exchange was short and the escalation to violence was quick. Both agree that John Gilleland drew his weapon out first, and both agree that he never articulated the purpose of his visit, which was to deliver Stinson's message of conciliation. The resulting gunfight may have grown out of a simmering disagreement between Gilleland and Tewksbury, one that they both personalized.

One can only speculate about what that disagreement might have been. But what both parties remembered of the encounter offers important clues. Stinson had already threatened prosecution, and as far as the Tewksbury and Graham brothers knew, nothing had changed. Gilleland and Ruiz were clearly Stinson's representatives on the ground. And they came riding up on Tewksbury property through the cold, uninvited, unannounced, and armed. Surely, for Ed Tewksbury at least, the purpose of their visit could not have been a peaceful one, and he was ready for what might happen. On the other side, whatever Ed Tewksbury's demeanor that morning, Stinson's cowboys thought him to be defensive, if not hostile. They could have simply delivered the message they were charged to give and then left the way they came. But Gilleland, according to his side of the story, chose to draw Tewksbury out, almost contemptuously, as if he were reluctant to let the Tewksburys off the hook. Why? Did Gilleland's slaveholding background color the way he looked upon the dark-skinned man who stood defiantly in front of him, challenging his authority?

Oscar Felton's warning to Constable Bunch, who had arrived at Felton's ranch with nine men to arrest the Tewksbury and Graham brothers, also illustrates how exaggeration shaped the events that followed.[34] Bunch arrived at Felton's ranch to discover that neither Elisha nor John had died from their wounds, but Felton and a neighbor warned Bunch that "a force of armed men from 14 to 20 . . . was in a strong position of defence [sic] at Tewksburys." Bunch doubled his posse.[35] In truth, the Tewksbury and Graham brothers totaled only seven, and with two already on their way to Prescott to press charges against Gilleland, there were only five left. Those five offered no resistance when the posse arrived. Clearly the information that Felton gave was wrong, but Felton's warning reveals how anticipation and misperceptions began to shape what settlers believed about their neighbors.

One might reasonably ask why either Gilleland or Tewksbury was armed at all that day if they were not expecting a confrontation. At least Hanchett interpreted Tewksbury's carrying a pistol as an indication of a personality prone to violence. Yet one must not forget that Apaches had raided through the valley only a few months earlier, killing eight Apache scouts and a dozen or more settlers, wounding others, and stealing horses from the Tewksbury and Rose ranches.[36] The settlers in Pleasant Valley certainly had not forgotten. While the army ended that particular raid with the Battle of Big Dry Wash in mid-July, memories of the raids were still fresh, and settlers remained on the alert. Keeping loaded weapons close at hand, for many Pleasant Valley settlers, simply made good sense.

Within this already tense environment, when disagreements festered and tempers were short, bloodshed was all too easily the result.

JOHNNY GRAHAM'S GAMBLE

The year 1883 was a bad one for the Tewksbury family. Even though Ed had been acquitted of the charge of attempting to murder John Gilleland, Frank died from measles in January while in Prescott for the trial.[37] It was a difficult loss for the close-knit brothers.

Perhaps in a desperate and foolhardy effort to raise cash, Jim Tewksbury joined George Blaine in robbing an Arizona Cooperative Mercantile Incorporated (ACMI) store in Woodruff. They may have believed that the store was vulnerable, given its location in a small Mormon settlement in the next county over, about thirteen miles southeast of Holbrook.[38] Either way, they left with $500, a pistol, and some peach preserves—but not before one of the store clerks recognized them. Even with their neckerchiefs pulled over their faces, they made a distinctive pair.[39]

Then, the Graham family irreparably broke with the Tewksburys over the summer months. If there was a single event that caused the split, it has been lost to time, and neither family spoke of it. There was a curious story circulating in the territorial press years later that attributed the break to a "Sallie Blevens [sic]" who was forbidden by her father to see her lover William Graham. The Prescott *Arizona Weekly Journal-Miner* entirely dismissed this account as "perfect ignorance of the situation," and, indeed, it was so; there was no Sallie Blevins, nor was the conflict between the Grahams and Blevinses. Nonetheless, the story appears to have served as Zane Grey's inspiration for casting the Pleasant Valley War in *To the Last Man* as a frontier story of Romeo and Juliet.[40] In truth, fissures in the Graham and Tewksbury friendship began to appear within a few months of the Graham's arrival in Pleasant Valley.[41] With James Stinson's scheme to stop the rustlers preying on his herd, those fissures grew into a clean split.

In the late fall of 1883, Johnny Graham met with Stinson and entered into a contractual agreement. In exchange for providing evidence that would lead to the arrest and conviction of anyone stealing Stinson's cattle, Stinson agreed to pay Graham 25 cows and 25 calves, worth $25 each. The contract was dated 14 November 1883, but it was not recorded with the county until the following spring, on 28 March 1884.[42] Offering $1,250 for such information was not unusual for Stinson. He had the reputation of wielding money as a tool to get what he wanted, and his herds were facing steady losses in Pleasant Valley. He wanted the theft of his investments stopped.

What Johnny Graham did next is significant. The day after the contract was recorded with the county, Graham visited the office of District Attorney Charles B. Rush in Prescott and filed a complaint against six of his Pleasant Valley neighbors: three Tewksbury brothers and three other Pleasant Valley residents. He swore that five months earlier, in October, his neighbors and former friends had altered the brands of cattle that belonged to Stinson, as well as cattle that belonged to him and to his brother Tom.[43]

Johnny's actions suggest a sequence of events that was not coincidental, but carefully planned and carried out to ensure that he would receive the promised reward. When $20 a month could rent a six-room house in St. Louis, $1,250 could go a very long way in the Arizona Territory.[44] Graham may have been motivated by a change of heart over his Tewksbury friends after Jim was caught robbing the ACMI store and after possibly witnessing the branding of cattle that he thought belonged to Stinson. Others in the area who knew the Grahams, however, had grave doubts about Johnny's integrity, especially when it came to cattle. "There was a lot of stealing," Osmer Flake recalled in his memoirs, "and by 1886 they were well organized, and were stealing hundreds of cattle and horses from our range. We knew they were being stolen, but could not find where they were being taken. We learned that the Blevins and Grahams had begun working together. Both had been stealing for a long time, and in fact it was largely the Grahams who had stolen Stinson's stock and driven him out of his range."[45]

If Flake was right, that the Grahams were intimately involved in the rustling ring preying upon Stinson's herd, then Johnny Graham's accusations against six Pleasant Valley neighbors had every appearance of an effort not only to throw suspicion off themselves, by accusing the others of theft, but to profit handsomely by it. In any case, whether Graham really believed that his neighbors were steal-ing cattle or whether he was playing Stinson for a fool, he surely knew that his accusations would injure his association with his Pleasant Valley neighbors. Apparently, he believed that it was worth the price.

Tom Graham's journal may provide insight into why Johnny was vulnerable to Stinson's offer. Although some pages of Tom's journal were torn out, what remains shows a codependent pattern in the relationship between the Graham brothers. By the time that Johnny was killed, he had borrowed $3,200 from Tom—approximately $90,000 in modern dollars. Then, about six weeks before Johnny died, Tom also recorded a cluster of sales of cattle and mares that Johnny made to Tom, totaling $3,800. Those sales could have been intended to satisfy Johnny's outstanding debt, but the terms of the sale are described as "for cash in hand," suggesting, instead, that Johnny sold the livestock to raise more revenue.[46] If so, he still owed Tom $3,200. Where did Tom get that kind of cash to make such purchases and loans? And where was that money going?

The Grahams lived no differently from any of their neighbors in Pleasant Valley, and they were not awash in material possessions. They rode in no fine rig, their cabin was rustic and no grander than anyone else's, their horses and tackle were ordinary, and their herds were about the size of the other small ranchers. Indeed, Tom reminded his sister that Johnny "was no great hand for any nice things."[47] Johnny possessed only a gold watch, a pin, a silver dollar, and few coins when he was killed.[48]

Where did the money go? At least one of the residents of Pleasant Valley remembered that when Ed Tewksbury met the Grahams, they were working in Globe City as "tinhorn gamblers."[49] Tom went to Pleasant Valley with dreams of becoming a cattle baron, but Johnny may never have left the gambling tables behind. Tom's journal shows that Johnny regularly took out a stream of loans over the winter months, when the Graham brothers were typically in the warmer elevations of Phoenix or Globe City.[50] By 1887, Johnny's borrowing rate had doubled from what he had asked for in 1885.[51] At least one ledger entry recorded a promissory note that Johnny made to Tom, to repay that loan within three months at eighteen percent annual interest—at a time when the national interest rates hovered between three and four percent annually.[52] Wherever the money was going, Johnny habitually needed cash, and he was accumulating debt at a rapid rate to get his hands on it.

It may well have been that Johnny was unable to stem gambling losses while he waited for his next big score. If this was where the money was going, then Johnny was a man desperate for capital, from whatever quarter. Stinson's offer of $1,250 in cattle to turn evidence against his neighbors may have been too great a lure to pass up. So, too, were the profits that illicit livestock promised. The catalyst that altered the nature of the Pleasant Valley War, turning settlers on each other, may have come from Johnny's need to raise income.

Based on Johnny's sworn statement, the grand jury subpoenaed six witnesses and spent the day of 7 June 1884 hearing their testimonies. This would become the second of the Pleasant Valley trials. Among the witnesses were Stinson, his ranch overseer Frances Marion McCann, J .D. Adams, Ed Tewksbury, and George Blaine.[53] At the end of the proceedings, the grand jury issued four indictments for grand larceny—in other words, cattle rustling—against six Pleasant Valley residents: John, Ed, and Jim Tewksbury; William Richards; Herbert H. Bishop; and George Blaine.[54] The defendants were all arrested that same day, though John Tewksbury and possibly Ed were able to post bail with the help of their Pleasant Valley neighbors Bob Sixby and Al Rose.[55]

The charges that Johnny Graham leveled at his neighbors were no small inconvenience. In the Territory of Arizona, grand larceny was a felony, and it could land you in jail for up to ten years.[56]

The following month, things went from bad to worse for Jim Tewksbury and George Blaine. Jim Tewksbury was already charged in all three indictments for grand larceny, and Blaine was charged in one count. Then, in early July 1884, another warrant was issued for the arrest of both men in connection with the ACMI store robbery in Woodruff the previous spring. To post bail for Jim, the Tewksburys turned to the Daggs brothers, prominent Flagstaff businessmen, with John putting up his ranch and all its assets as warranty.[57]

The criminal trial against six Pleasant Valley neighbors would prove to be a dramatic turn of events for both the accused and the accusers. The prosecution began with a recitation of all the testimonies before the grand jury that had resulted in the indictments against Jim and Ed Tewksbury and the others. The defense, however, introduced new evidence that devastated the credibility of Johnny Graham. After learning of the grand jury indictment, several Pleasant Valley residents came forward and testified that neither Graham brother was anywhere near the Tonto Basin on the dates that they allegedly witnessed the defendants altering brands of cattle from the Stinson and Graham herds. The defense then introduced a copy of Johnny Graham's contract with Stinson. The judge then turned to the jury and instructed: "If you believe the Grahams, find the defendants guilty. If you do not believe the Grahams, find the defendants not guilty."[58]

The jury did *not* believe the Grahams and found for the accused. Indeed, so damaging was this new evidence that Pleasant Valley residents J. J. Vosburgh and Al Rose filed a formal complaint against the Grahams for perjury.[59] A special grand jury was immediately impaneled, and it returned indictments against the Graham brothers. The court then issued a bench warrant for their arrest.[60]

The outcome of the trial had a dramatic impact on remaining charges. The following day, the district attorney entered a *nolle prosequi* (unwilling to pursue) in the other larceny charges against the Tewksburys, Blaine, Richards, and Bishop. Judge Sumner Howard then ordered the men discharged and their bail exonerated.[61]

Jim Tewksbury's trial for armed robbery also suffered for want of evidence. When the trial convened, the jury found him not guilty largely because the key witness failed to appear at the trial. Joseph Fish, the clerk who identified the masked robbers, was a Mormon polygamist who, in the interim, had fled to Mexico to avoid prosecution for bigamy.[62]

This was the moment, in previous tellings of the conflicts in Pleasant Valley, when the Grahams and Tewksburys developed a deadly animosity toward one another. Author Leon Hanchett went so far as to posit that the Tewksburys already blamed the Grahams for Frank Tewksbury's untimely death from measles as he traveled to Prescott over the winter months to testify in the shooting of John and Elisha Gilleland (even though the Graham and Tewksbury brothers were on the same side in that trial).

Without a doubt, it was a blow to the Tewksburys to be so quickly turned upon by men they had befriended, but what is actually more significant about this moment in their relationship is that no violence came of it. With the exception of John Tewksbury slapping Johnny Graham after the trial ended, for three years there were no other verbal or physical altercations between the two sets of brothers even though they lived within a few miles of one another.[63] It was as if, though equally wounded by the accusations of theft or perjury, both families simply allowed the matter to pass between them without further incident.

Others, however, were not as restrained.

SHOOTOUT AT STINSON'S RANCH

The settlement in Pleasant Valley was small enough that nearly everyone was affected in some way by the larceny and perjury trials. Although the accusations, the hearings, and the inconveniences of travel to distant courts were unpleasant, the cases were over by early summer. There was work to be done and a roundup to plan. Disagreements over cattle were not sufficient to cancel the annual event. Perhaps some even hoped that it would help smooth things over. A planning meeting was scheduled for Wednesday, 23 July 1884, at Stinson's ranch. Surprisingly, no one seems to have thought that this was a very bad idea.

George Blaine, William Richards, John Tewksbury, and Ed Rose rode out to Stinson's ranch, which was just a few miles north of John Tewksbury's ranch and a few miles southeast of the Grahams' place.

Waiting at Stinson's place were five hired hands, among them Marion McCann, who had recently testified in Prescott against Blaine, Richards, and the Tewksbury brothers. McCann was also a deputy sheriff for Maricopa County.[64]

Any pretense at civility withered quickly. McCann frankly told Blaine, Richards, and Tewksbury that he wanted nothing to do with them, and curtly—but quietly, he later said—dismissed everyone except for Ed Rose.[65]

Blaine and Tewksbury were incensed and blasted McCann. "We can go anywhere we damned well please!" Tewksbury protested.

"You damned son of a bitch," Blaine bellowed. "You have run this country long enough!" Blaine always had a short temper.[66]

"You damned, cowardly, son of a bitch," he thundered on. "You dare not come out on open ground!"

McCann had only a few days left in Stinson's employ and hoped to avert any trouble. But he also had a bad feeling when the men rode up. He listened to the tirade of profanities without reacting—until he'd had enough.[67] He picked up his Winchester and stepped away from the shade of the ranch house. He stopped directly in front of Blaine and turned to face him. William Richards, at this point, spurred his horse and left at full gallop.[68]

Cursing, Blaine also wheeled his horse around and began to follow Richards, but stopped abruptly after his horse took only a few strides. He yanked his horse around to face McCann, pulled his revolver out, and shot at him. The bullet whizzed by McCann as he jerked up his rifle and returned fire.

McCann's aim was sure. Blaine grabbed his throat as he tumbled off his horse with a thud and writhed on the ground, gargling wretchedly on his own blood.

Seeing this, John Tewksbury pulled out his pistol and shot at McCann, but his aim was hasty. He, too, missed. McCann returned fire and wounded Tewksbury, but not bad enough that he could not spur his horse and flee.

Two of Stinson's other men rushed over to Blaine, picked him up, and placed him in the shade. They washed off his wound with water as they sent others for help. Miraculously, the wound, though grave, was not mortal. When Blaine was stable enough to be moved, Ed Rose took him to his ranch with the help of some of Stinson's men.[69]

Not knowing whether Tewksbury and Richards were going to return with reinforcements, Stinson's ranch hands quickly fled to the neighboring Graham ranch. They need not have worried. Richards had had enough shooting and wanted nothing more to do with it, and John Tewksbury was too wounded to do anything even if he wanted to.

In the subsequent trial against McCann for assault with murderous intent, the judge found his actions to be reasonable self-defense, and the territory elected not to pursue charges against Blaine or Tewksbury, who were convalescing.[70] It was as if everyone involved—Stinson's men, Blaine and Tewksbury, and even the justice of the peace—wary of the heightened state of tensions between Pleasant Valley's neighbors, wanted to see things return to a more normal footing.

And so it did for a season. George Blaine remained under a watchful doctor's care.[71] He regained a measure of respect for enduring a three-hour-long surgery that removed an inch of bone and a molar that had been driven deep into his neck by McCann's bullet, all without anesthesia.[72] Mary Ann Tewksbury, John's wife, gave birth to daughter Bertha that October while he convalesced. Stinson's men and the other Pleasant Valley ranchers minded their own business and lay low for the rest of the year.

But Stinson still had unfinished business with the Graham brothers.

STINSON'S REVENGE

There was quite a stir in the Prescott courtroom when the judge ordered the arrest of Johnny and Tom Graham, immediately after the jury found the six Pleasant Valley defendants not guilty of the charges that Johnny Graham had leveled against them. With the Grahams behind bars for perjury, the shoe was now on the other foot. Court observers applauded the action, praising Howard for his "able and impartial administration of justice [that had] already secured for him the highest respect and strongest confidence of the honest, law-abiding citizens of the Third Judicial District."[73] After a week in the county jail, the Graham brothers convinced Stinson and former county sheriff John R. Walker to post bail for them, at $2,000 each.[74] Stinson, it seems, was in no rush to come to the Grahams' defense.

When the District Court convened for the October 1884 term, the attorneys, witnesses, and jury assembled in the Prescott courtroom and waited for the Grahams to appear. They waited in vain, for the Grahams never showed up.[75]

The court was nonplussed. As was often the case with territorial courts with limited resources, the case was simply set aside. A couple of cowboys caught in a lie was not terribly significant when there were more pressing matters before the court. So the Grahams escaped having to answer for themselves before the law—but not before Stinson. Their failure to appear in court meant that Stinson and Walker forfeited their bonds.[76] And Stinson, at least, was not a man to be trifled with. He surely took some measure of satisfaction from the events that followed, which he had already set in motion.

In the next county over, rancher William Atchison received a letter. He lived in Apache County, some eighty miles east of Pleasant Valley, and two of his cows had been missing for a year and a half. Those cows, the letter informed him, could be found in Pleasant Valley. They had been rebranded and were in the possession of Johnny and Tom Graham.[77] And there was someone there in Pleasant Valley who had seen those cows taken: Jim Tewksbury, who had been in the Grahams' employ. The letter was signed by James Stinson.

Atchison was a member of the Apache County Stock Association, and after the winter snows cleared, the association sent Carr Blassingame to ride out to Yavapai County to gather evidence for an indictment.[78] Blassingame was a Hashknife cowboy who had fallen in love with a local girl and settled down in northern Arizona, hiring on as the association's range detective.[79] In early May 1885, he rode out to Pleasant Valley, hoping to persuade Jim Tewksbury to swear out a complaint against the Grahams. Blassingame even offered to pay him for his time to help gather evidence.[80] Jim agreed, and they rode to a justice of the peace.[81]

The justice of the peace who listened to Tewksbury's complaint did something very curious. He sat down and wrote out the indictment, but then balked at signing it.[82] It was as if the charge that Jim made was a valid one, enough for the judge to sit down and write the indictment out by hand. But when all that was left to do was to place his signature on the document, the judge thought about what was likely to happen from that complaint. Nothing good could possibly come from escalating tensions within Pleasant Valley.

Blassingame was undeterred. He returned to the valley later that month to press the matter. If Jim could not secure an indictment in Yavapai County, he would gather enough evidence to make one stick in Apache County, where the cattle came from. Blassingame again rode out to the Tewksburys, and then, in the company of Deputy Sheriff Oscar Felton, Ed Rose, Bob Sixby, and Ed and Jim Tewksbury, they rode out to the Grahams' ranch.[83] The Grahams—Johnny, Tom, and nephew Louis Parker—were at the ranch when the party arrived.[84] No one recorded what that meeting was like for the Grahams when Blassingame came riding onto their property with the Tewksburys and other Pleasant Valley neighbors, but their testimonies during the subsequent trial provide a clue. Louis Parker testified that Jim Tewksbury and Johnny and Tom Graham "are on very bad terms."[85] Johnny Graham went straight to the point. Since he had charged them with grand larceny a year and a half earlier, "[We] have not been friends since."[86]

At the Graham ranch, Jim pointed out one of Atchison's cows, and Blassingame found the other. Blassingame inspected their brands. They looked like the work of what ranchers called "rawhide artists"—a brand forged with a straight iron that was often used in altering brands. The Grahams protested. These cows had once belonged to Atchison, they conceded, but he had sold the cattle to William Jordan Flake, who then sold the cows to them, and they were willing to sign a statement to that effect. Tom drew up the statement, and with this evidence in hand, along with Jim Tewksbury's testimony, Blassingame appeared before the Apache County grand jury in May 1885 and charged the Grahams with stealing Atchison's cattle. John and Tom Graham were indicted in Apache County for grand larceny, and Blassingame named as witnesses James Dunning Tewksbury, the father, and his three boys, John, Ed, and Jim. Osmer Flake, who was also subpoenaed as a witness for the territory, later recalled that the Grahams breathed out threats against the Tewksbury family if they testified against them.[87] If Flake's recollection was true, the Tewksburys paid the Grahams no heed.

The trial in St. Johns was now the fourth one to involve Pleasant Valley settlers, and the second one based on the charge of larceny. During the trial, the Graham brothers were resolute in their testimonies that the cows in question came with the herd they had purchased from Flake in 1882. Atchison, however, denied ever selling these cows to anyone. Further, Atchison stated that he had helped rebrand cattle that were bought by the Grahams and that none of those cattle had his brand. Osmer Flake was also present at that 1882 sale and also helped rebrand the cattle sold to the Grahams. He confirmed Atchison's testimony.

The case looked strong against the Grahams, but it was still circumstantial. The prosecution called for more witnesses, and the court held the case over to reconvene in a week and a half. In the interim, the Grahams left St. Johns to gather their own witnesses (they claimed). But when the court reconvened, and the attorneys, jurors, and witnesses were assembled, the Grahams once again could not be found. The judge immediately ordered a warrant for their arrest, and the witnesses were held for another three days as the court waited for the Grahams to return. The Apache County district attorney approached Oscar Felton, who was both a witness in the case and a Yavapai County deputy sheriff, and asked him to proceed to Pleasant Valley to arrest the Grahams. Felton refused. If Apache County wanted to pursue the Grahams, they would have to send their own man out to get them. Felton seemed to sense that a nasty fight was brewing, and he wanted no part of it. After three days of waiting, the case was set aside, and the jurors dismissed.

Again, the Grahams skirted the law. But the social impact of these two cases—the perjury hearing in Prescott, and the grand larceny hearing in St. Johns—was profound. They had two separate opportunities, in two different venues, to set the record straight and clear their names. They chose instead to flee both times.

The *Prescott Miner* summed up the reactions of many toward the Grahams. "The reckless disregard of the Grahams for the sanctity of their oaths," they began, "was demonstrated by the most unimpeachable testimony, and, that too, in a manner that left no doubt that they had been tempted by the prospects of the rewards, offered for the conviction of cattle thieves, gone into a wholesale conspiracy against the parties defendant. The arrests will have a most salutary effect in impressing in a most forcible manner the minds of the untruthful that the dignity of Judge Howard's court will not tolerate wilful [sic] and malicious perjury."[88]

This editorial might strike a modern reader as quaint and melodramatic. But it must be remembered that these were the days when a man's word meant something, and business agreements were often sealed with the simple shake of a hand. For Johnny and Tom Graham, to be so publically branded as liars by half a dozen neighbors, a jury of one's peers, a grand jury, and a judge, was, by nineteenth-century standards, to be declared less than a man.

The *Prescott Miner*'s editorial about the Grahams was shared across the territory, in newspapers from Kingman and St. Johns in the north to Globe City and Yuma in the south.[89] What's more, the Graham brothers were exposed as men who would turn against their neighbors for lucre. It was then of no coincidence that hereafter the Grahams' circle of friends in Pleasant Valley contracted. And with that contraction, they increasingly associated with drifters and strangers whose activities were highly suspect.[90]

4

TO SUFFER THE ARROWS
OF OUTRAGEOUS FORTUNE

Life in the Arizona high country slowed as winter descended upon the mountains. Pleasant Valley typically averaged a modest amount of snowfall—around eight inches—but the winter months of 1886–1887 were unusually mild.[1] The springtime runoff was vital to all manner of life that depended on the waterways of the Rim country, so the meager snowfall promised another dry spring to a region already parched by a decade of warmer winters and miserly rainfall. And another dry spring would make grass and water more precious, and competition for it keener.

The decade was also unkind to the Mormon colonies up on the Rim along the Little Colorado River. The crop yield was so meager between 1884 and 1886, in fact, that the Mormon settlements were dying. They could scarcely harvest enough to feed themselves, let alone ship to market, and they had to rely on surplus grain provided by Mormon settlements in Utah to continue going. Politically, they were also facing fierce opposition in the territory to what Mormons viewed as the Biblical practice of plural marriage. Several communities created anti-Mormon parties that were specifically aimed at circumventing Mormon political participation and aggressively enforcing laws that were designed to break the church. Some LDS leaders who practiced plural marriage were already in prison or were driven underground. Many Mormon families left the area to return home to Utah or to find more hospitable lands elsewhere in the West.[2]

The mild winter of 1887 was also something of a boon for some. Activities that usually had to wait until the roads became passable, such as traveling to Phoenix or moving livestock to market, could continue uninterrupted. It was on a winter trip to Phoenix that Tom Graham first saw sixteen-year-old Annie Elizabeth Melton, the daughter of the prominent Baptist minister, climbing a fig tree with her hair up in curlers.[3] She was fifteen years his junior, and full of spark.[4] To her, Tom must have looked like a man of the world, sitting tall in the saddle as he rode in from the mountains carrying a six-shooter. Soon enough, they would be stealing away from the watchful gaze of her parents.

The Daggs brothers also had their eye on Phoenix that winter, hoping to send a flock to market. They hired a sheepherder who began the journey to Phoenix, moving the Daggses' sheep along the route that ran just north of the Graham property. The Daggses had already lost seven hundred sheep just a few weeks earlier, stolen near St. Johns, and this sale would help make up the loss.[5]

But livestock on the move was always a risky venture. They could fall prey to any number of hazards along the trail. So could their handlers.

APOCALYPTIC ANTICIPATIONS

The policy of the U.S. Army to consolidate reservations was continuing to bear ill fruit. Tensions on the Apache reservation between warring clans escalated to the point that by the summer of 1885, several leaders could no longer endure the tension of being confined in proximity to traditional enemies. This, combined with the tension the reservation system already imposed on skilled warrior societies, forcing them to relearn their traditional lifeways, proved to be a combustible combination. One-hundred and fifty Apaches led by Mangas (the son of Mangas Coloradas), and others, fled the reservation in a desperate hope to recapture the life they once knew, guided by the powerful shaman Goyaałé. He was more commonly known by his Spanish name, *Jerónimo*.[6]

The runaways knew that the army would employ scouts from enemy clans to track them, so they took special care to conceal their escape route. Within an hour after their escape became known, the cavalry at Fort Apache mobilized in full force to search for the breakaways. Troops scattered in all directions trying to pick up their trail, including to the familiar raiding grounds of Pleasant Valley, but the military simply could not find them.

As soon as word spread that Apaches were on the loose again, communities near the reservation went into high alert. The level of anxiety over Apache discontent was already high in the settlements near the reservation, and gauging the level of Apache unrest was a common feature of northern Arizona newspapers, perhaps more than gauging the weather. Unfortunately, the news was often late, published only weekly, and often provided little accurate information. Thus, constant, relentless preparedness was the first defense. Settlers were never far away from their firearms.

The army called in more units to help track the runaways and transferred the 10th Cavalry of the famed Buffalo Soldiers from Texas to the Department of Arizona.[7] The trail of the Apaches was still a mystery until 10 June when Apache warriors in southern Arizona overwhelmed a detachment of the 4th Cavalry. After that attack, Apache scouts picked up their trail heading south toward the Sierra Madre in Mexico. To capture them if they reentered the United States, General Crook stationed troops at every known watering hole along the border and established a second line of soldiers paralleling the A&P Railroad tracks.

Apaches still slipped past the blue line of soldiers. Ulzana—who was also known by Americans as Josanie—and his band struck near Fort Apache with complete surprise on 23–24 November, killing two civilians and twenty White Mountain Apaches before they left.[8] The army spent the winter months of 1885–1886 in a deadly cat-and-mouse chase through the canyons of southern Arizona and northern Mexico. After a year of constantly being on the run, fatigue began to take its toll. Small groups of Apaches began to approach their pursuers to surrender. In time, even Geronimo himself would lay down his arms.

———

Turmoil among settlers stirred up from these attacks, in general, tended to ebb and flow with the seasons because outbreaks from the reservation tended to peak in the spring and summer months and die down over the winter. Sometimes that agitation arose not so much from what Apaches themselves did, but from the misperception of their activities by hypervigilant settlers (territorial newspapers were reasonably quick to publish corrections in the case of false alarms).[9]

The rash of settler unrest unleashed by Josanie's raid, however, was different. That state of alarm lasted much longer than previously, and the tenor reached an unusual height. Editorials throughout the territory openly speculated that a territory-wide uprising was at hand, and some newspapers began calling for an ultimate resolution: a final showdown between settlers and Indians. The state of alarm became bad enough throughout the territory that even Apache scouts, who served the army with distinction, fell under scrutiny, criticism, and distrust.[10]

Josanie's raid in the fall of 1885 was by no means the worst outbreak, and save for the tragic loss of human life, it was relatively unremarkable from previous raids. For most territorial newspapers, he was just another Apache threat, and reports of that outbreak never included his name. Yet that raid was another episode in a long sequence of violence, and the response that settlers had to this particular attack suggests that several communities were beginning to show signs of fatigue under the constant strain of deadly assaults. "Authorities at the agency," reported newspapers as far away as Tucson, "are on the alert in anticipation of further danger. . . . The people on the out-skirts of the reservation have been warned."[11]

Settler unrest cooled down with the coming of frost, but it warmed up again in earnest in the early spring of 1886. Reports of widespread Indian restlessness began to circulate among the territorial newspapers in May. Such news did not deter one group of Hashknife cowboys from moving their herds near the Apache reservation. They were nonetheless startled early one morning by a band of renegade Apaches who stole into the campsite and took provisions and ammunition. The cowboys gave chase, which resulted in a running gun battle between the renegades and the cowboys. Once again, settlers feared that an uprising was at hand. "It is feared by the people of Apache county that if these Indians come north they may incite the Navajoes [*sic*] to join them in a campaign of rapine and murder," the editors of the *Arizona Sentinel* reported. "Major Warren, general manager of the Aztec company, is very uneasy and left for the scene of trouble this morning."[12]

The editors of the *Clifton Clarion,* from a town south of the Apache reservation, speculated that an apocalyptic showdown with the Indians of the territory was at hand: "As things look now, there is probability of other fresh bands leaving the reservation and perhaps the best thing which could happen to New Mexico and Arizona would be for the entire reservation to turn loose, Chiricahuas, White Mountains, Mescaleros and Ex-Scouts. There would be war at our doors, but the thing would be settled finally and the reservation become a thing of the past."[13] The *St. Johns Herald* also devoted a heightened amount of press to covering the movement of Apaches on the reservation. "It is rumored that the White Mountain Apaches have broken out. . . . It seems to be the general impression that the hostiles now ravaging the country will use every effort to influence all malcontents to join them."[14] One *St. Johns Herald* report especially warned the settlers in the Tonto Basin that they were the next target of Apache attack.[15]

So great was the excitement about Apache outbreaks that summer that reports flew throughout the territorial newspapers like rumors passing from one settler to another.[16] Perhaps it was no surprise that in August, the Prescott newspaper *Arizona Weekly Journal-Miner* again waved the battle flag first raised by the *Clifton Clarion* in calling for a final showdown with native peoples. Commenting on the reluctance of national leaders to endorse a plan to remove Apaches from the Arizona Territory, the editors concluded: "If this is true, then the people of Arizona will be compelled to take the matter into their own hands and destroy the last of the human wretches."[17] The Globe City journal *Arizona Silver Belt* responded in kind: "Until the last Apache is removed, let the agitation go on."[18]

Even though some of the reports that year about pending violence later turned out to be false, the effects that such news had, in terms of the readiness and wariness required to defend one's life and property, took their toll on the settlers. "Great excitement was caused in Tonto Basin recently by the false report that 600 reservation Apaches had broken out," noted the *Daily Tombstone Epitaph*. "Settlers came in for protection from all directions."[19]

It is worth pondering for a moment the cost of that "great excitement." For those settlers who had the means, they incurred the expense involved in harnessing teams and supplies, driving to nearby towns, renting rooms to stay in, and quartering their livestock until the danger passed. For those who did not have the means, it meant that they had to barricade themselves to await an attack. Sometimes settlers would gather together at a defensible location, and other times they had to wait it out, on the alert, alone in their cabins. Either way, settlers were repeatedly subjected to an environment that demanded that they prepare to fight or flee.

THE TEXAS BLEVINSES

Just as tensions began to ease for settlers close to reservation lands, a Texas family arrived in the Tonto Basin and settled north of Pleasant Valley. They would eventually terrorize a good portion of eastern Arizona, for both whites and Indians.[20] Mormon pioneers John and Will Adams were their first victims. The Adamses had originally settled on Canyon Creek, about twenty miles northeast of the Pleasant Valley settlement, where the northwest corner of the White Mountain Apache Reservation meets the Mogollon Rim. There, the Adams brothers built a small log cabin and kept a modest herd of cattle.

Two other brothers, Andrew and Charlie Blevins, found that ranch to be the perfect spot for business. Andrew was on the run from the law—for horse theft, certainly, but rumors had it that he had also killed a deputy sheriff in Texas—and he went by the alias of Andy Cooper.[21] He savored the remoteness of the ranch that was, at the same time, close enough to large herds of cattle and horses and to the railroad.[22] So, at gunpoint, Cooper ordered the Adams brothers to leave or he would kill them on the spot.[23] The Adamses left Arizona.

According to family legend, Cooper's father, Martin J. Blevins, originally from Missouri, was forced to flee from Llano County, Texas, after a gunfight following a horse race.[24] Historian David Johnson argues that the Blevinses were implicated in stealing horses in the county.[25] Either way, they had to get out of town, and several members of the Blevins family left that county almost overnight and relocated to the Canyon Creek ranch.[26]

Despite the Blevinses' isolated location in the territory, their reputation spread quickly. Within a year of their coming to Arizona, the *St. Johns Herald* declared Andy Cooper "one of the boldest and most daring of these desperados," and the reference to "Canyon Creek" became a common metaphor for the Blevinses' operation.[27] The *Arizona Silver Belt* described the Blevinses as "roving desperados from Tonto Basin" engaged in stealing horses and cattle.[28] Glenn Ellison remembered what his father told him about the family: "He Sed the Blevins family a Tuff Gang come in & Took over & run the familys off."[29] Snowflake settler Lucy Hanna White Flake agreed with that assessment, describing the Blevinses as "the worst family of thieves and outlaws in the country."[30]

The Blevinses' reputation was well deserved. They quickly became one of the chief suppliers in the illicit livestock trade, preying upon the Mormon settlements atop the Rim and the Navajo and Apache reservations.[31] In April 1887, the Blevinses brazenly took 103 Navajo horses and openly drove them down to their ranch. A party of Navajos and white settlers intercepted them, and after a gun battle, the Indian horses were recovered. Even so, the Blevinses were criticized for escalating tensions between whites and Indians and blamed for the Reynolds Cattle Company losing a wandering herd of cattle to the Navajos, who refused to allow herders access to their land. "Such troubles are serious, and if the white men don't unite in putting a stop to this stealing from the Navajos, we may see terrible times along this river from it," the editors of the *St. Johns Herald* warned. "There are too many outlying and widely separated cow camps scattered around through this country to suffer from such a raid. This lawless and unresponsible element must be put down, or it will cost us dear."[32]

The Blevinses paid such warnings little heed. Bonnie Stevens Hunt recorded one very close encounter with an angry war party that was looking for the Blevinses:

> One of the Blevin's [sic] boys showed up at James Shelley's [in Heber, Arizona] to buy some potatoes. While they were in the cellar getting potatoes, a large band of Indians painted for war, rode into the valley crying out, "Blevins! Blevins!" They were very angry about their stolen horses. Mary Shelley had just finished baking twelve loaves of bread, her weekly chore. She pulled them from the oven and put them in her ample apron. She ran out to the Indians and began passing out loaves of hot, freshly baked bread. Being on the edge of constant hunger, the Indians gratefully accepted the loaves and rode away, not really knowing the men they were looking for were in the Shelley's cellar.[33]

Though Mormon settlers had little love for the Blevinses, Mary's quick thinking was widely credited for circumventing what could have been a bloody encounter for the Shelleys with the war party.

JOHN TEWKSBURY'S TRADEOFF

With an eye toward the Phoenix market, P. P. Daggs extended his sheep-raising business below the Rim by acquiring 160 acres in Pleasant Valley. That ranch served as a way station for his flocks as they moved down the trail that would become known as the Heber-Reno Sheep Trail Driveway, a stretch of about 160 miles from Holbrook to Punkin Center. In the late winter months of 1886, Daggs had seven thousand sheep moved to his Pleasant Valley ranch on their way to market.[34] Part of that flock, about one thousand sheep, also wintered on John Tewksbury's spread.

This simple business arrangement between John Tewksbury and Daggs, who had earlier helped the Tewksburys by posting bail for Jim when he stood trial for robbery, has been the source of much speculation. Some folklorists have interpreted Tewksbury's decision to allow sheep on his property as an act of vengeance against cattlemen, or more specifically against the Grahams. But John Tewksbury never broke with his cattlemen friends in Pleasant Valley, and there is no evidence that his cattlemen friends took offense to Daggs's sheep on Tewksbury land for a short season. Indeed, many of Tewksbury's friends, who would stand shoulder to shoulder with him during the violence to come, were small-time cattlemen in the valley. Further, the distance separating the Tewksbury and Graham properties was greater than the two-mile buffer that sheepherders and cattlemen traditionally observed in keeping their livestock apart, and the Stinson and Rose ranches lay in between.[35] There is no reason to believe that sheep on Tewksbury's property, three ranches away, would have particularly galled the Grahams.

While sheep were hardly new to the valley, there were two critical differences with the coming of the Daggs flock in the winter of 1886. The arrival of several thousand sheep doubled the strain on natural resources that Stinson's herd of cattle had created only a few years earlier. Taken together, Stinson's herd and Daggs's flock vastly outnumbered the collective livestock of the valley's settlers, and the smaller herdsmen felt the impact immediately. And perhaps more importantly, the introduction of so many sheep to an area already subjected to rampant thieving proved to be an irresistible lure for those involved in the trafficking of stolen livestock.

THE BEHEADED SHEEPHERDER

P. P. Daggs also struggled with the widespread theft that plagued the livestock industry in the territory. The year 1887 began with the loss of seven hundred sheep in January, taken in the direction of St. Johns.[36] Any number of parties could have been responsible. St. Johns borders the Navajo and Apache reservations, and families trying to feed themselves during the winter could have raided the flocks. Mexico was also the favored destination of stolen livestock, and Daggs's sheep could have disappeared in the black market economy of the borderlands.

Despite this loss, the sheep business was still lucrative. Just the previous month, in December 1886, William Pinkerton of New Mexico traveled to Arizona to purchase a carload of rams from Daggs, and "Charles Deusha"—most likely Tom Graham's friend Charlie Duchet—negotiated with Daggs to purchase sheep on shares.[37] It may have been during the filling of one of these orders, taking advantage of an unusually mild winter to move sheep from Pleasant Valley to market, that one of Daggs's sheepherders was murdered.[38]

Little is known about that sheepherder or the violent end to his life, but what is known is that his death was not an accident. His body was found in an alcove carved by a rivulet that feeds into Cherry Creek, just north of the Graham property. He was on the trail that would later be designated as the Heber-Reno Sheep Driveway, through which thousands of sheep passed on their way toward the Salt River Valley. The sheepherder's body was found with several gunshot wounds—and he was decapitated.[39]

Because so little survives about his identity, one can only speculate about who he was. Some territorial documents identified him as a Ute, others as a Navajo. If he was a Ute, he was far from home. As Ned Blackhawk shows in *Violence over the Land,* New Mexico was a major trade center where New Mexicans purchased Ute slaves for export elsewhere.[40] Thus, he may have come to the Arizona Territory as a young captive of raiding. He could also have traveled with the Mormon families that settled along the Little Colorado River in northern Arizona. If he was Navajo, however, he would have come with sheepherding skills common to Navajo families. He, too, would have been far from home, but under different conditions.[41]

One common account in Pleasant Valley lore is that Indian trackers hired by the Tewksburys found the sheepherder's body, as well as a set of tracks that led from the body to Graham land, implicating the Grahams.[42] It remains difficult to corroborate this account with reliable documentation. The discovery of the sheepherder's body certainly could have happened this way, yet critical elements to this oft-told tale are missing. If the Grahams were suspected, no one swore a complaint against them, no one took depositions of the trackers, and no one attempted to make any arrests in connection with the sheepherder's death—all despite the $1,500 that the Daggs brothers offered as a reward.[43] One might speculate that residents did not act because they feared the Grahams, but there is not a shred of evidence that the Graham brothers physically harassed anyone, let alone murdered anyone, or that residents had any previous reason to fear them.[44]

There is, nevertheless, compelling evidence to suggest who might have actually murdered the sheepherder and why. It was the role of the justice of the peace to oversee the coroner's inquest, impaneling a jury of local citizens, taking depositions from witnesses, and rendering a conclusion about the cause of death. In the case of the murdered sheepherder, however, Justice of the Peace William Burch believed that circumstances compelled him *not* to impanel a jury because, he feared, those responsible for the sheepherder's murder could be unknowingly asked to serve on the jury. Coroner Patrick Ford agreed, stating in his report that "no good" could come from holding the inquest.

Who were the factions that Burch alluded to? He used the term "clan" twice in his report to refer to parties responsible for the murder, and many have been quick to assume that Burch was referring to the Tewksburys and Grahams. But up to this point, both families had kept their distance from one another and no fighting had broken out between these former friends. Further, Burch's report specifically mentions the Daggs brothers and the sheepherder, implying that the Daggs and/or sheepherders may have been one of the factions, and that the other faction was in competition with Daggs. If this is what Burch intended, there were four possibilities in Pleasant Valley.

Hashknife cowboys had already clashed with the Daggs brothers. These cowboys were a rough bunch; some were on the run from the law in other jurisdictions for assault and murder, and they were known to kill each other over petty offenses. While some of the Hashknife cowboys fit the description of being lawless, the problem is that referring to a group of employees as a "clan" seems a curious reference.

The proximity of the sheepherder's body to the Graham property surely confirmed in the minds of at least some settlers that the Grahams had murdered the sheepherder. Yet it is important to keep in mind that the Grahams owned 160 acres, and that the alleged tracks were never followed to discover where the trail actually ended. It is possible, therefore, that the murdering party passed through part of the Graham property without the Graham brothers ever knowing. Secondly, as mentioned previously, there was no evidence up to that point that the Grahams had murdered anyone. Indeed, they had taken up no arms in the recent gun battles and were involved only in recovery efforts.[45] While there were those who certainly believed them to be engaged in the theft economy, no claim can be found that they had threatened anyone's life.

Even if the Grahams *had* murdered in the past, there is a great difference between shooting someone and beheading them. And this perhaps is the most compelling clue. Only one population in the territory was known to dismember their victims: Apaches.

Apaches were known raiders of livestock, and Pleasant Valley was a prime area of raiding activity. Apaches frequently mutilated the bodies of their victims, and beheading was a common practice.[46] And although the Apache wars had quieted during the winter of 1886 after Geronimo surrendered, Apache raiding parties were still being reported in Pleasant Valley as late as the summer of 1887.[47]

To be sure, no one in Pleasant Valley suspected that Apaches murdered the sheepherder despite the evidence of an Apache attack. Burch and Ford certainly appear to have believed that local settlers were involved, and their reluctance to probe any deeper is clear in their reports. Whoever murdered the sheepherder, it is clear that the settlers of Pleasant Valley began to look with increasing suspicion at one another in the mounting violence.

The sheepherder's murder was the first seismic jolt in the social relations that held the Pleasant Valley community together. In the previous five years, that small settlement had endured two murderous Apache raids, a flood of cattle imported from Texas that threatened land and water, an escalation of livestock theft, two gunfights between small and large ranchers, two larceny trials and a perjury trial, and another Apache outbreak that escalated territorial anxiety to a fevered pitch. Now a man had been murdered in their settlement, and even though he was an employee of the wealthy and well-connected Daggs brothers, county officials were too afraid to investigate.

The threat of death was certainly a fact of living in this part of the territory, being so close to the Apache reservation, and the law could only offer delayed protection, if it ever came at all. That, they knew well, but this was different. Death always stalked the settlement from the outside, and there was a certain sense of security that came from knowing that your neighbors, whatever their faults, were united in defending the community from external attack. This time, however, death had breached that sense of security. This was the first time that one of the settlers was suspected of murder.

While the sheepherder's death could have been attributed to Apaches, the settlers instead turned on each other with suspicion. Why? Again, the historical record is silent on the question, but the study of the human brain under such conditions offers some reasonable conjecture. The fight-or-flight response to danger and even the perception of danger, which allows for the best chance at survival, was never meant to be a long-term solution to crisis. That neurochemical bath that quickens the blood flow and stimulates muscles and nerves becomes toxic over time.[48] The acute stress response can turn into an acute stress reaction.[49] So, the stimuli that produce an intensely alert mind and quickened senses can also produce anxiety, restlessness, anger, depression, difficulty concentrating and sleeping, and overreaction to circumstances when exposure to that stimuli becomes chronic.

Fear of violence can become insidious. Anxiety preys upon the mind, and in the dark places of the soul, hope can give way to foreboding, trust to suspicion, and patience to intolerance. Chronic anxiety can warp perception and impair social engagement. Rumors have a way of feeding upon themselves, often with tragic results. Before the sheepherder's murder, social divisions within the community were already strained. Now, his grisly death quickened the hardening of those divisions, and neighbors increasingly began to suspect one another of fell deeds. In time, those dark suspicions turned to judgment, and judgment to execution.

So began 1887 in Pleasant Valley, where belief, suspicion, and fear undermined the relationships that had held that community together.

NI'GODIZNAA—EARTH MOVED

The spring months of 1887 were filled with tension, like the charged mountain air of the Mogollon Rim before a lightning storm. Someone, or some group, continued stealing livestock. Herders were being murdered on the open range. In March, Jake Lauffer, who boarded with Ed Rose in the Pleasant Valley settlement, brought charges against a couple of Hashknife men for stealing his horse. James "Jamie" Stott, one of the accused, came to the Arizona Territory in the employ of the Aztec Land and Cattle Company but left to set up his own ranch on the Mogollon Rim.[50] The other accused, however, Tom Tucker, was still riding with the outfit.[51] All three men would later play a role in the Pleasant Valley War. Within weeks of Lauffer's suit, four Mexican sheepherders had a running gun battle with twenty-five white American cowboys near Grant Station on the A&P railroad line.[52] Tensions continued to fester between the Aztec Land and Cattle Company and local ranchers, and rumors spread wildly that the Hashknife cowboys were going to run small-time ranchers, especially sheepherders, off their property.[53]

Then, in early May, a very unexpected event rocked the territory. On a Tuesday afternoon, without any forewarning, the earth shook violently for at least thirty seconds (some areas reported tremors that lasted longer).[54] Modern estimates place the strength of that earthquake at 7.2 on the Richter Scale.[55] The overall loss of life and damage to property was minimal in the territory for such an event, but that earthquake set in motion a sequence of human responses that played out with tragic effect.

The zone of damage stretched from El Paso in the east to Yuma in the west, and from St. Johns in the north all the way down to Mexico City in the south, where tremors caused cathedral bells to ring.[56] In the Arizona Territory, the quake was strong enough to destroy some homes, damage others, and alter the landscape.[57] Some residents in the towns ran out of buildings or jumped through windows as plaster and chandeliers crashed to the ground.[58] Others fainted as buildings seemed to sway to and fro, at least four feet from their original position.[59] In southern Arizona, where the earthquake appears to have been the strongest in the territory, mountains toppled and rocks cracked with a frightening thunder.[60] Great plumes of dust and debris flew skyward, making some of the mountains appear, for a time, as if the volcanos of old had returned.[61] In the lower elevations, water geysers shot up from the ground in some areas and caused parched creek beds to roar to life with raging water.[62] Some reports told of sheepherders who were found lying dead among their flocks from no apparent cause, and were presumed to have died of fright.[63]

Communities living side by side in the territory responded to that earthquake very differently in the aftermath and cleanup. White settlers continued to speculate about the likelihood of another earthquake, but they tended to shrug it off as a curiosity of the natural world.[64] In the Apache world, however, that same event had profound meaning, one that set off a round of intense social unrest.

Native communities saw in the tremor the promise of more upheavals to come: the great imbalance in Indian life brought on by white settlers would soon be leveled. In the weeks before the earthquake hit, Yavapai healer Echawmahu had been teaching that great changes were at hand if Indians of all nations united. After the earthquake, many flocked to the San Carlos Reservation to hear his message.[65] To the north, at a meeting between Mormon leaders and White Mountain Apaches, one of the Apache leaders proclaimed that the recent earthquake was because the earth was growing old, that there would be more of them, and that "the Lord would come in four years."[66] So powerful was that anticipation of restoration that over the late spring and early summer months of 1887, Mohaves, Yavapais, Coyoteros, and Yumas began gathering with Apaches near the western boundary of the San Carlos Reservation, close to Globe City, to await the day of reckoning. Nakaaidoklini's vision still lived.

From May to July of 1887, settlers throughout the territory kept a vigilant—if not anxious—watch as the gathering of Indians surged. With their numbers growing close to fifteen hundred, the tenor of their songs became more strident, and their dances more vigorous.[67] Ranchers along the reservation boundary began reporting that their horses had gone missing. When some of the horses were located, they showed signs of having been ridden hard, as if their riders had crossed great distances in a hurry. Other ranchers reported that Apaches had taken to cutting their hair short and dressing like Mexicans to purchase "arms, ammunition, and liquor."[68]

Alarmed by the actions of Apaches, newspapers across the territory once again raised the cry that expulsion or extermination was the only solution left.[69] "Reason laughs at the folly of expecting anything but evil from these human fiends," the editors of the Florence newspaper *Arizona Weekly Enterprise* argued. "And it protests against placing any faith in their promises or professions. As dangerous as ever, menacing foes to civilization, they should be beyond the ability to wantonly destroy human life and valuable property. . . . The people of Arizona demand their removal from the Territory in the name of humanity as well as of right and justice. The latest trail of blood leaves no other proper course open, and although the casualties so far are not great[,] the fact remains that their savage nature is unchanged by kindness and only awaits an opportunity to return to the bloody carnival they delight to revel in."[70] The following week, the Yuma journal *The Arizona Sentinel* joined the clamor, noting that "the *Tucson Citizen* has hoisted the black flag, and inscribed on its folds, 'Hark, from the tomb is a doleful sound,' for the murderous Apache devils. . . . We join the chorus," the *Sentinel* editors proclaimed, "and unhesitatingly endorse the position of the *Citizen*, that the Apaches must be removed from this Territory; if not, then it is the duty of Arizonians to kill them wherever and whenever they be found."[71]

Even the territorial governor Conrad Meyer Zulick reversed his earlier position of benevolence toward Apaches. Only nineteen months earlier, he had issued a proclamation to the territory warning settlers "not to take the law into your hands to punish the Apaches."[72] However, in July 1887, he gave a speech in Phoenix harshly criticizing Apaches and calling for their complete removal from the territory.

The fallacious humanization sentiment, that has persisted in quartering upon the Apache assassins, satiated with the bounties of a too generous

Armed Apaches on Hillside, 1886.
Photograph by C. S. Fly. Courtesy Library of Congress, Prints and Photographs Division,
LC-USZ62–55389.

government, mendacious to every obligation, cunning in their bloody
[and] wanton brutality; desolation and death amongst the sturdy pioneers
of Arizona, has been rebuked, none too soon. The bleached bones of the
murdered victims that are scattered on the hill-tops and in the valleys of
our fair land, are the silent but eloquent witness of a weak and erroneous
policy. . . . The cause of humanity and the obligatory necessities of our
advancing civilization demand their removal from the scenes of their
annual barbarities. Our cause is just, and must ultimately triumph.[73]

The same month, territorial representative Marcus Aurelius Smith left for Washington, D.C., to press Congress to expel Apaches from the territory.[74]

————◦•◦————

It was during this period of clamor and uproar that a herd of horses disappeared from the Blevins ranch, which was tucked beneath the Mogollon Rim.
Wandering livestock were not uncommon on the open range, but this was not
an ordinary time. Scores of Apaches and other nations had gathered to await a
great reckoning, settlers were crying out for a final solution, and ranchers near
the reservation were widely reporting the theft of horses.

Nor was the Blevins ranch an ordinary ranch. Their spread was situated precariously close to the Apache reservation, and the Blevinses were well known to the Navajos and the Apaches and widely disliked by them.[75]

In early August, the older Blevins boys, Andy Cooper, Charlie, and Hamp, turned a herd of horses out to graze while they went to Holbrook for a week to purchase supplies. The following morning, however, their father, Mart Blevins, discovered that the herd was gone. Mart returned to the cabin to inform his son John that he was going to track the horses while the trail was still fresh. Riding out with a neighbor, John Dement, they set out traveling south.[76]

Dement rode for two days with Blevins but returned after four without him. He told Ann Blevins that her husband wanted to continue looking for the herd, and that he parted with Blevins about a mile from the Middleton ranch.[77] Dement's news left her apprehensive. Mart had not taken supplies for a long journey, and Apaches had twice attacked the Middleton ranch before. She immediately sent the older Blevins boys to look for their father after they returned from Holbrook the next day.

When Mart Blevins continued on, tracking the horses alone, he rode into a storm of discontent. Was he concerned about the escalating unrest on the reservation—or was he even aware of it? They had picked the Canyon Creek ranch for their home base because of its very remoteness, so news may have been slow to reach them. Either way, Blevins took his life into his own hands when he rode south along the river beds that cut through reservation land. The Blevinses brazenly stole Indian horses and wantonly murdered the Indians who got in their way.[78] Navajos and Apaches knew the Blevinses by sight and by name. It was a bad time for a white man to be riding through Indian country alone. It was an even worse time for a Blevins to be tempting fate.

Mart would never return, and what happened to him has always been a mystery.[79] A Yavapai memoir may, however, hold a clue.

Mike Burns was an interpreter on the San Carlos Reservation at the time of the earthquake, and he observed the heightened anticipation of reckoning. In his memoir, *The Only One Living to Tell*, Burns recalled that in the days that followed the earthquake, a runner came to the San Carlos Agency bearing the news that a white man had been killed on the reservation. The white man had come upon an Indian encampment on the San Carlos River, and, after spending the night getting them drunk, they killed him. None of the soldiers or scouts sent out to investigate could determine the man's identity, nor could they determine where his assailants had gone. His body had been burned beyond recognition, and there were so many hoof prints where the man was killed, as if a herd had trampled the ground, that the trail of his murderers was obscured.[80]

Even if this wasn't Blevins, this man's fate was a real possibility that awaited him as he struck out alone through Indian country during this perilous moment.

Mart's disappearance was a significant moment in the story of Pleasant Valley, although the settlers at the time were likely unaware that the ground was shifting beneath them. It was not so much because he personally meant something to the settlers; the Blevinses were largely outsiders, who seemed to trail trouble wherever they went. But what followed his disappearance opened up underlying fissures in the social geography of the community, spewing forth torrents of fear, hatred, grief, revenge, and trauma.

The larger struggles that occupied the settlers also changed in the wake of his disappearance. The previous gun battles in Pleasant Valley tended to be between the large cattle operations and small-time ranchers. After the disappearance of Mart Blevins, however, strife became internecine. The settlers of Pleasant Valley squared off with one another with increasing vehemence, and those confrontations were not random. Factions created by the seemingly endless round of lawsuits and countersuits now hardened between those who were suspected of being engaged in the livestock black market—or at least supporting it in some fashion—and those who opposed that illegal market. Friendships broke, loyalties were tested, and new alliances arose from the heat of conflict. In some important ways, it became a battle between lawful pursuits and quick profit, or, as Herman argues, over whether the framework of civilization would ultimately survive the savagery of naked aggression.

SHOOT-OUT AT THE MIDDLETON RANCH

The Blevins boys searched for a day and a half, but, curiously, they had great difficulty picking up a trail. A herd of horses shouldn't have been that difficult to find. They would not have strayed too far from water, and there would have been hoofprints and droppings on the ground.[81]

The Blevins boys returned to their ranch, resupplied, and divided up, traveling in different directions. Hampton "Hamp" Blevins traveled east toward Pinedale and Heber and met up with some Hashknife cowboys to ask for help. Given their previous confrontations with Indians, and the direction where Mart was last seen, the Blevins boys may have concluded that it was safer to travel in larger numbers. John Paine, Tom Tucker (who was accused of stealing Jake Lauffer's horse), Bob Glaspie, Bob Carrington, and three other Hashknife cowboys volunteered to join the search for the elder Blevins.[82]

Hamp's asking these particular men for help may not have been coincidental. Before he met up with these cowboys, Hashknife manager J. E. Simpson had gathered the company together and issued an ultimatum: the rustling that was thinning the Aztec cattle herds by the company's own cow herders had to stop. Those who would not commit to do so were invited to leave the outfit immediately. Blevins's friends Paine, Tucker, and Glaspie chose to quit.[83] Though hardly a smoking gun, their choice is nonetheless suggestive of the nature of their association with the Blevinses. Hamp had served time in Texas for stealing horses with his older brother Andy, and he was given a compassionate release due to his epileptic fits.[84] In the Arizona Territory, the Blevinses were widely suspected of actively engaging in the theft economy, and the evidence seems to support that suspicion. Paine, Tucker, and Glaspie, furthermore, preferred to leave honest work rather than commit to not stealing from their employer. They, too, may have been actively involved in the livestock black market.

Whatever their previous association, these men, now unemployed, joined the Blevins search party. They seemed to know that they were riding into trouble. "There's a war going on down there," Will C. Barnes reminded them when he overheard their plans. "Maybe we'll start a little old war of our own," John Paine shot back, defiantly.[85] Before they left the Hashknife camp, they armed themselves for a possible confrontation. They borrowed "all the surplus ammunition in camp," Barnes remembered, and "they left . . . without a pack horse or supplies of any kind except those of war."[86]

The search party made slow progress, probably because they spread out, zigzagging back and forth along Canyon Creek, trying to pick up a trail. By 9 August 1887, they had managed to travel only about twenty miles in a southerly direction from the Canyon Creek ranch.[87] The trail was getting cold, the daytime temperatures were growing warm, and the cowboys were frustrated.[88]

The search party soon picked up the smell of meat being smoked and traveled in that direction.[89] It was the old Middleton place, where the Middletons had survived a siege during an Apache uprising six years earlier. Middleton had sold his place to George Newton, a Globe City merchant in watches and sewing machines. Newton traveled up to Pleasant Valley when occasion permitted, but on that particular afternoon, only two men were present: Newton's brother-in-law, George Wilson, and Jim Tewksbury. They were working together curing beef when the Blevins search party arrived.

In the many retellings of this story, so many Tewksbury family members and friends have been named as being present with Newton that afternoon that they could only have been tightly packed, shoulder to shoulder, in the small cabin. But George Wilson was adamant in his retelling of the events of that day, that only he and Jim Tewksbury were present. "I ought to know," he insisted. "It was my cabin."[90]

What followed is less contested.

As the search party rode up, Jim Tewksbury cracked open the cabin door. The distance between the front door and where the horsemen stopped was only about thirty yards.[91] The cowboys asked for supper, which was a customary thing to do on the range.

"No sir," came Jim's curt reply. "We ain't running no hotel here."

He held a cocked Winchester rifle in his other hand behind the door. George stood in a corner holding a shotgun, wide-eyed and frozen with fear.[92]

Some of the party angrily cursed as they turned their horses to ride away. "You black son of a bitch!" snarled John Paine.[93] In an instant, bullets from Tewksbury's Winchester burst out from Newton's cabin in deafening succession.[94]

Hamp Blevins immediately tumbled from his saddle, shot through the head. Seeing this, Tucker, Glaspie, and Carrington dug their spurs deep into horseflesh to flee, but another bullet ripped through Tucker's ribs underneath his arms and exited out the other side before he could get far. He still managed to ride out of range at full gallop, however. Other than a bullet through his shirt, Carrington was unscathed, but Glaspie was shot through the knee.[95] The bullet passed through his horse, which collapsed moments afterward.

Just as the others started to ride off, John Paine whirled around in time to squeeze off one shot, but his horse collapsed, mortally wounded, before he could fire again. Paine was pinned to the ground by his own horse as men shouted and horses crashed amid the steady gunfire from the cabin. As Paine struggled to free himself, one bullet tore an ear off. Once loose, he scrambled to find cover, but another bullet smacked him in the back after he had taken half a dozen steps. He slammed to the ground, dead, near Blevins's body.[96]

Carrington and Tucker rode hard until Tucker finally fell off his saddle from losing blood. Left behind, he lost consciousness and all track of time. Only a hard summer rainstorm common to the Mogollon Rim, followed by hail, revived him. He was alone, his horse was gone, and he could only move very slowly. For close to forty hours, he dragged himself along, inch by inch, until he collapsed from fatigue.[97] During the harrowing journey, a mother bear and cubs tried to attack him as he wandered, but he managed to frighten them off. Confused and probably delirious at times, he finally staggered up to the ranch of Al Rose, seventeen miles away.[98] Rose's ranch was still a good twenty-five miles from the Blevinses' ranch, but Bob Sixby, who was working as a ranch hand for Rose, took Tucker in, and dressed his still-open wound that had become infected with blowflies and maggots.[99]

Bob Glaspie fared a little better. After his horse collapsed, fatally wounded, Glaspie lay still until the shooting stopped and then crawled across open ground into a wooded area for concealment. There he waited until he could crawl back to his dead horse to retrieve his saddle and hide it in the woods. Then, binding his wound with his own underwear, and treating it with a little tobacco, he haltingly began the journey back to Canyon Creek. For two nights and three days, he slowly limped along the creek bed, until he finally reached the Blevins ranch. There he bore the tragic news to Ann Blevins about her boy Hamp, while the camp cook treated his wounds.[100]

Perhaps more importantly for the Blevinses, he gave the name of the man who killed Hamp: Tewksbury.

———•◦•———

Why had Jim Tewksbury fired on the search party? Some storytellers, writing long after this tragedy, have used this moment to illustrate the Tewksburys' violent streak. Whether Jim knew Blevins and the Hashknife cowboys, or what their business was on that fateful day, is unknown. But the Middleton ranch was in a remote clearing, miles away from the nearest neighbor and far from well-traveled paths.[101] Riders did not simply wander by. Rumors had been flying throughout the valley that Hashknife cowboys were coming after small-time ranchers, and Jim could clearly see that these men—most of whom were Hashknife cowboys—were well armed.[102] And this wasn't the first time in Jim Tewksbury's life when armed men came riding up, unannounced, and made trouble. Tewksbury was surely already on the alert, if not already on edge, from the murder of the sheepherder only a few months earlier. And as drums beat on the reservation less than three miles away, they were alone, in a remote cabin that Apaches had attacked before with fatal consequences, killing two neighbors. The Middletons had barely escaped with their lives.

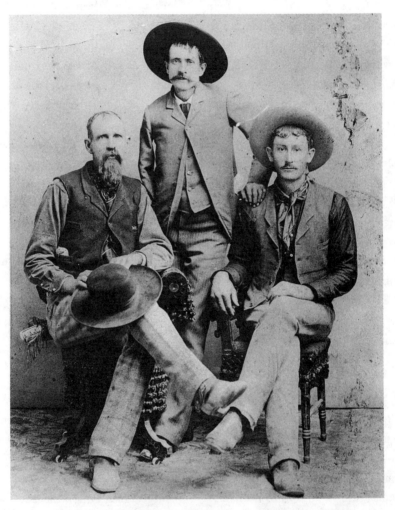

Red Holkam [Holcomb] (*seated, left*), Hampton Blevins (*standing*),
and John Black Blevins (*seated, right*), ca. 1885.

Courtesy Don Dedera Papers, Arizona Collection, Arizona State University Hayden Library, Tempe.

Jim Roberts, a friend of the Tewksburys, later insisted that Hamp Blevins was the one who drew first, and this may have been what Jim Tewksbury thought as he kicked open the door, raised his rifle, and fired on the retreating cowboys.[103] It is possible that Hamp attempted to draw his weapon, but it would have been difficult to do while holding the reins to his horse. In the only photograph known to exist of Hamp Blevins, he has only one arm. Jim, however, saw something threatening enough to provoke an immediate response. Psychologists speak of confirmation bias, the ability of the human mind to find in random events evidence that confirms one's suspicions.[104] Is it possible, then, that as Hamp pulled the reins on his horse with his one arm to return to the trail, his other sleeve, fluttering down by his gun belt, was tragically, mistakenly, interpreted in the anxiety of the moment by Jim Tewksbury as a reach for his weapon?

The news of Hamp's murder, on the heels of Mart's disappearance, was devastating to the Blevinses. Bob Glaspie insisted that they were simply asking for a meal at the Middleton ranch, and that their attack was entirely unprovoked, so the Blevins family surely viewed Hamp's death as a callous murder of a sickly lad who was simply looking for his father—a young man with only one arm who was shot through the head before he had a chance to try to defend himself, murdered by "desperado half-blood Indians" who still walked the valley.

How does a family like the Blevinses rectify the injustice of such a loss in their minds? How did Hamp's murder in a lonely dell eat upon their thoughts as days wore long, while they instinctively looked to the tree line, still holding on to the slimmest of hope, as families so often do for the missing, that Mart would emerge, riding back home? It is telling that the Blevinses made no effort to go to the law to file a complaint in Hamp's murder (Graham nephew Louis Parker would see to that). Andy Cooper, at least—the elder Blevins boy—had other things in mind.

Hamp's murder pulled the families of Pleasant Valley even deeper into a maelstrom. Jim Tewksbury and George Wilson fled from the Middleton ranch after the shooting, and when they returned days later, they found the ranch burned to the ground. Who did it and why was another wedge that drove Pleasant Valley families apart.

5

ENFORCEMENT WITH
EXTREME PREJUDICE

For all the folklore about the killings from the so-called Graham-Tewksbury feud, the hyperaggressive enforcement of the law was the principal reason for so many deaths during this conflict. More men died resisting arrest—or were presumed to be resisting arrest—than at the hands of either the Graham or the Tewksbury families. Some observers tried to group lawmen from several jurisdictions into a "Tewksbury faction," and Tom Graham at least charged that a conspiracy was behind the violence that his family suffered, but there is simply no evidence that lawmen from towns as far away as Prescott and Holbrook stood to personally gain anything by removing the Blevinses or the Grahams from a remote and obscure hamlet of the territory, especially on behalf of a family like the Tewksburys of very limited means and influence.

The aggressive posture of territorial lawmen was born in fear. In the face of a potential threat, they much preferred to shoot first and ask questions later—if they ever asked—than risk their lives. Indeed, so aggressive were some territorial lawmen that settlers believed that an arrest warrant was as good as a death sentence. "Commodore Owens, it was often said," quipped an Arizona newspaper about one of the territory's famed sheriffs, "would shoot not only 'at the drop of a hat, but before the hat was dropped.'"[1]

Within this ethos of enforcement, the guilt or innocence of the resisting party was entirely beside the point. Any action short of absolute compliance could get a suspect shot, if not killed, especially if that suspect was armed. This was a key to survival that the Tewksburys seemed to grasp early on. The Blevinses and the Grahams never did.

At the same time, territorial lawmen were not the only ones who acted preemptively with extreme aggression. As violence spiraled outward, pulling more people into its destructive path, settlers also assumed extreme postures, which

1887–1888 PLEASANT VALLEY CASUALTIES, BY ACTION

KILLED BY LAW ENFORCEMENT	KILLED BY SETTLERS	KILLED BY UNKNOWN OR APACHES	KILLED BY VIGILANTES	WOUNDED BY SETTLERS
Bill Graham	Hamp Blevins	Sheepherder	Al Rose	Tom Tucker
Andy Cooper	John Tewksbury	Mart Blevins	James Stott	Robert Glaspie
John Blevins	Bill Jacobs		James Scott	Joe Ellingwood
Mose Roberts	Harry Midleton		Billy Wilson	George Blaine
Sam Blevins	John Paine			
Johnny Graham				
Charles Blevins				

all too often led to hair-trigger responses to perceived threats. Tragically, the victims of such responses were as often the wrong ones as the right ones. But taking the time to make such determinations was a luxury when families believed they were facing imminent attack. As casualties mounted, all that mattered was protection. When the justice from territorial courts was slow and inconsistent, settlers drew upon their own codes of morality, which were as much tribal as they were biblical.

THE FUNERAL PYRE

After he fled the attack at the Middleton ranch, Bob Carrington continued straight to the Blevinses' ranch, where he and Charlie Blevins began recruiting others to return in force to the site. Who they turned to reveals the coalitions that had formed or were beginning to form among Pleasant Valley residents. Blevins turned to Johnny Graham and his nephew Louis Parker.[2] Graham recruited his neighbor in the north valley, Louis Naeglin, and neighboring ranchers Al Rose and Ed Rose. In all, about a dozen settlers rode out to the Middleton ranch on the afternoon of 10 August 1887, including storeowner Charles Perkins and ranchers Miguel Apodaca and Bill Voris.[3]

The mood among the burial party ranged from somber to seething. The Newton ranch was about a two-hours' ride south of the Graham ranch, and when they arrived, they found the place abandoned except for some hogs and chickens roaming freely.[4] The dead horses lay in the road, along with the undisturbed bodies of Blevins and Paine. The party immediately set about digging graves.

They left the horses where they fell, unburied; their mission was to bury their riders. Al Rose used planks torn from the freestanding corral fence to build rudimentary coffins. Once he finished, he piled the scrap wood against the corral fence, about seventy-five yards from the house.[5] After the bodies were buried, the party of settlers entered the cabin and cooked dinner before riding back.

As the party saddled up for the ride home, someone—most likely Charlie Blevins—muttered: "That damned shanty ought to be burned."[6] Most of the group left about the same time, but some momentarily straggled behind.[7] When the first group was about a half mile away from the ranch, flames began to leap through the cabin roof, and smoke filled the air.[8]

The burning of the Middleton ranch was another axis of tension within the Pleasant Valley settlement that more deeply drew lines between families.[9]

Earl Forrest raised the possibility that an Apache raiding party was actually responsible for the fire. Pleasant Valley resident Jim Roberts related that Jim Tewksbury and George Newton saw, shortly after the shooting, a large company of mounted Apaches on the hills watching them. Indeed, this may have been true, since an outbreak had been reported that summer, and burning settler property was a common Apache tactic, although none of the burial party reported seeing any Indian activity in the area. Regardless of who burned the cabin, the fire seems to have started no longer than ten minutes after the last members of the burial party left.[10]

Rumors about the arson reached Lydia and Mary Ann Tewksbury, and they quickly passed the news to George Newton, who had been staying with them. Newton rode out to investigate, and by the time he arrived at his property, the ranch was a total loss; the house, corral, and barn were completely destroyed by fire. Louis Parker, in the meantime, rode west to Prescott to swear out complaints for the murder of "John Pain & H. Blivens" against James Dunning Tewksbury, his three sons, Bill Jacobs, and Joe Boyer, and another complaint against J. R. Edmonson and John Roberts.[11] George Wilson was not far behind Parker, swearing out an arson complaint against members of the burial party: Al Rose, Miguel Apodaca, Louis Parker, William Bonner, and two unknown men.[12]

Parker was not connected to Paine or Blevins, but his willingness to make the three-day journey to Prescott reveals a deep motivation to bring charges against the men of the Tewksbury family. He did not witness the event, and it is difficult to imagine how he could have provided evidence to the justice of the peace in swearing out the murder complaints. He may have known Paine and the Blevins through the flow of stolen livestock, however, and many in the area already suspected that they were partners in crime. At the same time, the Grahams had used the court as a weapon against their rivals before—especially those who had testified against them in previous charges. Whatever Parker's relationship with the Blevinses and the Hashknife cowboys, he had to have known that his actions would drive the two families further apart.

THE FIRST GRAHAM TO DIE

One week after Blevins and Paine were buried at the Middleton ranch, twenty-one-year-old Bill Graham, the younger half brother of John and Tom, rode out to the Heber-Reno Sheep Driveway, the trail that ran along the northern boundary of Graham land.[13] Bill was a tall young man who, like his father, had fair hair and blue eyes. Few details are known about what motivated that particular journey, but he left the cabin early in the morning, perhaps at daybreak. Even in the higher elevations, the Arizona highlands could get quite warm in August as the day wore on.

Whatever Graham's destination that morning, he never made it. When he stumbled through the Grahams' cabin door a few hours later, he was trying to hold his intestines in. He was weak from profuse blood loss from a shot to the bowels and to his arm, and in shock.[14] The Graham brothers frantically sent for help.

Neighbors Bob Sixby and Al Rose patched him up as best they could, washing his bowels and sewing the torn flesh with needle and thread, but gut shots were fatal and everyone knew it.[15] Even if they could stop the bleeding, infection was sure to set in from perforated bowels. Before Bill died feverishly the next day, he told his story.[16]

He was ambushed on the trail, he said, and he repeated the names of men the Grahams had accused before of crimes: John, Ed, and Jim Tewksbury; Jim Roberts; John Edmonson; Herbert Bishop; and Joe Boyer.[17] There were two or three others that he did not recognize.[18] But it was Ed Tewksbury who fired the first shot from behind a tree, about forty paces away, and that shot hit him in the bowels. As he reached for his pistol, he was then shot in the arm. In all, Bill thought that about twenty shots were fired at him. He said that someone shouted that he would not be further harmed if the Grahams left the county.

Bill died painfully.

Johnny and Tom watched helplessly as their little brother sank into a fevered unconsciousness. With each passing hour, their anguish grew into rage against their neighbors. Bill had nothing to do with their quarrels with the Tewksburys, but now their treacherous nature was revealed. When Bill sighed his last breath, his brothers swore in bitter grief that they would avenge him.[19] The valley would never be the same.

———•◦•———

Yet who really shot Bill is not as clear as the Grahams believed. A standing assumption in the nineteenth century was that a dying man's declaration was sacrosanct. No one would knowingly lie when facing the end of life, they reasoned, so statements given with a man's last breath, especially in identifying his assailant, were considered unassailable.

Bob Sixby was actually the first to raise questions about Bill's account when he testified at the coroner's inquest. The bullet that disemboweled Graham, according to Sixby's observation, came from behind him (Al Rose was less sure from which direction the shot had come).[20] This is important: if Bill was shot from behind, it would have been difficult, if not impossible, to know with certainty who shot him, especially if a group were firing at him at the same time, as he stated.

The geography where Bill Graham was shot prompts more questions. It is flat, open ground with rather clear views from almost every direction, particularly because the trail slopes gently upward by perhaps twenty degrees. Graham land was good grazing land for cattle. The rolling hills were grassy, with few trees, and it was relatively free of boulders or other significant geographic formations. The grass was not high or thick enough to hide a kneeling man, and a man lying in the grass would have been relatively easy to see, given the upward slope of the land from the direction Bill was coming from. The trees that grow in the area are sparsely placed coniferous junipers, perhaps twelve to fifteen feet high, with narrow trunks no thicker than a man's thigh, and thin branches. One man may have been able to conceal himself, but it would have been difficult for a large group to do so, given the openness of the area and the sparseness of the trees.

Recent studies in the psychology of eyewitness identification suggest that the trauma of violence may have influenced what Bill recalled in the throes of dying. Several studies show that a number of environmental factors can have a dramatic influence on the accuracy of one's perception, such as "low levels of illumination, greater distance between the witness and the perpetrator, a brief amount of time for viewing the perpetrator, the experience of stress or anxiety on the part of the witness (sometimes based on the presence of a weapon)."[21] All of these elements were present when Bill Graham was mortally wounded and surely had an impact on forming what he believed happened.[22]

Ed Tewksbury and all the other men Bill accused always denied being present that morning, and someone else took the responsibility for shooting Graham, someone entirely unconnected to Parker's murder complaint. And he told a very different story.

Deputy Sheriff James D. Houck, a Civil War veteran, reported to other lawmen that he shot Graham in self-defense.[23] He pointed out the location where it took place, and he explained what happened.[24] His account was even published in three territorial newspapers.[25]

Houck typically studied the men he was charged with arresting to learn their habits. Once satisfied that he could predict their comings and goings, he would then rise well before dawn to take up a position where he could surprise them as they rose to start their day. So it was, very early one morning, that Houck took up a position just outside the Grahams' spread, where the trail from the Graham cabin met up with the trail that bordered their property. In the dark, he patiently waited to intercept Johnny Graham and serve him with a warrant—probably the bench warrant from skipping out of their larceny trial in Apache County. Finally at dawn, when a horseman approached from the direction of the Graham ranch, Houck stepped out from behind a tree and aimed his rifle at the rider.

"Throw up!" Houck commanded.

The horseman stopped and looked up, startled. It was then that Houck realized that the horse rider was not Johnny.

"I've got the wrong man," he called out, raising the barrel upward.

"I haven't!" Bill replied as he pulled his pistol out and fired a wild shot at Houck.

The more experienced Houck lowered his rifle and returned fire from about forty yards away, mortally wounding Graham.[26]

Leon Hanchett charged that Houck gave this account merely to cover for Ed Tewksbury because of their sheep connections. But it bears repeating that the Tewksburys were not sheep men, and that none of the previous gun battles in Pleasant Valley were over sheep or between the two families. Further, while

Houck had participated in roundups with the Tewksburys in the past, roundups were community events involving many. There is no evidence that Houck was especially close with the Tewksburys, or that he had any particular animosity toward the Grahams. Thus, there does not appear to have been any motive for Houck to take the blame for Bill Graham's death if he was not responsible for it. There were many who hated Houck for his aggressive policing, but he was never known for being a liar.[27]

Rather, the gun battle on 17 August 1887 bears all the marks of a tragic case of mistaken identities. The light was still dim as Graham set out at daybreak. Houck, who had waited in the cool of the early morning to intercept Johnny Graham, very likely turned his coat collar up and pulled his hat down low to stay warm. Even in summertime, the Arizona nights could still grow cold. Bill was new to the settlement, and both Ed Tewksbury and Jim Houck were mustachioed, dark-haired, dark-complexioned, and of similar build. Under such conditions, it would have been easy to mistake one for the other at forty paces.[28] Houck realized his mistake quickly, that Bill was not Johnny, but Bill did not. He fired on who he thought was an armed Ed Tewksbury attempting to waylay his brother.[29]

Two days later, Yavapai County Sheriff William J. Mulvenon left for Pleasant Valley from Prescott, with two deputies. News had not yet reached them of Bill Graham's death. Instead they carried arrest warrants for the murders of Paine and Blevins. On their way to the valley, they routed north through Flagstaff to pick up six more members of the posse.[30]

Amid reports of a pending Apache outbreak, the posse rode into Pleasant Valley almost a week after they set out from Prescott, not sure if they would encounter armed Apache renegades or resistant suspects.[31] They found neither. When they arrived at the Tewksbury ranch, the brothers had already left for the Sierra Ancha Mountains. Only Mary Ann Tewksbury, John's wife, and the family patriarch, James Dunning Tewksbury, were home, and they were not terribly cooperative with the sheriff.

The Tewksbury brothers knew their surrounding environment well and used it to good effect. Tucked away in the rugged crevices of the Sierra Ancha Mountains were several ruins of the ancient people who made their dwellings in the cliff walls before the Apaches arrived. The Tewksbury brothers used these ruins often when out hunting or, at times, when they were hunted.

Rather than follow into the mountains after the Tewksburys, Mulvenon

Andy Blevins, aka Andy Cooper, ca. 1880s.
Courtesy Don Dedera Papers, Arizona Collection, Arizona State University Hayden Library, Tempe.

took his posse several miles north to the Sixby ranch, where he sent a communiqué back to Prescott. The Tewksburys were in hiding, he reported, but he was confident that they would be found soon. In the following days, the posse rode through the valley serving warrants where they could.

Word spread quickly that the law was in town. Andy Cooper ordinarily stayed far away from lawmen, but his brother's murder demanded action. He rode to Pleasant Valley to the Graham ranch, and together they rode to the Perkins store to speak to Mulvenon. Cooper flatly told the sheriff that a war would start if the Tewksburys were not taken into custody.[32] George Newton also met with the sheriff and took him out to show him the burned-out buildings on his property. After almost two weeks, the sheriff's optimism waned that he would complete his charge. However, the posse had at least limited contact with the Tewksbury brothers on their twelfth day in the settlement. A messenger arrived informing the sheriff that the Tewksbury brothers would not leave the settlement—indeed, they could not because they feared what the Blevinses and Grahams would do if they were not there to protect their families. Upon hearing this, and being aware that each day on the trail was running up expenses for the county, the sheriff and posse returned to Prescott.[33]

The sheriff's departure marked a turning point in the community. While the Tewksburys succeeded in remaining with their families during this dangerous time, their success was the posse's failure, which provoked the Blevinses and the Grahams to resort to frontier justice.[34] With the Blevinses determined to avenge Hamp, the Grahams now had a formidable ally in planning their retribution. In a week's time, their actions altered the conflict within the settlement, shifting it into a civil war as neighbor turned on neighbor, allies on former allies, and friends on former friends.

"THE HEARTACHE AND THE THOUSAND NATURAL SHOCKS THAT FLESH IS HEIR TO"

"August the 19 Bill died at 10 oClock at night."[35] These words recorded in Tom Graham's journal are the only known statement that he made about the murder of his brother. That simple declaration, about such a pivotal moment in the lives of the Graham family, is so rich with potential insight. But in the end, it is still so frustratingly unrevealing about the man who wrote it, Tom Graham. Did he write that statement slowly and deliberately, carefully choosing each word to hold the grief that poured out from every stroke of his pen? Or were those words meant to scream with a rage that filled his soul? Perhaps, instead, it was simply a terse pronouncement from a hardened and stoic man.

"One can start anywhere in a culture's repertoire of forms and end up anywhere else," Clifford Geertz reminds us about the complexity of interpreting human expression.[36] Those few words can be read in different ways, and much of it depends on how one thinks about those who settled the West. Did they experience the pain of loss differently from the generations that followed them?

The question is an important one for this study. Did the settlers of Pleasant Valley experience fear, anxiety, and loss in ways similar to those of modern times, or were they made of sterner stuff? If they did experience what modern diagnosticians would term continuous traumatic stress, was their reaction the same as those of the present? Westerns tend to revolve around stoic characters, and it is well worth asking: What made them stoic? Delving into the inner lives of historical actors to probe what people were thinking and feeling in any historical moment is often difficult to do through conventional historical methods. But other disciplines that study the past provide compelling models for discerning the inner lives of settlers who endured the relentless fear, violence, and suffering of frontier conditions.

Kathleen Donegan's *Seasons of Misery: Catastrophe and Colonial Settlement in Early America* is especially helpful in uncovering from colonial narratives the intellectual and emotional chaos of sudden and unexpected violence, the relentless misery of starvation and poverty, and the utter dislocation of abandonment that came with colonizing the American wilderness. Turning the triumphal narrative of English settlement on its head, Donegan's study places "crisis—both experiential and existential—at the center of the story" of how English settlers understood themselves and their endeavor.[37]

The misery and crisis experienced by English colonists (what Donegan described as a psychic chaos) were also integral parts of the Spanish colonial experience. One might reasonably expect to see a different reaction to violence at least among the Jesuits who volunteered for service in the Americas. "The values and virtues related to martyrdom," Brad Gregory notes in *Salvation at Stake: Christian Martyrdom in Early Modern Europe*, "were integral to late medieval Catholicism."[38] And so Jesuits came from across Europe to live on the hostile frontier of New Spain, fully expecting to "share abundantly in Christ's sufferings" and to be "crucified with Christ" in emulation of the apostles of old.[39] Even then, however, with the sure knowledge that a martyr's suffering and death awaited them, and with the promise of glory in eternity, there are clues in the historical records that chronic trauma took its toll even on those who expected to die for their faith. Commenting on the work of the Jesuits in Apachería, one 1757 report noted: "Their lives are filled with bitter disappointment and continual mortification, oppressive and extreme heat, vermin and poisonous creatures, the rudeness and offensiveness of native character, the want of essentials and necessities; aside from all these are the other circumstances which provide an abundant harvest of suffering."[40] Indeed, as researcher Henrietta Stockel concluded in her study of Spanish colonizing, the "psychological stress" from unexpected raids was not only "debilitating" for the priests, but for their native parishioners, too.[41]

If the conditions on the frontier yielded a "harvest of suffering" for Jesuits, how much greater was the impact of violence and deprivation in the lives of the soldiers and settlers who came less fortified with the promise of glory from suffering and death? In 1774, Captain Nicolás Gil sent a picket of fifty soldiers under the command of Ensign Manuel Villa to recover the bodies of their captain and others who had been killed while chasing Indian raiders. Even though the Indians—presumably Apaches—had long fled the location by the time the soldiers arrived, the "soldiers were so frightened that they did not want to dismount," a colonial dispatch reported.[42] "It was obvious that a plan needed to be developed and implemented," historian Roberto Salmón observed, "to convince the troops to risk their lives."[43] John Kessell, who studied the Guevavi Mission in southern Arizona, concurred. "Not all of those who died in the following months were killed or mutilated by Apaches," he noted in *Mission of Sorrows,* "but the likelihood of such a grisly death gnawed at the resolve of the *gente de razón* who survived. A delegation of them went to Captain Anza. They wanted permission to abandon their homes in the San Luis Valley . . . [and] the sympathetic captain . . . approved."[44]

Apaches well knew the impact they had on Spanish settlers, Stockel argued. Fear was one of their most powerful weapons. They taunted, mocked, and screamed at the soldiers who rode into Apache territory. "Despite the anticipated rewards combat would bring," she noted, "many soldiers lost heart and courage, deserting their stations, while others simply refused to fight. New recruits seldom stayed long, many fleeing in terror after their first experience with the Chiricahuas. . . ."[45] In time, causing this very reaction, making settlers flee from fear, became one of the core strategies of Apache raiding. Rather than fighting, the villagers in some Mexican settlements, who endured constant raids, took to fleeing town at the first alarm of Apache attack and allowing Apaches to freely take whatever they wanted.[46]

The earliest records of Americans who dared enter Apache land in the Arizona Territory echo these same themes, even though some were more willing than others to openly acknowledge it. To be sure, these accounts were not written by the settlers of Pleasant Valley, but by contemporaries of the period. Apache fighter John C. Cremony was on his way to Doña Ana from Socorro in the New Mexico Territory when suddenly he noticed a column of dust rising behind him. Suspecting that it could only mean that an Apache attack was imminent, he spurred his horse and began a run for his life. For seventy miles, Cremony desperately rode as some forty Apache warriors bore down on him. At times the war party was close enough to send arrows whizzing by, and he in turn fired upon them with pistols. As they drew close, he could hear "their cries and yells," which he described as "fearful." Finally, as the town of Doña Ana came into view, he knew he was safe.[47]

Was Cremony's employment of the word "fearful" simply a rhetorical flourish to heighten the drama of his narrative, or does it begin to capture the impact of the moment when his fate hung in the balance? Cremony actually devoted more words to praising the qualities of his horse and to describing how he cared for it than he did to revealing his inner state, but there are clues in his narrative that are consistent with the sympathetic and parasympathetic responses to acute stress. Once he was within the safety of town, he simply could not rest, nor could he sleep. Even though he had been up since dawn and rode into town close to midnight, he remained wide awake, busying himself in the stable with the care for his horse until the sun rose. Then, after downing a hot whiskey toddy—a common medicinal of the day—exhaustion finally struck. He slept "all that day and the succeeding night."[48]

Important clues to this question of settler vulnerability to fear, anxiety, and loss also peek through the narratives of those who traveled through Apache country. Martha Summerhayes recalled her experiences as the wife of First Lieutenant John Wyer Summerhayes, first living at Fort Whipple (Prescott), Camp Verde, and then at Camp Apache.[49] All of these locations would have been well familiar to the settlers of Pleasant Valley. Summerhayes's memoir is especially important because she provides a window that looks past the gendered norms of expression for her day. "Women usually like to talk over their trials and their wonderful adventures, and that is why I am writing this, I suppose," she noted. "Men simply *will not* talk about such things."[50]

Summerhayes recalled one night of setting up camp in a thick grove of pines that, to her, looked primeval and untrodden. She and another army wife, along with their husbands and a few other officers, sat around the campfire after dinner talking about Indians.

"Injuns would not have such a big fire as that," one of the officers observed.

"No, you bet they wouldn't," another officer replied readily.

They sat in silence gazing into the fire, lost in thought.

Finally, another officer spoke up, uttering what was surely on the minds of the others: "Our figures must make a mighty good outline against that fire. . . . I dare say those stealthy sons of Satan know exactly where we are at this minute."

"Yes, you bet your life they do!" agreed the other officers.

The major turned to speak to Lieutenant Summerhayes, but the others overheard his comments. "Look behind you at those trees, Jack," he said. "Can you see anything? No! And if there were Apaches behind each one of them, we should never know it."

Everyone turned and looked into the thick blackness that lay beyond the reach of the firelight. Another long pause followed. The fire crackled as the wind blew through the pines.

Suddenly the silence was shattered by a crash in the woods. Everyone leaped to their feet and turned in the direction of the noise, straining to detect any movement in the darkness.

"A dead branch," someone finally concluded.

"D—d if I don't believe I'm getting nervous!" the major confided in a low tone to Lieutenant Summerhayes. He briskly wished all a goodnight.

"No element of doubt pervaded my mind as to my own state," Martha Summerhayes recalled as she watched the major quickly walking toward his tent. The thought that from behind each tree "a red devil might be at that moment taking aim with his deadly arrow" gave rise to a level of anxiety that she had never before experienced. She had survived a cyclone that for thirty-six hours tossed to and fro the ship she was on, until she had consigned herself to die by drowning. "But compared to the sickening dread of the cruel Apache, my fears then had been as naught . . . in this mysterious darkness, every nerve, every sense, was keenly alive with terror."[51]

One might argue that her fear was exceptionally keen because she was a civilian woman traveling through Apache country, while the hardened military men responded differently. But Summerhayes insisted otherwise. "I venture to say," she wrote, "that . . . not one will deny that he shared in the . . . apprehension which seized upon us."[52] At least one veteran from the Arizona Territory praised Summerhayes for speaking what he could not. "For what she's done, God bless her!" he wrote. "A friend of mine was in the shop and when I came to [reading about] Pringle's death, he said, 'Gurnett, that must be a sad book you're reading, why man, you're crying.'"[53]

Shortly after the Summerhayeses were transferred from the Arizona Territory, Charles B. Gatewood came to Fort Apache as the Commandant. Gatewood's prose was far more ascetic than Summerhayes's, but it is also clear from his memoir that fear on the frontier was a constant reality for settlers. "We are still aimlessly wandering around these mountains hunting for Indians that are not, & examining all sorts of rumors that have no shadow of foundation of truth in them," he complained. "Some of the settlers are wild with alarm & raise all kinds of stories to induce us to camp near their places, to protect them and buy grain & hay at high prices. Others are quiet & sensible and laugh at the fears of the timid." Making light of the "wild alarm" among the frightened settlers, he recorded the reaction of a prospector who fished near their camp as they searched for Apaches. Discovering tracks made by Apache scouts one morning, the prospector immediately fled "for parts unknown." "He is probably now spreading dismay through the country," he dryly noted.[54]

If those who settled the American West were made of sterner stuff, why would the prospector flee at discovering the tracks of Apache horses? What alarm would this frontiersman be raising, and why would other settlers react with equal alarm to his news? Why would settlers go to great lengths to try to induce the soldiers to remain close at hand? To be sure, some settlers, in Gatewood's assessment, were "quiet & sensible" when it came to rumors that Apaches were close. However, if the human brain has changed little in the intervening years, if the hypothalamus still responds in similar manner to threat and fear, then the growing body of scholarship on trauma can provide insight into how the settlers of the West, and of Pleasant Valley, reacted to the circumstances around them and why they may have acted as they did.

The psychological study of trauma as the product of chronic fear and violence did not develop in earnest until the Vietnam War, although the impact of combat on soldiers was known as early as the Civil War. Since then, psychologists have expanded the study of trauma beyond the battlefield to understand the role of chronic fear, stress, and violence in a variety of social contexts. One need not be a soldier in combat to be impacted by chronic fear and traumatic stress.[55] Indeed, trauma studies scholars have identified clues to chronic trauma in the writings of Homer, Shakespeare, and Charles Dickens.[56]

Eric Dean's *Shook Over Hell* has advanced the exploration of fear, suffering, and trauma among the generation of Civil War veterans, which has bearing on this study. Stoicism and silence in those subjected to chronic fear and violence are not indicators that they remain unaffected, he argues. Silence, instead, can often be the first articulation of trauma. "When one carefully examines accounts of men professing to be unconcerned about the dangers and terrors of war," Dean observed, "one often discovers that these stoic declarations of indifference hid a deeper fear and horror, held at bay for the time, but lurking within nonetheless."[57] The terror of battle, no matter the war, has been such a constant that American military experts challenge the idea that one can become seasoned to the violence of wounds, maiming, and death. "'Each moment of combat imposes a strain so great that men will break down in direct relation to the intensity and duration of their exposure . . . psychiatric casualties are as inevitable as gunshot and shrapnel wounds in warfare."[58] Even those who were not directly in the line of fire, but who simply witnessed the carnage of war, also suffered from trauma. In the letters and memoirs of Civil War nurses and doctors, Dean found descriptions of "symptoms of what we would today think of as PTSD."[59] Of the lives he studied, he found an increase in alcohol consumption and opiate addiction, violence, crime, and a lifelong struggle with insomnia, the constant fear of being under attack, and the need to constantly bear arms.

In seeking to understand the effects of unremitting random violence on a population, which differs from posttraumatic stress in that the stressors producing trauma are not in the past, but ongoing and seemingly relentless, Ignacio Martín-Baró pioneered the study of continuous traumatic stress. Fear, although a subjective and private experience, he argued, can acquire "an unsuspected relevance in social and political behavior" through creating a sense of vulnerability, hyper-alertness, a sense of impotence or loss of control, and an altered sense of reality that makes it impossible to objectively evaluate one's own experiences and knowledge. These conditions, Martín-Baró further argued, complement the findings of Joaquín Samayoa, who explored "the cognitive and behavioral changes caused by the necessity of adapting to war that bring about dehumanization." Those cognitive adaptations, according to Samayoa, are typically manifested by: "(1) selective inattention and a clinging to prejudices, (2) absolutism, idealization, and ideological rigidity, (3) evasive skepticism, (4) paranoid defensiveness, and (5) hatred and desire for revenge."[60]

Admittedly, the evidence of continuous traumatic stress in the lives of the settlers of Pleasant Valley is indirect, yet that evidence allows for a compelling interpretation. By virtue of time and location, the settlers of Pleasant Valley were subjected to a climate of continuous fear and violence as Apache clans close by struggled to convert to a life confined by reservations. Outbreaks swept through the settlement with regularity, and settler responses to such conditions can be found in articulate and inarticulate sources, from letters published in newspapers to the weapons they constantly bore, and to the way they constructed their homes as a last line of defense. Within this climate, hammered by chronic theft, competition from corporate cattle ranches, and a seemingly endless round of legal complaints and trials against one another, the settlement began to tear apart. By the time that settlers began to turn on each other with accusations and recriminations, leading to bloodshed, the settlers in Pleasant Valley had lived on the front lines of frontier warfare for years.

Perhaps what yields the most insight into the inner lives of Pleasant Valley settlers is how the death of Bill Graham fundamentally fractured the settlement. Three years earlier, the Graham brothers had fallen out with their friends, the Tewksbury brothers, over the disputed ownership of cattle. Accusations and counteraccusations flew, and they squared off in court. The Grahams lost their suit, and afterward, they simply parted ways. For three years, the two sets of brothers kept to themselves—not a word appears to have passed between them, although they lived just a few miles from one another. However, after Bill came stumbling back into the Graham cabin one August 1887 morning, bloodied with bowels in hand, everything changed. Before he died, he recited the names of many of the men that the Grahams fought before in court. The cold estrangement that existed between these neighbors and former friends now turned intimately murderous.

The Graham brothers knew the territorial judicial system well. They had used it numerous times before, charging neighbors with crimes that ranged from theft to murder. But neither Johnny nor Tom made any effort this time to involve the law in Bill's death. Why? Why did they believe that their brother, who was weakened by blood loss and on death's door, spoke with clarity about who shot him from behind that darkened morning, rather than the deputy sheriff who reported shooting him? Grief and rage can warp a person's understanding. How much more fragile would a person's judgment be from the effects of living in a climate of chronic fear for years? If living in a high-stress environment, where the exposure to violence and the fear of violence is unrelenting, has an effect similar to experiencing combat, how might such an effect shape how neighbors perceived one another over time? Could continuous traumatic stress have influenced the perceptions and judgments of those who had once called one another friends?

It is telling that when the Grahams chose to avenge their murdered brother, they never bothered to seek out the eight men Bill named. They only went after the Tewksburys, but not necessarily Ed—it appeared that any Tewksbury would do. And perhaps this was their intent all along. It was not an eye for an eye that they were after, but inflicting on the Tewksbury family the pain and suffering that comes from losing a loved one.

THE FIRST TEWKSBURY TO DIE

John Tewksbury rose early on the morning of Thursday, 1 September 1887.[61] It had been two weeks since Bill Graham was killed, and a little over three weeks since Hamp Blevins's death. After hiding out in the mountains, John and his brothers had quietly returned home when the posse left town.[62] They were surely glad to be back. Mary Ann was eight months pregnant with their second child, and Saturday was John's thirty-first birthday.[63]

During the night, however, something odd happened to one of the Tewksbury horses. It was not in the corral the next morning. It was not entirely a surprise that a horse would roam at night, but they were not taking chances. They still needed to keep their horses close. Bill Jacobs, a friend and business partner, agreed to go with John to find the horse. They armed themselves before leaving the cabin.[64]

They carefully followed the tracks across the creek that wrapped around the south and west of the ranch and corral. All the while, they listened for the sounds of the horse, and any other sound that might be floating on the early-morning air. Broadleaf cottonwood trees, about fifty feet high, lined the creek bed. Behind the cottonwoods was an area thick with scrub pines, manzanitas, and pine trees, so much so, that the ranch house could no longer be seen upon walking fifteen yards into the brush.

Their going was slow, partly because of the thick undergrowth that grabbed at their boots, and partly because of their cautious approach. It was almost impossible for them to be entirely quiet as they pushed deeper into the scrub. It was late summer, and the ground was lined with dried leaves, fallen branches of all sizes, and tree trunks. Thorny bushes and loose rocks covered the dry ground.

They continued cautiously advancing southward, as best they could, through the brush. Tewksbury's horse could be heard farther in, near another creek, Rock Creek, that runs along a canyon that now bears the name of Graveyard Canyon. Their vision was greatly limited by both the terrain and brush, and they had to pause periodically to listen for the horse.

About seventy-five yards in from the first creek bed, they turned westward and began walking along the north bank of Rock Creek. To their left, on the south bank of the creek, a wooded knoll rose sharply upward, some forty to fifty feet high at a steep angle. It was covered with tall pines all the way to the summit. Large boulders lay at the base of the knoll, carved out of the soil by the awesome power of earlier floodwaters. The terrain on their right was much flatter, with a gentle slope upward, but it, too, was thickly covered by trees and bushes. Wedged logs washed down the creek bed by torrential flooding lay all about the ground. It was easy for someone to hide among the rubble if they wanted.

Tewksbury and Jacobs advanced westward up the canyon, surely spurred on by the sound of the neighing horse up ahead of them. When they were about fifty yards in, a single gunshot exploded the morning air. John Tewksbury crumpled to the ground, dead from a shot to the back.

Jacobs instinctively froze, startled by the sight of Tewksbury lying motionless in pooling blood. Men silently emerged from the rocks and brush behind him. Jacobs knew them: Andy Cooper and Johnny and Tom Graham. There may have been others, too: Andy's brothers Charlie and John certainly had every reason to want to see Hamp avenged.[65] Instinctively, Jacobs lifted his hands up in the air as the men began approaching him with their weapons still trained at him. Another gunshot would give away their position, so when one of the gunmen got close enough, he swung his rifle at Jacobs like a bat to the head. Jacobs fell. In agony he clawed the ground, desperately trying to crawl away to safety.[66] Picking up a rock nearby, the gunman battered Jacobs's skull again and again until Jacobs finally collapsed and stopped moving.[67]

Satisfied that Jacobs was dead, the men quickly scanned the surrounding area for signs of anyone else that might have followed Tewksbury and Jacobs. Finding that the two had traveled alone, Johnny Graham pulled out a knife. Staring at John Tewksbury's body, he walked over, stooped down, and grabbed a handful of hair. As he jerked Tewksbury's head back and lay the blade at Tewksbury's hairline to scalp him, Tom Graham urgently hissed: "Don't be a heathen!"[68]

That caution was enough to call Johnny back from his frenzy, and he let go of Tewksbury's head. It wasn't the immorality of killing that gave Johnny pause, or even the mutilating of his neighbor's body. It was that the Grahams were white men after all, and they would not behave like Indians.

The conspirators hastily broke up. Andy Cooper mounted up and pushed hard with his companions to get to Holbrook. Johnny and Tom Graham, however, stayed behind. Looking toward the Tewksbury ranch, where Lydia, Mary Ann, and the children were, the Grahams began working their way through the brush. Their job was not finished.[69]

————◦•◦————

In the many retellings of this moment in the story of the Pleasant Valley War, about half of the settlement was present in the Tewksbury cabin that morning.[70] The list of witnesses subpoenaed for the coroner's inquest, however, suggests that only members of the immediate Tewksbury family were there: Ed and Jim, Lydia, her twelve-year-old son Thomas Shultes, eleven-year-old Gus Shultes, six-year-old Parker, and three-year-old Walter. Mary Ann Tewksbury would likely have been there with her three-year-old daughter Bertha, too.

The family was startled to hear gunshots in the distance, at about 8:30 in the morning, not long after John and Bill left the cabin. They listened, straining to hear anything else that might tell them what was going on. Thomas Shultes peered outside the cabin and saw what looked like gun smoke rising above the pines, about a quarter of a mile away.[71] As he walked out to the corral to get a better look, more gunshots began to ring out from the woods. Only this time, they were much closer. Bullets smacked the barn and popped in the dirt around him as he raced back to the safety of the cabin.[72]

For the next eight hours, gunshots rang out from the tree line of the creek bed to the south and west of the Tewksbury ranch. Thomas Shultes later told of how the children hid behind the stove for protection.[73] Bullet holes visible on the western eave of the Tewksbury barn, which still stands, suggest that some shots were randomly aimed. Perhaps it was to continue the terror, and perhaps it was because Johnny Graham, at least, had been drinking throughout the day. In all, it seemed to the Tewksburys that one hundred shots were fired at their property during the daylight hours.[74]

The guns finally fell silent as the sun set. The Grahams may have run out of ammunition (and probably whiskey). They used the cover of darkness to slink away.[75]

There would be no sleeping that night in the Tewksbury cabin. They did not know who was shooting at them, but Apaches were known to set fire on settlers' cabins as they slept, only to shoot them as they ran out for their lives. Who knew what malevolence these attackers were capable of.[76]

Estella Graham Hill revealed, decades later, that the Tewksburys' fears were correct. Were it not for Tom, Johnny Graham would have set fire to the cabin while the Tewksbury women and children were in it. Again, Tom pulled him back from acting out his pain and rage.[77]

Surely the family hoped for the best as the darkness settled in and the two men did not return. No one saw the direction they had taken, but John knew the area well, and he could handle himself.

As that long night passed into day, and neither man returned or gave some kind of signal, the nagging feeling that something was terribly wrong began to press on them.[78] The woods were quiet and gloomy. The Tewksburys kept their movements restricted that day. It was still possible that their assailants would return. It was still possible, too, that John had returned to their hideout in the Sierra Ancha Mountains to wait out the ambush. Time, which passed with aching slowness, would eventually tell.

On the third day that the men had not returned, vultures could be seen swarming in the air about a quarter of a mile away.[79] They were circling the area where Thomas had seen gun smoke rising through the pines. They all well knew what that bitter omen foretold.

No clear record establishes who first set out to try to investigate, although the condition of John's body, when found, is well known.[80]

It seems highly unlikely that Ed would have allowed his very pregnant sister-in-law to wander the rugged terrain in search of her husband. The signs were already troubling about what they might find, and their assailants might still be lurking in the area. The Tewksburys would have likely left behind as many as they possibly could in the protection of their cabin. Ed would have shouldered the responsibility himself to find his brother.

The emotions that tore through Ed as he made his way up the dry creek bed toward the circling vultures are not hard to guess. He would have traveled cautiously and on the alert, rifle at the ready, scanning the brush for any sign of danger. He could control his breathing and ignore the knot in his stomach as he carefully pressed forward through the brush, but his blood would have raced with anticipation of what lay around the bend.

Ed had lived all his life on the frontier and was as skilled as they came, but there was nothing in his twenty-nine years that could have prepared him for what he saw next. A wake of turkey vultures covered John's body like a black shroud, cawing and fighting over strips of sinew and flesh. They would yield only reluctantly to the anguished cries of the man who rushed at them, frantically trying to wave them off.

How long did it take Ed to process that scene, to grasp the incongruity of looking upon the brother who had, only days before, rushed into the arms of his expecting wife, and was now dead on the ground before him, ripped open in an almost unrecognizable bloody heap? What does such a moment do to a man? How long does the torturous imprint of that scene haunt his dreams at night and warp his thinking by day?

Lydia Tewksbury and her twelve-year-old son Thomas bore the responsibility of returning to the scene to cover the bodies with blankets until the law arrived.[81] They would likely have tried to protect the pregnant Mary Ann from seeing her husband's remains in such a state. It would take several more days before Justice of the Peace John Meadow could ride out from Prescott to conduct a coroner's inquest on the bodies at the scene of the crime. In the meantime, as news of the murders spread, some of the settlers were warning others to leave the bodies where they lay for fear that the murderers would exact revenge.[82] By the time that ten men could be found to convene a jury, the remains of both men were putrefying in the summer sun. "It was the awefulest mess you ever saw," Bill Voris remembered being told by his father, who had served as one of the jurors.

Jury members gagged throughout the inquest.[83] When the proceeding was over, there was nothing left to do but to shovel the rotting remains into Arbuckle Coffee packing cases and bury them where they lay.[84]

A legend arose that John's body had been partially consumed by hogs—or so a headstone erected to his memory, now faded beyond legibility, once testified. Where this information came from, however, is not entirely known.[85] Upon closer examination, it seems to be yet another curious assertion out of place in the many campfire stories that swirled like embers on the wind long after the conflict. Because hogs require frequent feed and watering, and are kept penned in order to keep them from damaging gardens and crops, the Tewksburys built their hog pen near Cherry Creek. In fact, territorial law required that hogs be penned.[86] John was found a quarter of a mile away in a rocky area largely devoid of vegetation and water. Why hogs would have been in such an unlikely area is unclear. It seems more likely that John's body was gnawed by any number of wild animals that would not pass up an available meal.

When Tewksbury and Jacobs were found, their rifles, pistols, and ammunition were missing.[87] In addition to their bodies being disturbed by animals, someone had plundered their weapons.

Another well-cherished tale is told that amid the hail of bullets, the Tewksbury women bravely marched out to bury their dead with shovels in hand, and that the assailants withheld their fire until the women had finished placing their men in the ground. The earliest known version of this account appeared five years later, in an 1892 story.[88] Raconteurs cherish this yarn because it illustrates the grit of frontier women and the so-called cowboy code of honor, that they would never shoot at a woman, even one from the enemy's side.[89]

But the story is yet another legend of the Pleasant Valley War. Mary Ann Tewksbury was a month away from giving birth to her son, and the Tewksbury women always disputed the tale.[90] Further, the vegetation is so thick and the terrain so hilly that the place where both Jacobs and Tewksbury fell is not visible from any part of the cabin, corral, or barn. It was impossible for them to know that the men had been killed until the vultures started to swarm days after the assault.

Closer to the truth, however, is that this was a turning point for many in the area, who had previously looked upon the Graham brothers with more sympathy. "Never in the annals of history have so-called civilized people taken such a cold-blooded and inhuman stand," recalled Drusilla Hazleton, whose sister was married to John Gilleland, the first man wounded in the violence. For her, leaving the bodies of Tewksbury and Jacobs in the open to rot, to be witnessed by John's family, "was the most cruel and barbarious [*sic*] incident of the entire Pleasant Valley War, equaled only by the atrocities perpetrated by the savage Apache Indians."[91]

MASSACRE IN HOLBROOK

When Andy Cooper and his companions fled Pleasant Valley, they pressed through the night to get up to Holbrook, keeping themselves awake with snorts of whiskey and tales of bravado. Their path took them past Dry Lake, where James Edward Shelley had camped for the night. Shelley was a schoolteacher and postmaster in Heber, who knew the Blevinses well; it was his daughter Mary's quick thinking that had spared Mormon settlers of disaster when a band of angry Indians rode up demanding the whereabouts of one of the Blevinses who had stolen their horses.

The night of Saturday, 3 September, was windless, and voices carried well over the flat high desert. As Cooper's party rode by Shelley's camp, he heard drunken voices laughing and boasting about a murder they had committed.[92] The rest of the Blevinses were already in Holbrook, having removed their belongings from their cherished ranch at Canyon Creek. They probably knew what Andy intended to do in Pleasant Valley, and looked to Holbrook as the perfect place to lie low after the killings.

Holbrook was one of the most lawless towns on top of the Rim.[93] Prior to the railroad running straight through the town, Holbrook was no more than a small cluster of Mexican homes founded sixteen years earlier at the ford of the Puerco and Little Colorado Rivers. Americans knew the hamlet as Horsehead Crossing, but it was rechristened "Holbrook" in 1880 after the chief engineer of A&P Railroad, H. R. Holbrook, when the town was designated as a regional terminus. That newfound status rapidly transformed the sleepy village into a lawless place as cowboys and sheepherders, with pockets full of cash after having delivered their livestock for shipment to markets elsewhere, crowded into saloons that sprang up seemingly overnight.

Alcohol, guns, and single men are a terrible combination. In 1886, twenty-six

Apache County Sheriff Commodore Perry Owens, ca. 1880.
Courtesy Arizona State Library, Archives, and Public Records, Phoenix, 97.7750.

men were killed by gunfire in a town of only 250 full-time residents. Reportedly, Holbrook was so notoriously lawless that the Salvation Army designated the town as a special target for evangelizing.[94]

Once in Holbrook, Cooper made it impossible to go unnoticed—even in that environment. He arrived in town Sunday morning and crowed openly on the streets that he had just killed John Tewksbury and some other man that he did not know. He was already well known to the residents there, and the fact that he and his family suddenly appeared in their town alarmed many.[95] To have an infamous horse thief and cattle rustler of Cooper's reputation moving his base of operations to their town was especially distressing to several citizens of Holbrook. As soon as word spread that Andy Cooper was in town, citizens immediately began to press Apache County Sherriff Commodore Perry Owens to do something about him.

Sheriff Owens was one of the more striking figures of the territory. Born to a large Quaker family in Tennessee, he left home at the age of twelve and struck out for the West.[96] He had a slight build, with blue eyes, brown hair, and a fair complexion. He was not given to much talk, but three things stood out about him: he wore his hair almost to the middle of his back (much longer than men did in his day); he did not drink, gamble, or womanize; and he was no pacifist.[97] He always wore pistols holstered with the handle turned forward, for he preferred to cross arms while reaching for his pistol.

Many dismissed him as a dime-store cowboy on the basis of his looks, only to discover too late that they had vastly underestimated him. Over his career as a lawman, he killed dozens of men and wounded scores more. Sheriff Owens was either feared or respected, depending on what side of the law you were on.[98]

On the strength of his reputation, Owens was elected sheriff of Apache County on the People's Ticket in 1886. Some saw the hand of Providence behind his election at a time when lawlessness reigned in the county. Although Owens served for only one term (at his preference), he was single-handedly credited with killing, jailing, or chasing out every thug and desperado; disrupting all the cattle-rustling rings; and restoring order to the county. When asked years later which experience as a lawman stood out, he recalled the day when he went to arrest Andy Cooper in Holbrook.

Owens had earlier sent notice to Cooper asking him to surrender on an outstanding warrant for stealing horses from Navajos.[99] Cooper did not respond. When Cooper and the entire Blevins family suddenly appeared in Holbrook, townspeople pressed Owens to go after Cooper.[100] So eager were some for the sheriff to do something about Cooper that Owens's bondsmen threatened to withdraw their support, and one citizen even accused him of being afraid of

Cooper. Owens would not act, however, until someone in Holbrook was willing to sign a complaint against Cooper.

Owens briefly left town on another law matter, and when he returned on Sunday, 4 September, a group of armed citizens met him at his office to help arrest Cooper. Owens thanked them for their offers of help, and told them that he would go alone.

"I'm paid to take risks like this," he told them. "Now all of you go home, you have families to think of. Besides, this is my job and I won't have you doing my job for me."[101]

As Owens approached the Blevins house, next to a blacksmith shop, he observed a horse tied out front and someone watching from the door. Inside were the family matriarch Mary Atkinson Blevins, twenty-five-year-old Andy Cooper, twenty-year-old John Black Blevins with his wife Eva and their baby, sixteen-year-old Artemissa Blevins, fifteen-year-old Samuel Houston Blevins. Also in the house were Mose Roberts, one of Cooper's business associates long suspected of stealing Indian horses, and a family friend, Amanda Gladden, with her nine-year-old daughter O'Beria and five-month-old daughter Grace. They had just finished their Sunday supper together.[102]

The front door shut as Owens neared. The house was in an L shape, with two doors in front and windows.

Owens walked around the horse, stepped up on the porch, and looked through the windows on his left and right. He could see Cooper and other men in the house. Owens knocked on the door.

Eva Blevins answered, holding her eight-month-old baby in her arms.

"Is Andy here?" Owens asked.

"Yes, of course," she replied, and called for Andy.[103]

Cooper stepped to the door. Eva took a step back but remained standing at the doorway, curious about what the sheriff wanted with her brother-in-law.[104] Cooper opened the door only halfway as he stuck his head out.

"How nice of you to call, Sheriff," Cooper said.[105]

"Cooper, I have a warrant for you," Owens quietly replied.

"What warrant?" asked Cooper.

"The same warrant that I spoke to you [about] some time ago that I left in Taylor—for horse stealing."

"Wait. . . ." Cooper replied.

"Cooper, no 'wait,'" Owens's voice rose slightly.

Cooper's pistol came into view. "I won't go!" he snapped.[106]

Owens raised his Winchester and shot from the hip through the door. Cooper collapsed with a guttural cry, shot through the stomach. He was still alive and visible through the window.[107] Eva stood frozen at the doorway, still holding her baby. Both were splattered with Cooper's blood.[108]

Twenty-year-old John Black Blevins yanked the door open to the left of Owens and shot at the sheriff. The bullet missed Owens but wounded the horse behind him.[109] As the horse jerked away from its post and ran down the street, Owens pivoted his rifle to his left and shot. John Black Blevins fell screaming, shot through the shoulder. To his right, Owens could see through the window that Cooper, though deeply in pain, was pulling himself along the floor. His gun was still in his hand. Owens shot through the wall where Cooper's shoulders would have been. Cooper stopped moving.

Owens backed away from the porch and stood in front of the house for a few moments, reloading his rifle while his wide eyes scanned the windows. Suddenly Mose Roberts jumped through an open side window with gun in hand and hid behind a buckboard wagon.[110] Owens sidestepped to his right and fired through the wagon. The bullet tore through Roberts's back and shattered his lung and shoulder. Spitting out blood, he staggered to the back door and slammed face-first onto the kitchen floor.[111]

Fifteen-year-old Samuel Houston Blevins burst through the front door, screaming in rage at the sheriff with John Blevins's bloody six-shooter in his hand. His mother, Mary, was right behind him, trying to pull him back into the house. Nine-year-old O'Beria Gladden ran to the doorway to see what the commotion was.[112]

"Don't shoot!" Mary shrieked, "He's my baby! He's all I got left!"

Struggling to break free from his mother, Sam leveled his pistol at the sheriff. Before the boy could squeeze the trigger, Owens fired his rifle once more, still aiming from the hip. The bullet tore through the young Blevins's upper body, and he collapsed at his mother's feet, knocking over O'Beria as he fell.[113]

In less than one minute, three lay dead or dying on the floor, and one was wounded. Owens was unscathed. Satisfied that the Blevinses would offer no further resistance, the sheriff laid his rifle across his arm. By that time, citizens came running up, armed and ready to help. Owens directed them to care for the wounded and see to the dead. Once the townspeople began tending to the Blevinses, Owens turned and numbly walked back to his office.[114] "I didn't think it would be proper for me to act [any further] under the circumstances," he later recalled.[115]

By all reports, the scene in the Blevins house was macabre. The bodies of men and a boy lay strewn about, ripped open by bullets. Blood was everywhere, pooling on the floor and splattered on the walls and furniture. The women and children who had been standing by the doors were so covered by blood splatter that they had to be cleaned off before they knew if they had been wounded.[116] The air reeked of spent powder and burned flesh. The screams of the living rent the air, and those who were not yet dead were in the last throes of life, crying in agony. Within days of having killed John Tewksbury, Andy Cooper lay on the floor begging for someone to shoot him and end his pain.[117]

"War is hell on the men fighting it," Jayne Peace Pyle sagely observed, "but it is also hard on the women and children who suffer through it, doing whatever is necessary to survive."[118] To their dying day, the Blevins women defended their sons and brothers, insisting that Cooper and Roberts were unarmed, and that the sheriff fired upon them unprovoked and without warning.[119] Some ninety miles away, another baby was born in Pleasant Valley. Still mourning the murder of her husband only a month earlier and surrounded by her mother and other women friends, Mary Ann Tewksbury gave birth in a small log cabin to a son. He would never know his father, but he would always bear his name: John Tewksbury Jr.

6
RUSTLERS ROUSTED

The Blevins ranch, widely believed to be pivotal to the black-market economy, had been eliminated. But two more remained: the Graham ranch and the Stott ranch.[1] For those who believed that their properties would never be secure until livestock thieves were eliminated, there was still work to be done.[2]

The territorial court system proved to be an unreliable avenue for justice for those who adamantly believed that the Grahams and Jamie Stott were deeply involved in rustling. Judgments could be purchased and so could witnesses. Even if a judge was not for sale, verdicts often rested on who had the more convincing story.

Thus, the line between the law and lawlessness in the territory was often quite blurred. Newspaper editors urged citizens to stand up against rustling rings. Stock associations urged members to "render all necessary aid" in their power to stopping and arresting anyone caught with cattle that did not belong to them.[3] A number of the settlers who pursued vigilante justice later became lawmen themselves, and those lawmen who were currently serving frequently acted as if they were little more than hired guns for the state.

There existed no professional training for lawmen of the territory. Experience with a weapon was always good, but more importantly, they simply had to be willing to live by their reflexes and instincts and take whatever hardship came in pursuit of their duties. Sometimes that pursuit looked something like justice. Other times, it did not.

As settlers grappled with what was happening and why, racial animosity reared its ugly head. The Indian ancestry of the Tewksburys and the mixed-race relationships of those who sided with them—"those injun sons of bitches"—became a frequent characterization. And that characterization, in turn, became a justification for what some tried to do to them.

ALLEGIANCES HARDEN

On the day that Apache County Sheriff Owens relented to community pressure and went to arrest Cooper in Holbrook, Yavapai County Sheriff Mulvenon met with Governor Zulick in Prescott to discuss the crisis in the Tonto Basin. Author Leland Hanchett saw meaning in both events occurring on the same day, and deduced that the territorial governor colluded with territorial and county law enforcement, and the Tewksburys, to acquire the Grahams' land. But Hanchett failed to articulate why that land was so valuable or what the alleged conspirators stood to gain from removing the Grahams from Pleasant Valley. Indeed, when the violence was finally over, no one Hanchett accused of wanting Graham land profited in any way from their fate or their property.

The governor likely met that day over several high-profile issues confronting the territory. Two days before that meeting, three cattle rustlers were found hanging from trees in Yavapai County.[4] The territory was actively pursuing leads in the murder of Samuel Shull at his home on the Mogollon Rim, with the governor himself putting up a five-hundred-dollar reward for information leading to the capture of the murderer.[5] And then there was the ongoing case of former Buffalo Soldier John Johnson. He had been scheduled to hang with Frank Wilson in August for the brutal murder of their employers, Samuel and Charlotte Clevenger, and the kidnapping and rape of their fourteen-year-old daughter. Both Johnson and Wilson were convicted, but while on death row, Wilson recanted his statement that Johnson was complicit in the murders and accepted sole responsibility. Johnson was not involved. Johnson's attorneys swung into action and appealed for a commutation of his sentence. At noon on the scheduled day of the hangings, Governor Zulick handed Mulvenon a momentary reprieve and gave Johnson until 23 September to provide evidence of his innocence.[6] And then there was Pleasant Valley: the fact that Zulick discussed the tensions in the valley at that 5 September meeting illustrated the growing concern that territorial officials had about the lawless state of affairs in the Tonto Basin. Zulick no doubt wanted to know what Mulvenon, as sheriff of Yavapai County, was going to do to put an end to it.

Five days after meeting with the governor, Mulvenon saddled up with three deputies on 10 September and left Prescott for Pleasant Valley to try to again serve warrants on the Tewksburys. Justice of the Peace John Meadows was already there to hold a coroner's inquest on the killing of John Tewksbury and Bill Jacobs.

His findings about who killed Tewksbury and Jacobs were inconclusive, since only the Tewksburys could testify about what little they had witnessed. He did confirm, though, that when found, Tewksbury appeared to have been shot in the back and that Jacobs appeared to have died from being bashed with a rock.[7]

Meadows was then summoned to the Graham ranch to hold an inquest on the body of Bill Graham. His conclusion, based on the testimonies of those who heard Bill's statement before he died, only confirmed to Johnny and Tom Graham what they already believed: Ed Tewksbury had murdered their brother.

By that point, the settlement had hardened into factions. Disagreements turned into enmity, enough to justify the taking up of arms against one another for slights both real and imagined. But the contours of those factions were curiously carved.

The Graham brothers tended to attract a curious mix of cowpunchers and drifters whose presence in the valley would likely have gone unnoticed had they not collided with history. Even friends of the Grahams barely knew these cowboys and asked few questions of them. The only discernible connection they had with the Graham brothers was through the black-market economy. Many settlers believed that the Grahams worked closely with the Blevinses in stealing livestock; they certainly sided with one another in a fight. The Blevinses in turn were believed to have had a close association with Jamie Stott, an easterner who lived on an isolated ranch east of the valley up on the Rim and another suspect in the livestock-rustling ring. Henry Midleton (no relation to the Middletons who had moved to Globe City) worked for Stott, and it was through this connection that he knew the Grahams.[8] Joe Ellenwood lived in Pleasant Valley with his wife for a brief period, but not long enough to make much of an impression on anyone.

Other settlers, like Jim Roberts and Joe Boyer, viewed the Grahams as thieves and rode with those willing to stand up to them. J. D. Houck later suggested in a playful reminiscence that he led the so-called Tewksbury faction (many years after the events of 1887, his daughter recorded his escapades as a knight-errant story, complete with medieval references and imagery). But it is hard to imagine how Houck could have effectively led anyone in Pleasant Valley, given that he lived a good two-day ride away, up on the Rim, and that as deputy sheriff he traveled often and widely throughout the county.[9] Houck certainly knew the Tewksburys through his travels, and he may have felt an affinity for them because his own children were half Indian. Perhaps more importantly, Houck, like many others, was sure to have viewed the Grahams and Blevinses as thieves. His allegiance as a lawman and as a stockman was in breaking the black market, and he knew that on the frontier, overwhelming force was often the quickest and most lasting method. He also knew that he could count on the Tewksbury brothers to hold their ground in a fight.

The Tewksburys' racial identities may have been one of the threads that tied them to others in the settlement. Their friend John Rhodes had three children with a Mexican woman, and Jim Houck was married to a Navajo.[10] At least one of their contemporaries understood the racial undertones in the tensions that tore the settlement apart. George Walter Shute, the grandson of William Middleton, whose ranch was attacked by Natiotish in 1881, recalled that the Grahams promised "to run the 'injun sons-of-bitches' out of the valley."[11] Another settler remembered that the Grahams openly referred to the Tewksburys as "damned blacks," language that likely came out into the open after their falling out.[12] The Grahams reportedly attempted to recruit the help of a band of Apaches living close to the Blevins ranch, on the reservation side of Canyon Creek, to attack the Tewksbury family and "kill off the damned blacks." That band was led by *tc'à'ndè-zn*, or John Dayzn, as he was commonly called by white settlers, and Dayzn knew whites well, having served as an Apache scout for the military.[13] He declined to get involved; the fight was not his. However, he warned, if he were to get involved, it would be on the side of the "damned blacks."[14]

SHOOT-OUT ON THE OPEN RANGE

How does a family process why such malicious violence was thrust upon them? To what narrative do family members turn to understand why their eldest brother died in such a horrific manner? The religious might struggle to accept his death as the mystery of God's will. The fatalist might accept that death comes to all, and that violent death was always the risk of settling a contested land. Or, for a family like the Tewksburys, all raised on the frontier and ably proficient in taking care of themselves, they might conclude that the sword of justice had to fall hard on their foes before they knew peace again.

Conditions had devolved so severely between neighbors by that point that no one left their homes alone and without being heavily armed, and everyone assumed the worst of former friends or strangers caught on open ground.

—◦—

The standard allotment of a homesteaded claim was 160 acres, or a half mile squared. So, to find someone out in the countryside or on unclaimed land should not have been an extraordinary thing in itself. Settlers often tracked their wandering cattle for a fair distance. But these were far from ordinary times. In previous years, neighbors would have greeted neighbors cordially and perhaps even offered help in finding the missing cattle. By late 1887, however, fear and suspicion vanquished neighborliness. Merely being seen within rifle range was enough to get you shot.

Early on a Saturday morning, 17 September 1887, Joe Ellenwood, Henry Midleton, and a few other Graham employees who were strangers to the settlement set out to track wandering cattle.[15] They traveled into the rugged hills that sit to the east of the Tewksbury claims, about a mile away from any of their homes.[16] Jim Roberts happened to see movement through the pines on the hills, and hurried to tell Jim and Ed Tewksbury. It looked as if men were trying to surround the Tewksburys, and they were armed. Further, at least one of the men was not unknown to the Tewksbury brothers: Ellenwood was implicated in the arson of the Middleton ranch, and if rumors were to be believed, he was at the murder of John Tewksbury.[17]

Miguel Apodaca was at his ranch house when he heard the unmistakable sounds of a gun battle booming through the valley at half-past seven in the morning. In all, about twenty-five shots were fired within the space of an hour. When the gunshots ended, men came racing back to the Graham ranch. The Grahams summoned Apodaca, Ed and Al Rose, and a few others to go retrieve two men who were severely wounded. The settlers cautiously rode out and found Midleton shot through the left leg, a little above the ankle, and his right knee utterly shattered by a bullet. Ellenwood was shot through the hip. After the two men were loaded on a wagon, they were offered whiskey.

"No," Midleton groaned. "I could not keep it in my stomach."

Jim Roberts and the Tewksbury brothers watched with loaded weapons as the rescue party carried off their wounded.[18]

The wounded men were bandaged up at Al Rose's place and given a place to recuperate. While Ellenwood's condition held stable, Midleton's did not. He declined rapidly with each passing hour. Within two days he was dead.[19]

Did Roberts and the Tewksbury brothers foil an ambush? Were Midleton and Ellenwood merely out searching for their own cattle? Even tentative evidence is lacking to answer either question with certainty. Neither Midleton nor Ellenwood ever stated what they were doing in the hills east of the Tewksbury claims, although others in the rescue party claimed that they were only looking for cattle. What is clear is that Midleton and Ellenwood vastly underestimated the danger of the terrain they were crossing. And if they were attempting an ambush, the Grahams had no interest in mounting another attack when they had the advantage in numbers.

For the Tewksbury brothers, they were not going to be caught unaware again after the death of John Tewksbury and Bill Jacobs, and they assaulted with extreme prejudice anything that even had the appearance of a threat.

SHOOT-OUT AT THE PERKINS STORE

Mulvenon and his deputies arrived in the north valley on Wednesday, 21 September 1887, where they rendezvoused with six more lawmen from neighboring Apache County.[20] Their aim was to capture the parties behind the recent killings in Pleasant Valley. Mulvenon's plan was to lay a trap for the belligerents.

At 3:00 A.M. the following morning, about fourteen members of the posse quietly rode through Pleasant Valley and took up a position at the Perkins store, which was still under construction.[21] The posse secreted themselves inside the stone-walled structure while the sheriff waited out in the open. Mulvenon refused to allow Charlie and Mollie Perkins to leave, to prevent word of the trap from getting out, and ordered them to stay with the posse crouched behind the walls in the cold.[22] An hour later, the rest of the posse, about six men, began a slow, circuitous route through the settlement, riding within plain sight of the Graham and Rose ranches. Once they were confident that they had been seen, they turned and rode out to the Perkins store.

Johnny Graham and Charlie Blevins mounted their horses and began to follow the decoy posse at a safe distance.[23] As they approached the Perkins store, the two cautiously began to circle the area, slowly drawing closer and closer to the structure, trying to look inside. Finally, when they were within range, Mulvenon stepped out into the open with his shotgun in hand.

"Put up your hands, boys!" Mulvenon ordered. "I want you!"

Upon seeing the sheriff—and possibly members of the posse peering from behind the walls—Graham and Blevins yanked hard on the reins to wheel their horses around. Johnny Graham began reaching for his pistol, but before he could draw his weapon, Mulvenon let go with a blast from his shotgun. Graham's horse collapsed dead, shot in the neck.

Johnny leaped off his horse and charged for the cover of the trees that lined the pathway to the Perkins store. At that same moment, Blevins, who was still on his horse, reached for the Winchester in his saddle, but before he could pull his weapon out, the posse let loose with a withering volley of shots. The simultaneous gunfire roared like a cannon exploding. Blevins pitched forward face-first with eight bullet holes through his body.[24] A second blast from Mulvenon's shotgun ripped away the flesh on Graham's right arm, while another ball tore through his ribs from side to side, just above the heart. Graham fell next to Blevins.[25]

Blevins was still moving, so J. D. Houck charged out from the walls of the Perkins store toward the two men, with rifle raised to shoot. Joe McKinney sprinted after him, right on his heels. When the two reached Blevins, McKinney grabbed Houck's arm and pulled him around.

"Don't shoot him, Jim!" he shouted.

"I wasn't going to unless he made a play," Houck protested.

They looked down at Blevins, whose legs were jerking. They reached down and cautiously rolled him over. He was dead.

They picked up his bloodied body and dragged it into the shade of the house. Some of the posse members gathered around Blevins to examine his wounds.[26] Other posse members tended to Graham, who was still clinging to life. They moved him to the shade and gave him a drink of water.

Mulvenon walked over and knelt down on one knee.

"Johnny, why didn't you put up your hands when I told you to—didn't you know me?" he angrily demanded.

Graham said nothing, but shook his head slowly from side to side.

"He knows he is a damned liar," Mulvenon exclaimed to the men standing around. "He knew me!"

Just then Osmer Flake and Glenn Reynolds rode up with additional posse members. The acrid smell of gunpowder and seared flesh hung in the air. A dead horse lay splayed on the road. As Flake dismounted and walked over to Mulvenon, the sheriff turned to Graham and asked if he recognized Flake. Graham said "yes" and spoke briefly with Flake.[27]

"Now, John," the sheriff continued. "You can't live but a short time, and may go at any time. You better tell me if Tom is in the Valley. If he is, I will send a man for him. He can stay with you while you live, and then ride off. I will not arrest him."[28]

Tom *was* in the vicinity, hiding with his nephew Louis Parker just up the road. But Johnny would not risk losing his remaining brother to aggressive lawmen. Tom was no longer in the valley, he insisted. And with that last protective act, he slipped in and out of consciousness, straddling life and death for an hour longer. He quietly died alone.[29]

One of the posse members climbed a tall pine tree with a spyglass to see if he could spot Graham and Parker.[30] He found them, saddling their horses and hurriedly making preparations to leave. He called down the news to the men below.

Tom Graham knew that the thunderous percussion of gunshots that rolled across the valley could not be good, and if Johnny had survived, he would be galloping toward them at any moment. Tom could wait, but not for long.

Some of the posse wanted to race toward the Graham ranch before Tom and Louis could get away, but Mulvenon hesitated. There had been enough killing for one day, and he had good reason to believe that Tom would not surrender peacefully. He did not want to provoke any more unnecessary deaths.[31]

Anxious moments passed for Tom and Louis as they sat on their horses, craning their necks in the direction of the gunfire, hoping to catch sight of Johnny racing toward them. When he failed to arrive within a reasonable time, Graham and Parker dug their heels into their mounts and leaned low in the saddle as they flew up the trail to escape what they believed was a pursuing posse. After they discovered that they were not being followed, they took up a defensive position to watch the trails until nightfall. When all signs pointed to the posse having left, they cautiously and quietly made their way back to their cabin.

Why would they return to the valley when they had so narrowly escaped with their lives? There was nothing left for them there anymore—save for a small sliver of hope. If Johnny survived the shoot-out, he may have made it back to the cabin.

Tom would have used the shallow creek bed that ran close to their cabin for cover as he quietly approached the cabin, pausing periodically to scan the horizon and listen for any telltale sounds of a posse in hiding. He also would have anxiously strained to listen for any signs of someone stirring in the cabin. Perhaps he cautiously called out to his brother as he neared, hoping for a reply.

Someone was in the cabin, though. Surely his heart sank when he pushed open the cabin door only to find Joe Ellenwood and his wife there. Johnny was gone.

It was then, while gazing about the cabin, that he began to fully grasp that Johnny was not coming back. Never again would he have his brother, friend, and constant companion by his side. One can still sense his tone of deep disappointment and disgust in the letter to his sister Margaret. "The folks at the house Was so Bad scared," he wrote. "They dident no eny thing and Beged for us to leave the house as thare Was 75 armed men Watching the house."[32]

There were not enough lawmen in the entire Tonto Basin to mount that kind of force, and Graham and Parker would not have been able to return to their ranch if there were. But Ellenwood's exaggerated count reveals the level of fear they felt about being in the same cabin with Graham and Parker, and they wanted them out. "We told the old Woman to keep her shurt on," Tom continued. "We got grub and my gold Watch."[33] Tom then ordered the Ellenwoods to place all of the Grahams' possessions into a locker, and then he and Louis Parker fled the valley once and for all.

The Grahams would no longer be a presence in the settlement, and perhaps more significantly, the livestock black market lost an important associate. The law was finally closing in on the rustling ring that for years had ruled the Mogollon nights.

Sheriff Mulvenon sent a member of the posse to ride out of the valley, too, but not after the Grahams. He was to bring word to Justice Meadows that his services were needed again, to hold an inquest over the bodies of Johnny Graham and Charlie Blevins. Within a matter of thirteen weeks, twelve men in the valley had been shot to death, one was missing and presumed dead, and four had been wounded.

When in Pleasant Valley, Meadows received word that another inquest was needed. Henry Midleton had died of the wounds he received near the Tewksburys' ranch. When Meadows convened an inquest at the Al Rose ranch on 23 September, the testimonies were one-sided. All witnesses were Midleton's remaining companions, and no one from the Tewksbury side was present. Meadows ruled that Midleton died as a result of gunshot wounds received from the Tewksburys. After the inquest was completed, Tucker, Glaspie, and Carrington took the opportunity to leave Pleasant Valley, never again to return.[34] George Newton took the opportunity of Meadows's presence to file a formal complaint about the burning of his ranch the previous month. First on his list was Al Rose, along with Miguel Apodaca, Louis Parker, William Bonner, and two other unknown persons.

After fleeing the valley, Tom Graham took up temporary residence in a Prescott hotel, where he filed a petition to the probate court to assume control of Johnny's estate. Louis Parker went into hiding, and Tom refused to divulge his whereabouts even to his own sister, Louis's mother, for fear that his letter might be intercepted.[35] Once Tom's work was completed regarding Johnny's estate, he then headed south toward the settlements in Maricopa County and chose the small village of Tempe to make a new home.

Not long after his arrival in the Salt River Valley, he married Annie Melton. And then, immediately, he published his story in the *Phoenix Arizonan*.

7

BLIND JUSTICE, MASKED JUSTICE

Within a few years of its founding, Pleasant Valley became an astonishingly litigious community.

There were, perhaps, no more than about twenty-five residents in Pleasant Valley between 1883 and 1888, but during this five-year period, they filed criminal claims against one another, or were implicated in criminal complaints initiated by others, sixteen times. That number is only half the story, however. Their time spent in the territorial courtrooms was actually twice that, because almost every case involved a grand jury trial first, before formal indictments were handed down, which then proceeded to a criminal trial. So, for almost every complaint filed, more often than not, a witness or a defendant faced a formal hearing twice. For that five-year period, nearly everyone in the community was involved as a witness or a defendant in over thirty court hearings, sometimes in different cases at once.

A very telling pattern emerges in looking at those complaints as a whole. The Grahams initiated more complaints against their neighbors than any other party. Of the sixteen Pleasant Valley court cases, the Grahams initiated seven. The Territory of Arizona, in comparison, initiated five, and the Tewksbury brothers, only two. The rest of the complaints came from individual residents. Clearly, the Graham family knew how to use the courts as a weapon.

Out of this poisoned soil grew a tangle of thorns that bore ill fruit. One fruit was the division that came from these lawsuits, as groups of residents were named co-conspirators in multiple rounds of indictments. Another fruit was the violence that spilled from the courtroom onto the open range. And still another was the vigilantism that arose as residents of Tonto Basin formed a shadowy alliance to enforce what the courts failed to do.

This last fruit, the alliance of masked vigilantes, took on the name "Committee of Fifty," although it is very likely that they were never fifty in number.

PATTERNS OF VIOLENCE IN PLEASANT VALLEY, 1882–1890

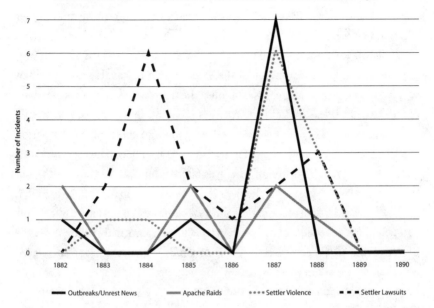

Courtesy Katie Jane Jones

There simply were not that many residents in the valley, but the name suggests that they saw themselves as acting on behalf of the majority.[1] However they saw themselves, this clandestine group was somewhat unique—as vigilantes go. Katherine Benton-Cohen observed in her study of the southern territory that "vigilante justice was often racially motivated and directed, just as it was in the South, and Tombstone had its fair share of racial prejudice."[2] This group, however, seemed to steer clear of any personal quarrels between the resident factions, and mixed-blood settlers were never targets. Rather, the vigilantes appeared to focus on the singular purpose of putting an end to the livestock black market.[3]

Decades after the bloody battles for control of Pleasant Valley were over, some family members began to share what they knew about this group. Some stories seem to corroborate one another, while others will always remain only rumor. Some of the suspected vigilantes were war veterans, and some were prominent ranchers in the outlying areas of the Tonto Basin. Some were rumored to be lawmen frustrated by the limitations of the territorial legal system.[4]

Whoever they truly were, this group of masked men on horseback, riding through the valley, imposed their will on the events that followed.[5]

DISCOURAGING WORDS

How did the settlers of Pleasant Valley make sense of this poisoned atmosphere? Western movies and novels often employ the persona of taciturn characters who are short on words and long on action, where "seldom is heard a discouraging word." But as with so much of the genre, such portrayals are more often caricatures than accurate representations. The truth of the matter is that many of the settlers in Pleasant Valley, whether combatants or witnesses, were keenly aware of the power of narrative and actively sought to control the information in circulation. They regularly sent letters to territorial newspapers or met with editors to assert their version of what was happening. And so it was with Tom Graham, who was eager to establish a different reputation in the Salt River Valley.

Graham's published account probably reveals more about what he wanted his new neighbors to believe about him than what he may have truly believed. Yet the narrative that he tenaciously clung to yields some insights into how he perceived what had happened in Pleasant Valley and why. In October 1887, Graham told a reporter that upon his arrival in Prescott, he willingly surrendered himself to Sheriff Halbert in Prescott, but the sheriff had no warrant for his arrest and let him go. He then went on to comment about his alleged role in the various gun battles that had taken place in Pleasant Valley.

He insisted that he was not present for any of it (although he makes no effort to provide an alibi for the killing of John Tewksbury and Bill Jacobs). When Hamp Blevins and John Paine were killed at the Middleton ranch, and when his brother Billy was shot, he was away in Phoenix. Neither he nor his brother Johnny was present when Ellenwood and Midleton were shot near the Tewksbury ranches. And when Sheriff Mulvenon's posse entered Pleasant Valley in late September 1887, he was busy shoeing a horse and had sent his brother Johnny to see if there were any warrants against him because he was willing to peacefully surrender. Moreover, he claimed that he never met any of the Blevinses until Mart Blevins passed by his ranch looking for stolen horses. Finally, he insisted that the events in Pleasant Valley were driven by "men of money [who] were trying to obtain control of ranches located, for honest purposes, by hard working and honorable boys."[6] On other occasions, Graham railed against national conspiracies as well.[7]

Tom's insistence that wealthy men conspired to take over Pleasant Valley found audience at least with his father, Samuel Graham, who made sure that his views were published in his hometown newspaper, the *Boone County Democrat*.

When the elder Graham received a tersely worded telegram from an Arizona justice of the peace that a son was killed and the other was missing, Samuel Graham initially believed that a son died from another Indian uprising. But from further news reports he learned of the violence that had been raging between the settlers. He set out immediately for Arizona, and when in Phoenix, he wrote to a friend back in Iowa. He found friends of his sons who told him that "a lot of desperados and half blood Indians undertook to clean out Pleasant Valley in order to get the range." They did so, he asserted, because his sons had "700 head of cattle here and one of the finest ranges and water privileges in the valley."[8] It is clear that to Samuel Graham, if not to Tom's friends as well, "half blood" Indians were equal to "desperados."

Tom Graham never identified who those wealthy interests were in the territory, or why they might wish to see the Grahams dead, other than that he thought his land was coveted by his neighbors.[9] His Pleasant Valley neighbors, however, would likely have found Graham's glowing view of his land curious. The earliest settlers had their pick of the land and passed over the parcel where the Grahams later settled, which was just under a mile from steady water, and chose instead to settle along the streams and creeks of the valley. Indeed, even as the Tewksbury brothers expanded their holdings and established their individual ranges, they much preferred to spread out along Cherry Creek in the south valley rather than to settle in the open ranges of the Tonto Basin.

After the violence in Pleasant Valley, the Tewksburys were no less eager to shape the narrative and, like the Graham brothers, they wrote letters to the editors of territorial papers or visited the printing offices personally. Like the Grahams, they saw themselves as innocents who simply acted to defend themselves when attacked. For the Tewksburys, however, it was not the land that their attackers were after; it was them. The Tewksbury brothers were keenly aware of how white settlers viewed Indians in general, especially living in a settlement that had been repeatedly hit by renegades. They furthermore understood their social position as children of an Indian mother, having experienced outright discrimination all their lives because of their color. It is no surprise, therefore, that the Tewksbury brothers repeatedly expressed their belief that there were people who wanted to exterminate their family.

Other settlers in the valley were also eager to rush their stories to print. Who authored these stories—whether a single settler or several—is not known because territorial newspapers would introduce these accounts only as "another dispatch from Pleasant Valley." Yet these anonymous authors, more than any other source, created the dominant narratives of Pleasant Valley that survive to this day. For all the efforts of the Graham and Tewksbury families to shape the narratives about them, they could never overcome the power of a good story. The view that Pleasant Valley was embroiled in its own range war or a blood feud—interpretations that neither the Grahams nor the Tewksburys ever used—made the most sense to Americans at the end of the nineteenth century. These interpretations drew upon the dominant language of community tension that was already current in the major story lines of the day—the Hatfields and McCoys, the Lincoln County War, and so on. Drawing upon these interpretations was also a way of pulling the Arizona Territory from the periphery of national events to the center.

In the end, once Tom permanently left the valley, there was no rush to acquire Graham land. He eventually sold his holdings at a time and to a person of his choosing. And except for John Tewksbury's murder, the other Tewksbury brothers died of natural causes, and their family long outlasted anyone who might have wanted them dead in Pleasant Valley.

THE ARSON TRIAL

Joe Ellenwood's wife knew what the sound of hoof beats meant as she cared for her husband, convalescing in the Graham cabin.[10] Rather than take any chance that the sheriff's posse would charge in with weapons raised, she steeled herself and walked out to meet them. Joe McKinney, who was riding posse with Mulvenon, recalled, "When Ellenwood's wife reached us she dropped down on the grass and Mulvenon advanced to where she was. She said 'I will tell you all that are in the house. My husband, Joe Ellenwood, is in there, and he is wounded and not able to get about. Miguel is in there also. They are all that are in there.'"[11]

Her actions soothed any desire the posse may have had to go in with guns blazing. Instead, they dismounted and served Apodaca with a warrant for the burning of the Middleton ranch. Once they were content that no one else was on the property, the sheriff and posse left the valley.

Al Rose and Miguel Apodaca rode with Mulvenon back to Payson for a preliminary hearing. They were arraigned before Justice of the Peace John Meadows on 27 September 1887. After an assault trial, a perjury trial, and two larceny trials, this was now the fifth trial involving Pleasant Valley settlers.

The territory never had a strong case going into the trial. None of the witnesses could—or would—testify that they saw who started the fire. Only Bob Voris's testimony provided any hint that Al Rose started it, but Voris was contradictory on the stand, and the territory failed to press him for clarity. During the trial, the defense attorney believed that there were menacing undertones from the witnesses for the prosecution toward Rose and Apodaca, and he privately advised his clients to leave the county for their health.[12] Miguel Apodaca, at least, found Wentworth's counsel wise and left promptly after the trial ended, never to return to the valley. The other defendants, though, were more confident of their well-being and returned to Pleasant Valley to resume their usual activities.

One of the codefendants, William Bonner, seemed to return to business with a new sense of invulnerability. He came to the Arizona Territory fleeing justice in Colorado and found haven in working for the Grahams. Bonner—which may have been an alias—was wanted for horse thieving and murder. While in Arizona, he seemed unable to straighten that bent.[13] Within a month of the arson trial, masked men held up the stage line running between Fort Apache and St. Johns, as well as the A&P train at Navajo Station. Bonner was strongly suspected of being one of them.[14]

If that suspicion was wrong, Bonner never had the chance to prove it. In mid-October, his bloated body was found about fifteen feet off the side of a well-traveled road, covered with sage brush. It appeared that he had been ambushed. Since his death came on the heels of the arson case, the *Arizona Weekly Journal-Miner* speculated that he had been killed "by members of the Tewksbury gang, as he belonged to the Graham faction." But his part was minimal in the arson case, and he was just as likely to have been waylaid for his plunder by partners in crime, if not more so. However he died and for whatever reason, the *Arizona Weekly Journal-Miner* would not lament his passing. "He participated in all manner of crimes that have stained the annals of Arizona," the editors concluded. "And there is no question but his death is a welcome one."[15]

AMBUSH AT THE HOUDON RANCH

Although one of the arson codefendants met a violent end, Al Rose had good reason to believe that he was out of harm's way after that trial concluded. The violence that had torn apart their small community appeared to be over. The Grahams were gone from the valley, and the sheriff had returned to Prescott. Rose had no hand in any of the gunfights, and all suspected rustlers were run out or dead. From the late summer to the early fall, life in the valley resumed its usual cycles of activity. Even on the Graham property, although the proprietors were gone, there were calves to brand and cattle to be rounded up and accounted for.

So, in the early fall, Al Rose rode out to the old Louis Houdon ranch, several miles away in the east valley. Houdon's place had been acquired by the Graham brothers, and Louis Naeglin and John Whatley were there overseeing Graham's cattle while Tom was away in Phoenix.[16] At the break of day on a cool November morning, Al Rose took some corn out to feed his horse. They had a full day ahead of them branding cattle and looking for strays, and the horses needed to be fed and watered.

Rose's horse was in a clearing, about one hundred and fifty yards from the cabin. As he was tending to his horse, the morning calm was interrupted by the sound of movement behind him. A group of armed men, about nine in number, suddenly emerged from the brush. They stood between Rose and the cabin, dressed in long coats, with collars turned up, and with faces covered.[17] Most held rifles or shotguns in their hands. To Naeglin and Whatley back in the cabin, they appeared to be white men, at a distance of a hundred yards or so, with two standing taller than the rest. Only something was different about this group. Whatley later described them as being "masked and fantastically disguised." And they began howling in an "unearthly" fashion.[18]

The old Swede was tough as nails and wasn't normally one to run. He was an infantryman who had "seen the elephant." His unit had seen action at Shiloh and Vicksburg.[19] But white men did not normally act like this, and Apaches did not ordinarily wear long coats and hats. Something was terribly wrong.

Rose immediately tried sprinting back toward the cabin, hollering at the other two men who were still inside. But he stopped short when he realized that he could not clear the line of men who blocked his path to safety. Rapidly searching for a way out or around them, he attempted again to run for the cabin but stopped, realizing that he could not escape.

"Well, all right!" he defiantly shouted, and threw his hands up.

Multiple shots bellowed forth, riddling Rose's body with bullets.

The masked men walked up to where Rose lay, and looked him over. Some bent down to peer into his face.[20] He was gone.

Naeglin and Whatley, who had been standing at the cabin door since Rose shouted out, witnessed the murder. They began to step out, but the masked men turned and pointed their rifles at them. They retreated behind the safety of the cabin walls and peered out from the gun ports. The masked men walked back into the brush and were not seen again.

By all accounts, Rose was only a secondary figure in the tensions that plagued the valley. He was never directly implicated in the rustling that underwrote the tensions in the valley, but he was implicated in the burning of the Newton ranch. Perhaps of greater significance, however, was that he made no secret of his likes and dislikes, and he clearly did not like his neighbors, the Tewksbury brothers, or the other Indian "half breeds" in the area. Further, many remembered him as a cantankerous soul and as an instigator who continually needled the Graham brothers into action. This was, perhaps, what cost him his life: he may never have pulled a trigger during the war, but he shot his mouth off once too often.[21]

TOM GRAHAM'S "PUT UP JOB"

Al Rose's older brother Ed learned of the killing from a deputy sheriff while on the trail to Globe City, and he returned to the settlement to bear the tragic news to Al's wife, Lizzie.[22] She immediately left the ranch in the care of Bob Sixby and moved with her two children to live with her mother and stepfather. Jayne Peace Pyle believed that Lizzie left the settlement in fear for her own life. Weariness and frustration certainly come through in a letter she wrote to Sixby several months later. "I can tell you the earnest truth, I don't know what to do. I am pretty well discouraged, but there is no use to give up. . . . I am getting tired of living among such a low class of people. It don't matter what you do, you can't please them all and I am getting tired and sick of living this way." The climate in the settlement had deteriorated to the point that she was left feeling suspicious, vulnerable, and alone. In time, she would return to Pleasant Valley. "All I got is there," she confessed, "and the only way is to keep still and say nothing."[23]

With the burial of Al Rose, the battles in Pleasant Valley died down over the winter months of 1887–1888. But with the thawing of the winter snows, newer fates began to swirl around the residents of Pleasant Valley like rivulets of water gathering speed as they moved downhill.

In early May, Ed Tewksbury and John Rhodes decided to stop for a drink while on the road. Bayard's Saloon was just a small cantina in a tiny settlement along the Salt River. Their visit did not end well. Neither John nor the other patrons were directly involved in the escalating tensions within Pleasant Valley, but temperatures were running high even for people on the periphery of events. John and another patron wound up firing their pistols at each other, "all the result of the Tonto Basin feud."[24] John was wounded in the hand, but two men received more serious wounds from John's bullet.[25]

Barely a week after that shoot-out, two of Tom Graham's employees broke into a Tonto Basin post office and store.[26] A reporter with the *Phoenix Arizonan* caught up with Tom Graham and asked for a statement. Why were his horses, his saddles, and his men implicated in a robbery? Graham obliged the reporter.

He was not thoroughly acquainted with the facts, he began, but he was certain that the entire affair was a "put up job" to prejudice opinion against him in his pending trials. It was his enemies who stole his horses and saddles, robbed the store, rode in the direction of his ranch, he argued, and then left the horses with his brand and tack to be found. It was all a scheme to implicate him. Yes, he conceded, Whatley was his employee, but Whatley had reported a few weeks earlier that two horses and saddles had been stolen from his ranch. Further, the distance between Watkins's store and the Grahams' ranch was too great to make it reasonable for anyone to abandon their horses before returning to his ranch. Finally, Graham insisted that he kept his ranch well supplied, so there was no reason for any employee of his to steal from anyone. He did not uphold crime, he concluded, and if Whatley was guilty, then "he would be glad to see him arrested and punished."[27]

The editors of the *Phoenix Arizonan* were unimpressed with Graham's explanation. "It is but natural," they concluded, "that Mr. Graham should wish to remove the suspicion left in the minds of persons who read the brief report of the burglary as published in the [Silver] Belt of May 12th, that his ranch is the rendezvous of thieves."[28] One "correspondent writing from Tonto" was even more direct about what Graham's neighbors thought of the robbery: "The people here are aroused and determined to put a stop to such work."[29]

LYNCHING AT BLACK CANYON RIM

With the Blevins family decimated and the Grahams run out of Pleasant Valley, Jamie Stott's place was the last ranch suspected of operating in the black-market economy. James Warren Stott was an unlikely cowboy and was among the more unlikely settlers to be suspected of dealing in stolen livestock. He was born and raised in a prosperous family in Massachusetts and moved out to the Arizona Territory solely for the thrill of adventure. People there knew him as Jamie or Jimmy.

By all accounts, he was a handsome young man, congenial and smart. Though he left Harvard University during his junior year, he was better educated than many of the settlers, perhaps for a hundred miles around in any direction, and he well knew it.[30] He counted on his intellect and quick reflexes to see him through whatever dangers he might encounter.

Stott built his ranch in an isolated canyon on top of the Mogollon Rim, close to the northern boundary of the Apache reservation. Stott's "Circle Dot" ranch, as he named it, was about midway between Pleasant Valley and Holbrook and a little farther up the trail from the Blevinses' ranch at Canyon Creek.[31] Stott was not believed to be involved in the actual thievery of livestock but in serving more as a middleman between the stolen goods and the market. His only crime may have been his carelessness about the origins of the livestock that always seemed available for sale by certain parties.[32] Either way, he certainly knew of the rumors. "Some people have judged me guilty without taking the trouble to investigate the charges or giving me a chance to defend myself," Stott complained to one of his Hashknife cowboy friends. "These men are not friendly to me so I shall not take the trouble to change their opinion."[33] Will Barnes told a different story, however.

Barnes spent a considerable amount of time trying to track stolen livestock as an agent of a livestock association. Like most investigators, he soon developed a working theory about who was involved in moving cattle through the supply chain. There appears to have been a clear consensus among the livestock agents that the trail led to Stott's ranch. If the trail led to anywhere else, no contemporaries spoke of it and its location has been lost to history.

Barnes knew Stott fairly well, so he diplomatically advised Stott that he was involved in a very dangerous occupation. Stott laughed off his concern. And why wouldn't he? It had been over a year since the Blevinses were killed and the Grahams run out of Pleasant Valley, and Stott's ranch was still in operation. Besides, he could take care of himself, Stott allegedly told Barnes while patting his six-shooter, stating that he'd like to see the hair color of the man who could get the drop on him. Sadly, events were already aligning so that he would get his wish, unexpectedly one August 1888 morning.[34]

About two weeks prior and some thirty miles to the south, another Apache outbreak drove the settlers of Pleasant Valley to abandon their homes. John Dayzn, an Apache clan chief who was friendly with the settlers, warned them of a pending attack. The residents of the settlement evacuated their homes and gathered at the Perkins store, where it was hoped that their greater numbers and the thick rock walls of the store would provide better protection in the case of assault. For four days, Pleasant Valley was a deserted village, save for the encampment around the Perkins store, where settlers vigilantly watched for Apaches.

On the fourth day, as the air was misty from summer rains, they sent scouts out. It was during that ride that the scouts discovered Jake Lauffer wounded in his cabin. Lauffer had set out to look for his horses and was shot from behind a tree. Later that same day, as they rode through the settlement, two other scouts were also shot at by two men who were seen riding straight for the deserted cabin of Lizzie Rose. The shooters went in, took a pair of field glasses and a picket rope, and then left. The scouts tried to trail the assailants, but lost them in a heavy downpour.[35]

Lauffer survived his wound, but his arm was permanently disabled. Despite the high tensions precipitated by armed Apaches in the area, Lauffer was convinced that he wasn't wounded by an Apache. Rather, he believed it was Jamie Stott who took revenge for the larceny charge that Lauffer had leveled against him. Lauffer swore out another complaint against Stott and two of his ranch hands, Jim Scott and Jeff Wilson, but this time it was for attempted murder.[36]

Early on the morning of 11 August, Stott arose, partially dressed himself, and casually headed out to the woodpile to gather kindling for the morning's fire. He was apparently unaware that there was a warrant for his arrest. Stepping outside of his cabin, though, he froze at the unmistakable sound of a bullet being chambered in a Winchester. "Hands up, Jim!" came the order from behind. With his hands in the air, he turned slowly to see Deputy Sheriff J. D. Houck standing beside the cabin with his rifle aimed directly at him.[37]

Stott got his wish, to see the hair color of the man who got the drop on him: Houck's hair was chestnut brown.

Houck and two deputies had been patiently waiting outside his cabin since dawn to serve warrants on Stott and his companions.[38] Seeing his predicament, Stott calmly invited Houck and the other two deputies to join him and his companions for breakfast. The lawmen agreed, and Stott prepared a meal for his captors, as well as for Scott and Wilson and for another guest at Stott's ranch, Mott Clymer.

Clymer was suffering from tuberculosis and had arranged to stay at Stott's ranch to regain his health in the mountain air. He later related that after the men had eaten, they sat around, joking, talking, and smoking until the deputies decided that it was time to head out. The deputies escorted Stott, Scott, and Wilson outside and placed them on their horses, handcuffed at the wrists with a chain passing through the arch of their saddles, and at the ankles with the chain running underneath each horse's belly. None of the arrested men made any protest.

As the deputies and their captives rode off down the trail, one dropped back and returned to the cabin. He informed Clymer that his friends were likely not going to return for some time, if ever, and that there was a horse left in the corral for Clymer to take his leave of the country.[39] His poor health notwithstanding, Clymer thought it was sound advice.

Houck later insisted that he and his deputies were overtaken on the trail by a group of masked men who demanded at gunpoint that he turn Stott and his companions over to them. Houck never said who the vigilantes were, and their identities have been a matter of lively speculation to this day. But there has been little disagreement, then or now, that among the vigilantes were some of the most prominent residents of the area, among them Colonel William Colcord, famed cowboy Tom Horn, and famed lawman Glenn Reynolds.[40]

What exactly happened next is not known, but the outcome was that Stott, Scott, and Wilson were hung that morning from a tall pine tree, and their bodies were left to twist in the wind. Snowflake resident Osmer Flake was one of the passersby who stumbled on the macabre scene after the vigilantes were gone, and he stayed long enough to formulate a theory of what had happened. From the tracks, Flake surmised that the three men's horses were led to where ropes were thrown over a strong branch. Their ankle restraints were removed and each had a noose placed around his neck.

Rumors later circulated that Scott and Wilson broke down and begged for their lives, while Stott was defiant, cursing and challenging each of the vigilantes by name to fight him one on one. Scott and Wilson were summarily hung without much fanfare as their horses were whipped from behind. But the grooved branch above Stott indicated that the rope from which he hung had cut into the bark like a saw as it was repeatedly pulled taught and slackened. Further, in a cruel nod to his privileged upbringing, someone had placed a red silk handkerchief around his neck before the noose was tightened. It appeared to Flake that Stott was very likely taunted and tortured by the vigilantes to discover who his accomplices were in the black-market economy. Was his windpipe accidentally crushed before he could speak or was his refusal to provide names his last act of defiance? We will never know. Once all three men were jerking at the end of a rope, the vigilantes rode off, leaving their bodies as a warning to other thieves.[41]

Over the following days, a number of travelers stumbled upon the shocking scene of three decomposing bodies dangling from a tree limb, but no one dared get close enough to bury the bodies. District Attorney A. F. Banta of Apache County finally rode out with four other men to convene a coroner's inquest. With little evidence other than the corpses, they could only conclude that their deaths had come at the hands of parties unknown. They rolled the badly decomposed remains in blankets and buried them in a nearby meadow.[42]

Whether Houck was complicit in the lynching of Stott, Scott, and Wilson, or simply an outnumbered lawman in the face of greater forces, he never escaped community censure for his role that morning. But he refused to concede complicity in the event and would fight anyone to defend his reputation.

In 1888, within days of the lynching, a young Mormon boy by the name of John Hunt went to the doctor's office in Holbrook with an earache. The doctor had a small, one-room office, with chairs on one side for a waiting area and the examination table on the other side. As the doctor lifted Hunt onto the table, J. D. Houck came into the waiting area. Suddenly, Ed Rogers, a range foreman for the Hashknife cowboys, burst into the office. Deputy Sheriff Frank Wattron came running in from behind.

Rogers charged up to Houck and accused him of hanging an innocent man when he hung Jimmie Scott. Rogers, who stood six feet tall, towered over Houck. "I didn't do it!" Houck protested loudly. Rogers called Houck a liar, along with a series of heated epithets. "At that they both jerked their six-shooters half way out of their scabbards with their thumbs on the hammers in full cock," Hunt recalled. "They stood face to face and called each other all the vile names they could think of. They were almost standing right over me and the Doctor. It looked and sounded like they would commence shooting any second and if they had they probably would have killed everyone in the room." To Hunt, the two looked like a pair of mountain lions squaring off against each other. "Houck called Rogers everything he could think of and cussed the outfit he was working for an everything that was connected with them." In the meantime, Wattron was excitedly pacing back and forth, "cussing a blue streak and trying to tell them there were different ways of settling their troubles without shooting." Even the doctor tried to cut in to calm the situation, but both men stood locked in position, glaring at one another with their hands on their weapons, neither averting their eyes from the other.

"I don't know how long it was, but it seemed like 30 minutes that they stood there arguing and that was one of the rankest worded battles I had heard," wrote Hunt. Finally, Rogers began to realize that he was outmatched in taking on Houck, but he did not know how to back down. Rogers then slowly reached over with his left hand and touched a release that ejected all six shells, and then backed out of the office. He had been standing so close to the boy that some of Rogers's shells hit him on the leg as they bounced off the wooden floor. Houck, however, stood with his hand on his pistol and eyes locked on the door for several minutes longer—it seemed to Hunt to be another thirty minutes—before he began to accept that Rogers was not going to reload and come back.[43]

———•———

When Secretary of War William C. Endicott submitted his annual report to Congress in 1888, he began by reflecting on the precarious situation in the Arizona Territory. "Between the first outbreak and their final surrender," Endicott wrote of the Apaches, they had "created a condition of panic and distress in New Mexico and Arizona difficult to describe. Men, women, and children were shot down, mutilated, and tortured, and *a reign of terror prevailed all along the boundary line*" (italics added). Apaches, Endicott warned, still posed a danger to settlers: "When relieved from control their violence and savagery was only limited by their powers of endurance. Once relieved from strict restraint we have no reason to believe that they would be peaceable; on the contrary, there is every reason to fear that numbers of them would return to the war-path again when the opportunity came."[44] Brigadier-General Miles, who oversaw the U.S. Army's Department of Arizona, expressed similar views in his report for that year. "The principal object of stationing troops at present in this department," he asserted, "is to hold under surveillance and restraint the thousands of turbulent and well-armed Indians living on the various reservations, and to give prompt and effective protection to the scattered settlements."[45]

The warnings these military leaders issued were not without reason. Even for troops on the ground, many of whom were seasoned Indian fighters, the conditions on the reservations in the Arizona Territory were like a powder keg waiting to explode. "San Carlos was such an undesirable place, a barren waste [that] no Indian would have stopped in, voluntarily," West Point graduate Thomas Cruse remembered. He had earned the Medal of Honor for his valor at the battle that ended Natiotish's raiding at Big Dry Wash, but he understood why Apaches had fled the reservation in the first place and why they were likely to flee again. "Here were held some four thousand fierce and restless savages with absolutely nothing to occupy them, while they saw their country filling up with white men," he reflected. "It was inevitable that the reckless, restless element should slip away to return to the ancient and natural way of living.[46] For Secretary of War Endicott, the mismanagement of the reservations was a critical contributor to the state of unrest among the Indians. "The condition of those at San Carlos was not favorable to their comfort or content," he wrote. "They chafed under restraint; the management was bad, corrupt, and dishonest. They complained that their blankets and stores were stolen and sold in the towns, probably with much truth. . . . It is sufficient to say that the Indians became turbulent and excited."[47]

THE TRIALS OF COURT

On 3 December 1887, the Yavapai County grand jury handed out indictments to fourteen men in connection with the murders in Pleasant Valley. Accused of murdering Hank Blevins and John Paine at the Middleton ranch were Jim Tewksbury, Ed Tewksbury, Joseph Boyer, James Roberts, George Newton, Jake Lauffer, and George Wagner. Accused of murdering John Tewksbury and Bill Jacobs near Tewksbury's ranch were Louis Parker, Tom Graham, Miguel Apodaca, William Bonner, Joseph Ellenwood, William Gould, and Thomas [Bob] Carrington.[48]

Yavapai County had a legal mess. Three of the seven residents of Pleasant Valley, who now stood accused of the murders of John Tewksbury and Bill Jacobs, had already been tried and acquitted for the burning of the Middleton Ranch. Of the thirty-five called as witnesses before the grand jury in the murder of Tewksbury and Jacobs, six were already facing charges in the murder of Bill Graham. And of those accused of killing Bill, several had previously testified in

St. Johns against John and Tom Graham for grand larceny.[49] The same problems that plagued the St. Johns trials a few years earlier also threatened the cases before the court now: they did not lack witnesses, just witnesses who were capable of and willing to provide clear and convincing evidence.[50]

To provide sufficient time for both the prosecution and the defense to prepare for these hearings, all four cases were scheduled for the June 1888 term.[51] However, when the court convened on 4 June, the county attorney stood and addressed the court. "In all probability," he announced, "the plaintiff would not be able to prepare for trial during the present term of this court," and moved for a continuance of all the cases until the November term.[52] The defense attorneys vigorously protested, but the court's docket was full and agreed to the continuance.[53]

In the interim, nine more defense witnesses, including law enforcement officers, were subpoenaed in the charge of murder against Ed and Jim Tewksbury, Boyer, Roberts, Newton, Lauffer, and Wagner. Curiously, no defense witnesses were called in the murder case against Parker, Graham, Apodaca, Bonner, Ellenwood, Gould, and Carrington. When the court convened in November 1888, the cases were again continued until the following June 1889 term.[54]

Such continuances were significant disruptions. The defendants and the witnesses totaled between thirty and thirty-five, and they often traveled in groups to Prescott. The journey to the county courthouse was a good three days on horseback over more than one hundred miles of rough terrain. There were no accommodations along the way, so they ate and slept outdoors, in any kind of weather. A trial could easily take up to ten days and cost perhaps $50 or more in travel, which was no casual amount for small-time ranchers and cowpunchers. Some of the witnesses reportedly skipped meals in order to afford the cost of appearing before the court.[55]

Others shouldered even greater personal sacrifices to appear in court. Tom Graham had to leave Annie in Tempe within days of their wedding to attend hearings in Prescott, and a few months after their daughter Arvilla was born, he was again called away to court. Such separations were hard on the young couple, and tensions grew between them.[56] Lizzie Rose, Al Rose's recent widow, subpoenaed as one of the witnesses, had to leave her children in the care of a neighbor who volunteered to take care of them during her absence.[57] Jim Tewksbury was already weakened from the effects of "quick consumption," a particularly aggressive form of tuberculosis. He nonetheless insisted on making the journey, but had to make several stops along the way to rest. Many who knew of his declining health wondered whether he would survive the journey at all.[58] When he finally made it to Prescott, his health was dire enough to make the town news. "James Tewksbury, of Tonto basin," the *Arizona Weekly Journal-Miner* reported after his cases had been continued, "is at Mrs. Dillon's, West Prescott, quite seriously ill."[59]

Love and death continued to weave their course through the lives that had become so intimately intertwined by violence. Jim seemed to get better while convalescing over the summer months, enough to be able to take walks along the streets of Prescott. Winter was coming, though, and Frank, who had also been ill, died during a Prescott winter. Jim sought the warmer climes of Phoenix, hoping to improve his health, but once there he took a turn for the worse.[60] He died in early December 1888. "During his stay in Prescott," the editors of the *Arizona Weekly Journal-Miner* were moved to write, "he won many friends by his quiet manners and gentlemanly deportment, who will regret to read of his untimely demise."[61] A week after Jim's passing, Ed's friend John Rhodes married Mary Ann Tewksbury, John Tewksbury's widow, in Pleasant Valley.[62]

Tom Graham took advantage of his time in Prescott to settle the outstanding probate matters in his brother's death. Then, when that was completed, Tom turned his back on the dreams of wealth that he and his brother shared in moving to Pleasant Valley. He left his herd of cattle to be looked after by others. His own fate was to be found elsewhere. In time, he would sell the land that he so highly praised. A year later he returned to the valley just once, quietly, and only for a moment, just long enough to reclaim some cattle, always under the watchful care of Charlie Duchet, a trusted companion with a fearsome reputation.[63]

Duchet, born Charles English, became one of the long line of questionable characters that seemed to gather around the Grahams, though Duchet was perhaps the wickedest of them all. He had the singular ability to leave behind a trail of blood everywhere he lived, having committed his first murders while still a boy. One knife fight in his youth left him disfigured for life, with scars across his face and head, and although his left arm was badly damaged from the fight, he continued raising hell. Upon his release from San Quentin, he headed for the Arizona Territory and changed his name to Duchet, perhaps in a quest to put his past behind him. It did not last. By the time he summoned a priest for his last rites in 1925, he had, by his own admission, killed at least thirty-five men.[64]

Not quite eight years earlier, when Johnny and Tom Graham moved to Pleasant Valley, there was money to be made in cattle because buyers were plentiful. But by the early 1890s, the eastern-owned outfits had flooded Arizona with thousands of cattle, and prices hit rock bottom.[65] Purchase agreements were hard to come by. Tom Graham found a buyer in the Phoenix area for some of his steers, but the buyer died before the purchase was finalized, and the manager of the buyer's estate refused to honor the agreement.[66] Graham sued the estate for breech of contract, and the estate administrator countersued.[67] When the case was finalized two years later, the court found for the estate. Graham was not only out of a sale, he was ordered to pay the defense costs.

8

"FROM HELL'S HEART"

When Tom Graham fled Pleasant Valley, he left with nothing more than what he could carry on his saddle. Fate had stripped him of the life that he had known: first Billy was cruelly gutted, and then Johnny had been shot down like a dog. Their land and livestock, which were now his by inheritance, were all left behind to be cared for by his few remaining friends. Louis was the only member of his family left to him, but they decided to go their separate ways for the sake of survival.[1]

Where does a man go who has lost nearly all? How does he begin to reassemble the pieces of a life now ripped away from him? Tom returned to the one thing he knew: the life he had left as a boy so many years ago, long before fate had struck her cruel blows. He returned to working the soil as a farmer. The Salt River Valley, where he started his new life, was a good three-days' ride by horseback from the killing field that Pleasant Valley had become. There were farther places in the territory where he could have dropped his bedroll, but one hundred miles must have seemed as good as a thousand for a man who desperately needed to put his past behind him.

So Graham lived for the next five years, assuming a quiet life and keeping a low profile while working several rural acres south of the small village of Tempe, named for the Vale of Tempe in Thessaly, Greece. It was there near the banks of the Salt River that he began to rebuild his life.[2] It was hard going, but with Annie Melton, he found a stability and companionship that he had sorely lacked.[3] They took up residence under a mesquite tree, fending off rattlesnakes and clearing three hundred cords of wood before building a modest house.[4] A year after losing Arvilla to dehydration, Annie gave birth to their second daughter, Estella, who lived.[5] In time, Tom's terrors eased, enough for him to stop sleeping with a gun. Eventually, he stopped carrying one altogether.[6]

The Salt River Valley, once difficult to reach by miles of daunting terrain, would not remain isolated for long. Visionaries with resources saw vast potential in the open land, and businessmen and financiers began laying the groundwork for its economic transformation. In 1888, investors succeeded in financing a railroad line through Phoenix, connecting the city to the Southern and Pacific line. With that improvement came quick changes. By the end of the nineteenth century, Phoenix became Arizona's major economic hub, reorienting the trade and traffic from the outlying settlements toward the Salt River Valley, even those one hundred miles away. Phoenix became a major destination for exporting Arizona horses, sheep, and cattle from the north country.

With an 1890 population of close to thirty-five hundred in the Salt River Valley (almost a 50 percent increase from the previous decade), it was still possible that the paths of Tom Graham and his former adversaries from Pleasant Valley would never cross.[7] Tom was no longer in the livestock trade, and Tempe remained separated from Phoenix by twelve miles of desert scrub.

But trouble has a peculiar way of finding some men.

Robert Bowen built the Tempe Hotel in 1890, and he prospered well enough to invest in cattle. He chose to keep a herd at a ranch in Pleasant Valley, and he hired one of the best cowboys around to tend them: John Rhodes. But John Rhodes was no ordinary cow herder. He was the brother-in-law of Ed Tewksbury, having married Mary Ann after John Tewksbury's murder. And he was Ed's best friend.

In late July 1892, on one of the cattle drives from Pleasant Valley to Tempe, Bowen had an auspicious conversation with Rhodes. Bowen mentioned that they were moving his cattle to the field next to Tom Graham's place.[8] Bowen later claimed to have no ill feelings toward Graham and that he had simply mentioned Graham's name in a reference to the pasture's location. But Bowen also knew of the previous difficulties in Pleasant Valley. He may have wanted to forewarn his business partner of a possible encounter.

Either way, Rhodes gave no reaction to the mention of that name.

———•———

Tom Graham rose early on the morning of 2 August.[9] The summertime temperatures in Tempe, Arizona, could peak over one hundred degrees at midday and he wanted to start out early on his journey in order to beat the heat.[10] He carefully loaded his wagon with his newly harvested sacks of barley and set out for the Hayden Flour Mill, about three miles away.

As he steered his wagon around large cottonwood trees that had fallen onto the road from a severe windstorm the night before, Graham was startled to hear the sounds of horses charging hard from behind. He turned to his left and in his peripheral vision he saw two riders bearing down hard on him with rifles raised. Graham tried to jump from the wagon as a single rifle shot shattered the quiet of the morning.[11]

The projectile drilled through the summer air at about five hundred miles an hour.[12] In the split second that it tore through Graham's body, the bullet punctured his left trapezius muscle just inches away from his vertebrae, and continued on a trajectory that shattered his spinal cord and grazed his trachea. The pressure cavity caused by the blunted slug exploded outward below his right jaw line, ripping out muscle and sinew. The force of that blast snapped his head back and sent his body flopping helplessly onto the fruits of his harvest.[13] Paralyzed from the neck down, he could only gasp for breath as he awaited the kill shot that would surely come from the gunmen.

The percussion of the rifle shot hung in the air as the wagon came to a stop at an odd angle in front of the home of Whitfield Cummings.[14] There the horses stood in the middle of the road, patiently waiting for their driver's command.[15] Graham's blood-splattered hat rolled aimlessly in the dirt road.[16]

The lead gunman pulled his horse to a hard stop behind the wagon while the second rider raced around the wagon and then headed for the cover of the trees lining the road.[17] The lead gunman held his rifle taut, still aimed at Graham, waiting for any movement. Except for the profuse flow of blood and shallow gasps, Graham could not move.

The kill shot did not come.

Instead, the gunman lowered his rifle and lightly nudged the flanks of his horse. He was a broad-shouldered, barrel-chested man with a dark complexion, who could easily be mistaken for a Mexican. As he approached the left side of the wagon, he stood in his stirrups to lean over and get a good look at Tom Graham's blood-splattered face. Their eyes met. Then, without saying a word, the dark cowboy settled back into his saddle and holstered his rifle. Spurring his horse, he galloped east toward the Superstition Mountains.[18]

The gunman would have escaped without a witness were it not for seventeen-year-old Mollie Cummings and her fifteen-year-old friend Grace Griffith.[19] They had just steered their buggy onto the road from Mollie's home when they heard the sound of a rifle discharge within close range, and then a dark cowboy emerged from where the cottonwood trees had fallen on the road, riding past at a fast gallop. He was in such a hurry that his horse brushed against their buggy as he rode by, startling the girls.

M. A. Cravath, newly hired as a schoolteacher, was taking advantage of the summer break to clear some cockleburs on the side of the road early that morning. Initially he paid no attention to the report of a rifle as he worked with his back to the road, but he noticed a man galloping past him on a large, light bay horse. Then the excited cries of a young woman at the Cummings house drew his attention.

Cravath ran toward the commotion and was the first to find Graham lying on his wagon.[20] Others in the neighborhood quickly gathered around Graham, lifted him off the wagon, and placed him on the rocking chair on the Cummingses' front porch. Doctors living in the area were summoned.

Dr. Fenn Hart was the first to arrive, and he immediately tried to stem the flow of blood, but there was not much he could do other than try to make Graham comfortable.[21] They then moved him to a cot on the porch and propped him up with pillows.[22] Except for his head, he could not move. He was paralyzed from the neck down, and even his head movements were very limited.

This wound was fatal, but the doctor tried to keep Graham's spirits up by telling him otherwise. Graham knew better. He slowly nodded no to each of Hart's encouragements.

"You mustn't give up that way," Hart protested. "You must be brave! We hope you will survive the shock and recover. There *is* a chance!"[23]

Again, Graham sluggishly shook his head no.

Reverend E. G. Roberts arrived and also tried to reassure Tom of his recovery, but Tom was already resigned to his fate. "I . . . don't . . . care . . . much," he tiredly replied. It . . . makes . . . but . . . little . . . difference . . . to . . . me."[24]

When Dr. Scott Helm arrived, Tom winked at his old friend. Helm was more direct with Graham. "Well, Tom," he quietly said as he gingerly pulled back the bandages to look over Graham's wound, "they have got you this time."[25]

"I . . . am . . . done . . . for," Graham whispered in gasps.[26] His words were beginning to slur as the opiates administered for pain were beginning to take effect.[27]

About an hour later, a handful of men gathered close to Graham. Among them were Charlie Duchet, John "J.J." Hickey, and Lon Forsee.[28] Duchet, Graham's long-time associate and right-hand man, was perhaps the only true friend Graham had. He also loathed the Tewksburys. Thirty-year-old J.J. Hickey was a justice of the peace in Phoenix. Forsee, a thirty-three-year-old merchant, was also a justice of the peace. He was determined to write out a murder complaint on Graham's behalf.[29]

Hickey bent in close. "Do you recognize me?" he asked. Graham nodded his head slightly.

"Tom, who shot you—did Ed Tewksbury shoot you?" prompted Hickey.

Graham slowly moved his head from side to side.

"Who shot you?" Forsee demanded.

Graham's lips and tongue were so affected by his wound that he could not move them without great difficulty. He could only rasp a response, barely audible.[30] Forsee leaned in with his ear toward Graham's mouth, ready with pencil and paper in hand.

"Roh-zzze."

Forsee could not make out what Graham said and looked up at the others. They debated what it sounded like. Rose? Rhodes? Was it John Rhodes? offered Duchet.[31]

Graham confirmed with a slight nod.

The men in the room began trying to remember when they last saw Rhodes in Tempe. Amid the discussion, Graham moved his head once again, as if to speak. The men grew quiet.

"Too-ssrree," he breathed out.

Toossree? Tewksbury?

"Was it Rhodes or Tewksbury who shot you?" asked Forsee.

"Both," he emphatically rasped.[32]

That these names had any meaning to the men who gathered around Graham, or that they immediately attached the names of Rhodes and Tewksbury to the question of who would shoot him, suggests that Graham did not live in complete anonymity in Tempe. Graham's friends had heard these two names from him before. Was it only after several beers that he spilled his story, or did he talk openly about the killings in Pleasant Valley? It was often enough at least to reveal that even though he had fashioned a new life for himself in the Salt River Valley, the ghosts of his past still haunted him.

"Did you see them, Tom, before they came up?" Hickey wondered.[33]

Graham slowly moved his head from side to side.

"You didn't see them before they came up?"

Slowly, Graham responded, managing only one garbled word with each labored breath: "I . . . seen . . . them . . . just . . . as . . . they . . . raised . . . their . . . guns . . . I . . . then . . . threw . . . myself . . . forward."

"Tom," Hickey pressed, "how far were they from you when they shot?"

"About . . . twenty . . . five . . . feet."[34]

Duchet stepped forward with Tom's wife, Annie, who had just arrived. "There is hope," Duchet assured her, "the doctor said so."

"No . . . there . . . is . . . no . . . hope . . . Charlie," Graham drowsily replied. "I . . . am . . . bleeding . . . inside . . . I . . . can . . . feel . . . it."

"I . . . know . . . I . . . can't . . . live." He slowly added. "I . . . am . . . satisfied . . . of . . . it."[35]

He asked Annie to bring their baby daughter close so he could kiss her good-bye. When Annie set the child down, she leaned forward to also kiss her husband, but sprang back in shock when she pressed his lips. He already felt cold and lifeless.

"He's dying!" she cried out.

Dr. Hart cautioned her about giving way to excitement and encouraged her to keep hope for recovery. Graham again shook his head no. "I'm . . . gone," he said.[36]

For a man who had lost nearly all that was meaningful to him in just a few short years, surely the hastening of death seemed a bittersweet resolution. He would miss his wife and daughter, surely. They had known happiness, hadn't they, despite their grief over losing their first baby? But the lingering ache of losing his brothers to violence, the years of living with fear in the back of his mind that capable men wanted him dead—indeed, of wrestling with the nagging instinct to look over his shoulder for the man who would end his life—never really went away. Now it would soon end, "a consummation devoutly to be wished," and he was satisfied with it.[37]

Within the hour, he lost consciousness.[38]

———•—•———

Reverend Roberts, Hickey, and Duchet left Annie to be alone with Tom in his final moments. They stepped outside and examined the road to see what tales tracks could tell. Graham stated emphatically that there were two shooters, but the two young girls who had stumbled across the murder only saw one man.

Horse tracks on the packed desert floor were not difficult to pick out near the place where Graham's wagon had come to a stop, and there were indeed two distinctive sets. One horse had an oblong shoe, and the other had a more rounded shoe. Both tracks appeared to have been made at the same time, and both could be seen circling the wagon. The men traced the tracks back to where the two horses had stopped earlier and tromped around near the fallen cottonwood trees, as if their riders had spent several minutes waiting in the brush. Two cigarette butts were also found on the ground, and there were marks suggesting that at least one person had dismounted and squatted for a time on his toes. The tracking party continued on, following the hoof prints down the road, but lost them after a quarter of a mile.[39]

Nevertheless, they had seen enough and were satisfied that Graham had identified his killers: John Rhodes and Ed Tewksbury.

———•—•———

Annie stayed by Tom's side for two more hours as he lingered at the edge of life, as if hesitant to irrevocably cross the great divide. Around 3:00 in the afternoon he finally gave up the last fight of his life.[40] Tempe lawmen set about tracking Rhodes and Tewksbury. John Rhodes was not hard to find. Constable Gallardo arrested him at 10:00 P.M.[41]

———•—•———

Tom Graham was a complex man who inhabited, it seems, different narratives. For those who stood by him throughout the violent clashes in Pleasant Valley and afterward, they saw in him the kinds of qualities that most men would want in a friend. For Siras Young, who oversaw Graham's ranches after he fled from Pleasant Valley, Graham was a likable man who made friends easily. Graham's devoted friend Charlie Duchet saw Graham as a man who most preferred peace to violence. "All children loved him," Mollie Cummings McTaggart said almost seventy years later, remembering the ride in his wagon that Graham had given her and several other neighborhood children, driving past the spot where he would be shot the next day. He was known as a quiet, considerate neighbor who adored his daughter and minded his own business.[42]

It was nothing short of a tragedy, then, that such an agreeable man could not, or perhaps would not, seek to resolve any misunderstandings with those who held decidedly different views about him. Mormon settlers in the communities surrounding Pleasant Valley who regularly set out to track and recover their stolen livestock were firm in their beliefs that Tom Graham was a principal operator in the rustling ring that preyed upon their livestock. They were not the only ones. Other Pleasant Valley settlers—some decidedly anti-Mormon—also came to the same conclusion, that Graham played a key role in their losing livestock in the thousands of dollars. And for the surviving Tewksbury brothers, Tom Graham was the friend who betrayed them for lucre and who kept them in and out of Prescott courts on a variety of trumped-up charges. Most grievous of all, he boasted of having killed their oldest brother, John.[43]

Perhaps there were elements of each narrative about Tom that were true. For those with whom he had no quarrel, he was an easygoing, peaceable man. But survival on the frontier had also taught him to be coldly practical. Some relationships were simply more profitable to keep than others. He might have disagreed with his brother Johnny in turning on the Tewksburys, but Johnny was his brother and his companion, and blood was thicker than water. This likeable man, when aggrieved, when deeply wounded by the loss of his half brother Bill, was relentless in seeing that justice was served. Loyalty to family and friends was a virtue he prized above all others.[44] And in lesser moments, he could gloat over his role in sending a man to an early grave. In many ways, he was no different from many. But perhaps his greatest flaw was that when disagreements arose in Pleasant Valley, and especially when they began turning violent, he never once tried to talk man to man with those who had differences with him. It was as if what others thought mattered not at all.

The stories that could reveal more about the man who would stand accused of his murder, Ed Tewksbury, are comparatively fewer and almost nonexistent in writing. Instead, their loyalty spoke loudly. When county sheriffs raised a posse of lawmen in the Tonto Basin to look for Johnny Graham and Charlie Blevins, it was Ed Tewksbury that the lawmen turned to as one of the dependable local men. When Globe City resident George Wilson needed a foreman to run his sister's ranch in Pleasant Valley in his absence, he trusted her place and her livestock to Ed. And several men in Pleasant Valley would ride for days with Tewksbury at a moment's notice; honest small ranchers just trying to make a living in the valley against whom no complaint had been raised. What it was about this man that allowed him to command this level of respect has never been fully articulated. He had many friends, and they would come ready to defend him if needed.

The Grahams, however, held a much darker view of Ed Tewksbury and his brothers, one they did not hesitate to press upon others. The Tewksburys were liars, and Ed was dangerous. Jim was seen robbing a Mormon ACMI store up on the Rim in Woodruff. Tom and Johnny swore in court that they witnessed the Tewksbury brothers branding calves that they knew did not belong to them. For holding the Tewksburys accountable before the law, they believed, Ed Tewksbury had callously shot their half brother in the bowels and left him to die a painful death.

Both sides of these narratives reveal the complicated nature of Ed Tewksbury. He was a man at home in the wide-open spaces of the frontier, having lived all of his life on it. He was not ordinarily given to much talk, but he knew ranching and horses better than most. His was a friendship that was true through thick and thin, and he could be counted on to come charging through the fire when things became dicey. Such friendships were rare, and good as gold on the frontier, and men loved him for it. He was also a man who would act to protect his own, regardless of what the law might say or do. So when Tom Graham threatened his best friend after five years of peace, Ed knew what had to happen.

The two men were more alike than not, though torn apart by misperceptions about each other that in time grew into an abiding enmity. There may have been a chance at reconciliation early on, after the first allegations against the Tewksbury brothers and other settlers were thrown out of court. But an encounter between the two oldest brothers afterward reveals how deeply betrayed the Tewksbury brothers felt. John Tewksbury accosted Johnny Graham after the trial and slapped him. The elder Graham did not respond, but after that moment, the two sets of brothers never had contact with one another again, even though they continued to live only two miles apart. The round of legal complaints that the Grahams filed against the Tewksburys must have seemed to the Tewksbury brothers as clear evidence of Graham harassment. And the Tewksburys' continual acquittals from those charges must have stoked the Grahams' frustration and increased their resolve not to let them get away.[45]

9

BURDENS OF PROOF

Already the West was changing when Tom Graham died. The native grasses that had made the Arizona meadows so appealing to cattlemen were gone in just a few decades through overgrazing. Ranchers began importing foreign, more invasive grasses to feed their livestock, and alfalfa growers in the Salt River Valley were kept busy meeting the increased demand.[1] The Ghost Dance, which may have been inspired in part by Mormon missions to the Indians, spread rapidly from the Nevada Paiute to other nations in the West who were eager to embrace its message that a spiritual cleansing from all things European would bring about a resurrection of their dead and a restoration of the Earth, as it was before the coming of the white man.[2] Wovoka's message was a peaceful one that anticipated the mutual cooperation among the Indian nations, but the message emboldened the Lakota to resist subjugation.[3] Their showdown with the 7th Cavalry in December 1890 resulted in the massacre of 150 Lakota Ghostdancers.[4]

At least some were already lamenting that an era was drawing to a close. "The West has changed," noted Emerson Hough from his office in Chicago. Hough was a prolific writer who romanticized the Old West for popular audiences. "The old days are gone," he continued, "the house dog sits on the hill where yesterday the coyote sang. The fences are short and small, and within them grow green things instead of gray. There are many smokes now rising over the prairie, and they are wide and black instead of thin and blue."[5]

Indeed, western farmers and labor unions found common cause and grew in political power, pushing a populist agenda that profoundly impacted national politics for several decades.[6] Citizens in the western territories demanded action from their representatives to put an end to the theft and violence that plagued the livestock trade. In his 1883 address to Arizona's Twelfth Territorial Legislature, territorial governor Frederick A. Tritle urged leaders to do more to curb the thefts, murder, and lawlessness that ran rampant in the territory. Arizonans sent a special appeal to the president to petition Congress for an appropriation of $150,000 to be used to mount a force of rangers who could pursue and arrest criminals, and help prevent raids from hostile Indians.[7] Livestock associations hired more rangers to investigate crimes and pursue the guilty, and local citizens in various communities privately financed special officers to put an end to the theft economy.

Changes were also in store for the Tewksbury family and their Pleasant Valley friends. Some of those changes would be cause for more merriment, others for mourning. Only a few years after the bloodshed ended, family patriarch James Dunning Tewksbury passed away in his Pleasant Valley home after lingering for a year after a stroke.[8] Death was not yet finished in Pleasant Valley. The following spring, in April 1892, George Newton left his home in Globe City for his ranch in Pleasant Valley. Bob Pringle, one of the men shot four years earlier by John Rhodes at Bayard's Saloon, was expecting his friend George to stop at his place that night. Newton never arrived.[9]

N. H. Price was the last person to see him when they met three miles south of the Salt River. The river had been dangerously swollen by the spring runoff, and Price tried to dissuade Newton from continuing on. But Newton was confident that he could safely cross. Four days later, when he failed to arrive, Pringle set out to see if he could find Newton. Making his way south to Globe City, Pringle found Newton's horses, about seventy-five yards south of Redman's Crossing on the Salt River. George's horse was still saddled, lazily eating grass on the banks of Coon Creek. The packhorse was dead, lying in a shallow pool of receding floodwater. There was no sign of George. His rain slicker, shoes, and spurs were still tied to his saddle, and his rifle lay on the sand. After reporting the news to Alice Newton, George's wife, Pringle set out again from Globe City at 3:00 A.M. the next morning to return to Coon's Creek with George's brother Harry and another friend, to see if they could find George's body. They were unsuccessful. Two weeks later, more of Newton's friends mounted another search to find Newton's remains, but they could only locate his pistol and gun belt, partially buried in a sand barge.[10]

Newton would not have been the first to tragically misjudge the dangerous undercurrents of an Arizona river swollen by winter runoff. William Middleton survived the Apache attacks in Pleasant Valley years earlier, only to drown in a Globe City creek.[11] But that did not stop later generations of storytellers from spinning conspiracy out of Newton's disappearance. Some writers speculated that Ed Tewksbury had a hand in it, or that one of the men who were accused of burning Newton's ranch house had finally exacted revenge. It is clear, though, that few people at the time—if anyone—suspected foul play.[12] His death was never referred to with any suspicion in the Globe City newspapers, and for the rest of the year, Alice Newton continued to run ads in the newspaper offering a $500 reward for anyone who could find his remains.[13]

SOUND AND FURY

When Tom Graham's friends held his hand to sign an "X" on the statement penned by Justice Forsee, John Rhodes was quickly placed under arrest. Rhodes was not known to have any quarrel with Graham, and his name was never associated with the violent conflicts of Pleasant Valley. He was not hard to find in town and he made no effort to resist arrest.[14] There was an attempt to give Rhodes a straw bond, which would have allowed him to remain out of jail, but citizens indignantly protested, and Rhodes was taken before Justice Roberts, who ordered him to be held in jail until his arraignment.

With Rhodes in custody, Charley McFarland, who would later run for sheriff, led a posse of thirty citizens to capture Tewksbury. The tracks of the gunman headed east toward the Superstition Mountains, but with every hour the gunman seemed to be widening his lead. After several hours of tracking him, McFarland's horse fell and the posse gave up the chase, convinced that once Tewksbury made it to the mountains, they would never find him.[15]

Enraged citizens in Tempe clamored for swift justice. Charlie Duchet prowled the streets of Tempe with a loaded shotgun. He seemed to reflect the restlessness of the residents, and as nighttime fell, conditions within that small community worsened. Public anger on the dusty streets grew more intense, to the point where the sheriff and his deputies began to fear that a lynching attempt was imminent. Sheriff Montgomery decided to immediately move Rhodes out of the Tempe jail to the county jail in Phoenix, where he would be better protected. The sheriff and his deputy readied the carriage, placed Rhodes between them, and employed two more armed men to ride out in front.

Despite his brave face, the specter of an imminent lynching was unnerving for Rhodes. When they finally neared the county jail eleven miles away, he leaped off the carriage and sprinted up the steps into the corridors of the building. After he was safely behind bars, he tried to laugh off his nervousness, joking with the other men in jail or with the curiosity seekers who came to look at him. There were, in fact, so many who came to gawk at him that Rhodes advised Sheriff Montgomery that he should be charging an admission fee.[16]

John Rhodes was arraigned on the afternoon of Friday, 4 August, just two days after Graham's murder. He confidently plead not guilty of the charge, and following legal protocol, Justice of the Peace Willis Oren Huson scheduled a preliminary hearing for 9 A.M. the following Monday to determine whether the territory had enough evidence to establish probable cause.[17] If the territory succeeded in persuading the judge, the prosecution of John Rhodes would then move to a trial by jury.

The following week, residents packed the courtroom and jammed the corridor and stairway at 10:00 A.M. on Monday morning, expecting a battle royal between two sets of highly respected attorneys.[18] Fifty-six witnesses had been summoned (though several had been subpoenaed by both the territory and the defense).[19] The hearing began with a few legal formalities discussed between the two sides. Then, Annie Graham dramatically appeared in the doorway with her one-year-old daughter Estella. They were both dressed in black. Onlookers respectfully parted as Annie marched forward with her daughter and took a seat near the front, causing a momentary stir of commotion.[20]

John Rhodes looked indifferent to the proceedings, gazing about the room with a mild curiosity but otherwise showing no other emotion. It was only when Charlie Duchet entered the courtroom that Rhodes showed any reaction at all. The two men instantly locked eyes, and Duchet glared at Rhodes with a withering malignancy that seemed to quail Rhodes, but he nonetheless returned the look with equal venom and never turned away until Duchet took his seat and was no longer visible in the audience. Among those who witnessed the moment, they were sure that Duchet's look revealed an impending homicide and that Rhodes well knew its meaning.[21]

The march of witnesses for the prosecution over two days failed to persuasively tie Rhodes to the murder. None of the witnesses knew Rhodes or could remember that they had ever seen him until the trial, and none were positive that he was the man they saw fleeing the scene of the murder.

Annie Graham seemed brave and stoic during the proceedings, even smiling on occasion, but privately her frustration grew with the weakness of the territory's case. In the hours after the trial, she raged in bitterness against Rhodes, that he was still alive while her husband was dead. Something had to be done, she repeated. Her father, a pastor, tried to console Annie and urged her to seek to forgive. He thought she was starting to come around.

Annie was absent from the courtroom as the trial reconvened the following morning. She spent the morning in weeping jags and could not seem to stop, but finally she was able to compose herself enough to attend the afternoon session. Only this time, something was different. When she entered the courtroom, she was alone, without her daughter or her mother, and her veil was thrown back.

Annie took her seat near the front and soon began weeping again. Her sobs could be heard throughout the courtroom while witnesses gave testimony. A neighbor who was present at the hearing brought Annie a glass of water. She stood up to drink, and began to look about the room. All eyes were focused on the witness who was drawing a diagram of the Tempe streets on the chalkboard. Suddenly, with a shriek that spoke of wound and fury, she lunged at Rhodes, shoving her dead husband's cocked .45 Colt revolver against Rhodes's back, still partially covered by the cloth handbag with which she had concealed it.[22] Without a moment's hesitation, she pulled the trigger.

As the hammer snapped down, it caught part of the handbag, enough to blunt the force of the firing pin striking the cartridge. Rhodes's life was spared by a thin piece of cloth.

The room erupted in pandemonium. Rhodes leaped to his feet, twisted around, and clamped down on Annie's extended hand as Sheriff Montgomery seized her from behind and other lawmen rushed over to subdue her. Sheriff Garfias and a few others wrenched Rhodes away from Graham and dragged him toward the judge's bench, where they sat him down. Startled audience members jumped out of their seats and fled toward the door and down the stairwell.[23] Within moments, the room was almost completely empty of spectators, save a few.[24]

Annie managed to shove the pistol between her knees and lock her legs together as lawmen frantically grappled to retrieve the weapon. One audience member raised a chair into the air to strike her if she attempted to shoot again.[25]

"Oh my God, *let me shoot!*" she screamed.

"Oh, do let me shoot!! Oh, God, let me shoot—he killed my husband! Oh

God, let me shoot! Oh, Jesus, let me shoot!"

Her father called out amid the throng of lawmen around her. "They're doing all they can!" he shouted over her wails.[26]

She continued screaming as she struggled against the lawmen who rushed her into the corridor. "Oh God, he killed my husband! I have no one!! They ain't doing anything! Oh, somebody help me!"

"Bring him out!" she implored her husband's friends as she was pushed into the jury room.[27]

Fearful that her plea would cause a riot among Tom Graham's friends, the bailiffs immediately sealed the doors to the courtroom until they were satisfied that order had been restored in the courthouse.

After that, Rhodes's composure cracked. Before, he looked placidly uninterested; now he looked pale and nervous. For the rest of the afternoon he sat facing the doorway, barely conscious of the proceedings while scrutinizing everyone who entered the room.

After that day, all spectators were examined and no one but officials were allowed to enter with weapons. Justice Huson announced that anyone with firearms in the courtroom would be punished for carrying a concealed weapon and for contempt of court.

Annie Graham was prohibited from attending the proceedings. She appeared the following day, but the bailiffs turned her away as she attempted to enter the courtroom. She tried to enter the courtroom a second time, but again the bailiffs refused her admittance. She reluctantly returned to her hotel.

A report in the *Arizona Republican* following Annie Graham's attempted murder in the courtroom illustrates how difficult it was for many to acknowledge the effects of violence. Some court spectators experienced serious emotional reactions to Graham's attack in the courtroom, but in reporting on those reactions, the newspaper struck a lighthearted if not sniggering tone. While the report acknowledged the seriousness of Graham's assault, it nonetheless described spectator responses as "funny incidents." One court spectator "who foremost but not alone fell down stairs was horribly guyed [ridiculed] yesterday. He is charged with having broken all sprinting records until he reached Frake's livery stable where he waited long enough to give his breath a chance to come up with him." One of the peace officers was reported to have experienced a more serious reaction, "suffering from nervous prostration contracted during the melee."

The term "nervous prostration" was commonly applied to the symptoms of a nervous breakdown, and its inclusion in the report of "funny incidents" reveals an indifference toward what we would now call posttraumatic stress. Given this kind of community censure—from those who "horribly guyed" one court spectator whose instinctive reaction was to flee from danger, and a press that publically called out a debilitated peace officer—it is easy to see why people of that day would eschew any mention of having been affected at all by the threat of violence.[28]

TERRITORY OF ARIZONA VS. JOHN RHODES

For five days, the prosecution presented witnesses for the territory, but they each lacked direct information that could place Rhodes at the scene of the murder, much less that he actually shot Graham. The defense presented a string of witnesses, from prominent citizens to obscure stable boys, who accounted for John Rhodes's activities from the moment he arose from his cot that morning until he was arrested later in the day, and insisted that he was never near the scene of the crime.

The defense attorneys hammered away at the credibility of the territory's key witnesses, arguing that Duchet first instilled the idea to the dying Tom Graham, and to those gathered around him, that Rhodes and Tewksbury were the shooters. Duchet would not allow himself to be boxed into an admission by Rhodes's attorney. "I don't think *I* said so," he replied to the accusation that he fed Tom the names of his old enemies. "Still, I might have said that was what *Graham* said."[29]

The final witness called by the defense was John Rhodes himself. His testimony about his activities and locations that morning conformed to those of the previous witnesses, although he only knew the general time by the sun. "I did not shoot Graham," Rhodes declared emphatically. "I had nothing to do with the killing; I know nothing about it. I saw Tewksbury on either the 7th or 8th of July and have not seen him since."[30]

He admitted that he had talked with Tewksbury about Tom Graham two months earlier, when Graham briefly visited Pleasant Valley. Graham's visit caused a considerable stir, and everyone talked about it. He had seen Graham nearly every day, since he worked in Tempe, but they never spoke. He never learned until recently where Graham lived, and it was only because he was in that neighborhood herding cattle.

When his examination concluded, the defense announced that it rested its case.

ARIZONA CELEBRITY

Sam Finley, one of the bartenders at the Tempe Hotel, was also a deputy constable. He drew the assignment to serve Ed Tewksbury with an arrest warrant and to bring him back to Tempe. If Finley had any concerns about confronting Tewksbury, he did not show it. Finley had worked the range with Tewksbury, previous to his moving to Tempe, and he thought that Ed would prove reasonable. So he rode to Pleasant Valley alone and unarmed.

When Finley arrived in Pleasant Valley, he simply asked where Tewksbury was and was eventually directed to George Wilson's ranch on the lower Cherry Creek. Once there, he informed Wilson of the purpose of his visit and asked for Tewksbury. Ed was out at Wilson's horse ranch about five miles away, Wilson replied. Finley asked George if he wouldn't mind retrieving Tewksbury while he waited at Wilson's ranch. Wilson returned four hours later with Tewksbury.[31]

A lynch mob had formed to intercept Tewksbury when he arrived in Tempe, so lawmen took Tewksbury 170 miles south to a jail in Tucson.[32] News of the lynch mob reached Pleasant Valley, and the next day nine men rode into Tempe, conspicuously armed with rifles and pistols at their side. They came to make sure that Tewksbury was protected, but perhaps more importantly, they wanted to make it clear that they stood by their friend.[33]

Even when things looked calmer, lawmen concluded that Tewksbury would be better protected in a Phoenix jail, rather than the Tempe jail, and Phoenix law enforcement coordinated his transfer from Tucson with the highest secrecy and security. When Tewksbury strode into the Phoenix jail, visitors and prison officials were astonished to see him, and even the deputy sheriffs in town refused to believe the news of Tewksbury's imprisonment until they saw him with their own eyes. Tewksbury seemed to take it all in with a measured sense of humor.[34]

Three days later, however, Tewksbury's mood turned darker.

"It's a funny thing to me," he told a reporter for the *Arizona Star,* "how those men that have so much to say against Rhodes can reconcile their statements with the truth. . . . I never heard Rhodes threaten anyone." How did he explain that his name was on the arrest warrant for Graham's murder? It was Charles

Duchet, Graham's longtime friend who had manipulated the events, he insisted. "Duchet is the prime mover of evil against us," he bitterly declared, "Everyone knows he is a man who would say anything to hurt us."[35]

CLOSING ARGUMENTS

For ten days, Tempe residents had been absorbed with news of the trial. Prominent on the front page of area newspapers were summations of the testimonies given that day, as well as editorial commentaries on how effective the attorneys had been. Conversations in parlors and on the dusty streets frequently turned to the trial, and although public opinion was divided on what the evidence revealed, the prevailing opinion was that the judge would order Rhodes to remain in custody, without bail, to await a grand jury. Thus, residents packed the courtroom, eager to hear the judge's verdict.

The room grew silent when it was the judge's turn to speak. Huson carefully looked over the packed courtroom. Then, he simply declared: "After carefully weighing the evidence, I find the alibi complete and therefore discharge the prisoner."[36]

With the clap of the judge's gavel, the courtroom remained oddly quiet. No cheers erupted from Rhodes's corner, or outrage from those who believed him guilty, although there were many furrowed brows as people slowly filed out of the courtroom. Outside the courthouse, men gathered in small groups to debate what had happened. Some insisted that the evidence clearly implicated Rhodes, and that this would not be the end of it. A few called for hanging Huson in effigy. Others looked upon Ed Tewksbury's sure conviction with even greater anticipation.[37]

John Rhodes was now a free man, but he refused to walk out of the courthouse. He preferred to spend one more night within the protection of iron bars. The next day, heavily armed friends from Pleasant Valley rode up to the courthouse, and when John Rhodes mounted his horse, they set their faces to the east and galloped away toward the mountains.[38]

10

THE TRIALS OF ED TEWKSBURY

The two men that Tom Graham named as his murderers had been captured, and one had already faced trial. But after hearing testimony from fifty-six witnesses, the territory could not prove that John Rhodes was at the murder scene, much less that he shot Graham. None of the witnesses could confirm the dying man's testimony because no one saw Rhodes at the scene of the murder.

The case against Ed Tewksbury looked stronger, but it still suffered from critical weaknesses. He more closely resembled the man that witnesses saw fleeing the murder, but no one actually saw Ed shoot Tom. What's more, Charlie Duchet was adamant at the Rhodes hearing that Tom Graham said that John Rhodes's bullet hit him, and that Ed Tewksbury's bullet missed. If Rhodes was now a free man for lack of evidence, could the territory convict Tewksbury for Tom Graham's murder?

WOULD-BE VIGILANTES

The preliminary hearing for Ed Tewksbury was set for Monday, 29 August 1892. But residents of Tempe, angered over the freeing of Rhodes, were anxious that the court would be unable to convict him, too. So about a week and a half before Tewksbury's hearing, a mob of angry Tempe citizens assembled late one Saturday night, probably well fueled by liquid courage. They rode to the outskirts of Phoenix and then divided into smaller groups to enter the city unnoticed. Their plan was to storm the county jail by surprise and hang Tewksbury.

Phoenix law enforcement was already well prepared for vigilantes. Seventeen well-armed men were stationed around the jailhouse, and scores of other officers roamed the streets in the blocks surrounding the jail. The strong showing of guards did not stop the Tempe mob from prowling around the jail howling for vengeance, however. So vehement were their threats that at one point during the night the sheriff grew alarmed enough to hand a pistol to Tewksbury and tell him to defend himself should the mob succeed in breaking into the jail.[1] When the dawn arrived, the mob finally abandoned their hope of seizing Tewksbury and rode back to Tempe.[2]

Community outrage nonetheless continued to boil in the days leading up to Tewksbury's hearing. Two of Phoenix's newspapers, the *Phoenix Herald* and the *Phoenix Gazette,* condemned Huson for releasing Rhodes. Then on Wednesday, 24 August 1892, thirty prominent residents of Tempe circulated a notice that a mass meeting would be held on the following Saturday at 3:00 P.M. Their purpose was to protest the killing of Tom Graham and the release of John Rhodes, and to raise support for the prosecution of Ed Tewksbury, scheduled to start the following Monday.[3]

Residents from Tempe and the surrounding communities gathered at the Tempe Free Reading Room on that Saturday afternoon. After the meeting was called to order, Charles Austin was made chairman, and Charles Taylor was appointed secretary.[4] Austin was the son-in-law of Whitfield Cummings and one of the trackers who followed the horse tracks from the murder scene. He was a member of the Good Templar fraternal society in Tempe and was known around town for the blackface minstrel performances that he would put on at the Tempe Dramatic Club. He would later run for justice of the peace. Charles Taylor, an agent for a local lumber company, was also known around town for his performances with a local glee club and for his active role in the local Republican Party.

Among the men who stood to speak at the meeting was Tempe Baptist minister M. M. Hitchcock, Tempe Justice of the Peace Lon Forsee, Charles Austin, and others.[5] Many who spoke insisted that Graham's dying statement in the presence of reputable citizens should have been sufficient evidence to convict Rhodes. Ever mindful of the power of narrative, the assembly drafted a resolution denouncing the effect that the murder could have on the community's reputation as a civilized town unless the murder could be "legally avenged." And of course, that resolution also deplored the fact that Graham had been murdered. Another resolution condemned Huson for setting Rhodes free, declaring that there had been sufficient evidence introduced during Rhodes's hearing to at least hold him for a formal trial, if not to convict him. Still another resolution called for a subsequent meeting to aid the prosecution in collecting testimony for the Tewksbury hearing and to raise $200 to help with the investigation.

During this time, John Rhodes was reportedly seen riding daily through the streets of Mesa City, east of Tempe, in the company of three other men. They were all heavily armed. Given the attempts on his life while in jail and the ongoing belief of many that he had gotten away with murder, it is no surprise that he wanted to travel well protected in the Salt River Valley. But some residents speculated that there was another purpose for his high visibility in the area: Graham's murderer had ridden directly through the main street of Mesa City in his escape. Although witnesses in Mesa City had already been subpoenaed for Ed Tewksbury's hearing, a well-armed Rhodes may have been riding up and down the streets between Tempe and Mesa City to silence anyone else along the murderer's route who might wish to come forward as a witness.[6]

TERRITORY OF ARIZONA VS. ED TEWKSBURY

As Justice of the Peace Horatio Wharton convened the preliminary hearing of Ed Tewksbury on Monday, 29 August 1892, the district attorney's office was once again pitting the attorneys in the Rhodes hearing against one another.[7] Both sides had clearly studied the court transcript from the previous hearing. Although the territory called the same witnesses who had testified against Rhodes, the prosecution worked to ensure that their case was stronger against the strategy the defense had used previously. Knowing that the defense would challenge the credibility of Graham's dying statement, each witness for the territory was asked about Graham's state of mind: was he rational? Each witness agreed that he was, as did the doctors who attended him. Every witness who testified that they saw Tewksbury fleeing the scene of the murder was asked to point him out in the courtroom.

The defense anticipated the prosecution's strategy and presented a different tactic. One court already found Rhodes's alibi persuasive enough to drop all charges. Therefore, they argued, if compelling evidence existed suggesting that Rhodes was *not* present when Graham was killed, then the dying man's testimony that he was shot by both Rhodes and Tewksbury could not be considered reliable. So they worked assiduously to poke holes in the testimonies of those who claimed to have seen Ed Tewksbury—or at least a man closely resembling Tewksbury—fleeing the scene of the crime. Did he have facial hair? Was his hat light or dark? What clothing did he wear? Was his horse a light bay or a roan? Did the horse have any distinct markings or not? Did he carry arms? The witnesses for the prosecution could not agree on these identifying details, and that lack of agreement—even outright disagreement at times—created room for reasonable doubt. If the man seen by all of the prosecution's witnesses was in fact Tewksbury, the defense maintained, he must have been a change artist of some renown. He must have been accompanied by a herd of horses of all different types to account for the different horses described by the prosecution witnesses. He must have been traveling with a hat and clothing store to wear the different articles of clothing the prosecution witnesses swore they saw. He must have carried a razor and cream with which to shave, all while galloping at speeds sufficient to be seen in Pleasant Valley on the same day of the murder!

After six days of testimonies, when both sides rested their cases, Justice Wharton surprised the courtroom by announcing that he would not render a decision that day. Instead, he would take the matter under advisement until 3 o'clock the next afternoon.[8] When the court reconvened, Wharton took up his seat on the bench. He seemed to be very aware of the potentially explosive nature of his ruling. The outraged citizens of Tempe were eager to see Tom Graham's killer brought to justice, and many residents from Pleasant Valley were in the courtroom, ready to defend Ed Tewksbury. Whatever ruling Wharton declared, it had to be carefully and methodically laid out for all present.

"This case I regard as a very important one," he began. "It is a question in which is to be considered the liberty, at least for the time, of an American citizen, and should not be passed over lightly."

There was no dispute that Thomas Graham was assassinated on the morning of 2 August, he continued. The question before the court was who was responsible. He then carefully reviewed the pieces of testimonies presented for the prosecution that he found compelling. Nearly all agreed that a dark-colored man wearing a light hat with a red band was seen at the murder, riding a bay-colored horse. Many witnesses—though not all, he conceded—identified Ed Tewksbury as that man. Some of the witnesses knew him from before, and others did not. But three more witnesses testified conclusively that they saw Ed Tewksbury in Tempe on the night before and the morning of the murder.

He dismissed the argument challenging the reliability of Graham's dying declaration. Citing the decision in *Commonwealth of Massachusetts vs. John W.*

Webster regarding an alibi, if the evidence presented is equally persuasive that the defendant committed the crime and that he was not present to commit the crime, the burden of proof rests with the alibi to raise reasonable doubt that the defendant committed the crime.[9] If it does not, the alibi defense fails. Measured against this ruling, Wharton found the testimonies weak of those who insisted that Ed Tewksbury was in Pleasant Valley on the day that Graham was murdered. None of the witnesses could conclusively testify how they knew the precise day and time that they saw Tewksbury in Pleasant Valley. All the testimonies were based on beliefs and impressions. "I have examined every authority that has been cited," he concluded. "And after a careful consideration of the matter, both as to the evidence and the law, I believe that there is but one duty left for me to perform: and that is, to say, under the law and the evidence, I believe there is a sufficiency of evidence to convince me that the defendant is guilty."

He ordered Tewksbury to be held without bail by the sheriff of Maricopa County to await trial.[10]

Tewksbury registered no reaction to the decision and betrayed no emotion. His friends, however, were bitterly disappointed and argued afterward that the court had erred in its judgment. Tewksbury later told reporters that he was disappointed, but expected nothing else from the judge.[11]

GRAND JURY DIFFICULTIES

Even though Judge Wharton found probable cause, only the grand jury was empowered by Arizona law to hand down the actual indictment for murder. Finding an impartial jury in Phoenix, however, proved challenging. In many jurisdictions that utilized the grand jury system, the selection of jurors was up to the county court, a board of commissioners, or another branch of the government. In the Arizona Territory, however, the selection of jurors was subjected to the same scrutiny as in a trial court, and both the prosecution and the defense had the opportunity to test potential jurors for their impartiality.[12] The complication with this system in the Arizona Territory was that the defense had the opportunity to screen the jury. In most cases, this was not a problem. In the matter of *Territory of Arizona vs. Ed. Tewksbury* (1892), however, it was.

For well over a month after Graham's murder, avenging his death was *the* topic of conversation on the streets and in the saloons. The newspapers closely followed the crime from the beginning and reported daily on the testimonies given in the trials for both Rhodes and Tewksbury. Testimonies were published either verbatim or summarized quite closely. Reporters seldom failed to include subtle comments on the credibility of the witnesses or the strength of either side's case, and most often that commentary was in support of the territory. Two Phoenix newspapers, the *Herald* and the *Express,* furthermore, took the lead in calling for swift justice against both men. The *Arizona Republican,* though somewhat more reserved, was not that far behind.

Tewksbury's case was the last one presented to the grand jury after it had heard all of the other cases on the docket. Before it was presented, Tewksbury's defense attorneys carefully screened jurors about their prejudices in the case. Six jurors who could not swear to their impartiality toward Tewksbury were dismissed, so the court extended the jury selection process to find four more jurors to serve.[13] Finally, by mid-November, after the court interviewed thirty-five potential jurors, the court found enough jurors to make a quorum. After two weeks of hearings, on 2 December 1892, the grand jury then handed down a murder indictment against Ed Tewksbury.[14]

Tewksbury's attorneys had not given up on waging a vigorous defense of their client and tried two different tacks. When Tewksbury was arraigned on 6 December, he was given until 15 December to enter a plea.[15] When that day came, Tewksbury did not answer the charge. Instead, his attorneys filed a plea of abatement, challenging the legality of the court's actions in dismissing part of the regularly constituted grand jury and convening a special grand jury solely to hear Tewksbury's case. This was a violation of the territory's law, they contended. The court scheduled a separate hearing on that motion for April 1893, four months later.[16]

Just days before the court convened to hear the plea of abatement, Baker and Campbell filed a second motion. This time it was to change the venue.[17] The news had not yet been made public, but president-elect Grover Cleveland had appointed one of Tewksbury's defense attorneys, Albert Baker, to serve as chief justice of the Arizona Territorial Supreme Court. Justice Baker would be responsible for the Third District Court, which was the court that was scheduled to hear Tewksbury's case.[18] The Maricopa court convened in April to hear the plea of abatement, but it was almost a moot issue by then. Nonetheless, the court issued a ruling ten days later disagreeing with the merits of the defense's assertion that convening a special grand jury solely to hear Tewksbury's case was illegal.[19] The hearing for a change in venue was next scheduled for another two months out. On 4 July, Tewksbury's case was transferred to the First District Court in Pima County, and Judge Sloan received the appointment to hear the case in Tucson.[20]

THE BATTLE FOR NARRATIVE CONTROL

By this time, Ed Tewksbury had been in jail for seven months. Over that time, another conflict had been growing. If the editorials in Globe's newspaper *Arizona Silver Belt* were any indication, commentaries of the trials grew into a war of words between the *Arizona Silver Belt* and the *Phoenix Herald,* and over the honor of Maricopa County and Gila County. Many in Gila County, where both Globe City and the Pleasant Valley settlement were located, were beginning to develop two firm beliefs about their neighbors in Maricopa County: that Tewksbury was being unfairly denied a swift trial, and that it was impossible for him to receive a fair trial in that county.

Furthermore, the *Arizona Silver Belt* grew critical of the clamor for swift vengeance by Phoenix and Tempe residents and for their attempts to lynch both men while already in the custody of the law. Lynching and attempted murder were felonies, the editors pointed out, yet Maricopa County officials made no effort to arrest any of the mob or Annie Graham, who attempted to assassinate John Rhodes in full view of the court.[21] Its editorials were equally critical of Phoenix newspapers for the way they covered the trial and of the Phoenix courts for dismissing the credibility of respected Pleasant Valley settlers in Tewksbury's preliminary hearing. The *Silver Belt* increasingly argued that only a change of venue would allow Tewksbury to receive a fair hearing.

HABEAS CORPUS

The formal trial of Ed Tewksbury got under way in mid-July 1893, within ten days of its move to Tucson.[22] But court continued the matter until 15 December, most likely to provide time for the Pima County district attorney's office to prepare for the case.[23] When the court once again convened in mid-December, the district courtroom was "crowded to suffocation" with spectators eager to witness what Tucson newspapers hailed as "the most interesting case ever tried in Arizona."[24] The newspapers could not help but note the large number of women filling the seats, eager to catch a glimpse of Ed Tewksbury.

The Tucson press demonstrated an almost prurient fascination with Tewksbury's appearance. His eyes were described as "black" and "restless," "fastened on each witness on the stand." He was unmistakably described as an Indian: "his skin is dark, his hair inky black, and his cheek bones are high and quite prominent," and his so-called half-breed status still warranted particular note (although he was incorrectly described as being half German and Cherokee).[25]

If he noticed the extra attention paid to him, he never let on. Each day he quietly sat by his attorney and listened intently to the testimonies. "Tewksbury is a man of few words," the *Daily Star* wrote of him. "One of those men that say little and think much."[26] He also seemed entirely unconcerned by Annie Graham's attendance. She came and went as she pleased, unrestrained by guards or bailiffs.

Onward the trial proceeded, much as it had in the preliminary and grand jury hearings. Finally, in late December, both sides rested. The defendant was allowed by territorial law to make a statement before the jury began deliberation. Characteristically, Ed declined. After the court gave the jury lengthy instructions, the jury then retired to the upper rooms of the courthouse at 3:30 P.M. to decide the fate of Ed Tewksbury.[27]

The jury deliberation dragged on into the night. Within a few days it would be Christmas Eve, and many spectators began to believe that the jury would be unable to agree on Tewksbury's guilt. When polled after several hours on the first evening, the jury stood eight to four for conviction. The following day at noon, two more jurymen swung over to convict. The jury now stood ten to two for conviction. Then, shortly before 3:00 P.M. the following day, the courtroom began to stir with excitement. The jury had reached a final decision.

When the attorneys for both sides were present in the courtroom, the bailiffs brought Ed Tewksbury in. The jury foreman stood and read the verdict: guilty of first-degree murder.

Tewksbury remained placid. He cast a momentary glance at his attorney as the verdict was read, but no other change came over his face upon hearing his fate. Given the Christmas holiday, the judge set sentencing for the following Thursday, 30 December.[28] The verdict made news from San Francisco to New York City.[29]

The Clerk of the Court in Tucson went to work the next day, which was his usual day off. It was a Saturday morning, but Christmas was in two days, and he wanted to return from the holidays caught up on all the paperwork. It was then that he made a startling discovery: when Ed Tewksbury was first arraigned in Maricopa County, he never filed a plea.[30]

What many saw as a legal trick on the part of the defense was instead a flaw in territorial statutes, and a monumental oversight on the part of the clerk of the Third District Court. Arizona Territory statutes allowed defendants one of three options in entering a plea: guilty, not guilty, or request a demurrer to the indictment to challenge the legality of the proceedings.[31] Tewksbury's attorneys chose the third option, and while the Third District Court adjudicated the plea for abatement, and then the plea to change venue, the clerk of that court failed to keep track of the fact that after the demurrer was settled, Tewksbury had not entered a formal plea to the charge. It was only months later that the clerk of the First District Court discovered the mistake of the Third District Court.

The defense immediately filed a formal motion to arrest judgment, set aside verdict, and open a new trial. The Tucson district attorney desperately searched the laws to prevent the court from declaring a mistrial. In the end, the territory had no other choice but to concede the point. The Third District Court in Maricopa County had failed to follow the law.

RETRIAL

More than a year after he surrendered, Ed Tewksbury remained in a legal limbo. He had been charged and tried, but had yet to know his fate. He would remain in custody for another year longer before he would receive a retrial.

The retrial was scheduled to begin on Wednesday, 2 January 1895, but several witnesses were late in arriving from Tempe, and the case was continued until the following morning.[32] At 10:00 A.M. on Thursday, the courtroom was again crowded with witnesses and spectators as the jury selection took place. It seemed that half the population of Tempe arrived on the morning train, but it was noted that few strange faces were among this large number of witnesses. Nearly all the witnesses had been present at the previous trials.[33]

By the early afternoon, only eleven jurors had been impaneled when the venire was exhausted. Judge Bethune ordered a special venire of twenty-five potential jurors for the following morning and adjourned court until the next day.

After the jury was completed Friday morning, the prosecution began its case at 2:00 P.M.[34] The testimonies of the witnesses at this trial differed little in substance from the testimonies that they had already given—five times before. They had first testified at the coroner's jury, then at the preliminary examination of John Rhodes and then of Ed Tewksbury, then before the grand jury in Phoenix, then at the trial in Tucson that was declared a mistrial. Now at Tewksbury's retrial, they were providing their same testimonies, against the same cross-examinations, for the sixth time. "No wonder that interest in this, the most celebrated murder case ever known in Arizona," quipped the *Phoenix Gazette*, "has waned of late."[35] Although many spectators still arrived early at the courthouse to get a good seat, there was little information that was substantially new for newspapers to report to their readers.

The trial continued into the next week. Both sides gave their closing arguments late in the afternoon on Wednesday, 9 January, and then the case was handed over to the jury.[36] At 9:30 A.M. the next morning, Judge Bethune asked the jury if they had reached a verdict. They had not, and Bethune ordered them to again retire to the jury room. For another day and half the jury deliberated Tewksbury's fate. When they filed into the courtroom at noon on Friday, 11 January, the jury foreman informed Bethune that they were hopelessly deadlocked. Seven stood for acquittal, five for conviction, and there was no budging on either side. Upon hearing this, Bethune had no choice but to discharge the jury.[37]

Tewksbury's attorneys requested that the court finally allow their client out on bail on the strength of his model behavior while in jail. Bethune took the request under advisement. The following month he set bail at $10,000, and described Tewksbury as "one of the best behaved prisoners ever confined in the Pima county jail."[38] Friends and supporters raised that amount on Tewksbury's behalf, and he finally walked out of jail after two and a half years. The following month, Judge Jerry Millay dismissed the case at the suggestion of the county board of supervisors. The case had already cost Maricopa County close to $20,000 in expenses, and there was by that point no confidence that the county could ever secure a conviction for the murder of Tom Graham.[39]

11

"WHAT DREAMS MAY COME"

Ed Tewksbury was still relatively young at thirty-five years old when he walked the streets of Globe a free man in 1895, but the world was a very different place. By then, the nation had acquired territory in the Pacific Ocean as American settlers overthrew the royal family of the Hawaiian Islands.[1] In the Caribbean Islands, the long struggle for independence in Cuba and Puerto Rico was gaining ground. Protests were breaking out throughout the United States in solidarity with Cubans and Puerto Ricans struggling for their independence.[2] Spain was beginning to realize that it would soon need to send thousands more soldiers to crush the rebellion if that once proud empire was to preserve its remaining possessions in the New World.

Still more changes lay ahead, some unimaginable. Santa Clara College professor John J. Montgomery had already launched the first successfully manned glider near San Diego in 1883. Author Victor Loughead, an aviation enthusiast and visionary, purchased the rights to convert Montgomery's glider into a powered aircraft and hired his brother Allan to build it. In so doing, they laid the foundation for what would eventually become the global aerospace technology corporation Lockheed Martin.[3] In 1902, just seven years after Tewksbury's release, an engineer in Detroit by the name of Ransom Olds would begin mass-producing the Oldsmobile.[4] The following year, the Wright brothers would take to the sky in North Carolina.[5] And a few years after that, a newly awarded Ph.D. recipient in Germany named Albert Einstein would publish "On the Electrodynamics of Moving Bodies," in which he would propose the theory of general relativity.[6]

The American economy enjoyed a heady expansion in the decades following the Civil War, fueled mostly by the railroads. As companies built regional and local rail lines to connect with transcontinental lines, not only did those industries benefit that were directly involved in the production of the engines and rail cars, but a host of peripheral industries also underwent rapid growth, from copper-producing mines in Arizona to timber in Oregon and steel in Pennsylvania.

The nation then pitched headlong into the worst economic crisis in its history. The railroad industry had been overbuilt, and expansion ground to a halt. Real estate hit rock bottom. New mines in the West flooded the precious metals market with silver, thereby driving the price of silver downward and ultimately weakening the value of the dollar still tied to a bimetallic standard. And a series of droughts devastated farms in the Midwest, so families once again looked to the West for a better future. But water in the West became so scarce in overgrazed grasslands that sheep and cattle died of thirst by the thousands.

Workers revolted in record numbers as a rash of strikes rolled across the nation. The United Mine Workers union clashed violently with nonstrikers and mine owners in 1894 over wage cuts in Pennsylvania, Ohio, and Illinois. The Pullman Strike that same year shut down much of the nation's transportation system over the summer. And populist Jacob Coxey organized the unemployed from western and central states into the "Army of the Commonweal in Christ" and marched on Washington, D.C., to demand a federal jobs program.[7]

Republicans successfully placed the blame for the depression on Democrats and won landslide victories in the state and congressional elections of 1894. By 1896, the presidential election would be fought over economic issues as Democrat William Jennings Bryan, who favored silver, squared off with Republican William McKinley, who favored gold. The economy would not begin to recover for another few years, but by then, the nation would be engaged in a war with Spain.

The Arizona Territory had changed, too. Territorial governor John Nichol Irwin faced a growing demand for statehood. Unwilling to wait for the U.S. Congress to pass enabling legislation, the territorial legislature authorized a constitutional convention in 1891, and voters passed the constitution created largely by Democratic delegates in December of that year. Congress, however, would not be bullied into action.

Storytellers and local historians of the Pleasant Valley War speculate that it was the news of that violent struggle that prevented Arizona from becoming a state. No territory so out of control, they reasoned, could be admitted to the Union. In actuality, it was Republicans who blocked the admission of another Democratic state into the Union. Gold-standard Republicans found particular fault with the establishment of silver as the legal currency in Arizona's proposed state constitution. The rallying cry of the Republican Party—that Democrats advocated "Rum, Romanism, and Rebellion"—hit the territory especially hard with its large Mexican Catholic population and Democratic leanings.[8] The territory would have to wait another twenty-one years for political winds to change before it was finally admitted to the Union, the last territory within the forty-eight contiguous states to join.

Many in the territory were hit hard by the depression and the drought at the turn of the century. James Stinson, who once owned one of the finest herds in the territory, had to sell off what was left of his livestock and leave the territory with his family in a teetering, secondhand wagon.[9] After years of steady losses from cattle theft, the Aztec Land and Cattle Company hired Burt Mossman in 1898 to clean up employee graft. He immediately fired two-thirds of the cowboys and pursued cattle rustlers with a single-minded focus. By the end of the year, he had placed eleven men behind bars for larceny, and the Aztec Land and Cattle Company finally started to show a profit. But the following winter crippled the company worse than the losses from cattle rustlers.[10] Thousands of Hashknife cattle froze to death during the winter of 1900–1901, and with the price of cattle dropping out the following spring, the Aztec Cattle Company was forced to liquidate its remaining holdings.[11]

Relations with the Apaches continued to remain tense for whites in the territory.[12] No longer were outbreaks the chief concern, but the fear of the loss of property remained very much alive for the homesteaders living near the Apache reservations. "The residents of Pleasant valley and vicinity have been wonderfully forbearing with the Cibicu [*sic*] Indians," the *Arizona Republican* declared at the end of 1895, referring to Apaches on the Fort Apache Reservation, "who have preyed upon the settlers for years, robbing ranches, in the absence of the occupants, and killing citizens' cattle whenever they wanted meat. So flagrant have these depredations grown that the business of stock raising in northern Gila county has been practically ruined."[13]

Bill Voris was one Pleasant Valley resident who was not as "wonderfully forbearing." He filed a complaint against two Apache Indians for cattle theft from the old Middleton ranch, and he rode with the deputy sheriff to the reservation to make the arrest.[14] When the posse found the encampment of "Chief Cooley," curious Apaches began to gather around the four white men who so brazenly rode into their camp. Through an interpreter, the deputy sheriff explained their charge, and the interpreter relayed back what was discussed among the Apaches. Cooley was not present, but Nantangotayz—Cooley's brother—came forward.

Nantangotayz had long distinguished himself as a formidable protector of his people. As a younger man, he had led the raid on the Middleton ranch, but time and age had broadened his view somewhat. He quietly listened to the purpose of the posse's visiting, and sent for one of the accused warriors. The posse placed him under arrest, and, as they began to ride away, one of the posse members called for the group to halt. He thought he recognized the other warrior that they were looking for among the forty or fifty Apaches gathered. At that moment, Loco Jim, a former Indian scout for the U.S. Cavalry, rode up and demanded to know why the warrior was being taken away. The warrior had stolen cattle, they explained, and he was under arrest. Loco Jim refused to allow them to proceed. The drought that had hit the ranchers hard had hit them, too, and his people were hungry.

By that time, the Apaches of the encampment began to gather around the posse again. Nantangotayz walked up to one of the posse horses and reached out to hold its reins, but the horse jerked its head away. He then extended his hand toward Bill Voris's horse. Voris insisted later that Nantangotayz was attempting to pull his rifle out from the saddle scabbard. Voris reached down and grabbed Nantangotayz by the wrist. As the two men began grappling with each other, the arrested warrior discharged a pistol that had been passed to him. Voris panicked. Nantangotayz, the stronger of the two, was getting the better of him, so Voris wrenched a hand free and grabbed the six-shooter at his hip. As he fired, Nantangotayz flung his head backward and the bullet missed. Voris then shoved the pistol down at the old warrior's chest and fired again. Nantangotayz fell forward, on his face, without uttering a word.

All hell broke loose. Apaches on the side of a hill, some sixty yards away, began firing at the posse, and the posse pulled their pistols out and fired back. After their first volley, posse members dug their spurs deep and began a hard run for their lives. With war cries that rent the air, Apaches leaped to their horses and gave chase.

The Apaches knew the trails well, and they took a pass that cut off the escape of the fleeing posse. On seeing that they had been outflanked, the posse members left the trail and urged their horses up the steep mountainside through the trees. It was now dusk, and the posse began to lose sight of each other as they zigzagged through trees and boulders. When Bill Voris regained the trail, he was alone, but he dared not look for his companions. Each man was on his own now. Avoiding the main roads and traveling the back trails, he rode hard through the darkness until he reached the Ellison ranch at about 1:30 in the morning. A few hours later, the other posse members straggled in, bruised and battered from their ride through the forest in the dark, but still alive.[15]

Experience taught the settlers of Pleasant Valley that the worst was not over. Everyone knew that the killing of Nantangotayz was like lighting the fuse to a bundle of dynamite.

The settler grapevine quickly passed news of Apache unrest. Jake Meadows (the younger brother of John V. Meadows, who had earlier served as justice of the peace for Pleasant Valley) arrived in Phoenix with upsetting information. He relayed to the editors of the *Arizona Republican* that the talk in Payson was about the "grewsome" murder of Perley Ellison and his family in retribution for Nantangotayz's murder.[16] The editors ran the story: "His statement is that Perley Ellison and family were murdered by Apaches in lower Pleasant valley nearly a week ago," the journal reported, "Ellison at the time of the murder was on his way with his wife and two babes to the ranch of his father in Cherry Creek valley, there to celebrate Christmas. No particulars were given as to the mode of killing." The editors went on to speculate: "If the killing has been done it must have been by the Indians of Cooley's camp, where Nan-tan-go-tayz was shot, or by John Dazin's band, both of which are at home along Cibicu and Canyon creeks, within a range of forty miles from Pleasant valley. They were much incensed over the killing of their sub-chief[,] and settlers nearby have been expecting reprisals from them." Three days passed until the *Arizona Republican* printed a tentative retraction, based on reports from other residents of Pleasant Valley.[17] After that, the story dropped entirely from printed circulation.

But the "Ellison sensation" was more than just another excited rumor. It illustrates how quickly rumors of violence circulated in the territory, even in parts far removed from the reservation. Residents of Payson, who were a long day's ride from the Apache reservation, were quick to believe and quick to disseminate very specific rumors of Apache retribution. Although the editors of the *Arizona Republican* cautioned readers that the report was unconfirmed, they nonetheless believed it important enough to rush the story to print. Perhaps they were simply trying to keep from being scooped by competitors, which was surely a factor. Ellison wasn't just any settler, after all; he was the brother-in-law of the territorial representative George W. P. Hunt.[18] Yet the published rumor highlights the nature of alarm that existed in the territory, one that depended on the rapid dissemination of information—veracity be damned—and one that was quick to assume the worst of their neighbors, the Apaches.

No uprising came of Nantangotayz's murder. A contingent of soldiers hastened to quell unrest at Cooley's camp, and posse members surrendered themselves to the legal authorities in Globe. Both actions seemed to have prevented Apaches from seeking their own justice, although residents continued to complain about lost or stolen livestock.

As the nation approached the end of the century, territorial governor L. C. Hughes proclaimed that Arizona had finally attained a sufficient population and enough taxable property to entitle the territory to admission as a state in the Union. No longer was the territory riven with the warfare, gun battles, and feuds of the Old West. "Her people have passed through the ordeal of conquering this territory from savagery to civilization," he declared. "Less than a quarter of a century ago the entire territory was in the hands of the Apache Indians. Now after a struggle of many years, in which a large number of pioneers, and many of their families were sacrificed, thousands of families have established homes in our mountains and valleys. In place of the war whoop, the voices of children in the school houses are heard, and on the Sabbath the churches, whose spires point heavenward, resound with the same songs of praise and devotion as ascend from the churches in far-off eastern states."[19]

And much of it was true. The Apaches no longer commanded the field of operations that they once enjoyed. They had, by the end of the century, been relegated to the periphery of the territorial economy. Yet their presence still defined much of the Arizona experience for the Americans who claimed their lands.

THE UNSPOKEN PRICE

Even Ed Tewksbury, that feared frontier "half-breed" from the lawless mountains of the Arizona Territory, who was so resoundingly condemned by the Phoenix newspapers, enjoyed a kind of rehabilitation. As he was out on bail awaiting the court's decision about what to do with his case, he was unanimously elected to a two-year term as precinct constable in Globe City.[20] Within a few years, he married Braulia López, and together with her five children they settled down to raise a family there.[21] Braulia bore Ed two more sons and a daughter.

John Black Blevins, the only survivor of the Blevins massacre in Holbrook, was convicted for attempting to murder Sheriff Owens. The citizens of Holbrook, however, believing that the Blevins family had suffered enough, petitioned the governor to commute his sentence.[22] The governor agreed. Once freed, Blevins settled down to become a respectable citizen. For a time, he hired on with the Aztec Land and Cattle Company as a cook, while also becoming a popular fiddle player for local dances. Eventually, he was hired on as a deputy sheriff in Holbrook, serving in the same office of the sheriff who decimated his family.[23]

John Rhodes also went on to a career in law enforcement, becoming the oldest serving Arizona Ranger. As was so often the case, a man who was good with a gun could be forgiven for many things in the Arizona Territory if he came in from the range.

Fate was not as forgiving for Ed Tewksbury. He would enjoy his newfound career as a lawman for only a short time. While in his forties he suffered a stroke while lifting heavy material at the United Globe Mine.[24] The years of heavy smoking to still his troubled nerves exacted a hefty toll.[25]

Tewksbury's health declined and he eventually contracted pneumonia. Then, in 1904, another stroke took his life. He was only forty-six years old. He left behind a wife and eight children. John Rhodes lived on for another fifteen years, peacefully passing away in January 1919. Mary Ann Tewksbury Rhodes lived to see the nuclear age, passing away in 1950 at the age of 88.

Louis Parker, the last of the Grahams of Pleasant Valley, fled the territory altogether in 1887 after his uncle Johnny died in the shootout with the sheriff and his posse. He left his uncle Tom and put Arizona behind him. On he rode for hundreds of miles before finally stopping in southeastern New Mexico, not far from the border with Mexico. He found a spread near the cattle camps established by Goodnight and Loving on the Pecos River, and he stayed in the cattle and horse trade. In time, he found the kind of prosperity and respectability that escaped the Grahams in Arizona.[26] Within a decade, he married and started a family. His mother Mary—Tom and Johnny Graham's sister—moved out to live with him before she passed in 1912. He survived her by only a few years, though, passing away at the age of fifty in 1921.[27]

Around the turn of the century, J. D. Houck also picked up and put the Rim country behind him. It had been his home for some twenty years, but with his wife and family, he moved south to Cave Creek, Arizona, about thirty-four miles north of Phoenix. He ran a store and continued herding sheep until the end of March 1921. After feeding his chickens one morning, he entered his home and announced that he had taken strychnine. He lay on the bed, asked for his shoes to be removed, and simply said that he was tired of living. The family immediately called the doctor, who tried to counteract the poison, but Houck died a few hours later.[28]

Violence has a way of spiraling outward, sweeping up the lives of people who were not directly involved, but who nonetheless had to live with its consequences. Four years after Al Rose's murder, Lizzie Rose married a Virginian who came to Pleasant Valley with the Ellisons' herd. They had two more children while living in Pleasant Valley but eventually relocated to southern California. Her second husband died early in the Great Depression. Three years later, in 1935, Lizzie decided that she had taken up "arms against a sea of troubles" long enough.[29] She hung herself at seventy-two years of age.[30]

Mary Blevins never recovered from the devastating loss of her husband and sons. She never remarried, and the remainder of her days were filled with melancholy. At her request, a sympathetic attorney acquired from the county the pistol that Andy Cooper had carried—the one that Sam Blevins used in trying to kill Sheriff Owens—and presented it to her. It was, in a way, a memento mori from that awful moment when everything changed. For the rest of her life, it was said that she could be seen walking the streets of Holbrook, "kind of lost or looking for something."[31] And even though John Blevins found respectable work in his later years, he carried a disease that he kept well hidden: he was an alcoholic. It was bad enough that his wife left him, and he eventually died late one night in a single-car accident.[32]

Annie Graham outlived all the men who once warred with one another over property and profit. After John Rhodes's trial, Annie left the territory with her daughter Estella. For a while they stayed with Tom's parents in Iowa and then they moved back in with her parents in Los Angeles. Her time away from the territory seems to have been a much-needed respite from the ordeal of the court trials for Tom's murder. While Ed Tewksbury sat in jail awaiting a retrial, Annie met Thomas Hagan, an Englishman twenty-two years her senior, and they were married in Los Angeles.[33] No longer alone to bear her burdens, she returned to the territory to see Ed Tewksbury's trial through. As difficult as it was for her to endure a repetition of Rhodes's trial, and to witness the second man accused of his murder go free, she seems to have handled the ordeal with greater composure.

But the demons of heartache and suffering continued to hound her. As the nation stumbled toward recovery after the Great War, Hagan died, possibly a victim of the Spanish Flu epidemic. The strain of loss was too great for Annie. Shortly after Hagan's passing, she had to be committed to an insane asylum in South Pasadena.[34] But her breakdown began long before her second husband died. Hagan was enamored with the Old West and would have lived in Arizona, but Annie begged him to get her out.[35] "Mama['s] mental breakdown began years before Hagan died," her daughter Estella recalled. "Persecution. Afraid. Snakes. Curtains down."[36] After she was released, Annie spent the remainder of her days in the care of her children.[37] Finally, in 1961, she passed away in Estella's Phoenix home at the age of ninety-four.[38]

Estella, Tom and Annie Graham's only living daughter, was merely a toddler when her father was murdered. But she grew up devoted to learning all she could about him, and her care of Charlie Duchet in his final years suggests that she held dear those who were close to her father. Duchet, for his part, seems to have become the kind of fatherly figure she never quite had. When he passed away in 1925 of pneumonia, Estella bore all his funeral costs.[39] She married Ed Converse, a wealthy industrialist, and they lived together near Ventura, California. Like her stepfather, Converse passed away in the 1920s, and Estella remarried her neighbor Ben Hill. Together they shared homes in Scottsdale, Arizona, and Santa Paula, California. When she passed away in 1981, she asked to be buried next to Charlie Duchet in the Maricopa County Cemetery, located about a mile from where her father was killed.[40]

———·•·———

It may be tempting to assume that the Indian nations, whose social structures included warrior societies and whose economies depended on raiding, would experience violence and loss differently. Was not the risk of violence and death simply a way of life for them? Quite the opposite. Apaches excelled in the art of stealth *precisely* to avoid the loss of one of their own, and the leader of a raiding party whose decisions resulted in the death of a clan member faced withering censure from the community. Economic activity does not change the human heart, and tragic loss is still tragic for those who experience it.

In 1904, the famed Apache warrior Goyaałé, better known by his *nom de guerre* Geronimo, reflected in his old age on how trauma had profoundly altered the course of his life.[41] He was twenty-eight years old when, in 1855, his clan traveled to Janos, Mexico. The town was thirty miles below the border with New Mexico, and they were led by Mangas Coloradas The Apaches were at peace, as far as they knew, and they traveled into Mexico to trade. While the men were in the village, a force of four hundred soldiers from Sonora attacked the families that remained behind, camped next to the Arroyo San Pedro that ran south of town. It was only when the men began their journey back to camp that they learned of the massacre from a few of the survivors who had escaped.

Following Apache custom, the unarmed men scattered and concealed themselves where they could carefully watch for soldiers. Only after night fell did the men slip silently into camp and bear witness to the bloody aftermath. It was then that Goyaałé, who was not yet known as Geronimo, discovered that his elderly mother, his young wife Alope, and his three small children were among the massacred.

There would be no fires lit in the campsite that night. Stunned and grieving, Goyaałé wandered aimlessly until he found himself at river's edge. He lost all track of time as he stood in front of the flowing waters, his heart cleaved in half, wishing for death himself but still achingly alive. "How long I stood there I do not know," he later recalled. "I stood until all had passed, hardly knowing what I would do. I had no weapons, nor did I hardly wish to fight, neither did I contemplate recovering the bodies of my loved ones. . . . I did not pray, nor did I resolve to do anything in particular, for I had no purpose left."[42]

Numbly he took his place at the emergency council as the survivors debated what to do. When votes were taken to fight or flee, he simply could not vote. Finally, Mangas Coloradas advised the survivors to leave the dead where they lay and return to their homes in Arizona with all haste.[43]

On the long journey back, Goyaałé straggled behind, neither eating nor talking for days. "There was nothing to say," he later recalled. At last he found his voice, enough to reach out to others who had lost their loved ones, but the going was still wrenching. When they finally arrived at their Arizona settlement, the decorations that his wife had strung up in their lodging, along with his children's playthings, were still there.

He burned everything.

Fire quickly erased the material reminders of his happier life, but the pain of extraordinary loss seared his soul for years afterward. No longer would he devote his life to healing, but to devastation and destruction. "I was never again contented," he explained. "Whenever . . . I saw anything to remind me of former happy days, my heart would ache for revenge upon Mexico."[44]

In the unholy baptism of blood that followed, Goyaałé was christened Geronimo from the cries of those who called out in vain to San Jerónimo for deliverance. Untold numbers of Mexico's soldiers and civilians died to satisfy Geronimo's revenge. In time, his lust for the blood of his enemies grew to include attacking American settlements north of the border. By then he had become a coldly efficient killer, and he left behind few survivors. Not even children escaped.

Some fifty years later, at the age of seventy-seven, Geronimo revealed the guilt that he carried.[45] The memories of those blood-splattered days were etched in his brain, and he could not shake them. Nightmares born in profound guilt still caused him to wake in terror. "Often, I would steal up to the homes of the white settlers and kill the parents," he recalled. "In my hatred, I would even take the little ones out of their cradles and toss them in the air. They would like this and gurgle with glee, but when they came down I would catch them on my sharp hunting knife and kill them. Now, I wake up groaning and very sad at night when I remember the helpless little children."[46]

It may be tempting to assume that Indian emotions were different from those of American settlers, and that they experienced the trauma of violence and loss differently. Many American soldiers and settlers told themselves as much in the days when they went to war over Indian land. But the truth was that neither side was that different from the other. At a profound human level, nearly everyone was indelibly affected by frontier violence and warfare, whether they were attackers, the attacked, or merely witnesses to such horrific deeds.

Wounds to the body heal in time. Wounds to the soul sometimes never do.

———

What does victory in this conflict mean when the survivors continued to suffer the costs of battle? To assume that trauma played no part in the inner lives of those who braved the settling of Pleasant Valley would be to deny the profound, if not enduring, emotional impact of constant exposure to violence and death.

Nineteen men in the Pleasant Valley War lost their lives violently, and of those who survived the conflict, some were permanently disabled. Others were stalked by depression, insanity, and suicide.

Five years after John Rhodes passed, Mary Ann disclosed a secret that she had held while both men were alive. In writing to her son, who wanted to know what she could tell him of the violence that had shaped their lives in Pleasant Valley, she disclosed what happened on the morning of 2 August 1892 as Ed and John waited among the fallen cottonwood trees on that dusty road outside the village of Tempe. Revealingly, she framed her comments by telling of her struggle to bury the memories of those traumatic days: "I have never tried to remember any more of or about it than I could help, as it was not a very pleasant memory." After a brief summation of events as she understood them, she concluded with this: "Uncle Ed killed Graham to keep Papa from doing it."[47]

She left no further clue about how she learned this. Did Ed confess his part, or did Mary Ann only surmise that her stepbrother was the one who killed Graham? Either way, her revelation begs contemplation: why would Rhodes, who had no known association with Tom Graham, want to kill him so many years later? Drawing from history, psychology, and literary studies allows for some reasoned speculation.[48]

Love and fear are powerful motivators. Rhodes's only tangible connection to Graham was through the experiences of Ed and Mary Ann. He took no part in the conflicts in Pleasant Valley, but he bore firsthand witness to the toll that the years of traumatic stress exacted from those closest to him: years of living with a wife who struggled to sleep, and when sleep finally came, only to wake up screaming in the night; years of watching his best friend try to calm frayed nerves through chain smoking or drown terrible memories in hard liquor. The only way that they would both finally know peace, the only way to save those closest to him from their demons, was to see that John Tewksbury's murderer finally met justice.

Winslow Constable Joe McKinney, who later served as an Arizona Ranger with Rhodes, suggested that it was Graham himself who spurred Rhodes to action. According to McKinney, while Rhodes was in Tempe tending Bowen's herd, reports began to reach him from several quarters that Tom Graham tasked Charlie Duchet to kill him.[49] Rhodes chose to ignore those rumors until the day he saw Graham pointing him out to Duchet.[50] "Don't you think that was long enough?" Graham called out with a wicked smile. Exactly what Graham meant by that statement is unclear, but Rhodes knew Duchet's terrible reputation and concluded that he had to act quickly to preserve his life. He immediately sent word to Ed to ride with haste to Tempe.

For Ed's part, he seems to have come to terms with the fact that the other man who boasted of killing his brother John still lived.[51] Ed traveled often to the Salt River Valley in the intervening years since the guns went silent in Pleasant Valley, and Graham was living in the open and was well known around town. For five years Ed made no attempt to accost Tom in any fashion.[52] Indeed, when Graham momentarily traveled back to Pleasant Valley to retrieve his herd, he came and went entirely unmolested. This much is clear from the historical record. Tom Graham's perceived threat to Rhodes, however, seemed to be a turning point: if Graham was going to break the truce, Ed would finish the war.

Ed seems to have understood that Rhodes intended to resolve the problem himself, but Ed wanted Rhodes to have no part in it. Ed knew what he had to do to save his friend, who was determined to see the matter through. He was a good man and a better friend, but he was no killer. Neither was Ed, but he could not bear the thought of John going to the gallows and of Mary Ann losing another husband to the Grahams. If anyone was going to kill Tom, it would be him.

Did the two men have one last final argument over Rhodes's intentions as they sat on their horses hidden by the cottonwood trees that early August, when Tom Graham suddenly came riding by?

Extreme circumstances can drive people to see only extreme options before them. Honor and dishonor, right and wrong, are all indulgent moralities when the choices seem limited only to the question of survival or death. So when Graham came into view, driving his team down the dusty road toward Hayden's Mill, it was Ed who spurred his horse first to get out ahead of Rhodes. In so doing, he blocked his friend's aim. It was Ed who shot Graham before Rhodes could get off a clear shot, and it was Ed who stayed at the scene until Rhodes had made good his escape.

Then Ed did something very odd for a man of his experience: he conspicuously galloped through the main streets of Tempe and Mesa City on his flight back to Pleasant Valley. He was a skilled frontiersman and would have known how to take more care in covering his tracks and in traveling the back routes. Did he panic in fleeing the scene and simply take the straightest route home?

Or, was exposure his purpose all along? On his way back home, as people began their day, Ed charged down the middle of the main street of Tempe and Mesa City, wearing a red bandana around the brim of his light-colored hat. Such behavior could have done nothing but provoke notice. And this may have been precisely his aim: by being so highly visible, he drew attention away from Rhodes, who quietly resumed his daily routine.

As he raced back to Pleasant Valley, Ed drew upon all his skills as a frontiersman to make the arduous journey back to his mountain home. Stories circulated in later years that he had stationed fresh horses at strategic locations and pushed each of them to their limits to arrive back in Pleasant Valley on the day that Tom Graham was shot. However he accomplished the feat, it is known that after momentarily purchasing supplies in the early afternoon and attending a dance that evening, he retreated to the solitude of a remote highland base camp among the horses he loved.[53]

He did what had to be done, as he saw it. He had evaded capture. No one had followed him. He was free. John Rhodes, as far as he knew, was safely back at work, also free.

Ed had done the seemingly impossible. Although he would later endure a lynching attempt, two trials, and three years in prison, Ed's alibi ultimately worked because everyone knew that he could not have traveled one hundred miles over mountainous terrain in only a matter of hours. Even experienced horsemen like Charlie Duchet never challenged the fundamental premise of Tewksbury's defense that a man could not cover such a distance within a few hours.

Again, the historical record is silent on what Ed did once he returned to Pleasant Valley, but scholarship on killing allows for some reasoned speculation about how he spent his time. After returning to the routines of his frontier life, Ed came to realize that something was terribly amiss, something that he had not anticipated. The crash of exhilaration and the rip current of guilt surely surprised and confused him that morning as he looked down his rifle barrel at Tom Graham. His quick action had saved his sister's husband and his best friend from the gallows, yes, but it was done in a most ignoble way: taking the life of a man who was unarmed, and whose back was turned. Ed could not shake any of it.

The mountains that had once been his refuge and delight were now stony and silent.[54] They would no longer offer their solace to him no matter where he turned. Alone with his thoughts, Ed found the days long and the nights even longer with the haunting memory of the eyes of his old friend helplessly looking up at him.[55]

Ed had lived to finally see the sword of justice fall upon the last man of a family that had caused his family so much misery. But whatever satisfaction he may have derived from being the last man standing was fleeting. Ordinary men who have taken human life, whether in crime or on the battlefield, report experiencing the same flood of emotions: first comes elation—a primal spike of exhilaration from the ultimate exercise of power and domination over another—and then a crash of terrible guilt that never really leaves the soul. Somewhere in the mind, at times on the conscious level and at other times in the subconscious, every moment of the act of taking human life replays again and again in vivid, excruciating, lurid detail.[56]

And it may have been thus for Ed. Killing Graham may have settled the score, as far as he was concerned, but there was a terrible price to be borne for the rest of his days. When Graham breathed his last, he took his suffering with him. Ed, however, lived daily with the knowledge that he had become a killer. No matter how just the cause may have seemed at the time that drove him to inflict a mortal wound upon Tom Graham, it was Tom's eyes, frightened, wounded, pleading, that stopped Ed in his tracks. For all the negative press excoriating Ed as a cold-blooded killer, the truth was that he could not bring himself to pull the trigger to finish Tom when he had him squarely in his rifle sight.

When George Wilson rode out to tell Ed that the law had finally come looking for him, Ed still had options. He knew the mountains better than most who tried to carve their lives out of the rugged terrain of the Tonto Basin. He still knew how to use the seemingly endless jigsaw of canyons to escape capture, as he and his brothers had done so many times before. Or, he could flee the area altogether, assume an alias, and live his life in the saddle, moving cattle from one place to another as so many men did who ran from the law. In the end, he gave himself up to an unarmed deputy without a word of protest. Why?

What is clear is that Sam Finley waited for four hours at Wilson's ranch house before Ed finally came riding up. That passage of time suggests that Ed's decision may not have come easily. He may have been paralyzed by indecision, common to those who experience traumatic stress. He could neither flee when the moment was at hand to do so, nor could he respond with haste to the summons.

Survivors often speak of a burden that comes from simply surviving, a weight that presses upon the soul that can call into question one's very existence. A tiredness may well have pressed upon Ed as he pondered his next move, one that would not leave. He could flee, yes, but he could not outrun the trauma that shrouded him. He had been worn down by the succession of tragedy that had been his lot. His youth was spent, sacrificed in the fight to preserve his family. That gnaw of loneliness and the guilt of survival probably seemed to grow inexorably over time: his mother had died long ago when he was but a child, and his father had now gone the way of all flesh. All of his brothers were gone, too, cut down by disease or violence in their prime. His sister, stepsister, and their families lived, yes, but only Ed remained of the close-knit sons of James Dunning Tewksbury who once gamboled like young bucks over the untamed wilderness of the Mogollon Rim.

In the end, no bribery or force would be necessary to induce Ed to go back with Finley to face justice. He had cast his die. Destiny now beckoned. He could do nothing else but follow.

"TO ALL THAT FORTUNE, DEATH AND DANGER DARE"[57]

So, I return to the question that animated this retelling of the Pleasant Valley War. Why were settlers who were neighbors, and who had once been friends and coworkers, unable to come together to settle their disagreements before their quarrels turned to murder? No party stepped forward to mediate disagreements, no town meetings were convened to settle growing community divisions, and no overtures to peace were ever made, from any side, when divisions turned deadly. Friendships, once broken, remained irretrievably shattered.

In probing the relationship of law, property, and what he termed "the geography of violence," Nicholas Blomley theorized that violence is inherent to landownership. His reflection on the question derived from the power of the state to enforce the laws relating to the rights of ownership.[58] And indeed, in many ways, the turn to violence in this corner of the Arizona Territory originated with the effort of the federal government to remove a skilled and motivated people from lands they knew and cherished, and restrict their movements to the confines of the reservation. Violence was thus endemic in the effort to lay claim to property still very much under contest for that generation dedicated to preserving the life they had known. Pleasant Valley was a dangerous land to inhabit, and for those who sought to settle it, violence grew out of the imperative to survive.

What drove these settlers to tempt such a fate? They certainly would not have been alone in believing the promises of the military and the territorial government, that the age of the Indian was over. They may well have had supreme confidence in themselves and in their abilities to have dominion over the untamed wilderness. Perhaps they were simply looking for adventure. All motivations were possible, but the historical documentation of who these settlers were and where they came from provides a compelling portrait. They were among the most economically exposed of their day: mostly single men who had few other options before them. They had no resources to purchase land, and only with their sweat and tears—and blood, if it came to it—could they aspire to landownership through occupation and improvement, if they could manage to hold on to the land.

Whatever led them to Pleasant Valley, the price to homestead this insecure land came with hidden costs. The fear of surprise attack by day and the theft of livestock by night prompted settlers to shape their lives around the expectation of sudden violence. Since the moment when settlers of the valley first began to clear the land, the military simply did not have the resources to patrol the sprawling borders of the Apache reservations, and the threat of sudden attack proved unyielding over time. There was no one else those settlers could turn to for help. They were on their own to bear the price of security. That mix of unrelenting danger, among single men with abundant firearms, proved to be a deadly combination when internal disagreements festered.

Pleasant Valley was not the only community in the territory wary of Apache raids, but it was uniquely constrained in ways that other communities were not. To the south of the reservations, the citizens of Globe City could rely on a civil structure, resources, and numbers for defense. The Mormon communities to the north were united by bonds of history, belief, leadership, and marriage, and protected by sufficiently good relations with Indians to moderate the worst perils of attack. Pleasant Valley was small, isolated, unprotected, and perilously accessible to well-motivated warriors.

This was a different kind of place than what exists in the popular imagination about the West. No "cowboy code of honor" guided the actions of the settlers of Pleasant Valley as that community turned upon itself. (Indeed, the very notion of "cowboy honor" would have appeared oxymoronic to many of the period.) To be sure, honor, as Herman applies the term, as the quest for civil society, is a useful framework for understanding the struggles over property in the West during the period. But what was different in this particular settlement was its racialized settlers who fought to preserve their rights to property, while white cowboys strove to undermine the law through quick profit on the black market.[59] And when the conflict ended, the white cowboys who engaged in that economy were killed and driven out. The half-Indian and mixed-marriage settlers won. Listening carefully to frontier voices further reveals that what settlers themselves prized most of all was not a code of honor but survival. No shame threads their narratives when they describe using whatever means they had to live another day. Instead, settlers seemed to pride themselves on their ingenuity and determination in outwitting their circumstances, however inglorious, ugly, or intemperate their actions were. They hid, they lied, they stole, they begged, and they submitted. They exploited weakness and seized advantages. They pounced on the innocent and ran from the powerful. Whatever it took to live another day they did, without hesitation or remorse, because survival was all that really mattered. In this part of the territory, the so-called "code of the West" was a luxury that no one could afford.

The story of the Pleasant Valley War is larger than an exploration of the human imperative to survive, however. This study has sought to understand a more complete story of that conflict by exploring how different actors understood the threat before them; how violence shaped their lives, perceptions, and decisions; and how those who survived the conflict continued to carry the legacy of violence. In curious ways, violence also fashions how the story of the Pleasant Valley War has been remembered. Karl Jacoby referred to the selective remembering of violence, as well as what the erasure of experience does for the present, as a "violence of memory." Popular legends about the Pleasant Valley War have forgotten how the contests over place between Apaches and settlers flowed into contests over space between settlers and, in the process, erased the racial identities of the Tewksburys to fit the conflict into the more familiar tropes of the Old West.

Seeking to more fully understand the ways in which violence shaped the course of the Pleasant Valley War also presents an opportunity to probe a growing area of study in the historiography of the field, the role of trauma in the settling of the West. For good reason, leading works in the field have thus far focused on the experiences of American Indians within the economies fostered by colonial Spain, and the impact of American domination in claiming the American West. This study of the Pleasant Valley War continues in that vein, but my interest is not solely on the experiences of the Indians, or even of the mixed-blood settlers of Pleasant Valley. I aim to understand how violence and trauma became its own dynamic within that conflict, driving the perceptions and actions of neighbors who had been friends to act against their better selves.

LEGENDS OF PLEASANT VALLEY

We look to the act of telling stories to give voice to that which we carry within, and in so doing, seek understanding, clarity, or healing. At other times, the stories we continue to tell are the means of perpetuating misunderstandings and injustice. Whatever our motivations, metaphors serve as tools in that process of telling stories, at times speaking in poetic parcels to larger truths about the human experience, and at other times masking the darker realities that we wish not to remember. The metaphors of "conquest," "settlement," and "pioneer" are stock expressions in the language of westerns, and they convey to most Americans qualities that we admire and wish to emulate: tales of the victor (and occasionally of the noble vanquished); the glories of struggle and triumph; the courage to trail blaze and to press forward at the vanguard of change. Even our national anthem intones: "then conquer we must, when our cause it is just" in its forgotten fourth verse. All these terms imply the successful imposition of will—*con quer*, literally "with will"—over some opposing force or obstacle.

In reflecting on the enduring persistence of the tales of the Old West, Patricia Limerick observed that "to most twentieth-century Americans, the legacy of slavery was serious business, while the legacy of conquest was not. Southern historians successfully fought through the aura of moonlight and magnolias, and established slavery, emancipation, and black/white relations as major issues in American history. . . . Conquest took another route into national memory. In the popular imagination, the reality of conquest dissolved into stereotypes of noble savages and noble pioneers struggling quaintly in the wilderness.[60] To be sure, the struggles over land, livestock, and lives in the West, and the price that was so dearly paid in that struggle, were anything but quaint. Yet, as Limerick reminds us, that reality has been lost in our narratives. Violence in westerns has come to be as commonplace as tumbleweeds.

It is telling that the word "pioneer" came to modern English from the terminology of the Anglo-Norman military. To be a *pëonier* was to be a foot soldier, and the term came to refer to one who was employed in the backbreaking work of the *peon*. What we have yet to incorporate into our narratives of the West are the experiences that some settlers endured as foot soldiers of the West. We are more accustomed to stories of stark fear in the face of violent death from war memoirs and are only now beginning to appreciate the prolonged, if not lifelong, cost of exposure to such conditions. But we expect a more stoic response from those who, in going "out West," marched into battlefields unprepared, at times unknowingly, and largely alone. We expect the saga of suffering and sacrifice to simply go on as another quaint struggle in the wilderness, where the victory of white settlers over the West and its people is assured once the opposition to the imposition of will is overcome. The brilliance of the ending that has become so associated with western movies, where the hero rides into the sunset amid epic orchestration as the production credits roll, is that it allows the story to close without ever having to deal with its messy aftermath.

The story of Pleasant Valley faded from national view, overshadowed by other western conflicts that more neatly fit with what national audiences wanted to see. Decades passed, and even when the myth of the Old West once again resurfaced during the Cold War and became the stuff of national narratives, where good vanquished evil and order triumphed over chaos, the story of Pleasant Valley remained largely forgotten, except in the works of local authors who kept the story alive.

To be sure, some have tried to make that clash align with the epic narratives of the West in print and on screen. It is telling that, in so doing, they have had to invent fictitious new characters to stretch the fit.[61] The Pleasant Valley War as *history,* instead, does not provide such affirmation. Rather, it reveals sides of our national story, if not the human experience, that we would rather not see. Enforcement of the law rested in the hands of men who were underfunded and untrained, and people died as a result. Freedom from governing institutions, which the frontier offered too easily, turned into civil chaos in the fight over property and resources. Progress came at great cost for some, and the rapidly changing economy drove others to madness as they clawed their way to survive. The Indians, although pushed onto reservations, did not fade away from significance, and they continued to shape the history of the West. In the Pleasant Valley War, there is no great story of chivalric behavior, or right and wrong, on which to hang the themes of the western. There were only desperate souls behaving most desperately.

There are stories that we tell about ourselves because we believe them to be true, and there are others we tell because we want them to be true. And sometimes, the truth matters not at all.

In a remote community in the Arizona territory, between the national narratives of Manifest Destiny and the "White Man's Burden," stories mattered as much as truth—maybe more. Amid the pressures that came with progress, the settlers of Pleasant Valley warred with one another over which of their own narratives would dominate about who they were and, perhaps more importantly, who their neighbors were. In the end, neither side won, really. Those who sought profit from seizing market opportunities and exploiting the weaknesses in law enforcement were either dead or driven from Pleasant Valley, and many of those who worked to secure their property and holdings at the point of a gun did not remain in the valley much longer, either.

But their stories remain alive in the tales told around the campfires of Arizona's high country. Fittingly, it is still a contested story. Passions run deep about what happened and who was right when that settlement battled itself. Each generation has written and rewritten the narrative in an attempt to find the truth, or to impose logic and coherence on that historic moment. In the process, Tom Graham's narrative found new champions among subsequent generations. So did Ed Tewksbury's. And their stories, like all good stories worth telling, continue to sprout new tendrils from the fertile soil of the mythic Old West.

NOTES

INTRODUCTION

1. Drusilla Hazelton, who was married to Justice of the Peace (and Gila County Deputy Sheriff) William Burch and sister-in-law to John Gilleland, recalled that "representatives of the law had a one-hundred mile horseback ride from any direction, and expenses for such expeditions were exorbitant . . . the sparsely settled counties in the territory could not afford the expense of too many of these invasions." Drusilla Hazelton, "Hazelton Manuscript, 1977," MS 344, Arizona Historical Society Library and Archives, 92.

2. A variety of authors who wrote about the Pleasant Valley War have expanded the death toll, although each work cites the same number of gunfights, with the same outcomes. The death toll utilized in this study—nineteen—is derived by triangulating between coroner inquests, trial records, newspaper accounts (which regularly devoted much attention to unnatural deaths in the region), and the records of many journal-keeping settlers in the region.

3. Barnes also served as one of the associate editors of the journal.

4. Will C. Barnes, "The Pleasant Valley War of 1887: Its Genesis, History, and Necrology," *Arizona Historical Review* 4, no. 3 (October 1931): 5–34. See also Will C. Barnes, *Arizona Place Names*, revised and enlarged by Byrd H. Granger (Tucson: University of Arizona Press, 1960).

5. Zane Grey, *To the Last Man* (New York: Walter J. Black, 1921), iv.

6. Some well-known claims of combatants in the Pleasant Valley War are not included in this study. Frederick Russell Burnham wrote of his extensive involvement in the conflict in *Scouting on Two Continents* (Doubleday, 1926). While there was an F. R. Burnham working a claim near Tucson in 1882, all other documentation places Burnham in California during the period of the Pleasant Valley War. Further, details provided in his memoir do not align with any known event or individual in that conflict. Tom Horn claimed in *Life of Tom Horn: Government Scout and Interpreter, Written by Himself* (Denver, Colo.: Louthan Book Company, 1904) that he served as a deputy sheriff during the conflict. While Horn was well known to the families in Pleasant Valley, the extant evidence does not place him in any of the events of the Pleasant Valley War, nor does it support his claim to have served as a deputy to any of the sheriffs mentioned.

7. Hazelton, "Hazelton Manuscript," 89. Hazelton recalled that the Daggs flock in Pleasant Valley was under the supervision of Bill Jacobs, and that the Daggses had offered the Tewksbury brothers a band of sheep on shares. Mary Rhodes also shared this view in the 1928 letter that she wrote to her son, which Hazelton copied and transcribed in "Hazelton Manuscript," 75–78, 89.

8. "Territorial," *Arizona Champion*, 12 March 1887, 3. (This and all other articles from territorial newspapers can be accessed from the Library of Congress's *Chronicling America: Historic American Newspapers* website: http://chroniclingamerica.loc.gov.; hereafter these newspapers will be cited by article title [if available], newspaper name, date, and page number.) Joseph T. "Joe" McKinney alleged that Jim Tewksbury stated that the Grahams lived a mile and a half from him, in "Reminiscences (Concluded)," *Arizona Historical Review* 5, no. 3 (October 1932), 202. While this may have been Jim Tewksbury's reckoning, using GPS coordinates from Jinx Pyle's *Pleasant Valley War* (Payson, Ariz.: Git a Rope! Publishing, 2009), 139, shows the John Tewksbury cabin over two miles distant from the Graham cabin. Further, by spring 1887, the two-mile law had been repealed, before John was killed. The *Weekly Arizona Miner*, 10 February 1882, 4, lists John Tewksbury's property at 320 acres.

9. Harold D. Jenkerson's thesis bends two western legends into one: that the Tewksburys discovered the Lost Dutchman's Gold Mine, and that the "feud" between the Grahams and the Tewksburys was over that gold. See Jenkerson, *The Bloody Pleasant Valley Feud*, vols. 1, 2, 3 (Datil, N.Mex.: Alegres Enterprises, 1998), and *Arizona's Bloody Gold: The Pleasant Valley Feud and The Lost Dutchman's Mine* (Datil, N.Mex.: Alegres Enterprises, 1998).

10. Leland J. Hanchett Jr., *Arizona's Graham-Tewksbury Feud* (Cloverdale, Calif.: Hanchett, 1994), viii.

11. Daniel Justin Herman, *Hell on the Range* (New Haven, Conn.: Yale University Press, 2010), xvi.

12. Ibid., xvii.

13. Ned Blackhawk, *Violence over the Land* (Cambridge, Mass.: Harvard University Press, 2006), 8, 26. In *Shadows at Dawn* (New York: Penguin Random House, 2009), 235, Karl Jacoby discusses understandable sensitivities in how Apache activities have been historically discussed in Spanish-speaking and English-speaking communities, which have portrayed Apaches as "wild" and "savage." That is certainly not my intention in this study. Part of what made Apaches so formidable is that they carefully trained for, planned, organized, oversaw, and executed forays to acquire food or goods. Thus, I employ adjectives such as "skilled" and "motivated" to suggest the impressive level of intentionality and expertise behind Apache effort.

14. The Fort Apache Reservation was the first Apache reservation, established in 1870 by the Military Division of the Pacific, which was then converted to the White Mountain Indian Reservation by the Department of the Interior in 1871. The Coyotero and Chilion Apaches were first assigned there, and they then became the White Mountain Apache Tribe. The reservation is currently known as the Fort Apache Indian Reservation, although it is also commonly known as the White Mountain Apache Indian Reservation. In 1872, the San Carlos Apache Indian Reservation was created, which is south of the Fort Apache Reservation, and in time, as various reservations were consolidated, San Carlos became the home of several bands: the Aravaipa, Chiricahua, Eastern White Mountain Apache, Jicarilla, Lipan, Mescalero, Pinal Apache, Pinal Coyotero, Pinaleño, San Carlos, Southern Tonto Apache, Tonto Apache, White Mountain, and Yavapai Apaches. See U.S. President, *Executive Orders Relating to Indian Reserves, from May 14, 1855, to July 1, 1902* (Washington,

D.C.: Government Printing Office, 1902). Jacoby provides an excellent overview of the fluidity and complexities of Apache social organization in *Shadows at Dawn*, 142–180, as do Lori Davisson and Edgar Perry in *Dispatches from the Fort Apache Scout* (Tucson: University of Arizona Press, 2016), xv, 19, 45. Since the focus of this study is on understanding the dynamics between the settlers of Pleasant Valley, however, I generally do not draw distinctions between Apache clans, nations, or reservation homes, unless the nuances of Apache identity are critical to understanding particular events. Territorial records tended to collapse Apaches together, and thus these sources do not often allow for greater nuance in establishing the identity of Apache raiding parties. For the most part, the Apaches who engaged the settlers of Pleasant Valley may have been Western Apache, although there is suggestive evidence that some Chiricahua Apache may have also participated in raids through the northern Arizona settlements.

15. The 1887 "Territory of Arizona" map, published by the Department of the Interior General Land Office, places the western boundary of the White Mountain Apache Indian Reservation near where it is today, at lat 34°10'36"N, long 110°78'28"W. My calculation of the distance between the reservation and Pleasant Valley is based on a straight line between the current western boundary and roughly the "center" of Young, Arizona, where the Young Public Library presently sits. Certainly, other ranches in Pleasant Valley were closer to the reservation, and other ranches were farther. Hiking the winding canyons that lay between Cherry Creek and the reservation makes the distance closer to eighteen miles, but Apaches preferred the camouflage of the mountains and tended to stay off common paths. The route they took to Pleasant Valley was probably shorter than following the creek beds.

16. Davisson and Perry, in *Dispatches from the Fort Apache Scout*, 26, suggest that Apaches' raids into Mexico were military in nature rather than economic, designed to slow the spread of Spanish expansion by making it costly.

17. Jacoby offers an excellent discussion of Apache thought processes and motivations when it came to raiding and warfare in *Shadows at Dawn*.

18. Jacoby, *Shadows at Dawn*, 3.

19. Continuous traumatic stress differs from posttraumatic stress in that the latter describes an event that is in the past, whereas the former seeks to recognize and understand the effects of conditions in which violence and the fear of violence are sustained over long periods or are seemingly never ending. See Gillian Eagle and Debra Kaminer, "Continuous Traumatic Stress: Expanding the Lexicon of Traumatic Stress," *Peace and Conflict: Journal of Peace Psychology* 19, no. 2 (May 2013): 85–99, and Garth Stevens et al., "Continuous Traumatic Stress: Conceptual Conversations in Contexts of Global Conflict, Violence and Trauma," *Peace and Conflict: Journal of Peace Psychology* 19, no. 2 (May 2013): 75–84.

20. Abraham Lincoln, "First Inaugural Address, Final Version," March 1861, The Lincoln Studies Center, Knox College, *Abraham Lincoln Papers at the Library of Congress*, http://memory.loc.gov/cgi-bin/query/r?ammem/mal:@field(DOCID+@lit(d0773800)) (accessed 27 Dec. 2017).

21. This estimate is based on the Great Register of Yavapai County, 24 September 1886, 20–21. Thirty men are listed, so, including wives and children, the aggregate population was perhaps closer to forty-five individuals. Since most of the men were single and bunked

together, the actual number of households was likely smaller than the aggregate. *Arizona, Voter Registrations, 1866–1955* (database on-line), Ancestry.com (accessed 1 Jan. 2018); original data from Great Registers (of Voters), Arizona History and Archives Division, Phoenix, Arizona.

CHAPTER 1. TERROR ON THE RANGE

1. Jacoby notes in *Shadows at Dawn*, 288, that alternative spellings of the Apaches' name for themselves, Ndee, Indee, or Nnēē, depend upon dialect.

2. John C. Cremony, *Life among the Apaches, 1849–1864* (San Francisco: A. Roman and Company, 1868), 43–44, 174–175, 180, 189–190; Jacoby, *Shadows at Dawn*, 149–50.

3. Apaches often used the dark to better position themselves for the fight the following day. Jacoby, *Shadows at Dawn*, 149–50.

4. See Ray Wheeler, "The Colorado Plateau Region," in *Wilderness at the Edge: A Citizen Proposal to Protect Utah's Canyons and Deserts* (Salt Lake City: Utah Wilderness Coalition, 1990), 97–100; John J. W. Rogers and M. Santosh, *Continents and Supercontinents* (New York: Oxford University Press, 2004), 86–87; Ellen Wohl, *Islands of Grass* (Denver: University Press of Colorado, 2009), 18–19, 23; Theodore Steinberg, *Down to Earth: Nature's Role in American History* (New York: Oxford University Press, 2002), 4–6; Donald L. Baars, *Red Rock Country: The Colorado Plateau, A Geologic History* (Albuquerque: University of New Mexico Press, 1983), 204–208.

5. U.S. Geological Survey, "Geologic Provinces of the United States: Colorado Plateau Province," http://geomaps.wr.usgs.gov/parks/province/coloplat.html (accessed 29 Dec. 2012).

6. See Marisa Repasch, Karl Karlstrom, Matt Heizler, and Mark Pecha, "Birth and Evolution of the Rio Grande Fluvial System in the Past 8 Ma: Progressive Downward Integration and the Influence of Tectonics, Volcanism, and Climate," *Earth-Science Reviews* 168 (May 2017), 113–64; James W. Byrkit, "Geographical Focal Areas of the Southwest," *Land, Sky, and People: The Southwest Defined* 34, no. 3 (Autumn 1992), http://jsw.library.arizona. edu/3403/geog.html (accessed 6 Sept. 2017); and Richard Hereford, Robert H. Webb, and Scott Graham, "Precipitation History of the Colorado Plateau Region, 1900–2000," U.S. Geological Survey Fact Sheet 119–02, http://pubs.usgs.gov/fs/2002/fs119–02/ (accessed 29 Dec. 2012).

7. See C. David Whiteman, *Mountain Meteorology: Fundamentals and Applications* (New York: Oxford University Press, 2000), 21–23.

8. See Northern Arizona University Ecological Restoration Institute, "Apache-Sitgreaves National Forest," http://www.eri.nau.edu/en/arizona/apache-sitgreaves-national-forest (accessed 30 May 2013); and Arizona Game and Fish Department, *Hunting & Fishing*, "Big Game Species," https://www.azgfd.com/hunting/species/biggame; ibid., "Furbearer Species," https://www.azgfd.com/hunting/species/furbearer; ibid., "Predator Species," http://www.azgfd.gov/h_f/predators_species.shtml; ibid., "Small Game Species," https:// www.azgfd.com/hunting/species/smallgame; Town of Payson, Parks, Recreation and Tourism Department, *Payson, Arizona's Cool Mountain Town*, "Hunting," http://www. paysonrimcountry.com/hunting (accessed 14 Dec. 2017); Arizona Game and Fish Department, http://www.azgfd.gov/h_f/hunting_fishing.shtml (accessed 30 May 2013); and "Visit

the 'Rim Country,'" https://www.paysonrimcountry.com/mountain-recreation/tabid/59/ Default.aspx (accessed 29 Dec. 2012).

9. "From the White Mountain Reservation," *Arizona Weekly Miner*, 19 March 1875, Image 2, *Chronicling America: Historic American Newspapers*, Library of Congress, https://chroniclingamerica.loc.gov/lccn/sn82014898/1875-03-19/ed-1/seq-2/ (accessed 18 Dec. 2017).

10. Thomas Edwin Farish, *History of Arizona* (Phoenix, Ariz.: Filmer Brothers Electrotype Company 1925), 2:241–47; 294, 297–98.

11. Jerry Stewart and Luann Maner, "History of Snowflake, AZ," www.jerrystewart.org/snowflakeaz/history.html (accessed 29 May 2013).

12. *Apache County Centennial Book* (St. Johns, Ariz.: Apache County, 1979), 3, 12, 46; Wayne Davis, *St. Johns Arizona Stake: Centennial, 1887–July 23, 1987* (St. Johns, Ariz.: The Church of Jesus Christ of Latter-day Saints, Arizona Stake, 1987), 57.

13. Davis, *St. Johns Arizona Stake*, 29–32.

14. Frontiersman Seth Kinman, who was among the first whites to settle near Eureka in Humboldt County, California, noted in his memoir, *Seth Kinman's Manuscript and Scrapbook* (Ferndale, Calif.: Ferndale Museum, 2010), 29, that "Jim" Tewksbury married a woman from the Bear River Clan. The Bear River Clan may have been ancestors of the Bear River Band of the Rohnerville Rancheria that presently resides in the area. See Dolan H. Eargle Jr., *Native California: An Introductory Guide to the Original Peoples from Earliest to Modern Times* (San Francisco: Trees Company Press, 2000), 111.

15. Other stories describe James Dunning Tewksbury's Indian wife as Shoshone or Hupa, but Kinman offers the clearest hope for establishing her tribal identity, given his association with Tewksbury. There is no evidence to support the speculation among settlers of Pleasant Valley that the oldest Tewksbury brothers were not of the same Indian mother.

16. Sherburne Friend Cook, *The Conflict between the California Indian and White Civilization* (Berkeley: University of California Press, 1976); William F. Strobridge, *Regulars in the Redwoods: The U.S. Army in Northern California, 1852–1861* (Spokane, Wash.: Arthur H. Clarke Company, 1994); Gary Scharnhorst, *Bret Harte: Opening the American Literary West* (Norman: University of Oklahoma Press, 2000); William B. Secrest, *When the Great Spirit Died: The Destruction of the California Indians, 1850–1860* (Fresno, Calif.: Quill Driver Books, 2002).

17. The 1870 U.S. Census shows Jas. D. Tewksbury living in Pacific, Humboldt County, with his children, but the 1875 Nevada State Census lists J. D. Tewksbury only with fourteen-year-old F[rancis] Tewksbury, and twelve-year-old J[ames] in Elko County, raising stock. See *Report Booklet Published for the State in 1876* (Carson City, Nev.: State Publishing Office, 1876); *Nevada State Census, 1875* (database online), Ancestry.com (accessed 17 Jan. 2018).

18. Tewksbury is alternatively spelled Tuxbury, Tewksberry, Tewesbury, and Tewsherry in territorial documents. Crigler's name also appears as Crigger. The Phoenix newspaper *Territorial Expositor*, November 1879, 2, lists the marriage date as 4 November, with the reception taking place at the schoolhouse in Tempe.

19. Genealogical researchers are not entirely clear about the children born to Lydia Tewksbury's first two marriages, and the documentary trail is scant. Some family trees list the children born to Lydia and Rufus Crigler as Dolph and Mary Ann, whereas others

list only Mary Ann. The names of the children born to Lydia and David Shultes are also somewhat contested. Some family trees list Anna or Hannah Shultes, Thomas Andrew Shultes or Shoultes, and Gustavus Adolphus Shultes. Some family trees indicate that the name of the youngest Shultes child was Gustane.

20. *Arizona, County Marriage Records, 1865–1972* (database on-line), Ancestry.com (accessed 1 Jan. 2018); original data from County Marriage Records, Arizona State Library, Archives, and Public Records.

21. Northern Gila County Historical Society, *Rim Country History Illustrated*, 70.

22. Joe Boyer testified that he had known Ed Tewksbury since 1878 in Testimony of Joseph Boyer, *Territory of Arizona vs. Ed Tewksbury* (1892), 583–84, University of Arizona Main Library, Special Collections. Hazelton, in "Hazelton Manuscript," 79, cites Walter Tewksbury as saying that the four oldest brothers were in Pleasant Valley as early as 1877. Barnes, in *Arizona Place Names*, 112–18, recorded that John Tewksbury arrived in Globe in 1879.

23. According to Barnes (*Arizona Place Names*, 112–18), Albert Rose built a stockade in 1877 and was thus the first settler, but the 1880 census shows Al Rose farming in Wheatfields, north of Globe. Edvard Roos from Sweden, also known as Edward Rose, appears to have been the first to take up residence in the valley. However, Al Sieber's 1889 deposition in support of Garret "Bob" Sixby's claim for Indian depredations states that he first met the Sixby brothers in 1877 when they asked directions to Pleasant Valley. See deposition transcribed by Richard Pierce, PDF in possession of the author. Sixby is alternatively spelled Sigsby or Sixsby. Garrat is alternatively spelled Garret.

24. Outbreaks that swept through Pleasant Valley came from both the San Carlos and the Fort Apache Indian Reservations.

25. Regarding the Tewksburys, Barnes also stated that John Tewksbury arrived in Globe in 1879 and returned shortly thereafter to California for his brothers and livestock, after which he settled in Pleasant Valley. For Al Rose's residence in 1880, see *Tenth Census of the United States, 1880*, Schedule 1, Inhabitants of Wheatfields in the County of Maricopa, State of Arizona, 19 June 1880, Enumeration District 19, page 14 (NARA microfilm publication T9, 1,454 rolls), Records of the Bureau of the Census, Record Group 29, National Archives, Washington, D.C. See also Hazelton, "Hazelton Manuscript," 68.

26. Estimated on twelve square miles of land. Four households are listed for Pleasant Valley in Schedule 1, Enumeration District 24, County of Yavapai, Territory of Arizona, June 1880, *1880 U.S. Census* (database on-line), Ancestry.com (accessed 28 Dec. 2017); original data from *Tenth Census of the United States, 1880* (NARA microfilm publication T9, 1,454 rolls), Records of the Bureau of the Census, Record Group 29, National Archives, Washington, D.C.

27. *Weekly Phoenix Herald*, "From Saturday's Daily," 3 April 1884, 3, https://chronicling-america.loc.gov/lccn/sn83025459/1884-04-03/ed-1/seq-3 (accessed 18 Dec. 2017). Geographically speaking, the Tonto Basin is defined today as the region lower than where Pleasant Valley resides, south of the Sierra Ancha Mountains and incorporating parts of the Salt River and Roosevelt Lake. See Charles A. Ferguson, Steven J. Skotnicki, and Wyatt G. Gilbert, "Geologic Map of the Tonto Basin, 7.5′ Quadrangle, Gila and Maricopa Counties, Arizona," *Arizona Geological Survey Open-File Report 98-16* (August 1998), 1, 7, http://repository.azgs.az.gov/sites/default/files/dlio/files/2010/u14/ofr-98-16.pdf (accessed 14 Dec.

2017). Historically, however, and still in popular usage, the term "Tonto Basin" refers to areas that include the transition zone starting at the Mogollon Rim, south to the Sierra Ancha and Mazatzal Mountains, where Pleasant Valley is found. For this reason, the Pleasant Valley War was also referred to as the Tonto Basin War.

28. Katherine Benton-Cohen found a similar distribution in 1880 Tombstone, in *Borderline Americans* (Cambridge, Mass.: Harvard University Press, 2009), 51.

29. G. O. "Bob" Sixby letter to "Dear Sister," 19 December 1887, transcribed by Cheryl Sigsbee. PDF copy in possession of the author. It is unclear why Garrat was called "Bob."

30. The 1851 Census, St. Armand West, Missisquoi County, Canada East (Quebec), Schedule A, Roll C 1127, page 17, line 32, lists Canada as the birthplace of the Sixbys. See also page 61, line 3 of that census. Settlers refer to the elder Sixby as Bob Sigsby, but federal census and territorial tax records record him as Garret, or Garrat, Sixby living with Charles Sixby in Pleasant Valley. See also Great Register of Yavapai County #2429, page 36, *Arizona, Voter Registrations, 1866–1955* (database on-line), Ancestry.com (accessed 13 March 2017); original data from Great Registers (of Voters), Arizona History and Archives Division, Phoenix, Arizona. For Al Rose's service, see *U.S. Civil War Draft Registrations Records, 1863–1865* (database on-line), Ancestry.com (accessed 13 March 2017); original data from *Consolidated Lists of Civil War Draft Registrations, 1863–1865*, NM-65, entry 172, 620 volumes (NAI: 4213514), Records of the Provost Marshal General's Bureau (Civil War), Record Group 110, National Archives, Washington, D.C.; *U.S. Civil War Pension Index: General Index to Pension Files, 1861–1934* (database on-line), Ancestry.com (accessed 13 March 2017); original data from *General Index to Pension Files, 1861–1934* (T288, 546 rolls), National Archives and Records Administration, Washington, D.C. See also Company "E" 17th Illinois Infantry, http://civilwar.illinoisgenweb.org/r050/017-e-in.html (accessed 13 March 2017). In 1883, Rose married Elizabeth Marie "Lizzie" Koehn in Globe, and Francis Winfred "Frank" Rose was born in 1884. Frank Rose died in California, and the California Death Index lists his mother's maiden name as Roehn. "Delayed Justice," *Arizona Silver Belt*, 16 June 1888, 3, mentions two Rose children, although some family trees at Ancestry.com only list Francis Winnifred "Frank" Rose as the child of Al and Lizzie Rose. It is not clear if Lizzie Rose lived in Pleasant Valley at the time of Frank's birth.

31. Little is known about Louis O. Houdon. Jacob Lauffer is most frequently referred to as Jake, but also as Jack, and Lauffer is also spelled Lauffler and Lawford in territorial records. For Lauffer, see *Arizona, Voter Registrations, 1866–1955*, Great Register of Gila County, Arizona, #263 Lauffer, Jacob B., *Arizona, Voter Registrations, 1866–1955* (database on-line), Ancestry.com; original data from Great Registers (of Voters), Arizona History and Archives Division, Phoenix, Arizona. Joseph Boyer's information is found at Census Enumeration of Maricopa County, 1882, #164, *Territory of Arizona Census Records, 1876, 1882* (database on-line), Ancestry.com (accessed 17 Jan. 2018); original data from Territorial Census Records, Arizona History and Archives Division, Phoenix, Arizona; and Schedule 1: "Inhabitants in Pleasant Valley, in the County of Yavapai, in Territory of Arizona, 1 June 1880," 436, 1880 U.S. Federal Census (database on-line), Ancestry.com (accessed 17 Jan. 2018); original data from *Tenth Census of the United States, 1880* (NARA microfilm publication T9, 1,454 rolls), Records of the Bureau of the Census, Record Group 29, National Archives, Washington, D.C.

32. Lydia Tewksbury's two children with David Shultes, still living at home in Pleasant Valley in 1887, were Thomas Shultes, born in 1874, and Adolphus Gustavus Shultes, born in 1875. Her two children with James Dunning Tewksbury were Parker, born in 1881, and Walter, born in 1884. Mary Ann Tewksbury, John's wife, had one child: Bertha, born in 1884 (John Tewksbury Jr. was born one month after his father's murder, in 1887). Lizzie Rose had two children: Francis Winifred Rose, born in 1884, and Norman Allen Rose, born in 1885.

33. Jayne Peace Pyle, *Women of the Pleasant Valley War* (Payson, Ariz.: Git a Rope! Publishing, 2014), 32. Pyle calls the child Hannah.

34. Elizabeth Marie "Lizzie" Koehn married Albert Rose at Globe in 1883. Lizzie Rose's parents may have been Jews who immigrated from Germany.

35. Pyle, *Women of the Pleasant Valley War*, 20.

36. Jayne Peace Pyle, in *Women of the Pleasant Valley War*, 76–78, speculates that the Crouches knew the Tewksburys before moving to Pleasant Valley.

37. Amanda Conner arrived with her husband Samuel J. Conner and six children in 1885. They lived either on Cherry Creek or on Rose Creek, according to Jayne Peace Pyle in *Women of the Pleasant Valley War*, 157, but the Great Register for Gila County shows the Conners living in Grapevine, Arizona, which is farther south on Cherry Creek, near Roosevelt Lake, in October of 1886 and 1888. It is perhaps twenty-six miles away from Pleasant Valley. Lillie Chardon Gentry arrived in Pleasant Valley in 1886, a few years after her husband Martin had already established himself there as a sheepherder (and took an Apache wife). His ranch was near the Ellison's Q ranch, about six miles from Pleasant Valley as the crow flies, but closer to seventeen miles weaving through the canyons that lay between the Q Ranch and the Pleasant Valley settlement. Jayne Peace Pyle speculates in *Women of the Pleasant Valley War*, 161, that Molly Perkins arrived in 1886. Records on the Perkinses are scant, but the Great Register of Maricopa County, Arizona, shows Charles Perkins living in Phoenix in October 1886, so their arrival was perhaps later. They had no children from the union.

38. It is possible that this core group included Mary "Mollie" Perkins, since she lived within the heart of the settlement, but her arrival was perhaps as late as the spring of 1887, and the Perkinses appear to have left the valley sometime after the year ended. Further, the Perkinses had no children, so she may not have participated in the kind of networking that is often found among families with children.

39. Other cabins and barns from the period still exist in Young, Arizona, in various states.

40. If John Tewksbury built the cabin, it was before his death in 1887, and it is likely that he would have had the help of at least his brothers Ed and Jim, if not other Pleasant Valley neighbors. According to the Pioneer Living History Museum, the "Flying V" cabin was later used by George Newton as a line rider's cabin.

41. These holes are also referred to as "loopholes"; see Works Project Administration, *Arizona: A State Guide* (New York: Hastings House, 1940), 460. Other mention of gun ports built into cabin walls can be found at "Saucy Redskins," *Weekly Arizona Miner*, 10 December 1870, 3; "The Apache War," 28 October 1871, 3; "More Apache Murders," 12 October 1872, 2; "Brave and Cool Men," 7 May 1882, 3—all three in the *Arizona Citizen*; and "Held Up Again," *Clifton Clarion*, 17 August 1887, 2. See also Vance Wampler, *Arizona* (Phoenix, Ariz.: Quail Run Publications, 1984), 196. The Ellisons built a fort on their property, as

mentioned in Pyle, *Women of the Pleasant Valley War*, 107–8.

42. Natale A. Zappia, in *Traders and Raiders* (Chapel Hill: University of North Carolina Press. 2014), explores the people who lived along the Colorado River. Ann Hyde, in *Empires, Nations, and Families* (Lincoln: University of Nebraska Press, 2011), focuses more on the nineteenth century.

43. Joshua Watts, in his Ph.D. dissertation, "The Organization and Evolution of the Hohokam Economy Agent-Based Modeling of Exchange in the Phoenix Basin, Arizona, A.D. 200–1450" (Arizona State University, 2013), explores various theories about trade, focusing on the Hohokam economy in central Arizona.

44. James F. Brooks also refers to this as the "slave and livestock trade" in *Captives and Cousins* (Chapel Hill: University of North Carolina Press, 2002), 214. See also H. Henrietta Stockel, *Salvation through Slavery* (Albuquerque: University of New Mexico Press, 2008), 82–83.

45. Brooks, *Captives and Cousins*, 214–216.

46. Stockel, *Salvation through Slavery*, 82nn43, 44.

47. Håmålåinen, *The Comanche Empire*, 23–26.

48. Blackhawk, *Violence over the Land*, 18–20, 70–80, 88–89, 140–44; and Timothy Braatz, *Surviving Conquest: A History of the Yavapai Peoples* (Lincoln: University of Nebraska Press, 2003), 63–66.

49. Carlos R. Herrera, *Juan Bautista de Anza* (Norman: University of Oklahoma Press, 2015), 19, 29. See also David J. Weber, *The Spanish Frontier in North America* (New Haven, Conn.: Yale University Press, 1992), 206.

50. Blackhawk's *Violence over the Land* discusses the Ute, Southern Paiute, and Navajo trade during this period, and Pekka Håmålåinen's *Comanche Empire* focuses on the activities of the Comanches in New Mexico.

51. Dan L. Thrapp, *The Conquest of Apacheria* (Norman: University of Oklahoma Press, 1979), 7, and Hubert Howe Bancroft and Henry Lebbeus Oak, *History of Arizona and New Mexico* (Albuquerque, N.Mex.: Horn and Wallace, 1962), 170.

52. See Stockel, *Salvation through Slavery*, 106n94, 82n42.

53. Weber, *The Spanish Frontier in North America*, 206, 209. Also Robert Brown, *The Races of Mankind* (London: Cassell, Peter, and Galpin, 1873–76), 1:181, and Herrera, *Juan Bautista de Anza*, 29–30.

54. Jacoby, *Shadows at Dawn*, 157–58.

55. Stockel, *Salvation through Slavery*, 43–44. Also Blackhawk, *Violence over the Land*, 28–29.

56. Stockel, *Salvation through Slavery*, 86, and Thrapp, *Conquest of Apacheria*, 8. Also see Wampler, *Arizona*, 182, and Davisson and Perry, *Dispatches from the Fort Apache Scout*, 26, 29, 116.

57. "Joseph Fish Manuscript," 3, State of Arizona Department of Library and Archives, State Archives.

58. "Treaty with the Republic of Mexico, Feb. 2, 1848," *A Century of Lawmaking for a New Nation: U.S. Congressional Documents and Debates, 1774–1875*, 930–32, http://memory.loc.gov/cgi-bin/ampage?collId=llsl&fileName=009/llsl009.db&recNum=983 (accessed 19 Dec. 2017).

59. Thrapp, *Conquest of Apacheria*, 8n5.

60. James Calhoun, Indian Agent, Santa Fe, New Mexico, to Colonel W. Medill, Commissioner of Indian Affairs, Washington, D.C., 15 October 1849, in Thomas Butler King, *Report in Relation to California and New Mexico, in Response to Senate Resolution of Jan. 17, 1850*, 213–14, *Nineteenth Century Collections Online*, http://tinyurl.galegroup.com/tinyurl/3NB7WX (accessed 9 May 2016).

61. Wilson likely used "Ute" somewhat generically, since Southern Paiutes were also active in the region. See Blackhawk, *Violence over the Land*, 119–75.

62. John Wilson, Indian Agent at the Salt Lake, California, to the Honorable Thomas Ewing, Secretary of the Department of the Interior, 4 September 1849, in Thomas Butler King, *Report in Relation to California and New Mexico, in Response to Senate Resolution of Jan. 17, 1870*, 108, *Nineteenth Century Collections Online*, http://tinyurl.galegroup.com/tinyurl/3NB7WX (accessed Dec. 28, 2017).

63. Jacoby, *Shadows at Dawn*, 149.

64. *Arizona Silver Belt*, "Correspondence, Wilcox, A.T. Sep. 3, 1883," 8 September 1883, 3, http://memory.loc.gov/cgi-bin/ampage?collId=llsl&fileName=009/lls1009.db&recNum=983 (accessed 18 Dec. 2017).

65. Reprinted in *Arizona Weekly Citizen* (Tucson), 4 March 1883, 4. See also *Arizona Weekly Citizen*, 18 February 18, 1883, 3, and 8 April 1883, 3.

66. Reprinted in "Prescott Journal: 'The Wounded Bird Flutters,'" *St. Johns Herald*, 30 July 1885, 1. See also Emerson Oliver Stratton, *Pioneering in Arizona* (Tucson: Arizona Pioneers' Historical Society, 1964), 52–53, and William Henry Bishop, *Old Mexico and Her Lost Provinces; A Journey in Mexico, Southern California, and Arizona, by way of Cuba* (New York: Harper and Brothers, 1887), 491.

67. Pyle, *Women of the Pleasant Valley War*, 130.

68. Alternatively spelled in documents as Nakaidoklini or Nock-ay-det-klinne.

69. Benton-Cohen explores the Apaches Wars, from Nakaaidoklini to Geronimo, in *Borderline Americans*, 63–71.

70. Jerome Greene, *Indian War Veterans* (Havertown, Pa.: Savas Beatie, 2007), 326–31, and Odie B. Faulk, *The Geronimo Campaign* (New York: Oxford University Press, 1993), 22–25.

71. Faulk, *The Geronimo Campaign*, 24. See also Aleshire, "Edge of Tragedy," and Pyle and Pyle, "Nock-ay-det-klinne and the 'Apache Uprising,'" http://www.paysonroundup.com/nock-ay-det-klinne-and-the-apache-uprising/article_c8293238-06b0-5812-8849-5f3021fc7498.html. Accounts of the Apache attack on Pleasant Valley are found in "Telegraph," *Arizona Weekly Citizen*, 16 July 1882, 1; "Miscellaneous Telegrams," *Phoenix Herald*, 21 July 1882, 1; "Renegades Raked!" ibid., 2; *Arizona Sentinel*, 22 July 1882, 2; "The Indian Outbreak," *Tombstone Weekly Epitaph*, 22 July 1882, 1; "Raiding in Pleasant Valley," ibid., 2; "An Indian Raid," ibid., 29 July 1882, 4; and *Arizona Weekly Citizen*, 30 July 1882, 1.

72. Rebecca Robbins Raines, *Getting the Message Through: A Branch History of the U.S. Army Signal Corps* (Washington, D.C.: Center of Military History, United States Army, 1996), 52.

73. The wording is not altogether clear in the earliest published report of the attack,

dated 8 September 1881, but it appears to place the attack on Friday, 30 August 1881, in "From Globe," *Arizona Weekly Citizen*, 11 September 1881, 3. Based on the coordinates of the ranch location provided by the Arizona Pioneer and Cemetery Research Project and the western boundary of the Fort Apache Indian Reservation, http://apcrp.org/MIDDLETON%20 RANCH/Meddleton%20Ranch%20Master.htm.

74. Ownership of this ranch changed over time and was alternatively referred to as the Middleton ranch, the Newton ranch, the Vosburg ranch, or the Flying V ranch during the period of this study. For a brief explanation of the ranch's ownership, see *Arizona Republican*, 24 December 1895, 1. For the sake of narrative consistency, I refer to the ranch as the Middleton ranch.

75. The 1880 U.S. Federal Census lists twenty-two-year-old Henry Moody living with his fifty-nine-year-old father Alexander. Both are listed as stock raisers in Schedule 1, Enumeration District 20, County of Maricopa, Territory of Arizona, June 1880, 9, *1880 U.S. Census*, Ancestry.com (accessed 28 Dec. 2017); original data from *Tenth Census of the United States, 1880* (NARA microfilm publication T9, 1,454 rolls), Records of the Bureau of the Census, Record Group 29, National Archives, Washington, D.C. Twenty-six-year-old George L. Turner Jr. and sixty-five-year-old Deputy Marshall George Turner Sr. are listed as boarding in Globe in Schedule 1, Globe, County of Pinal, State of Arizona, 21 June 1880, 20, *1880 U.S. Federal Census*, Ancestry.com (accessed 28 Dec. 2017). Original data from *Tenth Census of the United States, 1880* (NARA microfilm publication T9, 1,454 rolls), Records of the Bureau of the Census, Record Group 29, National Archives, Washington, D.C.

76. Earle A. Forrest, *Arizona's Dark and Bloody Ground* (Tucson: University of Arizona Press, 1979), 74–75; Don Dedera, *A Little War of Our Own* (Flagstaff, Ariz.: Northland Press, 1988), 32–33.

77. Hattie Middleton Allison, "An Indian Raid," *Arizona Cattlelog*, November 1953, 12–21.

78. "Town and County," *Salt River Herald*, 9 November 1878, 3.

79. Nantangotayz was later identified as a leader of this group in the *Arizona Republican*, 17 January 1896, 4.

80. Allison, "An Indian Raid," 18. The *Arizona Weekly Citizen*, 18 September 1881, 1, reported that "Mr. Barton Sr." led a rescue party to the Middleton ranch and buried the bodies of Turner and Moody.

81. "Globe, September 5," *Weekly Arizona Citizen*, 11 September 1881, 3, and "The Indian Butcheries," ibid., 18 September 1881, 1.

82. *Pinal Drill*, 24 September 1881.

83. Allison, "An Indian Raid," 18.

84. Ibid.

85. Ibid.

86. Ibid.

87. Dedera, *A Little War of Our Own*, 31, and Forrest, *Arizona's Dark and Bloody Ground*, 332. Vosberg was also spelled Vosburgh. The 1880 U.S. Federal Census lists thirty-one-year-old J. J. Vosburg as a Wells Fargo agent in Schedule 1, Globe, County of Pinal, State of Arizona, 19 June 1880, 18, Ancestry.com (accessed 28 Dec. 2017); original data from *Tenth Census of the United States, 1880* (NARA microfilm publication T9, 1,454 rolls), Records of

the Bureau of the Census, Record Group 29, National Archives, Washington, D.C.

88. "A Bloody Record: Killing of an Indian Chief Revives a Story," *Arizona Republican*, 17 January 1896, 4. Jacob Piatt Dunn, *Massacres of the Mountains* (New York: Harper and Bros., 1886), 746–47; Odie Faulk, *The Geronimo Campaign* (New York: Oxford University Press, 1993), 24–25; Robert Wooster, *The American Military Frontiers* (Albuquerque: University of New Mexico Press, 2001), 262; Bob Boze Bell, "The Battle of Big Dry Wash: Al Sieber and U.S. Troops vs. Na-ti-o-tish's Apaches," *True West* (1 August 2007), https://truewestmagazine.com/al-sieber-a-us-troops-vs-na-ti-o-tishs-apaches/ (accessed 30 May 2013); Tom Horn, *Life of Tom Horn: Government Scout and Interpreter, Written by Himself* (Santa Barbara, Calif.: Narrative Press: 2001), 82.

89. Joseph Harrison Pearce, "Pearce Reminiscences, 1903–1957," 26, Pearce Papers, Arizona Historical Society Library and Archives, Tucson. Also see Thomas R. McGuire, *Mixed-Bloods, Apaches, and Cattle Barons* (Tucson: University of Arizona, 1980), 42.

90. "A Bloody Record: Killing of an Indian Chief Revives a Story," *Arizona Republican*, 17 January 1896, 4, and Al Sieber deposition (1889), PDF in possession of the author. Colvig is spelled Colwick in Sieber's deposition.

91. Jacoby describes how the underlying principle in organizing raids was speed and stealth, and thus Apaches moved in small numbers to find food or plunder. War parties were qualitatively different in purpose, and large numbers were to their advantage. See his *Shadows at Dawn*, 149–52.

92. Report filed by Sergeant Fred Platten, 3rd Cavalry, quoted in Dedera, *A Little War of Our Own*, 32. See also *Arizona Weekly Citizen*, 30 July 1882, 1.

93. See Dedera, *A Little War of Our Own*, 31.

94. Ibid., 32–33.

95. "Items from the South, More Murders by the Apaches Reported from the Arizona Mountains," reprinted in Glenn R. Ellison, *Back Trackin* (Globe, Ariz.: Tyree Printing, 1975), 10–11. Further reports of the Apache attack on Pleasant Valley can be found in *Arizona Weekly Citizen*, 5 February 1882, 4; *Phoenix Herald*, 21 July 1882, 1, 2, 3; and *Arizona Sentinel*, 22 July 1882, 2.

96. See James L. Haley, *Apaches* (Norman: University of Oklahoma Press, 1981), and Robert M. Utley, *Frontier Regulars: The United States Army and the Indians* (New York: Macmillan, 1973).

97. Robert Voris remembered that the trip to Globe took about three days, but one could make it in two by pushing the horse hard, in Robert Voris and Dale Stuart King, "The Pleasant Valley War," oral history interview by Clara T. Woody, 23 March 1976, transcript and three sound cassettes available from Arizona Historical Society Library and Archives, http://catalog.azhsarchives.org/cgi-bin/koha/opac-detail.pl?biblionumber=203. Transcriber Rhonda Kaesberg spelled Voris's name as "Vorris." For the sake of consistency, I use the spelling found in court documents, with one *r*.

98. Johnny Graham's father, Samuel, was born in Blair Atholl, Perth, Scotland, but John was born in Antrim, Ireland, where his mother was from.

99. Accounts are unclear as to whether Tewksbury met Johnny or Tom Graham first, or both at the same time. See Dedera, *A Little War of Our Own*, 38. Drusilla Hazelton, in

"Hazelton Manuscript," 72, recalled that it was Ed who invited Johnny to look at the valley. Mary Ann Tewksbury Rhodes confirmed that Ed invited Johnny Graham to Pleasant Valley in her 1924 letter from Mary Rhodes to her son, photocopied and transcribed in "Hazelton Manuscript," 75–79.

100. Voris described the Grahams as "tin horn gamblers" in Globe, which was a common term for "crooked gamblers," in Voris and King, "The Pleasant Valley War," oral history interview, 42.

101. McGuire, citing a late-nineteenth-century study of the cattle industry, found that beef prices reached their peak in 1885 but held steady throughout the decade; see McGuire, *Mixed-Bloods, Apaches, and Cattle Barons*, 47 and 95, figure 16.

102. Mary Rhodes 1924 letter, transcribed and reprinted in Leland J. Hanchett Jr., *They Shot Billy Today* (Cave Creek, Ariz.: Pine Rim, 2006), 45–47. Hazelton recalled in "Hazelton Manuscript," 82, that the Tewksbury brothers were all employed by Stinson to oversee his cattle.

103. Estella Hill described her grandfather as a "refined, very tall, large, Scotsman but raised in Belfast, Ireland, blue eyes, grey hair, used to be a red beard," in "Estella Graham Converse Hill Dictation," 22 January 1962, 6, Don Dedera Papers, box 44, file 8, Arizona State University Hayden Library, Arizona Historical Foundation (hereafter cited as Dedera Papers).

104. Graham family information compiled from Iowa State Census Collection, 1856, Boone Township, Boone County, 42–43, Boone Country Historical Society; 1860 U.S. Federal Census, Des Moines Township, Boone County, 3; 1880 U.S. Federal Census, Des Moines Township, Boone County, 18.

105. Also listed as Mary Eve Lent Goetzman.

106. The *Boone County Democrat* described the Graham boys as "well known to all old timers. They were adventurous, and have been all through the west, from Alaska to Mexico," in "Bloody Work: Killing of the Graham Boys, in Arizona," 5 October 1887, 5.

107. "Estella Graham Converse Hill Dictation, January 22, 1962," 1, Dedera Papers, box 44, file 8.

108. Andrea G. McDowell, "From Commons to Claims: Property Rights in the California Gold Rush," *Yale Journal of Law & the Humanities* 14, no. 1, http://digitalcommons.law. yale.edu/cgi/viewcontent.cgi?article=1249&context=yjlh (accessed 5 July 2017). See also Robert V. Hine and John Mack Faragher, *The American West* (New Haven, Conn.: Yale University Press, 2000), 261, 266–67.

109. The 1885 Washington Territorial Census shows Allen Blair Graham married to Lucy Parman Graham, with nine-year-old Blair and six-year-old Jessie born in Washington. This places Allen in the Washington Territory as early as 1876, Blair's birth year. See Census of the Inhabitants of Tacoma, in the County of Pierce, Territory of Washington, 56–57, *Washington State and Territorial Censuses, 1857–1892*, Ancestry.com (accessed 29 Dec. 2017); original data from *Washington Territorial Census Rolls, 1857–1892*, Washington State Archives (M1, 20 rolls), Olympia, Washington.

110. "Estella Graham Converse Hill Dictation, 22 January 1962," 1–2, Dedera Papers, box 44, file 8. According to Hill, Tom Graham worked for Elias Jackson "Lucky" Baldwin,

a prominent developer in California, but she provided no further information about what he did as an employee of Baldwin.

111. Hill (in ibid.) stated that Tom Graham provided lumber for the railroads being built in the Arizona Territory.

112. Osmer D. Flake relates that his father, William Jordan Flake, paid Stinson 450 head of cattle every year for three years, starting in 1878, and in 1881 Stinson moved about 800 head of cattle to Pleasant Valley, in "Some Reminiscences of the Pleasant Valley War and Causes That Led Up to It" (unpublished ms. in Levi S. Udall Papers, Film 9355), 1.

113. Hazelton, "Hazelton Manuscript," 68–83.

114. Arizona Historical Society Library and Archives, Portraits—John Graham (photo file), photo number 4885, http://catalog.azhsarchives.org/cgi-bin/koha/opac-detail. pl?biblionumber=41258&query_desc=kw%2Cwrdl%3A%20John%20Graham. Information about the portrait date and location is found on the back of the portrait.

115. Arizona Historical Society Library and Archives, Portraits—Graham, Mr. and Mrs. Thomas H. (Anne Melton) (photo file), photo number 4886, http://catalog.azhsarchives. org/cgi-bin/koha/opac-detail.pl?biblionumber=41259&query_desc=kw%2Cwrdl%3A%20 Thomas%20Graham. Information about the portrait date and location is found on the back of the portrait.

116. Johnny testified that he moved to Pleasant Valley in August 1882, in Statement of Johnny Graham, *Territory of Arizona vs. John and Thos. H. Graham*, 13 June 1885. Tom testified that he moved to Pleasant Valley in September 1882 in Statement of Thos. H. Graham, *Territory of Arizona vs. John and Thos. H. Graham*, 12 June 1885.

117. Pearce, "Pearce Reminiscences," 31.

118. Forrest, *Arizona's Dark and Bloody Ground*, 34.

119. Hazelton, "Hazelton Manuscript," 72.

120. Ibid., 82.

121. James Tewksbury testified in *Territory of Arizona vs. John and Thos. H. Graham* (1885), that the Grahams purchased their herd from William J. Flake and Isaac Turley. Thomas Graham's testimony also mentioned the purchase of cattle from George Bagnall.

122. Flake, "Some Reminiscences," 3.

123. Hazelton, "Hazelton Manuscript," 87.

124. See Michno, *Settlers' War*, 321–24; Brisbin, *The Beef Bonanza; or, How to Get Rich on the Plains* (1881); and Baron von Richthofen's *Cattle-Raising on the Plains of North America* (1885).

CHAPTER 2. FRONTIER ENTREPRENEURS

1. Patricia Nelson Limerick, *The Legacy of Conquest: The Unbroken Past of the American West* (New York: W. W. Norton, 1987), and William G. Robbins, *Colony and Empire: The Capitalist Transformation of the American West* (Lawrence: University Press of Kansas, 1994).

2. Apache County Centennial Committee, *Lest Ye Forget* (St. Johns, Ariz.: Apache County Centennial Committee, 1980), 14.

3. Pearce, "Pearce Reminiscences," 27–30.

4. *Bouteloua oliogostachya*, in U.S. Department of Agriculture, *Grasses of the Arid*

Districts (Washington, D.C.: Government Printing Office, 1888), 11. See also Fred W. Croxen, "History of Grazing on Tonto," www.rangebiome.org/genesis/GrazingOnTonto-1926.html (accessed 30 May 2013).

5. "Thirty-fifth United States Colored Troops (First North Carolina Colored Volunteers)," http://battleofolustee.org/35th_usct.html (accessed 30 May 2013); Cyrus H. Bates, "Address on the Life and Character of Hon. Edward W. Kinsley," in Albert W. Mann, *History of the Forty-fifth Regiment, Massachusetts Volunteer Militia: "the Cadet Regiment"* (Jamaica Plain, Mass.: Brookside Print, 1908), 447–448, Ancestry.com (accessed 15 Dec. 2017).

6. The *Arizona Champion* devotes extensive coverage to the formation of the Aztec Land and Cattle Company in its 26 June 1886 issue, page 2.

7. William S. Abruzzi places the arrival of the train in 1881, but the *Arizona Champion* writes about the inaugural train leaving Albuquerque for Holbrook, Arizona, on 21 October 1883. See Abruzzi, "The Social and Ecological Consequences of Early Cattle Ranching in the Little Colorado River Basin," *Human Ecology* 23, no. 1 (March 1995): 75–98; and "The All Year Route" and "'All the Year!' Grand Opening of the New Line, Sunday, October 21, '83," *Arizona Champion*, 27 October 1883, 2.

8. Anderson, "Hashknife Ranch" and "Continental Land and Cattle Company," *Handbook of Texas Online*.

9. "The Arizona Cowboy," *Arizona Champion*, 20 September 1884, 1. Bishop also noted in *Old Mexico and Her Lost Provinces*, 491, that "the term cowboy, once applied to all those in the cattle business indiscriminately, while still including some honest persons, has been narrowed down to be chiefly a term of reproach for a class of stealers of cattle, over the Mexican frontier, and elsewhere, who are a terror in their day and generation."

10. Benton-Cohen explores similarly pejorative views of cowboys held in southern Arizona, for the same reasons, in *Borderline Americans*, 52–53.

11. Pearce, "Pearce Reminiscences," 28–29.

12. Ibid., 29.

13. Farnsworth details Hashknife cowboy harassment of Mormon settlers in "The Hashknife Cowboys and the Snowflake Saints," *True West* 42, no. 5 (May 1995): 40–43. James Pearce also details how he was driven off his land by cattle companies in James Pearce Interview, 9 January 1921, MS 184, Brigham Young University, Harold B. Lee Library, Tom Perry Special Collections.

14. For examples of annual sheepherder and cattleman balls in the county, see "Annual Meeting of the Mogollon Live Stock Association," *Arizona Champion*, 11 April 1885, 2; for seasonal "rondeos," see "Time of Holding the Spring Rondeo," ibid., 25 April 1885, 3; and for mutual cooperation regarding stolen livestock, see the $500 reward offered for "the arrest and conviction of any person illegally driving off, selling, or otherwise disposing of any horses, cattle, sheep or mules, belong[ing] to or legally controlled by any member of this association," in ibid., 9 January 1886, 4.

15. "Territorial," *Arizona Champion*, 12 March 1887, 3; *Arizona Silver Belt*, 19 March 1887, 4; *Mohave County Miner*, 5 March 1887, 2. The Hashknife outfit sued the Daggs brothers for forcible entry and detainer on property they claimed, but the Daggses prevailed. See *Arizona Champion*, 16 July 1887, 3.

16. "Murdered and Cremated," *Arizona Champion*, 12 March 1887, 3; and "A Cowardly Murder," *Daily Tombstone Epitaph*, 10 March 1887, 4.

17. "Territorial," *Arizona Champion*, 2 April 1887, 2.

18. Ibid., 19 December 1885, 3.

19. *Arizona Journal-Miner*, 18 March 1887, 4 (filed under Thursday, 17 March 1887).

20. Hazelton recalled in "Hazelton Manuscript," 92, that most lawmen were at least one hundred miles away.

21. "Prescott Journal: 'The Wounded Bird Flutters,'" *St. Johns Herald*, 30 July 1885, 1.

22. Louis W. Parker was the son of John and Tom's older sister, Mary, who married David H. Parker. Ralph E. Twitchell's *Leading Facts of New Mexican History* (Cedar Rapids, Iowa: Torch Press, 1912), 373, however, indicates that Louis's father was "D. U. Parker . . . a Methodist minister."

23. Osmer Flake, *William J. Flake: Pioneer, Colonizer* (N.p., 195–?), 117. Louis Parker was in Pleasant Valley as early as April 1884, according to Johnny Graham's testimony in the St. Johns trial. See also Flake, "Some Reminiscences," 8. Lucy Hannah White Flake, granddaughter of William J. Flake, recorded in *To the Last Frontier* (N.p., 1976), 109–10, that fresh tracks from their stolen livestock "led to Canyon Creek, the home of one of the worst family of thieves and outlaws in the country."

24. McGuire, *Mixed-Bloods, Apaches, and Cattle Barons*, 47.

25. Brian Roberts, *American Alchemy* (Chapel Hill: University of North Carolina Press, 2000), 204–205. Johnny Graham mentioned that he also worked in the lumber industry in Statement of Johnny Graham, *Territory of Arizona vs. John and Thos. H. Graham*, 13 June 1885.

26. Forrest wrote in *Arizona's Dark and Bloody Ground*, 51, that Tom Graham freely predicted that "some day he would become one of Arizona's cattle kings." Clara T. Woody and Milton L. Schwartz also state that "Tom Graham was an ambitious man. He dreamed of quick prosperity and firmly believed that he would soon be rich." See Woody and Schwartz, *Globe, Arizona* (Tucson: University of Arizona Press, 1970), 113.

27. "Estella Graham Converse Hill Dictation," 22 January 1962, 4, Dedera Papers, box 44, file 8. Hill remembered "Gruell" as a Mexican, but the *Arizona Silver Belt*, 18 September 1886, 3, reported a story about Tom Graham and "Ross Gruell" who rode together. Orville Ross Gruwell was the son of William Orville Gruwell who purchased the Blevins's Canyon Creek ranch, and the younger Gruwell was later arrested in Phoenix for rustling. "Grewell [*sic*] is well known throughout the territory. He was one of the active participants in the famous Tewksbury and Graham Tonto Basin War"; see "Pair of Alleged Horse Thieves Jailed," *Arizona Weekly Journal-Miner*, 9 August 1905, 2.

28. Arizona Live Stock Ranchmen's Association appears to have formed in the southern territory, perhaps around Tucson. See "Territorial Topics," *Arizona Silver Belt*, 26 January 1884, 3; and "Territorial Topics," ibid., 16 August 1884, 3. Stockmen of Apache County formed the Apache County Stock Association (also referred to as the Apache County Stock Grower's Association) in June 1884. See "Territorial Items," *Arizona Champion*, 14 June 1884, 2, and "Local News," and "General Round-Up," *St. Johns Herald*, 16 April 1885, 3. The Central Arizona Live Stock and Ranchmen's Association formed in Globe. See "Association of Stockmen," *Arizona Silver Belt*, 25 October 1884, 3. It is worth noting for this study that

J. J. Vosburgh served as secretary of the organizing committee, and then as vice president of the association. The *Arizona Weekly Citizen* reported on the formation of the Southern Arizona Live Stock Association on 15 November 1884, 2. Stockmen in Phoenix gathered in late March 1885 to organize a livestock association, as reported in "Live Stock Association," *Weekly Phoenix Herald*, 26 March 1885, 2. The *Arizona Weekly Citizen* mentions a Pima County livestock association in "Important! Notice to Stock Men," 11 April 1885, 3. There is mention of the Apache County Stock Growers Association in "General Round-Up," *St. Johns Herald*, 30 April 1885, 2. The Arizona Live Stock Association met in Tucson on 16 April 1885. It is unclear whether this organization was the same as the one mentioned by the *Arizona Silver Belt* a year earlier, but representatives of the Southeastern Stock Growers Association, Stock Growers Association of Tombstone, and Stock Growers Association of Gila County were present at this 1885 meeting. See "Territorial Meeting of Stockmen," *St. Johns Herald*, 30 April 1885, 2. The *St. Johns Herald* also mentions the Yavapai County Stock Grower's Association in "Territorial Items," 21 May 1885, 3, and reported on the formation of the Territorial Live Stock Association of Arizona, probably to organize the northern associations, on 1 September 1887, 1. The Mogollon Protective Association, based in Flagstaff, appears to have been formed in 1887; see "Stock Notes," *Arizona Champion*, 5 May 1888, 4. Barnes also observed in *Apaches and Longhorns*, 132, that the livestock associations were founded specifically because of rustling.

29. Article XXII, "Constitution and By-Laws of the Pinal County Live Stock Association," *Arizona Weekly Enterprise*, 3 September 1887, 1.

30. "Territorial Meeting of Stockmen," *St. Johns Herald*, 30 April 1885, 2.

31. Ibid., 1 September 1887, 1.

32. Article XX, "Constitution and By-Laws of the Pinal County Live Stock Association," *Arizona Weekly Enterprise*, 3 September 1887, 1.

33. Vincent M. Flake, "Early Day Brands of Northern Arizona," in S. Eugene Flake, *James Madison Flake* (Bountiful, Utah: Wasatch Press, 1970), 158–59.

34. Hazelton, "Hazelton Manuscript," 82.

CHAPTER 3. BLOOD OF THE COVENANT

1. According to Leland J. Hanchett Jr., George Wilson stated that they were on particular alert because they had been warned that Hashknife men were trying to eliminate sheep men, yet neither Newton nor Jim Tewksbury owned sheep. See Hanchett, *Arizona's Graham-Tewksbury Feud*, 55–59. Forrest also alleged, in *Arizona's Dark and Bloody Ground*, 69, that sheepherders were given until 10 August to leave the valley. Mormon settlers also heard rumors that the Hashknife cowboys "were going to drive out the 'Mormons' and did not want them about their ranches." See "Joseph Fish Manuscript," 27.

2. James P. Herman notes that the meaning of the word "stress" has undergone substantial change in the scientific communities that study the phenomenon. His use of the term, which is the one that I adopt in this study, is that stress is "a real or anticipated threat to homeostasis, or an anticipated threat to well-being." Herman, "Central Nervous System Regulation of the Hypothalamic-Pituitary-Adrenal Axis Stress Response," 117–53.

3. See Andrea Tone, *Age of Anxiety* (New York: Basic Books, 2008), 1–26, and Brant

Wenegrat, *Theater of Disorder* (New York: Oxford University Press, 2001), 117–19; "Americanitis elixir" was the common term given to over-the-counter drinks designed to counter
the effects of fatigue, such as Dr. Pepper, Coca-Cola, Pepsi, and so on.

4. Beard's previous study on the medical phenomenon was *Neurasthenia (Nerve Exhaustion): With Remarks on Treatment* (1879).

5. George Miller Beard, *American Nervousness* (New York: Putnam, 1881), 6–7.

6. Ibid., vi. See also Greg Eghigian and Gail Hornstein, *From Madness to Mental Health*
(Piscataway, N.J.: Rutgers University Press, 2009), 175–79. For a broader overview of mental
health in the period, see Eric Caplan, *Mind Games* (Berkeley: University of California
Press, 2011).

7. Benton-Cohen provides an excellent exploration of the changing dynamics of race
in southern Arizona toward the end of the century in *Borderline Americans*.

8. See, for example, *Pinal Drill*, 13 January 1883, 1, denigrating Mexican mining law.

9. *Arizona Champion*, 18 June 1887, 2.

10. "The World in Brief," ibid., 4, and "Removal or Extermination," ibid., 2 July 1887, 2.

11. *Arizona Journal-Miner*, 18 March 1887, 4.

12. Republished in "What Am I to Do?" *Arizona Champion*, 8 October 1887, 1. For other
examples of commentaries calling for extermination, see *Pinal Drill*, 20 January 1883, 2;
Arizona Weekly Citizen, 25 June 1887, 1, 25 June 1887, 4, and 11 June 1887, 2; "No Conflict
of Interest," *Arizona Weekly Enterprise*, 25 June 1887, 2; *Arizona Sentinel*, 11 June 1887, 2;
Clifton Clarion, 15 June 1887, 2.

13. Ed Tewksbury reportedly wore white gloves, but these were impractical for day-to-day
use on the frontier, so they may have been worn only at dances or other dress occasions, as
was common in the day. See L. J. Horton manuscript, "Pleasant Valley War," folder 5, Doc.
box 18, "Articles of Research for a Book," folder 5. See also Hanchett, *They Shot Billy Today*, 4.

14. Horton, "Pleasant Valley War." Dedera places the confrontation between Gladden
and Tewksbury during fall 1886 in *A Little War of Our Own*, 110. However, Herman, citing
Horton, identifies William Gladden, not George Gladden, as the man whom Tewksbury
assaulted, in *Hell on the Range*, 126. I have been unable to locate any record for William
Gladden in Arizona at this time.

15. Dave Johnson, "G. W. Gladden—Hard Luck Warrior," *National Association and
Center for Outlaw and Lawman History Quarterly* 15, no. 3 (1991): 1, 3–6.

16. Benton-Cohen found that for the community of Tres Alamos in southern Arizona, the
Apaches served as the racialized "other" that allowed white Americans to lay race aside and
find common cause with their Mexican neighbors. That bond, forged out of fear of Apaches,
underwrote social cohesion and cooperation for a time within the community. Something
of a similar dynamic could be found within the Pleasant Valley settlement but to a more
complicated degree. The Tewksburys' color was often noted, but for those who depended on
them, their racial identity seemed to matter little, if at all. And still, their closest friends seemed
to come predominantly from other mixed-race families. For those who found themselves in
opposition to the Tewksburys, on the other hand, the Tewksburys' color and their race became
much more discursively significant, as if noting their color carried sufficient explanatory
power in why they were to be opposed. See Benton-Cohen, *Borderline Americans*, 45–46.

17. Forrest erroneously records the date as 1886 in *Arizona's Dark and Bloody Ground*, 47.

18. Gilleland is alternatively spelled "Gilliland" in territorial records, and for the sake of consistency, I am using the spelling that Gilleland's sister-in-law Drusilla Hazelton used in "Hazelton Manuscript." Woody and Schwartz described Gilleland as "a heavy-drinking, hot-tempered young Texan" in *Globe, Arizona*, 109.

19. Woody and Schwartz, *Globe, Arizona*, 98.

20. To "vent" a cattle brand (from the Spanish verb *ventar*) was an acknowledgment of sale that included having both old and new cattle brands on the cowhide. Hazelton provides a different account of Gilleland's visit, that he instead rode out "to inquire about some butchered beeves," which then turned into a gunfight, in "Hazelton Manuscript," 99. Dane Coolidge's version corroborates this portion of Hazelton's account in *Arizona Cowboys* (Tucson: University of Arizona Press, 1938), 149, although there are great discrepancies as well between these two accounts. In general, I rely on Hazelton as the more reliable testimony, given her lifelong relationship with Gilleland, as opposed to Coolidge's single visit. Coolidge was an itinerant photographer and writer who traveled through Arizona in 1916, and he published his travelogue twenty-two years later in 1938. Coolidge's version of the shootout appears to have been the basis for many subsequent versions written about this confrontation, although Hazelton directly challenges several points of Coolidge's version.

21. Woody and Schwartz, *Globe, Arizona*, 116.

22. James D. Tewksbury letter to the editor, dated 12 January 1883, and published in *Arizona Gazette*, 27 January 1883, 3.

23. Woody and Schwartz, *Globe, Arizona*, 116.

24. Hazelton also contests the affidavits filed by the Graham and Tewksbury brothers, which stated that Gilleland fired his weapon. According to Hazelton (in "Hazelton Manuscript," 99), "Mr. Gilleland did not fire a shot."

25. Hazelton's version (ibid.) has both Graham brothers firing their weapons at John Gilleland.

26. Coolidge's version has Gilleland wounded in the shoulder, but Hazelton, in "Hazelton Manuscript," 99–101, insists that a single shot passed through both of Gilleland's elbows and that he was maimed for the rest of his life. Curiously, although Coolidge states that Gilleland told him that "a bullet went into my back, and lodged in my shoulder," he includes this detail that appears to corroborate Hazelton: "Thought I'd bumped my crazy bone against the horn while my horse was pitching around." See Coolidge, *Arizona Cowboys*, 149.

27. Hazelton, "Hazelton Manuscript," 99.

28. James D. Tewksbury letter to the editor, dated 12 January 1883, published in *Arizona Gazette*, 27 January 1883, 3.

29. Yebing Yang et al. defined acute stress as "a series of physiological and psychological responses generated after stressful events, that are manifested mainly by cognitive, emotional, and behavioral changes as well as somatic symptoms," in Yebing Yang, JingJing Tang, Yuan Jiang, Xufeng Liu, Yunfeng Sun, Xia Zhu, and Danmin Miao, "Development of the Acute Stress Response Scale," *Social Behavior and Personality: An International Journal* 39, no. 5 (2011), 714.

30. See David C. Geary, "Fight-or-Flight Response," in *Encyclopedia of Social Psychology*,

ed. Roy F. Baumeister and Kathleen D. Vohs (Thousand Oaks, Calif.: Sage Publications, 2007), 352, and "Fight-or-Flight Response," *Encyclopedia of Neuroscience*, 1571. Other studies have focused more on related aspects of this reaction, such as the startle response. See Terry D. Blumenthal and Joseph C. Franklin, "The Startle Eyeblink Response," in *Methods in Social Neuroscience* (New York: Guilford Press, 2009), edited by Eddie Harmon-Jones and Jennifer S Beer, 93; M. Koch, "The Neurobiology of Startle," *Progress in Neurobiology* 59, no. 2 (October 1999): 107–28; and Robert C. Eaton, *Neural Mechanisms of Startle Behavior* (New York: Plenum Press, 1984).

31. Surveying psychological studies on the effects of stress on judgment, Mark Staal found that "in general, judgment and decision making under stress tend to become more rigid with fewer alternatives scanned. Furthermore, there is evidence that individuals tend to rely on previous responses (typically when they are familiar and well-learned), regardless of previous response success. Thus, in addition to experiencing greater rigidity, individuals may tend to persist with a method or problem-solving strategy even after it has ceased to be helpful." Staal, "Stress, Cognition, and Human Performance: A Literature Review and Conceptual Framework," *NASA Scientific and Technical Aerospace Reports (STAR)* 44, no. 13 (July 5, 2006), 68.

32. Citing a 1996 study by Carl Remsburg, Darin M. Clay argues that "while you are in this [fight-or-flight] mode, you are unable to concentrate, your judgment suffers and your judgments may be wildly inappropriate." Further drawing on R. M. Ayer's 1990 study, Clay argued that in the aftermath of an intense experience, one can continue to have a "heightened sense of danger, anger . . . [or] the 'Mark of Cain' (an assumption that others blame or shame them)," in "Understanding the Human Physiological and Mental Response to Critical Incidents" (School of Law Enforcement Supervision Session 18, 2001, Criminal Justice Institute, University of Arkansas Systems), http://www.cji.edu/site/assets/files/1921/darin_clay.pdf (accessed 1 Aug. 2017), 16–17.

33. "From Tuesday's Daily," *Weekly Phoenix Herald*, 9 February 1883, 3. Jayne Peace Pyle speculates in *Women of the Pleasant Valley War*, 163, that John Gilleland's mother, Emily Gilliland Felton, removed the bullet from John, cleaned the wound, and nursed his recovery. Pyle, citing Felton family sources, spells Gilleland as Gilliland.

34. Felton had recently been appointed deputy sheriff by Sheriff William Mulvenon to oversee the Tonto Basin. "From Wednesday's Daily," *Weekly Arizona Miner*, 23 January 1885, 3.

35. Dedera, quoting Burch's report to Judge Louthian, in *A Little War of Our Own*, 44.

36. "Items from the South, More Murders by the Apaches Reported from the Arizona Mountains," reprinted in Ellison, *Back Trackin*, 10–11. See also Northern Gila County Historical Society, *Rim Country History Illustrated*, 63.

37. Dedera, citing the *Phoenix Herald*, places the date of Frank's passing sometime before 20 January 1883, in *A Little War of Our Own*, 49.

38. Between present-day Yavapai County and Apache County lies Navajo County, which was established in 1895. During the period of the Pleasant Valley War, however, Yavapai County and Apache County shared a border.

39. Krenkel, *Life and Times of Joseph Fish*, 242.

40. "An Albuquerque Dispatch Says . . . ," *Tombstone Epitaph*, 5 November 1887, 2. There are several aspects to this story that are wrong: the Blevinses did not have a daughter; William Graham grew up in Iowa and did not cross paths with the Blevinses, who were from Texas prior to coming to Arizona; and the fighting in Pleasant Valley was never between the Graham and Blevins families. Bill O'Neal cites Coolidge's observation that the fight between the two families originated when "one of the Grahams [made] love to the wife of one of the Tewksburys." O'Neal, *Cattlemen vs. Sheepherders* (Austin, Tex.: Eakin Press, 1989), 168n11, and Coolidge, *Arizona Cowboys*, 150. Only John Tewksbury was married at this time, so if there was any truth to this, the wife in question would have been Mary Ann Tewksbury. There were certainly some in Pleasant Valley who held to this scenario as the cause of tension between the two families, but Drusilla Hazelton entirely dismissed the idea in "Hazelton Manuscript," 93.

41. Although Johnny Graham filed a complaint against the Tewksburys for cattle theft a year after his arrival in Pleasant Valley, he testified in the St. Johns hearing that he did not speak to Tewksbury again after the cattle drive in October 1882. He did not give the reason why.

42. A hand-recorded copy of the agreement was entered into the trial records as evidence as "Exhibit no. 1, *Territory of Arizona vs. Tewksbury and Wm Richards*, 12 July 1884." It is found in *Territory of Arizona vs. Edwin Tewksbury, John Tewksbury, James Tewksbury, George Blaine, William Richards, and H. H. Bishop*, District Court, 3rd Judicial District, Yavapai County, June term A.D. 1884, Indictment for Grand Larceny, Yavapai County District Court Criminal Cases, 1883–1884, 50.14.9, and Yavapai County District Court Criminal Cases, 1883–1884, 50.14.10. Record Group: 113 Yavapai County, Subgroup 8: Criminal Division, 1865–1965 (hereafter cited as *Territory of Arizona vs. Tewksbury et al.* (1884); Record Group and Subgroup hereafter cited as RG and SG, respectively.

43. Johnny Graham complaint, 29 March 1884, *Territory of Arizona vs. Tewksbury et al.* (1884). Johnny Graham's 29 March 1884 complaint against Edwin, James, and John Tewksbury, offered as evidence in *Territory of Arizona vs. Tewksbury et al.* (1884), states that the Tewksbury brothers altered the brands of sixty-two cattle belonging to James Stinson and Johnny Graham. However, in his Apache County testimony in *Territory vs. John Graham and Thos H. Graham* (1885), Johnny Graham, while referencing his larceny complaint against the Tewksburys, also included his brother Thomas when listing who the Tewksburys allegedly stole from. It is possible that Johnny Graham may have filed several different complaints against the Tewksburys, which was a common practice, and only the complaint regarding Stinson's herd, as well as his own herd, were included in the evidence presented in *Territory of Arizona vs. Tewksbury et al.* Thomas Graham's brand and John and Thomas's jointly used brand were registered four days previously, on 25 March 1884. Some lay historians have asserted that in registering these brands, the Grahams double-crossed Ed Tewksbury, who allegedly owned cattle together with the Grahams. However, there is no evidence that Ed Tewksbury owned cattle jointly with any of the Grahams. For the description of the Graham brand and cattle markings, see Arizona Historical Society Library and Archives, Portraits—Tewksbury, Edwin (photo file), "Mr. & Mrs. Edwin Tewksbury, ca. 1897," photo #62447. This photo is actually a picture of the brand register for Thomas Graham's TE brand, dated 25 March 1884, 1:10

o'clock, Yavapai County. It is annotated as "Smooth crop off the left ear, and a crop and slit in the right ear. JT brand registered by John and Thomas Graham, smooth crop off left ear, and crop and half under bit with right ear," with the same date and time.

44. Joseph D. Weeks, *Report on the Average Retail Prices of Necessaries of Life in the United States*, "Average Rates of House Rent: Missouri," 106, from *Census of Population and Housing, 1880*, Tenth U.S. Census (1880), U.S. Census Bureau (Washington, D.C.: Government Printing Office, 1886), https://www.census.gov/prod/www/decennial.html (accessed 18 Dec. 2017).

45. Flake, *William J. Flake*, 124–26.

46. "Yavapai Co. A.T. Pleasant Valley August the 2= 1887," "Pleasant Valley, August -2= 1887," and "Dated Phoenix AT Feb 18 1887," Dedera Papers, box 43, file 42.

47. "Phoenix A.T. July the - 31 - 1888, Dear Sister," 4, Dedera Papers, box 43, file 42.

48. Ibid., 3–4.

49. "Tinhorn gamblers" was a common term for "crooked gamblers." See Voris and King, "The Pleasant Valley War," oral history interview, 42.

50. "Estella Graham Converse Hill Dictation," 22 January 1962, 3, in Dedera Papers, box 44, file 8.

51. From Dedera's transcribed notes "Tom Graham's Diary from Estella," Dedera Papers, box 43, file 24.

52. "Phoenix, A.T., Feb. 18 1887," transcribed promissory note, Dedera Papers, box 43, file 24. For 1880s interest rates, see Louise Yamada Technical Research Advisors, "200+ Years of U.S. Annual Interest Rates," published in Lawrence Lewitinn, "Here's 222 Years of Interest Rate History On One Chart," Talking Numbers, 18 September 2013, https://finance. yahoo.com/blogs/talking-numbers/222-years-interest-history-one-chart-173358843.html (accessed 31 Aug. 2017). See also Pflaum, Duncan, and Frye, "Historical Averages and the 'Real Rate' of Interest" (Kansas City, Mo.: Spectrum Economics, March 12, 1997), www. spectrumeconomics.com/wp-content/uploads/pdf/Historical-Averages-and-The-Real-Rate-of-Interest.pdf, 2 (accessed 31 Aug. 2017).

53. Jefferson Davis "J.D." Adams was born in Texas, and lived in Maricopa County in 1880. See "Maricopa, Arizona, Enumeration District 020," page 124D, *1880 U.S. Federal Census*, Ancestry.com (accessed 18 Dec. 2017); original data from *Tenth Census of the United States, 1880* (NARA microfilm publication T9, 1,454 rolls), Records of the Bureau of the Census, Record Group 29, National Archives, Washington, D.C.

54. Johnny Graham's sworn complaint resulted in four grand larceny cases: *Territory of Arizona vs. Thomas Graham and John Graham* (1884); *Territory of Arizona vs. Edwin Tewksbury and James Tewksbury* (1884); *Territory of Arizona vs. Edwin Tewksbury, John Tewksbury, James Tewksbury, George Blaine, William Richards, and H. H. Bishop* (1884); and *Territory of Arizona vs. James Tewksbury and William Richards* (1884). See also *Weekly Phoenix Herald*, 12 June 1884, 3. All three Tewksbury brothers, along with William Richards, Herbert H. Bishop, and George Blaine, were charged with stealing cattle from Stinson, as well as cattle from Thomas Graham's herd. Jim and Edwin Tewksbury were charged with stealing two head of cattle.

55. *Territory of Arizona vs. Edwin Tewksbury, John Tewksbury, James Tewksbury, George*

Blaine, William Richards, and H. H. Bishop (1884). Also noted in court documents as *Territory vs. Tewksbury et al.*

56. Grand larceny was defined in the territorial statutes as theft involving property exceeding $50 in *Revised Statutes of Arizona Territory, 1901* (Columbia, Mo.: E. W. Stephens, 1901), Title 13: Crimes Against Property, 1263, and Title 15: Offenses Against Stock Raisers, 1284–1287.

57. William Daggs posted bail for Jim Tewksbury and George Blaine in Apache County. See *Territory of Arizona vs. James Tewksbury and George Blaine* in Tewksbury Family, Surname Vertical File, Sharlot Hall Museum Library and Archives.

58. "Full and Complete Vindication On Of [*sic*] District-Attorney Rush," *Arizona Champion*, 25 October 1884, 2.

59. *Territory of Arizona vs. Thomas Graham and John Graham* (1884).

60. See verdict, John L. Taylor, Foreman, 11 July 1884. The wording of the court record, in *Territory of Arizona vs. Tewksbury et al.* (1884), filed on 1 July 1884, seems to suggest that H. H. Blaine and Ed Tewksbury introduced the Stinson contract into the proceedings.

61. See *Territory of Arizona vs. Tewksbury et al.* (1884), Indictment no. 2, Record of Action, filed 16 July 1884.

62. Krenkel, *Life and Times of Joseph Fish*, 242.

63. Testimony of J. W. Richards, "heard of them only of their slapping one of the Graham boys' jaws. . . . Heard the [Tewksbury] boys speaking of it the morning we left; heard the Graham boys speak about it, John Graham," *Territory of Arizona vs. F. M. McCann* (1884).

64. Testimony of Marion McCann, *Territory of Arizona vs. John and Thos. H. Graham*, 13 June 1885, Record Group 100—Apache County, Subgroup 04, Arizona State Library, Archives, and Public Records.

65. Charles Cameron described McCann's dismissal as "good naturedly," saying to Blaine and the others, "Go on, I do not want to have any trouble with you," in Testimony of Chas. Cameron, *Territory of Arizona vs. F. M. McCann* (1984). See also *Weekly Phoenix Herald*, 12 June 1884, 3.

66. Blaine reportedly boasted at a Prescott supply store, upon purchasing 45 caliber cartridges, that he was going to "clean out some of the damn Stinson gang," in the *Weekly Arizona Miner*, 25 July 1884, 3, https://chroniclingamerica.loc.gov/lccn/sn82014897/. Ten years later, Blaine would shoot an unarmed drunken miner for refusing to obey orders when he was in Blaine's custody. Blaine was given a twenty-five-year sentence for murder. See *Mojave County Miner*, 10 February 1894, 3; 17 February 1894, 3; 14 April 1894, 3. Blaine was later judged to be insane and was sent to the state insane asylum. The wounds received by McCann were blamed for his mental instability; see *Mojave County Miner*, 11 August 1894, 3.

67. "Shooting Scrape in Pleasant Valley," *Weekly Arizona Miner*, 25 July 1884, 2, and *Arizona Silver Belt*, 26 July 1884, 3. See also "Telegraph," *Arizona Weekly Citizen*, 26 July 1884, 2, and "Local Matters," *Arizona Champion*, 26 July 1884, 3.

68. See statement of Jeff Adams, one of Stinson's employees, in the *Weekly Arizona Miner*, 25 July 1884, 2.

69. "Local Matters," *Arizona Champion*, 26 July 1884, 3; *Arizona Silver Belt*, 26 July

1884, 3; "Telegraph," *Arizona Weekly Citizen*, 26 July 1884, 2, and "Tonto Troubles," ibid., 9 August 1884, 3. See also Hanchett, *They Shot Billy Today*, 189–90. Some eight months later, McCann would track and kill a horse thief near Reno Mountain in the Tonto Basin. See *Arizona Weekly Citizen*, 18 April 1885, 2.

70. Notes of *Territory of Arizona vs. F. M. McCann* are found in Dedera Papers, box 47, file 4.

71. "An Ugly Wound," *Arizona Silver Belt*, 29 November 1884, 3.

72. "A Nice Surgical Operation," ibid., 13 December 1884, 3.

73. *Arizona Sentinel*, 2 August 1884, 1.

74. *Territory of Arizona vs. Thomas Graham and John Graham* (1884).

75. "Local News," *St. Johns Herald*, 2 July 1885, 3.

76. "From Thursday's Daily," *Weekly Arizona Miner*, 17 July 1885, 3; *Arizona Silver Belt*, 25 July 1885, 4; *St. Johns Herald*, 6 August 1885, 4.

77. Atchison lived in Springerville according to the 1880 U.S. Census. See also "William Atchison, Atchison-Pilling Company (1853)," *Mormon Pioneer Overland Travel, 1847–1868*, website of Church of Jesus Christ of Latter-day Saints, https://history.lds.org/overlandtravel/pioneers/55691/william-atchison (accessed 20 Dec. 2017); and *St. Johns Herald*, 19 May 1887, 3.

78. Robert Carr Blassingame is also spelled Robert Carre Blassingame in territorial documents.

79. Ellen Greer Rees, *Greer Men and Ellen C. Greer* (N.p., 1953), 9, 65.

80. Evidence of James Tewksbury, *Territory of Arizona vs. John and Thos. H. Graham*, 13 June 1885.

81. Most likely it was John Meadows, who had jurisdiction over Pleasant Valley. He is alternatively listed as J. V. Meadows in court documents.

82. Evidence of James Tewksbury, *Territory of Arizona vs. John and Thos. H. Graham*, 13 June 1885.

83. Felton was appointed deputy sheriff over the Tonto Basin by Sheriff Mulvenon. See *Weekly Arizona Miner*, 23 January 1885, 3.

84. Testimony of R. C. Blassingame, *Territory of Arizona vs. John and Thos. H. Graham*, 12 June 1885.

85. Testimony of Louis Parker, *Territory of Arizona vs. John and Thos. H. Graham*, 12 June 1885.

86. Statement of Johnny Graham, *Territory of Arizona vs. John and Thos. H. Graham*, 13 June 1885.

87. Flake, "Some Reminiscences." Also see Flake, *William J. Flake*, 109–10.

88. *Arizona Miner*, as quoted in "Arrested for Perjury," *Arizona Champion*, 26 July 1884, 1. Also see "Territorial Items," *Arizona Sentinel*, 2 August 1884, 1.

89. See also "Disgraceful State of Affairs in Apache County," *Arizona Silver Belt*, 11 July 1885, 2; "Disgraceful State of Affairs in Apache County," *Arizona Champion*, 18 July 1885, 2; and *St. Johns Herald*, 23 July 1885, 2.

90. Woody and Schwartz, *Globe, Arizona*, 122.

CHAPTER 4. TO SUFFER THE ARROWS OF OUTRAGEOUS FORTUNE

Author's note: I am indebted to Professor Tennille Marley (White Mountain Apache) at Arizona State University for her language help.

1. Figure 2.0–10, "Arizona NOAA Climate Division 2 (Northeastern Arizona; Coconino, Navajo, and Apache Counties) winter (November–April) precipitation departures from average, 1000–1988, reconstructed from tree rings," www.azwater.gov/AzDWR/State-widePlanning/WaterAtlas/EasternPlateau/PlanningAreaOverview/Climate.htm; also see "Oldest Settler Says This Was Mildest Winter Experienced in Tonto Basin," *Arizona Champion*, 10 March 1887, 4.

2. William S. Abruzzi, *Dam That River!* (Lanham, Md.: University Press of America, 1993), 34–35.

3. Annie was the daughter of Reverend William A. Melton, who was a prominent Baptist minister in southern California and Arizona. Reverend Melton pastored the First Baptist Church in Florence, Arizona. See "Churches," *Arizona Weekly Enterprise*, 30 April 1887, 3, and "Estella Graham Converse Hill Dictation," 22 January 1962, 1, Dedera Papers, box 44, file 8.

4. "Interview with Mrs. John McTaggert [Mollie Cummings], 8 December 1961," 1, Dedera Papers, box 42, file 40.

5. *Apache County Critic* (Holbrook) advertised in January 1887 a reward for seven hundred stolen sheep from the Daggs herd, taken in the direction of St. Johns.

6. Edwin R. Sweeney, *Mangas Coloradas* (Norman: University of Oklahoma Press, 2011), 91.

7. Douglas C. McChristian, "Dress on the Colors, Boys!," in *Buffalo Soldiers in the West*, edited by Bruce A. Glasrud and Michael N. Searles (College Station: Texas A&M University Press, 2007), 91–92; Thomas R. Buecker, "One Soldier's Service," in ibid., 117; Thomas A. Britten, "The Black Seminole Indian Scouts in the Big Bend," in ibid., 150; Faulk, *The Geronimo Campaign*, 104–105. See also John A. Hamblin, "The Freight Lines," and "How I Was Almost Traded to the Indians," in Apache County Centennial Committee, *Lest Ye Forget*, 126, 152.

8. Faulk, *The Geronimo Campaign*, 58, 71–76.

9. See, for example, *Arizona Weekly Citizen*, 4 September 1886, 4.

10. *Daily Tombstone*, 2 February 1886, 2. See also *Arizona Silver Belt*, 17 April 1886, 3, and "Visitation from Apache Scouts," *Arizona Weekly Citizen*, 24 April 1886, 3.

11. "Telegraph," *Arizona Weekly Citizen*, 5 December 1885, 2.

12. "White Mountain Apaches," *Arizona Sentinel*, 29 May 1886, 2.

13. "More Apache Hellishness," *Clifton Clarion*, 2 June 1886, 2.

14. *St. Johns Herald*, 3 June 1886, 2.

15. Ibid., 3.

16. "More Apache Hellishness," *Clifton Clarion*, 2 June 1886, 2; "Restless Scouts" and "The Red Devils," *Daily Tombstone*, 5 June 1886, 3; "Another Victim," "An Indian Scare," and "Chief Natches," *Arizona Weekly Citizen*, 12 June 1886, 4; and *Arizona Champion*, 19 June 1886, 4, 5.

17. *Arizona Weekly Journal-Miner*, 18 August 1886, 2.

18. *Arizona Silver Belt*, 2 October 1886, 2. See also *Arizona Weekly Citizen*, 10 July 1886, 3; *St. Johns Herald*, 15 July 1886, 1; *Arizona Silver Belt*, 17 July 1886, 2, and 24 July 1886, 2; *Arizona Sentinel*, 24 July 1886, 2; and "The Apache Chief" and "The Apaches to Go," *Daily Tombstone*, 25 August 1886, 3.

19. *Daily Tombstone Epitaph*, 9 June 1886, 3.

20. The Blevinses appear to have moved to Arizona in February 1887. See Martin J. Blevins, 20 February 1887, letter to "Delila and Gim," Doc. box 199, folder 7, Sharlot Hall Museum Library and Archives. Blevins alternatively wrote his middle initial as a J. or a P.

21. *Mohave County Miner*, 17 September 1887, 2. Oz Flake speculated that Cooper was the half brother of the Blevins boys, but I have not been able to verify this claim. See Lester Flake, *Tales from Oz* (N.p.: Les Flake, 19–?), 37.

22. *St. Johns Herald*, 28 April 1887, 3, and "Work for Our Officers," *Arizona Weekly Journal-Miner*, 4 May 1887, 3. For further reports of the Blevinses' Canyon Creek ranch serving as a hideout and rendezvous point for rustlers, see *St. Johns Herald*, 26 May 1887, 3, and 7 July 1887, 3; *Clifton Clarion*, 17 August 1887, 2; "The Pleasant Valley Feud: More Killings Reported," *Arizona Silver Belt*, 27 August 1887, 3; and "Apache County Rustlers," *Arizona Weekly Citizen*, 27 August 1887, 4.

23. Martin Blevins wrote to "Delila and Gim" in Texas, 20 February 1887: "Tell your paw that I think that he could do better out here than he can do where he is for he can get a good home here for nothing. . . ." See also Woody and Schwartz, *Globe, Arizona*, 245n6, and Annie Richardson Johnson and Elva Richardson Shumway, *Charles Edmund Richardson* (Tempe: Ariz. Publication Services, 1982), 194.

24. Susie Wise Oakley, "Descendants of Heinrich Christoff SHULTZ–Notes," Ancestry.com (accessed 1 Jan. 2017); notes in possession of the author. See also A. G. Report 1900, Index Card Collections. Austin, Texas: Texas State Library and Archives Commission.

25. David Johnson, *Mason County "Hoo Doo" War, 1874–1902* (Denton: University of North Texas Press, 2006), 22.

26. Dedera, *A Little War of Our Own*, 81, 83–84; Hanchett, *They Shot Billy Today*, 150–51.

27. *St. Johns Herald*, 11 August 1887, 2. Also see *Clifton Clarion*, 17 August 1887, 2; "Apache County Rustlers," *Arizona Silver Belt*, 27 August 1887, 1; "Apache County Rustlers," *Arizona Weekly Citizen*, 27 August 1887, 4.

28. *Arizona Silver Belt*, 10 September 1887, 4. The *Arizona Silver Belt* quoted the "San Francisco Chronicle of the fifth" that Cooper's warrant for horse stealing was issued in March 1886. See also "Items from Down the River," *St. Johns Herald*, 7 April 1887, 3. The *Arizona Weekly Journal-Miner* reported that Cooper was wanted in Texas for killing a deputy sheriff, in "Our Territory," 14 September 1887, 2.

29. Ellison, *Back Trackin*, 128.

30. Flake, *To the Last Frontier*, 109.

31. Ibid. See also *St. Johns Herald*, 1 September 1887, 2, and "Bloody Tragedy," *Arizona Weekly Journal-Miner*, 7 September 1887, 2, 3.

32. "Items from Down the River," *St. Johns Herald*, 7 April 1887, 3.

33. Bobbie Stephens Hunt, *Those Days Are Gone Forever* (Mesa, Ariz.: Mead Publishers, 2002), 5, and "Items from Down the River," *St. Johns Herald*, 7 April 1887, 3.

34. Hanchett reports that one thousand sheep belonged to John Tewksbury in *They Shot Billy Today*, 57–58. George Walter Shute, in *The Pleasant Valley War* (Phoenix, Ariz.: N.p., 1954), 10, offers a different account, stating that the sheep in question were strays, about fifteen in number, found by Jim and Ed Tewksbury.

35. The distance between the Graham ranch and John Tewksbury's ranch measures just over two miles on a map but was longer following the trails used between the ranches.

36. *Apache County Critic*, January 1887, advertised a reward offered by the Daggs brothers for seven hundred sheep stolen from them and believed to have been taken near St. Johns, northeast of Pleasant Valley over the Rim.

37. *Arizona Champion*, 4 December 1886, 3.

38. Ibid., 19 March 1887, 1.

39. *Arizona Silver Belt*, 12 February 1887, 3; "Weekly Matters," *Arizona Champion*, 19 February 1887, 3; and "From Friday's Daily," *Arizona Weekly Journal-Miner*, 16 February 1887, 3. Barnes erroneously cites a 12 February 1887 news report as the "Globe Silver Belt," in "The Pleasant Valley War of 1887," 32. Also see Zane Watts, "A Piece of History Passes through Town," *Payson Roundup*, 10 September 2010. The Heber-Reno Sheep Driveway was an old military road built in 1868, and according to Drusilla Hazelton, was the main road into the valley. See Hazelton, "Hazelton Manuscript," 72. See also Edward N. Wentworth, *America's Sheep Trails* (Ames: Iowa State College Press, 1948), 256–57.

40. "Investigation of Killing of Ute Indian in Tonto Basin in February 1887," filed 23 March 1887, Yavapai County, RG 113, SG 5, "Crime," Series 9, box 4, file 75, Arizona State Library, Archives, and Public Records. See also Southern Ute Indian Tribe, "History of the Southern Ute," www.southernute-nsn.gov/history (accessed 25 June 2013). Ash identifies the sheepherder as Jose Chavez, and cites a 1 September 1887 edition of *Coconino Sun*, but the *Coconino Sun* did not begin publication until 1891. Further, he places Chavez's death in 1885, two years earlier than the murdered Ute sheepherder. See George Rickard Ash Jr., "Frontier Authority" (Ph.D. diss., University of Arizona, 1973), 55–56, 97–98. For discussion of the trade in captive Utes, see Blackhawk, *Violence over the Land*, 141–44.

41. There is speculation that the sheepherder's body was not found where the U.S. Forest Service officially marked the spot, but up on the hill, fifty yards south of the Forest Service marker, but there appears to be no record of who is buried in that unmarked burial site. Joseph Fish recorded that the sheepherder was Mexican, in "Fish Manuscript," 687. Zachariae, however, writes that the sheepherder was Charlie Etcity, brother-in-law to James Houck, in *Pleasant Valley Days*, 33, 159. While Houck's wife, Beatriz Gurulé Houck, was Navajo, I have been unable to link her to a Charlie Etcity; from the Fran Carlson Collection, 1870–1990, MSS 72, box 2, file 4. (Note on this collection: When the Arizona Historical Foundation closed in 2012, its holdings were placed in various archives in the Southwest. The Fran Carlson Collection, 1870–1990, however, appears to have been deaccessioned and has no permanent repository anymore. Author is in possession of notes.) Mary Ann Tewksbury Rhodes asserted that the sheepherder was, in fact, an Indian in her 1928 letter to her son, copied and transcribed in "Hazelton Manuscript," 75–78, 89. Hazelton believed the sheepherder to be Navajo, in ibid., 90. However, Globe researcher Clara Woody cites Nook Larson that the sheepherder was Basque, although she agrees the sheepherder was brother-

in-law to Houck, in Voris and King, "The Pleasant Valley War," oral history interview, 1, and Woody and Schwartz, *Globe, Arizona*, 130, 135.

42. "Fish Manuscript," 687. Hazelton, citing Mary Ann Tewksbury Rhodes, also states that Indian trackers "trailed the horses ridden by the killer to the Graham ranch [although] it was never made known who actually did the killing" ("Hazelton Manuscript," 97). The source of this claim may have come from "Territorial Topics," *Arizona Weekly Citizen*, 19 February 1887, 2, which cites "A Payson correspondent of the *Prescott Courier*" as its source that the Daggses hired Indians who tracked the murderers to their house. Who the Payson correspondent was, from twenty-five miles away from the scene of the murder, and how they would be in possession of the facts of the investigation, is unclear from all available information. Drusilla Hazelton asserted that "the Tewksburys had Tom Graham charged in St. Johns for the crime but for lack of evidence or some other reason he was exonerated of all blame" ("Hazelton Manuscript," 92), but Yavapai County had jurisdiction in this matter, not Apache County (St. Johns), two counties over. There is no record in either Yavapai County, Apache County, or territorial newspapers that a charge was made or a trial was held in this murder.

43. "$1500 Reward," *St. Johns Herald*, 6 January 1887, 3. See also *Arizona Champion*, 19 February 1887, 3.

44. Woody and Schwartz cite Barnes's *Arizona Historical Review* article ("The Pleasant Valley War of 1887") as their source for the oft-repeated story related to the sheepherder's death, that the herd was driven over a cliff, but Barnes does not describe this event. There appears to be no evidence that Daggs lost sheep at this time and in this manner. The Daggs brothers did not lack for attention from the territorial press, which noted their out-of-town visitors, business interests, and political activities with regularity. So it is unusual for the loss of $90,000 in sheep (according to Woody) to have no mention, as far as can be found, in the territorial newspapers. Finally, it is unclear where the cliff would have been from which the sheep were alleged to have been driven. The terrain in and around the Graham ranch is certainly hilly, but there is no cliff of sufficient height along the trial where the sheepherder was found that fits Woody's description. See Woody and Schwartz, *Globe, Arizona*, 130, and 247n7.

45. James McClintock, cited by Barnes, stated that Tom Graham would shoot at a coffeepot or a frying pan of a sheepherder as a form of moral suasion, in "The Pleasant Valley War in 1887," 33. If true, none of the accounts have him actually murdering a sheepherder, but only firing warning shots to keep sheep moving along the trail and away from his property.

46. See "John Rope" in Keith H. Basso, *Western Apache Raiding and Warfare* (Tucson: University of Arizona Press, 1971), 178.

47. The *Arizona Champion*, 11 June 1887, 2, reported that feuding clans led to a recent Apache outbreak from the reservation that resulted in the murder of four to five Apaches and one white settler. Jim Roberts also reported that after the August 1887 shooting at the Newton ranch, a raiding party of Apaches descended on the cabin (in Forrest, *Arizona's Dark and Bloody Ground*, 71–72). Glenn Ellison recalled that Roberts was accidently present during the shootout at the Newton ranch; see Glenn R. "Slim" Ellison Collection, MSS-35, box 1, folder 3, Manuscripts, "Back Trackin." However, I have been unable to verify this.

Others who were later arrested and tried for burning the Newton ranch also blamed Indians. It is interesting that previous to this 1887 murder, the *Weekly Arizona Miner* reported a murder in 1872 of an Austrian sheepherder, and the theft of his sheep, that bore similarities to the murder of the Daggses' sheepherder. Two miles south of Fort Whipple, in Prescott, Apaches murdered the sheepherder, took his sheep, and smashed his head beyond recognition with rocks. See *Weekly Arizona Miner*, 25 May 1872, 3.

48. Of the neurochemicals released in response to danger, John A. Russell and Michael J. Shipston observed: "From the earliest formulation of concepts of stress it has been convincingly established that central to automatic physiological coping responses to stressful stimuli (stressors) are the sympathetic-adrenomedullary (SAM) and hypothalamic-pituitary-adrenocortical (HPA) neuroendocrine systems. The rapid responses of these systems liberate into the system biologically powerful chemicals . . . and these hormones have bodywide actions to mobilize energy, increase bloodflow to essential organs and to optimize brain activity to deal with the emergency." Russell and Shipston, *Neuroendocrinology of Stress* (Hoboken, N.J.: John Wiley & Sons, 2015), 31.

49. Kenneth J. Thiel and Michael J. Dretsch argue that "at the core of an acute stress response is the initiation of the fight-or-flight response, which is characterized by its sympathetic-adrenal medullary components that serve as the first response to prepare the body for the energy resources it will require." Thiel and Dretsch, "The Basics of the Stress Response: A Historical Context and Introduction," 76. The acute stress response differs from an acute stress reaction in terms of its duration. The acute stress response, according to the *Encyclopedia of Public Health* (ed. Lester Breslow [New York: Macmillan Reference, USA, 2002]), 8–9, is "a transient disorder that . . . usually subsides within hours or days." Similarly, "an important distinguishing characteristic of stress," according to "Stress," in the *Encyclopedia of Neuroscience* (ed. Marc D. Binder, Nobutaka Hirokawa, and Uwe Windhorst [Springer Berlin Heidelberg, 2009]), 3856, "is its duration. Acute stress is defined as stress that lasts for a period of minutes to hours, and chronic stress as stress that persists for several hours a day or weeks or months." Further noting the effects of long-term exposure to stress-released hormones, Russell and Shipston state that "these hormones are so powerful, with deleterious actions when high levels are maintained" (*Neuroendocrinology of Stress*, 31).

50. *St. Johns Herald*, 23 August 1888, 2. From a letter that Stott wrote to his sister, he seems to have believed that the horse was his. See Hanchett, *They Shot Billy Today*, 243.

51. The *Arizona Silver Belt*, 26 March 1887, 3, took the unusual move of publishing verbatim the judgment of the Globe justice of the peace in the case of *Territory of Arizona vs. James Stott and Thomas Tucker*. See also "A Globe Justice Scored," *Arizona Weekly Journal-Miner*, 30 March 1887, 3.

52. "Desperate Fight," *Arizona Champion*, 16 April 1887, 3.

53. Forrest asserts in *Arizona's Dark and Bloody Ground*, 56, that sheep were driven out of Pleasant Valley by the spring.

54. Tremors can vary in duration and intensity. The *Daily Tombstone Epitaph*, 4 May 1887, 1, reported in "Earth Shaking" that the quake lasted "for a full 30 seconds," whereas the Globe *Arizona Silver Belt*, 7 May 1887, 3, reported in "The Earthquake" that the quake

lasted for 20 seconds. The *Arizona Weekly Citizen* published a report from the Olive Mining Camp in the territory, on 7 May 1887, 2, titled "Telegraph," that the quake lasted for three minutes. The *Daily Tombstone Epitaph* carried an account from a reader, in "Tucson Badly Shakes," on 4 May 1887, 4, stating that the quake lasted for four minutes. The report from Fort Apache had the quake lasting three minutes long, as did the report from St. David in "The Shake at St. David," *Daily Tombstone Epitaph*, 5 May 1887, 1. For further descriptions of the earthquake and its impact, see "Solomonville Siftings," *Clifton Clarion*, 11 May 1887, 3, and "General News," *Arizona Weekly Enterprise*, 14 May 1887, 1. Residents in Phoenix reported feeling tremors about a week later in "The Quake at McDowell," *Arizona Weekly Journal-Miner*, 11 May 1887, 4.

55. Susan M. DuBois and Ann W. Smith, *The 1887 Earthquake in San Bernardino Valley, Sonora* (Tucson: University of Arizona Press, 1980), 7.

56. Frank Neumann, *Earthquake Investigation in the United States* (Washington, D.C.: Government Printing Office, 1953), 8–9. See also "The Earthquake," *Arizona Silver Belt*, 7 May 1887, 3; "Local News," *St. Johns Herald*, 12 May 1887, 3, and 19 May 1887, 1; and "Earthquake Notes" and "General News," *Arizona Weekly Enterprise*, 14 May 1887, 1.

57. "The Quake at McDowell," *Arizona Weekly Journal-Miner*, 11 May 1887, 1, 4.

58. "Tucson Badly Shakes," *Daily Tombstone Epitaph*, 4 May 1887, 4, and 7 May 1887, 1; *Arizona Champion*, 7 May 1887, 2; *Arizona Weekly Enterprise*, 7 May 1887, 4.

59. *Daily Tombstone Epitaph*, 4 May 1887, 1. For reports around the territory on the extent of disruption and swaying from the earthquake, see "Tucson Badly Shakes," *Daily Tombstone Epitaph*, 4 May 1887, 4, and "The Shake at St. David," ibid., 5 May 1887, 1; "A Volcano," *Arizona Weekly Citizen*, 7 May 1887, 3; "A Volcano," *Arizona Weekly Enterprise*, 7 May 1887, 4; "El Temblor en Nogales," *El Fronterizo*, 7 May 1887, 3; *Arizona Weekly Journal-Miner*, 11 May 1887, 1; and "Solomonville Siftings," *Clifton Clarion*, 11 May 1887, 3.

60. *Daily Tombstone Epitaph*, 4 May 1887, 1.

61. "A Volcano," *Arizona Weekly Enterprise*, 7 May 1887, 4.

62. Ibid. A report from Benson tells of the flow of the San Pedro River suddenly stopping, causing the river to become dry, before it resurged with water two feet higher than before, in "A Volcano," *Arizona Weekly Citizen*, 7 May 1887, 3.

63. *Arizona Champion*, 7 May 1887, 3.

64. See "Telegraph," *Arizona Weekly Citizen*, 7 May 1887, 2; "The Earthquake in Hermosillo," and "News from Altar, Mexico," ibid., 14 May 1887, 1, 4; *Arizona Weekly Journal-Miner*, 11 May 1887, 2; *Arizona Silver Belt*, 14 May 1887, 2; *St. Johns Herald*, 19 May 1887, 1, 2; "Defying Earthquakes," *Arizona Sentinel*, 28 May 1887, 1; "Earth Upheavals," *Arizona Weekly Enterprise*, 2 July 1887, 1; "Earth Upheavals," ibid., 31 December 1887, 2, and "Creation's Works," 1 December 1888, 1.

65. See Mike Burns, *The Journey of a Yavapai Indian: A 19th Century Odyssey*, edited by Susan L. Rockwell (Princeton, N.J.: Elizabeth House, 2002), 147–52, and Mike Burns, *The Only One Living to Tell: The Autobiography of a Yavapai Indian*, edited by Gregory McNamee (Tucson: University of Arizona Press, 2012), 147–58. See also Braatz, *Surviving Conquest*, 204–206.

66. *Arizona Weekly Citizen*, 2 July 1887, 3; "The Evil Influence of Medicine Men," *Arizona*

Silver Belt, 25 June 1887, 2. Fish also recorded a meeting between Mormon leaders and Apaches in Linden, Arizona, where one of the chiefs made a similar prediction; see "Fish Manuscript," 27.

67. "Telegraph," *Arizona Weekly Citizen*, 2 July 1887, 2; *Arizona Weekly Journal-Miner*, 6 July 1887, 2; *Arizona Champion*, 9 July 1887, 2. For the size of the gathering of nations to the ceremonies at Coyote Holes on the San Carlos Reservation, see Burns, *The Only Living One to Tell*, 150, and Braatz, *Surviving Conquest*, 206.

68. "Apache Depredations," *Arizona Weekly Enterprise*, 9 July 1887, 2. See also *Arizona Weekly Journal-Miner*, 6 July 1887, 2. For the remainder of the year, territorial newspapers would carry reports of Apaches stealing cattle as well. See "The Evil Influence of Medicine Men," *Arizona Silver Belt*, 25 June 1887, 2, and 2 July 1887, 2; "Telegraph," *Arizona Weekly Citizen*, 2 July 1887, 2; *Arizona Weekly Journal-Miner*, 9 July 1887, 2; *Arizona Weekly Enterprise*, 13 August 1887, 2, and 10 September 1887, 2; "An Arizona Feud," *Los Angeles Daily Herald*, 25 September 1887, 1; "Resisted Arrest," *Arizona Weekly Journal-Miner*, 28 September 1887, 3; *Clifton Clarion*, 28 September 1887, 2.

69. Famed scout Al Sieber, born in Germany, was also wounded during this period by the Apache Kid in a dispute, which prompted the Kid and about seventeen others to flee the reservation. Before they were caught, one miner was killed. See "Rebellious Indians," *Arizona Silver Belt*, 4 June 1887, 3; *Arizona Sentinel*, 11 June 1887, 2; "Telegraph," *Arizona Weekly Citizen*, 11 June 1887, 1; and "The Indian Situation," ibid., 11 June 1887, 4.

70. *Arizona Weekly Enterprise*, 11 June 1887, 2. Also see *Clifton Clarion*, 15 June 1887, 2.

71. *Arizona Sentinel*, 18 June 1887, 2. See also "A Scalp Bounty," *Arizona Weekly Enterprise*, 18 June 1887, 3; *St. Johns Herald*, 14 July 1887, 1; *Arizona Weekly Citizen*, 18 June 1887, 2, 25 June 1887, 1 and 4, and "Telegraph," 2 July 1887, 2. For an overview of the hostile positions taken by several territorial newspapers toward Apaches, see "The Arizona Press on the Indian Question," *Arizona Silver Belt*, 18 June 1887, 2.

72. Richard Gorby, "Arizona's Governor Zulick Fell into Political Disfavor," 13 September 1997, https://sharlot.org/library-archives/index.php/blog/arizonas-governor-zulick (accessed 17 Jan. 2018).

73. "Our Own Loved Arizona," *Arizona Weekly Enterprise*, 23 July 1887, 2.

74. See Steven Adolph Fazio, "Marcus A. Smith, Arizona Politician" (master's thesis, University of Arizona, 1968), 17, http://arizona.openrepository.com/arizona/bitstream/10150/551996/1/AZU_TD_BOX263_E9791_1968_201.pdf.

75. Dedera cites an interview with Victoria Fredonia Shults Gilliland, in which she stated that her father exchanged Martin Blevins's land in Texas for a herd of horses, and Dedera, in *A Little War of Our Own*, 272n10, speculates that these were the horses that Mart was looking for when he went missing. However, given that the Blevinses had been implicated in the theft of over one hundred Navajo horses only a few months earlier, it seems more likely that the herd that went missing in July 1887 was a different herd from the one they brought from Texas, and quite possibly yet another herd stolen from Indian land, or from nearby settlements. See *St. Johns Herald*, 7 April 1887, 3. Gilliland's headstone lists her name as Fredonia Victoria Shults Gilland. Her father, Martin Van Buren Shults, married Angeline Mahalia Blevins. Angeline and Mart Blevins were first cousins, once

removed. Victoria's second husband, James Millard Gilliland, does not appear to be related to John Cullen Gilleland.

76. Allison manuscript "The Blevins Family: An Episode in the Pleasant Valley War," quoted in Dedera, *A Little War of Our Own*, 118. Also see Forrest, *Arizona's Dark and Bloody Ground*, 60. Dement is variously spelled Demint and Demmit in territorial records. See *U.S. Civil War Soldier Records and Profiles, 1861–1865*, Ancestry.com (accessed 17 March 2017); Alphabetical Seventh Iowa Volunteer Cavalry Roster, http://armysw.com/seventhcav/7thCavalryroster.pdf (accessed 17 March 2017); and National Archives and Records Administration, *U.S. Civil War Pension Index: General Index to Pension Files, 1861–1934*, Ancestry.com (accessed 17 March 2017); original data from *General Index to Pension Files, 1861–1934* (T288, 546 rolls), National Archives and Records Administration, Washington, D.C.

77. "Arizona News," *Arizona Weekly Enterprise*, 20 August 1887, 2.

78. "Items from Down the River," *St. Johns Herald*, 7 April 1887, 3, and 1 September 1887, 2. For widely spread accusations that Cooper and the Blevinses were openly stealing livestock from white settlers, see *St. Johns Herald*, 11 August 1887, 2; *Clifton Clarion*, 17 August 1887, 2; "Apache County Rustlers," *Arizona Silver Belt*, 27 August 1887, 1; and "Bloody Tragedy," *Arizona Weekly Journal-Miner*, 7 September 1887, 3. Cooper was initially hailed by the Prescott press for killing Indians but was resoundingly criticized for it in the St. Johns press. See "An Indian Killer," *Arizona Weekly Journal-Miner*, 6 January 1886, 1, and *St. Johns Herald*, 1 September 1887, 2.

79. The *St. Johns Herald* reported on 1 September 1887, 2, that "'old man Blevins'—was recently found dead," with no further information about the reported discovery. Two weeks later, on 15 September 1887, 2, the *St. Johns Herald* further stated that Blevins's remains were "found in the brush in Pleasant Valley," but again provides no further details about where, in what circumstance, or how they knew that the remains were of Blevins. See also "Territorial," *Arizona Champion*, 24 September 1887, 2. Two weeks later, the journal stated about Mart Blevins: "The father's bones are perhaps bleaching in some wild and unfrequented spot, the flesh having been torn from them [by] wild animals, as his body has never been found," in "Local News," 6 October 1887, 3. If a body had been found, it is curious that there is no record in county archives of a coroner's inquest being conducted, no mention of an inquest in the territorial press, and no record of any follow-up in the territorial court system. Shute makes a unique claim that Blevins's horse was found "on the range, still saddled, showing that something violent had happened" (*The Pleasant Valley War*, 11). Earle Forrest relates two different stories about the death of Mart Blevins: the first was that Navajos murdered Blevins while looking for the horses that were stolen from them; the second account, included in this narrative, is that Blevins disappeared in search of the herd of horses that his sons had recently acquired. Barnes favored the latter story because Susan Amanda McFarland Gladden wrote in her memoirs that she had moved onto the Blevins compound after her husband deserted her, and she saw Mart leave to search for the missing horses. Both accounts may actually be factual. The Blevinses were well-known horse thieves to the Navajos and Apaches, and all accounts agree that the Blevins boys deposited a herd on their ranch before leaving for Holbrook.

It is possible that Navajo raiders seeking to recover their horses ambushed Mart Blevins, who, in tracking the lost herd, appeared to be in pursuit. Of the Blevinses' Canyon Creek ranch, the *Arizona Silver Belt*, 10 September 1887, 4, reported that "the Indians complain that whites are taking stolen horses on the reservation and secreting them there." Further adding to the theory that Indian raiders killed Blevins is that two different skulls were found many years later in the area where Blevins was believed to have traveled. One skull had a spike driven through it, and the other was found with a rusty rifle leaning against the tree where the skull had been placed. Although the skulls could not be identified, some locals believe that the rifle belonged to Blevins. As discussed in the manuscript, whites typically shot their victims and left their bodies to be found. Apaches, on the other hand, were known to torture their victims and mutilate their bodies, which included beheadings. See Forrest, *Arizona's Dark and Bloody Ground*, 57–59, and Barnes, "The Pleasant Valley War of 1887," 34. The *Arizona Weekly Citizen*, in recounting the history of the Pleasant Valley War, stated, in regard to Blevins, that "although his body was never found, it is now known that he was murdered," 6 August 1892, 2, but that journal provides no more detail as to how it was known that Blevins was murdered. A firearm in the collection of Young resident Frank Chapman, found years later in Valentine Canyon, in the north corner of the Flying V horse pasture, is believed, by some who knew him, to be the rifle that Blevins carried. Dane Coolidge alleged that Sheriff Commodore Perry Owens killed Martin Blevins in a shootout, but his account came decades after the fact, and no other contemporary believed this. See Larry D. Ball, "Commodore Perry Owens," *The Journal of Arizona History* 33, no. 1 (Spring 1992), 40–41. Dan L. Thrapp claimed in *Encyclopedia of Frontier Biography* (Lincoln: University of Nebraska Press, 1991), vol. 1: A–F, 127, that Tom Horn killed Blevins.

80. Burns, *The Only Living One to Tell*, 156–57.

81. Dedera, citing a manuscript by Samuel Haught in his possession, writes in *A Little War of Our Own*, 272n11, that Tom Graham hired six men to kill the Tewksburys for $1,000 apiece, but they were warned by "Old Man Ketcham . . . who sent a runner." Dedera's source appears to have been Samuel A. Haught, who lived in Texas until 1915 and was not a witness to these events.

82. Carrington may have been an alias, since he appears in no other records before or after the Pleasant Valley War. Further, his first name is alternately reported in territorial records as Robert, Bob, or Thomas. I refer to him in this manuscript by the name by which he appears to have been most commonly known—Bob—although, curiously, he is referred to as Thomas in court cases. Glaspie is also spelled Glasspie or Gillespie in the territorial documents, and I use the spelling most frequently found. Paine is also spelled Payne. Other Hashknife men named in the search party were Tom Pickett, Buck Lancaster, McNeal Roxey, and Beck, in Dedera Papers, box 42, file 12. Voris made an intriguing assertion that Johnny Graham organized the group of men to drive the Tewksburys out but was not with them because he rode to the reservation to recruit Apaches to help. All other accounts instead have the party searching for Mart Blevins, and it remains unclear how any of the Blevins search party would have known that any of the Tewksburys, much less all of them (as Voris claims), would be in that remote cabin the day they rode up, rather than in their own cabins

some five miles to the northwest, as the crow flies (even farther following the winding washes). See Voris and King, "The Pleasant Valley War," oral history interview, 19–20.

83. "Local News," *St. Johns Herald*, 18 August 1887, 3, and "Tewksbury-Graham," *Tombstone Epitaph*, 27 August 1887, 3.

84. The "Texas State Penitentiaries Certificate of Prison Conduct," dated 15 April 1885, indicates that eighteen-year-old Hamp, who pled not guilty to horse theft, was sentenced to five years' confinement and served nine months and twenty-five days. His habits were described as intemperate, his education was limited, and his health was not good when received, and bad as of his release. One doctor stated that he was unfit for manual labor, and two others certified that he had a "nervous disease of an epileptic character," in Dedera Papers, box 42, file 16. See also Pyle, *Women of the Pleasant Valley War*, 150.

85. As quoted in Dedera, *A Little War of Our Own*, 119.

86. Ibid. Further accounts of Paine's merciless bullying can be found in Pearce, "Pearce Reminiscences," 33–35, and Niels and Lars Petersen Family Organization, *The Petersen Family of Gannebro Huse* (Pinedale, Ariz.: Petersen Publishing, 2000), 54–58, and "Fish Manuscript," 27–28."

87. "Tonto Basin," *Arizona Champion*, 3 September 1887, 3; "Resisted Arrest," *Arizona Weekly Journal-Miner*, 28 September 1887, 3; and "Tonto Basin," *St. Johns Herald*, 29 September 1887, 3.

88. "A Deplorable Affair," *Arizona Silver Belt*, 20 August 1887, 3.

89. George Wilson told Ellison, "They was inside makin Jerkey when the men rode up and ask for sumpin to eat" (Ellison, *Back Trackin*, 128–29).

90. The story that several were in the cabin may have originated from the report in the *Arizona Weekly Citizen*, "Globe A. T., August 15th," 20 August 1887, 2, which, although stating that the "other side of the story has not yet reported," nonetheless asserted that eight men were in the cabin. At the same time, other news reports stated that neither Tucker nor Glaspie knew who shot them. Forrest (*Arizona's Dark and Bloody Ground*, 79) asserts that Jim Roberts and Joseph Boyer were in the cabin along with Newton and Tewksbury. Shute (*The Pleasant Valley War*, 11) asserts that in addition to Roberts and Boyer, Ed and Jim Tewksbury were also there. However, Glenn Ellison, in *Back Trackin*, 128–29, quotes Wilson, who insisted that only he and Tewksbury were in the cabin that day. Ellison's manuscript asserts the same point but has slightly different wording: "Geo Wilson sed it was my place & only Jim T. & me was there." Ellison later clarified that Roberts was present, but not in the cabin, in Glenn R. "Slim" Ellison Collection, MSS-35, box 1, file 3, Manuscripts, "Back Trackin." Tucker's version of the encounter, printed in "A Deplorable Affair," *Arizona Silver Belt*, 20 August 1887, 3, and "A Deplorable Affair," *Arizona Weekly Citizen*, 27 August 1887, 3, tells only of seeing James Tewksbury. Flake's account, though usually accurate, is less credible here. He wrote that Lydia Tewksbury was standing at the door when Jim Tewksbury dropped a Winchester over her shoulder and began firing. No other account places her at the scene, and the scenario of Jim intentionally firing a rifle within inches of his stepmother's ear stretches credulity.

91. Forrest, *Arizona's Dark and Bloody Ground*, 71. The *Tombstone Epitaph*, quoting the "Flagstaff Champion," states that a woman answered the door, and this report was

likely the source of many other stories that recount that Lydia Tewksbury was present at the shooting. See *Tombstone Epitaph*, 20 August 1887, 1.

92. See Hanchett, *Arizona's Graham-Tewksbury Feud*, 55–59, for a discussion of George Wilson's account, both at the time, when he denied that he was present and presented witnesses to corroborate his claim, and years later, when he told stories about his being present after all.

93. Voris and King, "The Pleasant Valley War," oral history interview, 20. Tucker's account was published in *Arizona Weekly Citizen*, 27 August 1887, 3.

94. Jim Roberts reported that Hamp Blevins drew first. See Hanchett, *Arizona's Graham-Tewksbury Feud*, 55–59. Voris reported that John Paine drew first, in Voris and King, "The Pleasant Valley War," oral history interview, 20–21.

95. "A Deplorable Affair," *Arizona Weekly Citizen*, 27 August 1887, 3.

96. Some of the published accounts of the shoot-out appear to have come from Tucker. See *Arizona Weekly Enterprise*, 20 August 1887, 2, and "A Deplorable Affair," *Arizona Weekly Citizen*, 27 August 1887, 3. See also the report by Bob Glaspie in the *Arizona Republic*, 28 August 1955, and Forrest, *Arizona's Dark and Bloody Ground*, 66–65. Forrest alleges that cattlemen chased the Middleton ranch party into the mountains and lay siege, but given the remote location of the Middleton ranch and the sparse population of the valley, that scenario seems high improbable. See Forrest, *Arizona's Dark and Bloody Ground*, 77–79.

97. "A Deplorable Affair," *Arizona Weekly Citizen*, 27 August 1887, 3.

98. Hazelton, in "Hazelton Manuscript," 114, has Tucker and "Gillespie" both arriving at the Sixby ranch. Pyle, however, indicates in *Pleasant Valley War*, 139, that by 1886, the Sixby ranch was owned by Jacob Haigler. John W. Haigler's article "Jake Haigler," published in *The Benkelman Post*, 9 September 1949, also places Haigler in the Arizona Territory by 1886. Further, by 1887, Sixby appears to have been a boarder and ranch hand at the Al Rose ranch, rather than at the Haigler ranch. Finally, given that the Rose ranch is more centrally located and close to Cherry Creek, it seems more logical that Tucker found his way to that ranch.

99. After his recovery, Tucker appears to have fled to Tularosa, New Mexico, according to the 1900 census. He returned to Arizona, however, eventually becoming range foreman for the Wabash Cattle Company at Salt Lakes, north of St. Johns. See "Disastrous Fire," *St. Johns Herald*, 25 September 1897, 4. Bob Voris confuses Glaspie with Tucker, and claims that Glaspie died of his wounds in Voris and King, "The Pleasant Valley War," oral history interview, 22.

100. Robert Marion Glaspie arrived in the territory in 1886, coming from Texas, where his family name was known as Gillespy. For details about Glaspie's life in New Mexico, see the interview with Glaspie's wife Sunana "Nana" Elmira Glaspie, in William R. Ridgeway, "The Not-So-Pleasant Pleasant Valley War," *Arizona Days and Ways*, 28 August 1955.

101. Allison, "An Indian Raid," 14.

102. Hazelton, "Hazelton Manuscript," 136.

103. Hanchett, *Arizona's Graham-Tewksbury Feud*, 55–59.

104. See Raymond S. Nickerson, "Confirmation Bias," *Review of General Psychology* 2, no. 2 (June 1998): 175–220; and Scott Plous, *The Psychology of Judgment and Decision Making* (New York: McGraw-Hill, 1993), 233. Barbara Tuchman also used these insights in her study of warfare in *The March of Folly*.

CHAPTER 5. ENFORCEMENT WITH EXTREME PREJUDICE

1. "Nervy Sheriff Who Never Flinched," *Weekly Journal-Miner*, 18 June 1919, 5.

2. Louis is cited as a Graham nephew in several sources, and he appears to have been the son of Mary Graham and David Parker, but I am unable to confirm this through genealogical records.

3. See Statement of Bill Voris, *Territory of Arizona vs. Al Rose, Miguel Apodaca, Louis Parker, William Bonner, Richard Roe, and John Doe* (1887), Payson Precinct, Yavapai County, RG 11 Yavapai County, SG 8 Superior Court, Criminal Division, 1865–1965, Arizona State Library, Archives, and Record Division (hereafter cited as *Territory of Arizona vs. Al Rose et al.* [1887]). Apodaca's first name, Miguel, is also spelled "McGill" in territorial documents.

4. *Arizona Champion*, 3 September 1887, 3; *Mohave County Miner*, 17 September 1887, 1.

5. Statement of Bill Voris, *Territory of Arizona vs. Al Rose et al.* (1887).

6. Statement of Louis Naeglin, *Territory of Arizona vs. Rose et al.* (1887).

7. Statement of Ed Rose; Statement of Louis Naeglin, *Territory of Arizona vs. Al Rose et al.* (1887).

8. Al Rose testified that the party was a quarter mile away, whereas Louis Naeglin testified that the party was a half mile away. The time estimates are my own, based on an average walking speed of a horse at about 3–4 miles an hour on even ground. See Testimony of Al Rose, *Territory of Arizona vs. Al Rose et al.* (1887).

9. Newton charged that Al Rose and Miguel Apodaca burned his property, citing the statements of William Voris, Dick Williams, Charles Perkins, and Anton Besong. See statement of George A. Newton, *Territory of Arizona vs. Al Rose et al.* (1887).

10. Forrest, *Arizona's Dark and Bloody Ground*, 71–72, and Voris and King, "The Pleasant Valley War," oral history interview, 10, 23–24. For other mention of Apaches burning cabins in the Arizona Territory, see Wampler, *Arizona*, 196. The *Arizona Weekly Enterprise* reported on 20 August 1887, 2, on the other hand, that "Citizens learning of the [shooting] affair, assembled and burned his house and partially destroyed his corrals."

11. Criminal complaint, in the Justice's Court, Precinct of Payson, County of Yavapai, Territory of Arizona, *Territory of Arizona vs. John Tewksbury Sr. [sic], John Tewksbury Jr., James Tewksbury, Ed. Tewksbury, William Jacobs, Joseph Boyer*, 14 August 1887. This complaint does not appear to have gone to trial and was likely refiled with different defendants.

12. Wilson swore out a complaint 23 September 1887. See Hanchett, *They Shot Billy Today*, 82–83.

13. "Tonto Basin," *Arizona Champion*, 3 September 1887, 3.

14. The researchers with the Workers of the Writer's Program of the Works Projects Administration hold that Joe Ellenwood found Bill and brought him to his cabin, in *Arizona, A State Guide* (New York: Hastings House, 1940), 460.

15. "Interview with Mrs. Estella Converse Hill," daughter of Tom Graham, 2, Dedera Papers, box 44, file 8.

16. Statement of G. O. Sixby in Coroner's Inquest Over the Body of William Graham, RG 113: Yavapai County, SG 4, file 66. Estella Hill stated that Graham lived four days, rather than one, in "Estella Graham Converse Hill Dictation," 22 January 1962, 4, Dedera Papers, box 44, file 8.

17. Hanchett, *They Shot Billy Today*, 87. Edmonson's name appears very little in surviving records, and what his role in the events was, or what his relationship was to the Grahams or the Tewksburys, is unclear. See *Arizona Weekly Journal-Miner*, 12 October 1887, 3; *Arizona Silver Belt*, 10 November 1888, 4. Edmonson is not named in the formal indictment for murder, and he may have only served as a witness.

18. Samuel Graham reported in a letter to friends in Iowa that when he arrived in the Arizona Territory, his sons' friends informed him that only four men ambushed "Willie" as he went in search of horses. The elder Graham did not name his son's assailants in that letter, but he does allude to their having seven hundred head of cattle and "one of the finest ranges and water privileges in the valley" as a motive for the killing, in *Boone County Reporter*, 12 October 1887, 5.

19. Estella Hill described the wound as "practically disemboweled," although Rose's and Sixby's descriptions were less dramatic in their statements at the coroner's inquest. Nonetheless, Hill stated that both Johnny and Tom "swore over [Bill's] grave," in "Estella Graham Converse Hill Dictation," 22 January 1962, Dedera Papers, box 44, file 8. She later said: "The Bill Graham killing . . . profoundly affected Tom. That's when he went to war," in "Interview with Mrs. Estella Converse Hill," 2, Dedera Papers, box 44, file 8.

20. Testimony of G. O. Sixby, transcribed and published in Hanchett, *They Shot Billy Today*, 114.

21. Kyle J. Susa and Christian A. Meissner, "Accuracy of Eyewitness Descriptions," in *Encyclopedia of Psychology and Law*, edited by Bryan L. Cutler (Thousand Oaks, Calif.: Sage Publications, 2008), 286.

22. See also Christian A. Meissner and John C. Brigham, "A Meta-Analysis of the Verbal Overshadowing Effect in Face Identification," *Applied Cognitive Psychology* 15, no. 6 (2001): 603–16; Christian A. Meissner, Siegfried L. Sporer, and Jonathan W. Schooler, "Person Descriptions as Eyewitness Evidence," in *Handbook of Eyewitness Psychology*, ed. R. Lindsay et al. (Mahwah, N.J.: Lawrence Erlbaum, 2006), 3–34; and Siegfried L. Sporer, "Describing Others: Psychological Issues," in *Psychological Issues in Eyewitness Identification*, ed. Siegfried L. Sporer, Roy S. Malpass, and Guenter Koehnken (Hillsdale, N.J.: Lawrence Erlbaum, 1996), 53–86.

23. James D. Houck ran away from home at the age of fifteen and served in the 31st Wisconsin Volunteer Infantry Regiment, which, among other engagements, participated in the Battle of Shiloh, and the sieges of Atlanta and Savannah. See Martha Houck Lee, "Magazine of Feud Is Decried as Inaccurate," *Arizona Republic*, n.d., in Dedera Papers, box 44, file 12. Also, see James D. Houck headstone, Greenwood Memory Lawn Mortuary and Cemetery, Cave Creek, Ariz.; *U.S. Civil War Pension Index: General Index to Pension Files, 1861–1934*, and *U.S. Army, Register of Enlistments, 1798–1914*, 56. For information on the Wisconsin 31st Regiment's service, see Civil War Archive, "Union Regimental Histories," http://www.civilwararchive.com/Unreghst/unwiinf3.htm#31st (accessed 7 Sept. 2017).

24. Several family trees found on www.Ancestry.com list Houck's complete name as "James Denny Houck," whereas parish records from the Sacred Heart Cathedral in Gallup, New Mexico, list his full name as "James Dennis Houck"; from Fran Carlson Collection,

1870–1990, MSS 72, box 2, file 4 (notes in possession of author). Houck provided his account to William McLeod Raine, which was published in "The War for the Range," *Frank Leslie's Popular Monthly* (September 1930), 440.

25. "Tonto Basin," *St. Johns Herald*, 29 September 1887, 3; "Tonto Basin," *Arizona Weekly Enterprise*, 8 October 1887, 4.

26. Flake favored Houck's account in "Some Reminiscences," 11. Woody and Schwartz and Forrest also relayed Houck's account in *Globe, Arizona*, 135–37, and *Arizona's Dark and Bloody Ground*, 89–95, respectively. Houck clearly believed that the Grahams were dangerous in warning Mulvenon about the possibility of an ambush by the Grahams, as reported in "Tonto Basin," *St. Johns Herald*, 29 September 1887, 3, and "Tonto Basin," *Arizona Weekly Enterprise*, 8 October 1887, 4.

27. Fran Carlson speculated that Houck's marriage to an Indian woman may have been the source of the negative views that some had of him. Carlson also believed that Martha Houck Lee's statements that her father was honest and fair were corroborated by similar comments made of him by his neighbors. "Both of the Linville sisters that I interviewed," she recorded, "remembered him as kind and honest." "Interviews with Martha Houck Lee, October 22–23 1931," from Fran Carlson Collection, 1870–1990, S1, box 1, file 6, "Carlson Houck Interviews" (notes in possession of author).

28. John A. Hunt, who knew Houck, described him as "very dark—looked like a Mexican," in "Verbal Battle Between Jim Houck and Ed Rogers," 2, John Addison Hunt Biography, The Huntington Library, Art Collections, and Botanical Gardens.

29. Dedera rejected Houck's account, arguing that Houck knew all along that Bill was not John because Bill was large and "fleshy" like his brother Tom, whereas John was of slighter build. However, Dedera does not include a source for this physical description of the Grahams.

30. The sheriff named the others as Constable E. F. Odell, John W. Weatherford, and Fletcher Fairchild of Yavapai County. Forrest has this occurring on the day before; see *Arizona's Dark and Bloody Ground*, 80.

31. "Arizona News," *Arizona Champion*, 20 August 1887, 2.

32. Forrest, *Arizona's Dark and Bloody Ground*, 80.

33. See Hanchett, *Arizona's Graham-Tewksbury Feud*, 62, citing accounts by Mulvenon and John Weatherford published in the *Prescott Weekly Courier* and *Flagstaff Champion*, both in 1887 and found in the State Archives.

34. Hanchett, *Arizona's Graham-Tewksbury Feud*, 83–84.

35. William Shakespeare, *Hamlet*, act 3, scene 1, *The Complete Works of Williams Shakespeare*, "The Tragedy of Hamlet, Prince of Denmark," http://shakespeare.mit.edu (accessed 20 Dec. 2017). Tom Graham Diary (transcribed), page 2, Dedera Papers, MS 280, box 43, file 24.

36. Clifford Geertz, *The Interpretation of Cultures* (New York: Basic Books, 2000), 453.

37. From the description of Kathleen Donegan's book *Seasons of Misery: Catastrophe and Colonial Settlement in Early America* on the University of Pennsylvania Press's website, www.upenn.edu/pennpress/book/15167.html.

38. Brad S. Gregory, *Salvation at Stake* (Cambridge, Mass.: Harvard University Press, 1999), 250.

39. Galatians 2:20; 2 Corinthians 1:5–7; Romans 5:3. From the Internet Sacred Texts Archive, *The Polyglot Bible*, sacred-texts.com, http://sacred-texts.com/bib/poly/index.htm (accessed 20 Dec. 2017).

40. Anonymous Jesuit describing life in northern Mexico, Mexico City, 1757, quoted in Stockel, *Salvation through Slavery*, 40. Also quoted in Burrus, *Misiones norteñas mexicanas de la Compañía de Jesús, 1751–1757*, 81.

41. Stockel, *Salvation through Slavery*, 45.

42. Viceroy Antonio María Bucareli, Estracto de Novedades, Mexico, 26 November 1774 (enclosed with Bucareli to Arriaga, no. 1614), Archivo General de Indias, Sevilla, Spain, Audiencia de México, 514, as cited in Roberto Mario Salmón, *Indian Revolts in Northern New Spain* (Lanham, Md.: University Press of America, 1991), 129n10.

43. Salmón, *Indian Revolts in Northern New Spain*, 123.

44. Kessell, *Mission of Sorrows*, 166.

45. Stockel, *Salvation through Slavery*, 72–74.

46. Geronimo, *Geronimo's Story of His Life* (Taken down and edited by Stephen Melvil Barrett. New York: Duffield, 1906), 69, 71–73.

47. Doña Ana, New Mexico, was later renamed Las Cruces.

48. Cremony, *Life among the Apaches*, 74–79.

49. John Wyer Summerhayes retired from the army as a Major Quartermaster. See Arlington National Cemetery Website, http://www.arlingtoncemetery.net/jwsummerhayes. htm (accessed 20 May 2016).

50. Summerhayes, *Vanished Arizona*, 104. Martha Summerhayes also noted that soldiers, in particular, "never like to talk much about such things," 87.

51. Ibid., 82–84.

52. Summerhayes commented on the gendered differences in narrative styles in ibid., 312–13.

53. Letter from William A. Gurnett, dated 2 January 1909, reprinted in Summerhayes, *Vanished Arizona*, appendix, 318.

54. Charles B. Gatewood, *Lt. Charles Gatewood & His Apache Wars Memoir* (Lincoln: University of Nebraska Press, 2005), 173.

55. Psychologists Tess Neal and Carl Clements find that exposure to chronic fear can have the same impact of having experienced actual violence. "Diagnostic criteria for PTSD," they note in citing the *Diagnostic and Statistical Manual of Mental Disorders* (DSM 5), "include having experienced, witnessed, or been confronted with an event or events that involved threatened or actual death or serious injury, or a threat to the physical integrity to the self or others" (Neal and Clements, "Prison Rape and Psychological Sequelae: A Call for Research," *Psychology, Public Policy, and Law* 16, no. 3 [2010]), 289.

56. See Laurie Ellinghausen, "'Shame and Eternal Shame," *Exemplaria* 20, no. 3 (2008): 264–82; Richard Kearney, "Writing Trauma," in *Making Sense*, ed. Bandy Lee, Nancy Olson, and Thomas P. Duffy (New York: Peter Lang, 2015), 131–43; and Marie-Luise Kohlke and Christian Gutleben, *Neo-Victorian Tropes of Trauma* (Amsterdam: Editions Rodopi, 2010). For even earlier studies of stress in ancient literature, see Francesco M. Galassi et al., "Fight-or-Flight Response in the Ancient Egyptian Novel 'Sinuhe' (c. 1800 B.C.E.)," *Autonomic Neuroscience: Basic and Clinical* 195 (February 2016): 27–28.

57. Eric T. Dean, *Shook Over Hell* (Cambridge, Mass.: Harvard University Press, 1997), 72.

58. Ibid., 70, 74. Dean quotes L. H. Bartemeier et al.'s "Combat Exhaustion" (*Journal of Nervous and Mental Disease 104 (1946)*: 358–89, 489–525), from John Keegan, *The Face of Battle* (New York: Random House, 1976), 329.

59. Dean, *Shook Over Hell*, 78, 80.

60. Ignacio Martín-Baró, "Political Violence in War as Causes of Psychological Trauma in El Salvador," *International Journal of Mental Health* 18, no. 1 (Spring 1989), 15.

61. Sources do not agree on the date of Tewksbury's murder. At the coroner's inquest, Lydia Tewksbury stated that it was the morning of 1 September. Tewksbury descendant Bill Brown places the date at Saturday, 3 September, in "Letter from Bill Brown to Don Dedera, 1/7/88," Dedera Papers, box 42, file 48. Two territorial newspapers agree with Brown's murder date, "More Blood," *Arizona Weekly Journal-Miner*, 14 September 1887, 4, and *St. Johns Herald*, 15 September 1887, 2. Dedera, however, places the date at 2 September 1887, in *A Little War of Our Own*, 135. I use the date stated in the official coroner's report.

62. Shute claimed in *The Pleasant Valley War*, 13, that the Tewksburys often fled to Willow Creek at the base of Sombrero Butte.

63. John Tewksbury's birthdate is cited in "Letter from Bill Brown to Don Dedera, 1/7/88," Dedera Papers, box 42, file 48. John Tewksbury Jr. (later adopted by John Rhodes) was born in 1887, according to his military registration, and the 1900 U.S. Census. Some family trees at Ancestry.com (accessed 14 Dec. 2012) place the birthdate at 3 October of that year and indicate that John Jr. was possibly the third child born to John and Mary Ann Tewksbury, but the 1900 U.S. Census lists only two children—Bertha and John—born to Mary and John Tewksbury.

64. Lydia Tewksbury's testimony places their departure at about 8:00 A.M., after breakfast, and states that she heard firing at about 8:30 A.M. See her statement at the coroner's inquest, reprinted in Hanchett, *They Shot Billy Today*, 18–19. Hazelton recalled that Jacobs had worked as an agent for the Daggs brothers in Pleasant Valley; see "Hazelton Manuscript," 89.

65. Cooper was heard on the trail to Holbrook boasting about the murder, and he was clearly talking to someone. See Dedera, *A Little War of Our Own*, 141.

66. "Estella Graham Converse Hill Dictation," 22 January 1962, 4, Dedera Papers, box 44, file 8.

67. Dedera provided a more detailed, if not more colorful, description of this killing, citing Bob Voris's interview with Clara Woody, in *A Little War of Our Own*, 135–36. Since Bob Voris was born in 1902, and therefore not present during the killings, I draw from the testimonies given at the coroner's inquest. See "Evidence of Thomas Shultes," 10 September 1887, Coroner's Inquest of John Tewksbury and William Jacobs, RG 6, SG 5, Crime, Series 9, box 4:15, roll 50.25.66, Arizona State Library, Archives, and Public Records. See also Hanchett, *They Shot Billy Today*, 18–19. Woody probably drew from the *St. Johns Herald*, 29 September 1887, 3, in describing Jacobs's wounds as three shots in the back, and Tewksbury's wounds as one shot in the back of the neck, and his head smashed in by a rock. See Woody and Schwartz, *Globe, Arizona*, 137.

68. "Estella Graham Converse Hill Dictation," 22 January 1962, 4, Dedera Papers, box 44, file 8.

69. Ibid.

70. Bob Voris stated that Ollie Crouch was in the Tewksbury cabin the morning that John Tewksbury and Bill Jacobs were killed, and that they left to find her missing horse. Jayne Peace Pyle calls into question several aspects of Voris's claim in *Women of the Pleasant Valley War*, 77–78. Pyle also discusses the merits of the different accounts of who was in the Tewksbury cabin during the siege in ibid., 59–60.

71. See Thomas Shultes's statement at the coroner's inquest, reprinted in Hanchett, *They Shot Billy Today*, 19.

72. One account has it that Shultes stoically turned and walked back toward the cabin, unwilling to run for fear of showing cowardice. However, at the coroner's inquest, Shultes stated that he ran to the cabin. See ibid. Also see Lydia Tewksbury's testimony at the coroner's inquest in Hanchett, *They Shot Billy Today*, 18–19.

73. Pyle, *Women of the Pleasant Valley War*, 43.

74. Some accounts have Ed Tewksbury riding out for help amid a hail of bullets, but there is no information about who he returned with or to what effect. Lydia Tewksbury's testimony at the coroner's inquest estimated that one hundred shots were fired that day. See transcribed and reprinted statement in Hanchett, *They Shot Billy Today*, 18–19.

75. Don Dedera, in *A Little War of Our Own*, 275n6, cites a 1960 interview with Leland Shelley, whose grandfather James Edward Shelley told of overhearing drunken cowboys ride by his camp in early September 1887, laughing about the murder on their way to Holbrook.

76. Shute, in *The Pleasant Valley War*, 17, claimed that Ed Tewksbury voiced this concern.

77. "Estella Graham Converse Hill Dictation," 22 January 1962, 4, Dedera Papers, box 44, file 8.

78. "Mary Ann Tewksbury . . . always claimed that she did not learn of John's death until 2 or 3 days after, even though she feared so when he did not return," from Bill Brown Notarized Statement 10/14/92, Dedera Papers, box 42, file 28.

79. Popular accounts tell of the assault lasting for ten days. However, Lydia Tewksbury testified at the coroner's inquest that John's body was discovered on the third day. Clearly, they felt safe enough by then to leave the cabin and look for him. See transcription of Lydia's testimony in Hanchett, *They Shot Billy Today*, 18–19.

80. *Arizona Silver Belt*, 10 September 1887, 4, reported that the bodies of Tewksbury and Jacobs were discovered by Tewksbury's wife, Mary. I have been unable to corroborate this report with any other source, and for the reasons I argue in the manuscript, I do not believe this report is accurate.

81. See Lydia Tewksbury's and Thomas Shultes's statements at the coroner's inquest, transcribed and printed in Hanchett, *They Shot Billy Today*, 18–19.

82. "The Pleasant Valley War," *Arizona Silver Belt*, 1 October 1887, 3. The story that has grown from this initial account, which deserves further scrutiny, is that the Grahams stood guard over the bodies of Tewksbury and Jacobs until they were consumed by hogs. This story appears to have originated from the October 1887 *Arizona Silver Belt* report that "disinterested persons who asked to be allowed to bury them were warned by members of the Graham faction to keep away, that any one attempting to bury the corpses would forfeit their lives." Subsequent accounts have never identified who the "disinterested persons"

were who wished to bury the men, and many oft-cited secondhand accounts assert that the Grahams stood guard over the bodies for several days to prevent a burial. However, since it was common practice to hold a coroner's inquest at the scene of the crime, it is out of place, and seems unlikely, that anyone would be asking to bury the bodies *before* the official investigation was completed. Further, these secondhand stories presume that the Grahams prevented the justice of the peace from conducting the investigation so that hogs could complete their work, but there is no evidence in any territorial records of anyone hindering or preventing a coroner's inquest. Had this been the case, anyone so doing could easily have been charged with obstruction of justice, which did not happen in this case. Finally, when the justice of the peace arrived in the settlement, all evidence indicates that he traveled alone, without the protection of the county sheriff's office, which also suggests that he neither expected to encounter resistance nor did he fear to enter the crime scene.

83. "The Pleasant Valley War," *Arizona Silver Belt*, 1 October 1887, 3.

84. Hazleton, "Hazelton Manuscript," 140; Voris and King, "The Pleasant Valley War," oral history interview, 55–56.

85. There are no statements about hogs at the death site from Tewksbury family members; from the witnesses called at the coroner's inquest; from statements from members of the coroner's jury, either at the time of the inquest or later; or from the official report penned by Justice of the Peace John Meadows, who conducted the inquest. Further, the earliest report of the death of John Tewksbury states nothing about hogs, and seems to suggest that the bodies of both Tewksbury and Jacobs were in the same condition when the coroner's inquest was held as when they were initially found. The *St. Johns Herald* reported that "on or about the 2d of September, John Tewksbury and Wm. Jacobs were killed by the Graham party. They were shot about half a mile from the house of John Tewksbury. His wife found the bodies, but could get no one to bring them in, so she covered them up, one with a blanket and the other with a wagon sheet, *in which condition they were found when Judge Meadows arrived to hold the inquest. . . .*" (italics added), "Tonto Basin," 29 September 1887, 3. See also "Tonto Basin," *Arizona Weekly Enterprise*, 8 October 1887, 4. The earliest account of John Tewksbury's body being "almost devoured by hogs" appeared in the *Arizona Weekly Journal-Miner* the day before the *St. Johns Herald* report, on 28 September 1887, 4. The *Arizona Weekly Journal-Miner* stated that it pulled together information from "letters arrived here to-day, in the southern mail, from Payson, to a private individual, giving meager details of the bloody event. These letters were from four different parties, who are not connected with either of the opposing factions, and all agree as to the facts. One is dated the 18th instant, the day on which the last fight occurred, and the latest was of date of the 20th instant, all of them being from reliable citizens of that section." This story in the *Arizona Weekly Journal-Miner*, that the body of John Tewksbury was "almost devoured by hogs," provides no further information or context to understand what "almost" meant. Did "almost" mean that they had to shoo away hogs that were rooting about at the site of the murder, or that hogs were attempting to consume the corpse when the coroner and jury arrived, or that they actually ate the bodies? There are other elements to the *Arizona Weekly Journal-Miner's* account that are difficult to reconcile with corroborating evidence.

Why was only John Tewksbury's body desecrated by hogs, and not Jacobs's body as well, which was lying next to Tewksbury's? This claim that hogs devoured Tewksbury nonetheless became a significant part of the lore because it illustrated the depth of hatred between the two families, that the Grahams would prevent the burial of Tewksbury and Jacobs even though their bodies were molested by hogs.

86. Fred W. Croxen noted that a fence law was passed in the [18]70s requiring that hogs be penned, in "History of Grazing on Tonto," a paper presented at the Tonto Grazing Conference in Phoenix, Arizona, November 4–5, 1926.

87. Testimony of Thomas Shultes, transcribed and reprinted in Hanchett, *They Shot Billy Today*, 19.

88. "Murdered," *Arizona Republican*, 3 August 1892, 1. Since at no time did the Tewksburys live in or near Phoenix, and Tom Graham was the only one from that conflict who did, it seems likely that Graham was the origin of this story. See also "Fear Tewksbury-Graham Feud of Pioneer Days Is to Be Revived," *Coconino Sun*, 24 September 1920, 13.

89. This version can be found in practically all popular accounts. See, for example, Forrest, *Arizona's Dark and Bloody Ground*, 100–101; O'Neal, *Cattlemen vs. Sheepherders*, 50–51; and Shute, *The Pleasant Valley War*, 17. Dedera is more circumspect about this legend in *A Little War of Our Own*, 136-37, and Jayne Peace Pyle, in *Women of the Pleasant Valley War*, 41, is perhaps the only lay historian to openly challenge this popular story.

90. "Mary Ann Tewksbury denied to her grave any part in the burial of her husband, John Tewksbury, or William Jacobs. She always claimed that she did not learn of John's death until 2 or 3 days after, even though she feared so when he did not return," in William D. Brown Notarized Statement, 10/14/92, Dedera Papers, box 42, file 28. See also Hazelton, "Hazelton Manuscript," 145, and Zachariae, *Pleasant Valley Days*, 34. Voris also denied the veracity of the tale in Voris and King, "The Pleasant Valley War," oral history interview, 59.

91. Hazelton, "Hazelton Manuscript," 142.

92. From Dedera's copyedited notes "Joan Baeza, *Arizona Highways*, October 1960," Dedera Papers, box 130, file 11. Dedera also cites a 1960 interview with Leland Shelley, who told the same story, of his grandfather's overhearing drunken men ride by his camp in early September 1887, laughing about the murder on their way to Holbrook, in *A Little War of Our Own*, 141, 275n6. See also Adele B. Westover and J. Morris Richards, *Unflinching Courage* (Joseph City, Ariz.: John H. Miller, 1963), 493.

93. The Blevinses sold their Canyon Creek ranch to William Orville Gruwell. His name is also spelled Gruell or Grewell. Gruwell makes his first appearance in territorial records on 23 September 1887 as a witness in the death of Henry Midleton, and again on 16 November 1887 as a juror in the inquest on Al Rose's body. He also testified on 23 September that he had been living in the area ("some distance") about a month. For a description of early Holbrook's lawlessness, see Jan MacKell, *Red Light Women of the Rocky Mountains* (Albuquerque, University of New Mexico Press, 2011), 88.

94. *St. Johns Herald*, 7 April 1887, 3.

95. "More Rustlers Killed," *Arizona Champion*, 10 September 1887, 3. On Cooper's reputation as a rustler, see "Four More Men Killed," *Mohave County Miner*, 1 October 1887,

2; "Local News," *St. Johns Herald*, 22 September 1887, 3; "Good Work," *Tombstone Epitaph*, 10 September 1887, 4; and *Arizona Weekly Citizen*, 6 August 1892, 2. Drusilla Hazelton states that Annie Graham, Tom's wife, said that her husband also claimed to have killed John Tewksbury. The pistol Tom Graham carried, which Annie possessed after his death, is said to have been taken from John Tewksbury's body. Hazelton, "Hazelton Manuscript," 148–51. See also Hanchett, *Arizona's Graham-Tewksbury Feud*, 75.

96. Flake, *Tales from Oz*, 35.

97. Perry Owens, as quoted in "A Terror to Outlaws, the Sanguinary Record of a Quaker in Arizona," *The Climax*, 20 June 1894, 1.

98. For a detailed discussion of Perry's background and history, as well as the reaction to his aggressive job performance as sheriff, see Larry D. Ball, "Commodore Perry Owens," *The Journal of Arizona History* 33, no. 1 (Spring 1992): 27–56.

99. Owens told of sending a letter to Cooper, before the shootout, in his interview with *The Black Hills Union*, 15 February 1895, 3. See also Testimony of Deputy Sheriff Frank Wattron, reprinted in Hanchett, *They Shot Billy Today*, 165.

100. Owens, as quoted in "A Terror to Outlaws," *The Climax*, 20 June 1894, 1. See also *The Mason County Journal*, 29 June 1894, 4.

101. Flake, *Tales from Oz*, 37. See also Flake, "Some Reminiscences," 8–9. Will C. Barnes, who states that he witnessed the shoot-out, provides slightly different wording in how Owen responded to the armed citizens, but the intent conveyed is the same as Flake's. See Barnes, *Apaches and Longhorns*, 148.

102. Roberts had been employed by the Aztec Cattle Company, but was among the number of cowboys who quit when given the ultimatum to stop stealing from the company. See "Bloody Tragedy," *Arizona Weekly Journal-Miner*, 7 September 1887, 3. Grace Elnor Gladden was five months old. See Susan Amanda McFarland Gladden, "Payson Pioneer Cemetery," www.paysonrimcountry.com/WesternHeritage/PioneerCemetery.aspx (accessed 25 June 2013). See also Punkin Center Homemakers, Tonto Basin Research Collection, box 1, folder 2, "The History of the Tonto—Manus. (Pioneer Profiles)—c. 1976. John MacDonald."

103. Eva Blevins, as told to Robert Allison, "The Blevins Family: An Episode in the Pleasant Valley War," unpublished manuscript, Arizona Pioneer's Historical Society, 1936, quoted in Dedera, *A Little War of Our Own*, 149. Both Forrest and Dedera give variations of the wording of the exchange between Owens and Cooper, but do not disagree on the sequence or the intent of the exchange. See Forrest, *Arizona's Dark and Bloody Ground*, 117–18, and Dedera, *A Little War of Our Own*, 144–47.

104. Blevins, "The Blevins Family: An Episode in the Pleasant Valley War," quoted in Dedera, *A Little War of Our Own*, 144–47.

105. Flake, *Tales from Oz*, 37. Flake does not state that he was present in Holbrook at the time of the shooting, and he appears to be drawing from Owen's testimony that was reprinted in the *Apache Critic*. A portion of the transcription of that testimony can be found in Dedera, *A Little War of Our Own*, 146–47, whereas Hanchett provides a fuller transcription in *They Shot Billy Today*, 308–10.

106. Owens later stated that Cooper opened the door "about a foot and . . . stuck a gun out," in "A Terror to Outlaws," *The Black Hills Union*, 15 February 1895, 3. See also

Testimony of C. P. Owens, 6 September 1887, recorded by Justice of the Peace D. G. Harvey, and transcribed and reprinted in Hanchett, *They Shot Billy Today*, 308–10. Hanchett's preservation and transcription of this testimony is important because Owen's deposition appears to be missing from the inquest records of the Justice of the Peace Court, Apache County, 1882–1947 in the Arizona State Archives, Filmfile #57.2.3. Barnes offered a similar recounting of the exchange at the doorway from "my memory of the affair, which I have been at some pains to refresh and confirm," and, although he mixed up the names of the Blevins brothers, he wrote that "all of us standing on the depot platform [perhaps thirty yards away] heard him plainly" (*Apaches and Longhorns*, 148–51). The Blevins women offered a substantially different account from that of Owens at the same inquest, each stating that none of the slain men were armed. Regarding this discrepancy, Marshall Trimble sagely observed that "slain outlaws often grow halos," and other eyewitnesses to the shooting or the aftermath testified to the existence of weapons on or near the deceased. See Marshall Trimble, *Arizona Outlaws and Lawmen* (Charleston, S.C.: The History Press, 2015), 55–56. See also "Local News," *St. Johns Herald*, 8 September 1887, 3.

107. Flake, *Tales from Oz*, 38.

108. Blevins, as quoted in Allison, "The Blevins Family: An Episode in the Pleasant Valley War," Dedera Papers, box 42/OV1, file 2.

109. Barnes notes that the horse was shot between the eyes, but still ran about a hundred yards before it collapsed, in *Apaches and Longhorns*, 149.

110. Roberts is also identified as "Mote" in territorial records. See "Jury Verdict," 15 September 1887, reprinted in Hanchett, *They Shot Billy Today*, 226; Owens, quoted in "A Terror to Outlaws," *The Climax*, 20 June 1894, 1.

111. Testimony of Sam Brown, reprinted in Hanchett, *They Shot Billy Today*, 225; Flake, *Tales from Oz*, 38.

112. Punkin Center Homemakers, Tonto Basin Research Collection, box 1, folder 2 "The History of the Tonto—Manus. (Pioneer Profiles)—c. 1976. John MacDonald."

113. Flake, *Tales from Oz*, 38–39.

114. Ibid., 38.

115. Owens, as quoted in "A Terror to Outlaws," *The Climax*, 20 June 1894, 1. Genealogical records list 4 September 1887 as the death dates for Albert Charles Blevins and William Hampton Blevins, but other sources cite 9 or 10 August 1887 as the death date for Hampton Blevins.

116. See transcribed statement of Eva Blevins in Pyle, *Women of the Pleasant Valley War*, 143.

117. James H. McClintock quoted Holbrook newspaper editor W. H. Burbage, in *Arizona, Prehistoric, Aboriginal, Pioneer, Modern* (Chicago: S. J. Clark, 1916), 467.

118. Pyle, *Women of the Pleasant Valley War*, 59.

119. Dedera, citing Allison interview with Evelyn Blevins, in *A Little War of Our Own*, 276n28. Amanda Gladden, the wife of the late George Gladden, was also present at the shooting and later testified that none of the Blevins men, or Roberts, were armed. See "Testimony of Amanda Gladden," reprinted verbatim in *They Shot Billy Today*, 225. Jayne Peace Pyle published a transcription of Eva Blevins's account in *Women of the Pleasant Valley War*, 143–44.

CHAPTER 6. RUSTLERS ROUSTED

1. The *Arizona Weekly Enterprise* reported that "it is stated to be a fact that [Stott's] ranch was the headquarters of men known to be thieves, and that he acted as a go-between [for the Grahams and Blevinses]," in "Bloody Tonto Basin," 8 September 1888, 1.

2. Hanchett vigorously contests the assertion that Stott was involved in horse theft (*They Shot Billy Today*, 240–69). What is clear, and uncontested, however, is that contemporaries in the area suspected him of being part of the theft ring, and they acted on that suspicion. See *They Shot Billy Today*, fn 554.

3. Article XX, Pinal County Livestock Association, "Constitution and By-Laws," *Arizona Weekly Enterprise*, 3 September 1887, 1.

4. "Stock Notes," *Arizona Champion*, 3 September 1887, 1.

5. "Paid the Penalty," ibid., 13 August 1887, 3, and "Telegraph," *Arizona Weekly Citizen*, 20 August 1887, 1.

6. Parker Anderson, "True Crime: Frank Wilson and the Clevenger Murders." Sharlot Hall Museum Library and Archives, https://sharlot.org/library-archives/index.php/blog/true-crime (accessed 21 Dec. 2017).

7. Andy Cooper was reported to have stated that he smashed Tewksbury's head with a rock in "Resisted Arrest," *Arizona Weekly Journal-Miner*, 28 September 1887, 3. This version was also carried in "Four More Men Killed," *Mohave County Miner*, 1 October 1887, 2. However, Thomas Shultes testified at the coroner's inquest that "Wm. Jacobs . . . looked as though he had been hit with a rock at top of head," and that "John Tewksbury had no bruises upon [his] head." Lydia Tewksbury, who also testified at the inquest, made no mention of head wounds, only that she "thought [I] saw bullet wound in back of John Tewksbury." Testimony of Lydia Tewksbury and Testimony of Thomas Shultes, transcribed and reprinted in Hanchett, *They Shot Billy Today*, 18–19. The coroner's inquest ruling mentions no details about the kinds of wounds found on Tewksbury or Jacobs, or, for that matter, the condition of the bodies when found, stating only that "deceased came to death by gun shot [*sic*] wounds fired by parties unknown." See RG 113, Yavapai County, SG 4 Justice Court Inquests (Folder #1–180) (1867–1895) Box 1; Coroner inquests in RG 113, SG 4, 1:66 Tewksbury, John; Jacobs, William; Graham, William, 9/1887. There is no record of Cooper interacting with John Tewksbury prior to Tewksbury's murder, and the discrepancy between Cooper's reported boast and Shultes's testimony may have been because Cooper mistook Jacobs for Tewksbury. At the same time, however, if Cooper's murder of Tewksbury was motivated by revenge for his brother's murder, the act of smashing Tewksbury's skull would suggest a deeply personalized act of aggression directed specifically at Tewksbury.

8. The spelling of Midleton's name in this study is consistent with his gravestone in Young, AZ, although territorial documents spell his name "Middleton."

9. Houck's Tank is close to 167 miles from Young, AZ.

10. Rhodes is sometimes spelled Rhoades in territorial documents. Regarding Houck's wife, researcher Fran Carlson concluded: "She could have been all Navajo—both parents," in Fran Carlson Collection, 1870–1990, MSS 72 (notes in possession of author). Family tradition holds that John Rhodes's first wife, Trinidad Lopez, was born in Sonora, as indicated in

the 1920 U.S. Census, although the 1860 U.S. Census indicates that she was born in the New Mexico Territory. For Lopez family lore about John Rhodes, see Tobi Lopez Taylor, "Trinidad Lopez and the Naco Cemetery," *Archaeology Southwest* 20, no. 4 (Fall 2006), 13.

11. Shute, *The Pleasant Valley War*, ii, 4, 7. Shute's father was a peace officer during this period, and Shute himself later served as a former district attorney of Gila County, from 1908 to 1912.

12. This is according to Robert Voris in Voris and King, "The Pleasant Valley War," oral history interview, 18.

13. Grenville Goodwin, *The Social Organization of the Western Apache* (Tucson: University of Arizona Press, 1969), 579.

14. Voris, in Voris and King, "The Pleasant Valley War," oral history interview, 19. See also *Arizona Silver Belt*, 10 September 1887, 4, and Dedera, *A Little War of Our Own*, 116. Regarding John Dayzn also known as Char-ne-say, see Goodwin, *Social Organization of the Western Apache*, "Appendix C, Tag Bands, Fort Apache," 579. Dayzn is alternately spelled Dazen in territorial documents.

15. Ellenwood's name is alternatively spelled Ellingwood. Hazelton asserts that the name "Ellenwood" was an alias for Tom Pickett, who was employed as a Hashknife cowboy during this time and was wounded in Pleasant Valley. She described Picket as "a seasoned warrior from the Lincoln County, New Mexico war and former running mate of Bill the Kid" ("Hazelton Manuscript," 108). There was a Tom Pickett who later served as sheriff in Arizona, from 1912 to 1914. See Mitchel P. Roth, *Historical Dictionary of Law Enforcement* (Westport, Conn.: Greenwood Press, 2000), 265. If Ellenwood was Pickett's alias, the identity of his wife remains a mystery.

16. See Testimony of Al Rose, Coroner's Inquest, Yavapai County, RG 113, SG 4, 1:69 "Middleton, Henry" 10/1887.

17. See Hanchett, *They Shot Billy Today*, 133.

18. Roberts later told this to Winslow Constable Joe T. McKinney (alternatively spelled Mckinney). See Hanchett, *Arizona's Graham-Tewksbury Feud*, 79.

19. Hanchett places the date of Midleton's death on 20 September 1887, but Miguel Apodaca estimated that Midleton died within two days of being shot. See Hanchett, *They Shot Billy Today*, 278, and Testimony of Miguel Apodaca, reprinted in ibid., 282.

20. The posse consisted of Deputy Sheriff J. D. Houck, Winslow Constable Joe McKinney, and Osmer Flake from Snowflake.

21. Hanchett dates the Perkins store ambush as 22 September 1887 in *They Shot Billy Today*, 168. However, Individual Records at familysearch.org dates the deaths on 21 September 1887; other sources cite 4 September 1887 as the death date; see also Forrest, *Arizona's Dark and Bloody Ground*, 35.

22. Zachariae, *Pleasant Valley Days*, 131.

23. Albert Charles Blevins was the second son of Martin Blevins.

24. W. J. Mulvenon statement, Coroner's Inquest, RG 113, SG4 1:68, file "Graham, John; Blevins, Chas. 10/1887."

25. Ibid.

26. Flake, "Some Reminiscences," 14.

27. Hanchett, quoting Joe T. McKinney, "Reminiscences," *Arizona Historical Review* (April, July, October 1932), in *They Shot Billy Today*, 332.

28. Ibid.

29. Flake, "Some Reminiscences," 14. Estella Hill believed that Johnny died cursing the sheriff, in "Estella Graham Converse Hill Dictation," 22 January 1962, 4, Dedera Papers, box 44, file 8.

30. Flake, "Some Reminiscences," 14.

31. Ibid.

32. Phoenix A.T. July the 31= 1888, transcribed letter, 2–3, Dedera Papers, box 43, file 24.

33. Ibid.

34. Forrest, *Arizona's Dark and Bloody Ground*, 66–67.

35. Tom Graham letter to Mary Parker, Phoenix A.T. July the 31= 1888, Dedera Papers, box 43, file 24.

CHAPTER 7. BLIND JUSTICE, MASKED JUSTICE

1. Jayne Peace Pyle lists only twenty residents of the Tonto Basin as members of the vigilante committee, in *Women of the Pleasant Valley War*, 176. Shute estimates that there were thirty, in *The Pleasant Valley War*, 21.

2. Benton-Cohen, *Borderline Americans*, 61.

3. Barnes asserted in *Apaches and Longhorns*, 157–58, that this group consisted of "reputable citizens, determined to put an end to the reign of lawlessness that for some time had terrorized the entire region."

4. "Colonel" Jesse W. Ellison is frequently mentioned in second- and thirdhand accounts as a leader of this group. The title "colonel" was honorific, but he nonetheless served in the Kiowa and Comanche wars in Texas, and as a Confederate soldier, according to Roscoe Willson, in *Arizona Republic*, 16 July 1967. Bob Voris told Clara Woody of meeting Jesse Ellison, who was at an advanced age, and asking who was involved in the vigilante committee. Ellison reportedly relented, and named his sons-in-law Houston Kyle and Bud Campbell, Glenn Reynolds, Bill Colcord, Harvey Colcord, William McFadden, and John Rhodes. See Voris and King, "The Pleasant Valley War," oral history interview, 67–68. Still more residents have been named in other second- and thirdhand accounts.

5. Shute's 1954 manuscript is perhaps the first to discuss this vigilante group; see *The Pleasant Valley War*, 21–22. Zachariae later collected family stories about this group in *Pleasant Valley Days*, 28–29.

6. Reprinted in Hanchett, *They Shot Billy Today*, 128–29.

7. Letter from Tom Graham to "Dear Sister [Mag?]," 31 July 1888, reprinted in Dedera, *A Little War of Our Own*, 206–207.

8. Hanchett, *They Shot Billy Today*, 130–31.

9. Hazelton recalled that James Stinson tried to buy out both the Graham and Tewksbury brothers when he moved his cattle to Pleasant Valley. Allegedly, Stinson "wanted the whole country to himself and made every effort to keep everyone out," and the Grahams and Tewksburys "refused to negotiate with Stinson." It is possible that Tom Graham may have been referring to this effort by Stinson, but no evidence supports that Stinson made

an offer to the Grahams for their land, or sought to drive them to sell their land, or hired others to do so. Hazelton notes that the number of available men to work Stinson's cattle was under a dozen, so it does not seem likely that he would wish to drive his workforce away. See Hazelton, "Hazelton Manuscript," 68–74.

10. The documentary record on Joe Ellenwood is scant, and I have been unable to find any mention of his wife's first or maiden name.

11. McKinney, "Reminiscences," *Arizona Historical Review* 5, no. 3 (October 1932), 201.

12. Defense attorney John C. Wentworth's account of the trial is found in Jess G. Hayes, *Boots and Bullets* (Tucson: University of Arizona Press, 1967), 60–63.

13. "Local News," *St. Johns Herald*, 17 November 1887, 3.

14. *Tombstone Epitaph*, 5 November 1887, 2; *Arizona Weekly Enterprise*, 5 November 1887, 2; *St. Johns Herald*, 10 November 1887, 2, and "Local News," ibid., 17 November 1887, 3; "Mail Robbery," *Arizona Weekly Journal-Miner*, 9 November 1887, 4.

15. "Mail Robbery," *Arizona Weekly Journal-Miner*, 9 November 1887.

16. The Houdon ranch was located along the banks at the confluence of Spring Creek and Walnut Creek. See Pyle, *Pleasant Valley War*, 150. Dedera notes in *A Little War of Our Own*, 278n40, that the Rose children believed that they were present that day at the Houdon ranch, although there is no corroborating evidence for this.

17. Testimony of John Whatley, 16 November 1887, Inquest on the Body of Albert Rose, Pleasant Valley Precinct, filed 15 November 1887, Arizona State Library, Archives, and Public Records, RG 113 Yavapai County, SG 4 Justice Court Inquests, Folder #1–180 (1867–1895), box 1; Coroner Inquests 1:73 Rose, Albert, 11/1887.

18. "Pleasant Valley," *Tombstone Epitaph*, 19 November 1887, 1.

19. The Illinois Civil War Project, "17th Illinois Infantry Regiment: Three Year Service, May 24, 1861–June 4, 1864," http://civilwar.illinoisgenweb.org/reg_html/017_reg.html (accessed 14 March 2007).

20. How Rose was killed has been subject to disagreement. His companions insisted that they heard about twenty shots fired at close range. Whatley testified at the coroner's inquest that Rose appeared to have about eleven bullet wounds in his body, and a buckshot wound to his face, in John Whatley Testimony, reprinted in Hanchett, *They Shot Billy Today*, 275–77. See also *Tombstone Epitaph*, 19 November 1887, 1, and *Arizona Silver Belt*, 26 May 1888, 3. Sixby also reported eleven gunshot wounds on Rose's body in the *Prescott Courier*, which was reprinted in the *St. Johns Herald*, 17 November 1887, 1. Rose's son, however, reportedly remembered seeing his father's body draped over a horse with just two bullet wounds, and this is the number that Oz Flake cites in *William J. Flake*, 118. Constable Joe McKinney later wrote in his memoirs that only Glenn Reynolds fired at Rose with a shotgun (Hanchett, *They Shot Billy Today*, 335). Robert Voris insisted that Al Rose was hung, instead, and that Naeglin was coerced by the vigilantes into altering his testimony (Voris and King, "The Pleasant Valley War," oral history interview, 68–71). Jayne Peace Pyle took Voris's claim further in writing that Rose was "shot, hung, and shot again" (*Women of the Pleasant Valley War*, 48). None of the impaneled witnesses testified to any other wounds but gunshot, and six jurors of the coroner's inquest, as well as the coroner, concluded: "We find that deceased came to his death on or about the first of Nov 1887 by gunshot wounds

inflicted at the hands of parties unknown to us." See RG 113 Yavapai County, SG 4 Justice Court Inquests, Folder #1–180 (1867–1895), box 1; Coroner Inquests 1:73 Rose, Albert, 11/1887.

21. Dedera cites several contemporaries who also viewed Rose as an instigator and agitator in *A Little War of Our Own*, 277n3. The *Clifton Clarion* published on 16 November 1887, 2: "One theory of the killing of Al Rose is to the effect that he was shot by the Graham faction, because of a defection on his part from their ranks. He was shot to death by nine masked men."

22. "Local News," *Arizona Silver Belt*, 5 November 1887, 3.

23. Transcription reprinted in Pyle, *Women of the Pleasant Valley War*, 88.

24. *Clifton Clarion*, 23 May 1888, 2.

25. *Arizona Silver Belt*, 12 May 1888, 3. See also "A Salt River Shooting Scrape," *St. Johns Herald*, 31 May 1888, 1; and "From Tuesday's Daily" and "Our Territory," *Arizona Weekly Journal-Miner*, 16 May 1888, 3.

26. One of the men, John Whatley, was Graham's foreman and had been at the Houdon ranch when Al Rose was murdered. Whatley is also spelled Whately and Watley in territorial documents.

27. *Arizona Silver Belt*, 26 May 1888, 3.

28. "A Salt River Shooting Scrape," *Arizona Weekly Citizen*, 19 May 1888, 3; *Arizona Silver Belt*, 26 May 1888, 3.

29. "Robbery at Tonto," *St. Johns Herald*, 24 May 1888, 2.

30. Barnes, *Apaches and Longhorns*, 153–54.

31. Ibid., 159. Also see Forrest, *Arizona's Dark and Bloody Ground*, 195, 208–209.

32. Barnes asserted in *Apaches and Longhorns*, 154, that Stott's ranch was where horses stolen from the north were traded for those stolen from the south. Flake also believed this in "Some Reminiscences," 4–5.

33. Forrest, quoting from a letter by F. A. Ames, an acquaintance of Stott, in *Arizona's Dark and Bloody Ground*, 210.

34. Barnes, *Apaches and Longhorns*, 154. See also Flake, *Tales from Oz*, 28–31, and Forrest, *Arizona's Dark and Bloody Ground*, 195.

35. "Pleasant Valley Pleasantries," *Arizona Weekly Enterprise*, 1 September 1888, 3. See also "From Monday's Daily," *Arizona Weekly Journal-Miner*, 5 September 1888, 3A; "Territorial Items," *Mohave County Miner*, 15 September 1888, 2; and *St. Johns Herald*, 20 September 1888, 2.

36. The judge found in *Territory of Arizona vs. James Stott and Thomas Tucker* that the horse in question belonged to Lauffer, but he was not convinced that the evidence showed that Stott and Tucker actually took the horse, and found for the defendants.

37. Houck's method of serving warrants can be seen in the shooting of Billy Graham. Like many territorial lawmen of the day, he aimed to catch the accused by surprise with a chambered rifle pointed at that person before commanding surrender.

38. Joseph Fish identified Pleasant Valley resident Bill Voris as one of the deputies, in Fish Manuscript, 690.

39. Clymer's given name may have been Floyd, according to one memoir. See Forrest, *Arizona's Dark and Bloody Ground*, 375.

40. Zachariae, *Pleasant Valley Days*, 37, 128. Some accounts also name Jim Tewksbury,

but Shute denies that any of the Tewksburys were involved with this group. See *The Pleasant Valley War*, 23.

41. Flake, *Tales from Oz*, 30–31. Flake also told of riding up to a group of men he knew were from Pleasant Valley and carefully engaging them in conversation about what he discovered to see if he could learn any further details. From the looks and reactions he received, although no one stated so, he believed that his reading of the evidence was accurate.

42. Barnes, *Apaches and Longhorns*, 156–58. *Arizona Pioneer and Cemetery Research Project*, Stott, Scott and Wilson Cemetery, www.apcrp.org/STOTT-SCOTT-WILSON/ Stott_Scott_Wilson_Cem_082507.htm (18 Dec. 2017), describes the location as "Arizona Hwy 280 to Forest Service Road 300. Southeast to Mogollon Rim Road, to Hangman's Trail, Northeast on Hangman's Trail which is just past Black Canyon Road 300 to 400 feet, Northeast on Hangman's Trail 1/4 mile, graves are on right of the trail" (accessed 18 Dec. 2017).

43. John A. Hunt, "Verbal Battle Between Jim Houck and Ed Rogers," 2, John Addison Hunt Biography.

44. William C. Endicott, "Report of the Secretary of War," 30 November 1888, *Annual Report of the Secretary of War* (Washington, D.C.: Government Printing Office, 1888), 7.

45. Nelson A. Miles, "Report of Brigadier-General Miles," Headquarters Department of Arizona, 8 September 1888, in *Annual Report of the Secretary of War for the Year 1888*, 126.

46. Thomas Cruse, *Apache Days and After* (Caldwell, Idaho: Caxton Printers, 1941), 186.

47. Endicott, "Report of the Secretary of War," 30 November 1888, *Annual Report of the Secretary of War*, 6. See also Lori Davisson and Edgar Perry, *Dispatches from the Fort Apache Scout* (Tucson: University of Arizona Press, 2016), 126. Jacob Piatt Dunn's observations in *Massacres of the Mountains* (New York: Harper and Bros., 1886), 15, although writing about Colorado reservations, could well describe the problems in administering the Arizona reservations.

48. Although Bonner had been dead for a year, his name still appears on the indictments for the murder of John Tewksbury and Bill Jacobs.

49. *Territory of Arizona vs. Louis Parker, Thomas Graham, Miguel Apodaca, Thomas Carrington, William Bonner, Joseph Ellenwood, and William Gould*, Indictment for Murder, 2 December 1887, RG 113—Yavapai County. (All hearings were held in 1888.)

50. See "Court Calendar, Territorial Criminal," *Arizona Weekly Journal-Miner*, 29 May 1889, 3; "District Court Calendar, June Term, 1888, Territorial Criminal Cases," ibid., 30 May 1888, 3; "Court Calendar, November Term, 1888, Territorial Criminal," ibid., 14 November 1888, 4; and "Local News," *Arizona Silver Belt*, 15 June 1889, 3.

51. *Arizona Silver Belt*, 9 June 1888, 3.

52. J. J. Hawkins was law partner to District Attorney J. C. Herndon. *Territory of Arizona vs. Thomas Graham, Louis Parker, Miguel Apodaca, Thomas Carrington, William Bonner, Joseph Ellenwood, and William Gould*, "Booking Sheet," James M. Wright, District Judge, 4 June 1888. Also see court calendar published in *Arizona Weekly Journal-Miner*, 14 November 1888, 4.

53. Attorney General Herndon was an Arizona delegate to the National Democratic Nominating Convention that met in St. Louis the following week. See "Herndon and Barry

Our Delegates," *Clifton Clarion*, 9 May 1888, 3; *St. Johns Herald*, 17 May 1888, 2. President
Cleveland was renominated at this convention. Hanchett speculated in *They Shot Billy
Today*, 133, that Herndon's motive was to keep the Grahams occupied in court.

54. "Court Calendar, November Term, 1888, Territorial Criminal," *Arizona Weekly
Journal-Miner*, 14 November 1888, 3, and Yavapai County District Superior Court, Criminal
Register of Action, 1884–1894, 219–22, Arizona State Library, Archives, and Public Records.

55. "Delayed Justice," *Arizona Silver Belt*, 16 June 1888, 3.

56. See "Prescott Arizona 1887, Dear Annie," Dedera Papers, box 43, file 24.

57. "Delayed Justice," *Arizona Silver Belt*, 16 June 1888, 3; "Wednesday's Edition," *Arizona
Weekly Journal-Miner*, 14 November 1888, 3.

58. "Delayed Justice," *Arizona Silver Belt*, 16 June 1888, 3.

59. "Local Notes," *Arizona Weekly Journal-Miner*, 27 June 1888, 3.

60. Tewksbury descendant Bill Brown states that Jim went to Phoenix to kill Tom
Graham, reasoning that he was already going to die and had nothing to lose, in William
D. Brown notarized statement, 10/14/92, Dedera Papers, box 42, file 28. It is not clear if Jim
attempted to kill Graham during this time. Jayne Peace Pyle speculates in *Women of the
Pleasant Valley War*, 25, that he did not do so because he died before he could do it. While
it is certainly possible that this was Jim's motive in moving to Phoenix, Tempe was still
eleven miles away, and there were hotels in Tempe where he could have stayed to bring
him closer to where Tom Graham lived, on the outskirts of town.

61. *Arizona Weekly Journal-Miner*, 12 December 1888, 1. See also *Arizona Silver Belt*, 8
December 1888, 4, and *Arizona Weekly Enterprise*, 8 December 1888, 2.

62. They were married by Reverend Samuel Ezell, at Mary Ann Tewksbury's home,
Yavapai County Marriage Records, Arizona History and Archives Division, Phoenix,
Arizona. Also see *Arizona Marriage Collection, 1864–1982* (database on-line), Ancestry.
com, https://search.ancestry.com/search/db.aspx?dbid=7847 (accessed 17 Jan. 2018). John
Rhodes brought to the marriage three children from a previous relationship with Trinidad
Lopez in Tucson: Juan Francisco (John Frank), Ernestina Clara, and Guillermo (Willy).
See Tobi Lopez Taylor, "Trinidad Lopez and the Naco Cemetery," *Tobi Taylor's Journal*,
http://www.tobitaylor.com/blog/ (accessed 22 July 2017). In addition to the two children
she had with John Tewksbury, Mary Ann bore seven more children with John Rhodes.
See Pyle, *Women of the Pleasant Valley War*, 30.

63. Duchet is alternatively spelled Deushay, DuShey, Del Shay, Doesha, and Doesah
in territorial newspapers. Hanchett uses the spelling "Dushea," and references another
possible spelling of "DeShay," in *They Shot Billy Today*, 286–95. I have elected to follow
the spelling used in the court transcripts. The *Arizona Champion*, 4 December 1886, 3,
refers to the "Deusha bros.," but I have been unable to connect that reference specifically
to Charles Duchet, although that same spelling is used in the "Official Business," *Arizona
Republican*, 28 September 1920, 7, and "Early Days Recalled by an Old Timer," *Coconino
Sun*, 11 March 1921, 1, in clear reference to Charles Duchet. The *Arizona State Miner* further
noted on 28 March 1925 that Duchet came to the Arizona territory to establish himself as
a sheepherder, but makes no mention of brothers, in Doesha, Charles "Charley," Surname
Vertical File, Sharlot Hall Museum Library and Archives.

64. Duchet's physician, Dr. H. A. Hughes of Phoenix, recorded his many interviews with Duchet, including his final confession, in the 1930s. Logan D. Dameron, Hughes's great-grandson, typed the manuscript that is now known as the Dameron manuscript. It is reprinted verbatim in Hanchett, *They Shot Billy Today*, 286–95. Hughes clearly states that Duchet's surname by birth was English—which is what the Tewksburys insisted—but Duchet testified at the trial of John Rhodes that his "true name" was Duchet, although for a time he went by the name of his stepfather, Ingrahm. It is possible that the court transcriber misinterpreted Duchet's pronunciation of "English." See Court Transcript, 174.

65. Pearce, "Pearce Reminiscences," 28.

66. The Dameron manuscript states that Graham moved three hundred head of cattle from Pleasant Valley. See Hanchett, *They Shot Billy Today*, 295.

67. "Local Brevities," *Arizona Republican*, 22 March 1892, 4.

CHAPTER 8. "FROM HELL'S HEART"

Author's note: The quote used as the chapter title comes from Herman Melville, *Moby-Dick: An Authoritative Text*, edited by Hershel Parker and Harrison Hayford (New York: W.W. Norton, 1967), 426.

1. "Local News," *St. Johns Herald*, 9 June 1887, 3.

2. James H. McClintock, *Mormon Settlement in Arizona* (Phoenix, Ariz.: Manufacturing Stationers, 1921), 232.

3. "Married," *Arizona Weekly Journal-Miner*, 12 October 1887, 3.

4. "Estella Graham Converse Hill Dictation," 22 January 1962, Dedera Papers, box 44, file 8, 5.

5. Estella Hill related that Arvilla contracted diarrhea while Annie's mother was away, and the young mother did not know how to treat her, in "Estella Graham Converse Hill Dictation," 22 January 1962, box 44, file 8, 5. The Graham tombstone at the Phoenix (Arizona) Pioneer and Military Memorial Park, where Tom and Arvilla Graham were buried, gives Arvilla's birthdate as 14 December 1887. Her death in Phoenix was briefly noted almost a year later, in *Arizona Weekly Journal-Miner*, 14 November 1888, 3.

6. "Interview with Mrs. John McTaggart [Mollie Cummings], 8 December 1961," Dedera Papers, box 42, file 40. Earlier descriptions of the Grahams in Pleasant Valley also have them well armed, but Tom Graham was clearly unarmed when he was killed in Tempe.

7. U.S. Department of the Interior, Census Office, "Table 5—Population of States and Territories by Minor Civil Divisions, 1880 and 1890," 60.

8. Testimony of Robert Bowen, 424–25, *Territory of Arizona vs. Ed. Tewksbury* (1892), University of Arizona Main Library, Special Collections, Tucson, Ariz., filed as "Recorder's Transcript of Preliminary Examination 1892," AZ 142, hereafter cited as *Territory of Arizona vs. Ed. Tewksbury* (1892).

9. "Murdered," *Arizona Republican*, 3 August 1892, 1.

10. Testimony of E. M. Rumberg, *Territory of Arizona vs. Ed. Tewksbury* (1892), 79.

11. *Phoenix Gazette* described two shots ringing out "in almost perfect unison" on 4 August 1892, but three witnesses in court describe hearing only a single shot. The newspaper

report is reprinted in Hanchett, *They Shot Billy Today*, 136–37. Either way, if two shots were fired, Graham had only one wound.

12. The bullet's speed is based on 850 feet per second, or 580 miles per hour, the average speed of a modern .45 caliber bullet. The precise speed of the projectile that punctured Graham's body would depend on unknown variables such as the amount of powder used in the cartridge.

13. This wound is similar to the neck wound that President John F. Kennedy experienced in Dallas. For a detailed discussion of the "Thorburn response" and how the body reacts to such a wound, see http://mcadams.posc.mu.edu/thorburn.txt (accessed 27 Dec. 2012).

14. Cummings is variously identified in U.S. Census data as William Cummings or as Whitfield Thornton Cummings, and in Phoenix newspapers as W. T. Cummings.

15. Testimony of Fen J. Hart, *Territory of Arizona vs. Ed. Tewksbury* (1892), 103.

16. Testimony of Grace Griffith in the John Rhodes preliminary hearing, reported in "The Beginning," *Arizona Republican*, 9 August 1892, 1.

17. Testimony of J. J. Hickey, *Territory of Arizona vs. Ed. Tewksbury* (1892), 135, 141; Testimony of Charlie Duchet, ibid., 160.

18. "Interview with Mrs. John Taggart, Dec. 8, 1961," 3–4, in Dedera Papers, box 42, file 40.

19. Mary Eleanor "Mollie" Cummings, the third daughter of W. T. Cummings, is identified solely as Mollie Cummings in the court transcript.

20. Cummings may have referred to Cravath when she recalled that "our hired man was cutting weeds in alfalfa behind the trees, and he came out and caught the horses" in "Interview with Mrs. John Taggart, Dec. 8, 1961," 5, in Dedera Papers, box 42, file 40.

21. Testimony of Fen J. Hart, *Territory of Arizona vs. Ed. Tewksbury* (1892), 344. Hart was later elected mayor of Tempe, from 1894 to 1896. Hart's first name was spelled "Fen" in the court transcript, but he spelled it "Fenn."

22. Testimony of W. T. Cummings, *Territory of Arizona vs. Ed. Tewksbury* (1892), 117.

23. Testimony of Fen J. Hart, *Territory of Arizona vs. Ed. Tewksbury* (1892), 95–97.

24. Testimony of E. G. Roberts, *Territory of Arizona vs. Ed. Tewksbury* (1892), 375. Roberts was pastor of the Methodist Episcopal church, *Tempe City Directory*, 137.

25. "The Dying Man's Declaration Is Reproduced in Court," *Arizona Republican*, 12 August 1892, 1.

26. Judge John J. Hickey, alternately referred to in the territorial records as John, Jack, or J.J. Hickey, testified that Graham "gasped between every word as he said it," Testimony of J. J. Hickey, *Territory of Arizona vs. Ed. Tewksbury* (1892), 351.

27. Helm, who both administered to Graham and conducted the autopsy, testified that Graham had been given opiates to ease his pain (see *Arizona Republican*, 3 August 1892, 1). However, in later testimony, Dr. Hart insisted that Graham had received no opiates, although he conceded that some "stimulants" were administered to him. Hart did not describe what those stimulants were. See *Arizona Republican*, 11 August 1892, 1.

28. Forsee was also serving as justice of the peace, *Tempe City Directory*, 131. Hickey had been previously employed with the Southwest Detective Agency, and was also serving as a notary public at the time of Graham's death. Graham also had a mortgage through

the Western Investment Banking Company, of which Hickey's brother, Phillip K. Hickey, was a director and cashier. See *Arizona Republican*, 19 September 1893, 1, and 12 January 1894, 4. The *Arizona Republican* also lists Hickey as the assistant city marshal, but there is no further indication as to whether he served in this capacity at the time of Graham's murder. See *Arizona Republican*, 1 November 1893, 5.

29. Testimony of Fen J. Hart, *Territory of Arizona vs. Ed. Tewksbury* (1892), 345, 353–54; See also Testimony of Lon Forsee, ibid., 359.

30. Of the questions put to Graham, Judge Hickey testified: "He didn't talk very plain, and I had to lean over very close to hear him, within about a foot of his face so I could hear and understand what he was saying," Testimony of J.J. Hickey, *Territory of Arizona vs. Ed. Tewksbury* (1892), 351. See also Testimony of Fen J. Hart, ibid., 347.

31. Testimony of Joseph D. Crouse, *Territory of Arizona vs. Ed. Tewksbury* (1892), 349. There was disagreement among witnesses as to whether Graham used the first names of Rhodes and Tewksbury or merely their last names. Annie Graham and Charlie Duchet remembered Graham identifying his assailants by first and last names. However, W. T. Cummings, whose house Graham was taken to, testified that Graham used only last names. See *Arizona Republican*, 12 August 1892, 1.

32. Testimony of J.J. Hickey, *Territory of Arizona vs. Ed. Tewksbury* (1892), 351, and Testimony of E. G. Roberts, ibid., 375–76.

33. Testimony of J.J. Hickey, *Territory of Arizona vs. Ed. Tewksbury* (1892), 355–57.

34. Ibid., 352.

35. Testimony of Charlie Duchet, *Territory of Arizona vs. Ed. Tewksbury* (1892), 165–66.

36. "The Dying Man's Declaration Is Reproduced in Court," *Arizona Republican*, 12 August 1892, 1.

37. Shakespeare, *Hamlet*, act 3, scene 1.

38. "The Third Day," *Arizona Republican*, 11 August 1892, 1.

39. Almost all who were present at the Cummings house as Graham lay dying went out to examine the tracks made by the assassins. Discussion of the quality of the ground, the imprints made on them, the shape of the horseshoes, the spacing of the hoof prints, and each witness's ability to interpret tracks therefore constituted a significant part of the examination and cross-examination of the thirty-seven witnesses called for the plaintiff in *Territory of Arizona vs. Ed. Tewksbury* (1892). For example, see Duchet's testimony, *Territory of Arizona vs. Ed. Tewksbury*, 156–66, 174–76.

40. The official time of death was never recorded, and the attending physician could only recall that it was within fifteen minutes before or after 3:00 P.M.

41. See *Phoenix Gazette*, 4 August 1892. Also see Hanchett, *They Shot Billy Today*, 136.

42. "Interview with Mrs. John McTaggart, 8 December 1961," 2, Dedera Papers, box 42, file 40.

43. Hazelton, "Hazelton Manuscript," 146. See also Mary Ann Rhodes, 1924 letter, transcribed and reprinted in Hanchett, *They Shot Billy Today*, 45–47.

44. "There is no friends of the grahams Can say But What Tom Graham stayed with his friends don't never go back on a friend if it Costs your life," he wrote to his sister, in September the 7= 1890 Dear Sister, Dedera Papers, box 43, file 24.

45. An editorial in *Hoof and Horn* stated that the original disagreement between the two families was over the worth of a horse, but it provided no further details about that moment. The editorial was reprinted in *St. John's Herald*, 1 September 1887, 1.

CHAPTER 9. BURDENS OF PROOF

1. Whiteley, *Miracle on the Salt River* (Charleston, S.C.: The History Press, 2014), 16–17.

2. Nelson A. Miles, "The Future of the Indian Question," *North American Review* 152, no. 410 (January 1891), 8–9. See also Lawrence G. Coates, "The Mormons and the Ghost Dance," *Dialogue: A Journal of Mormon Thought* 18, no. 4 (Winter 1985), 94–102.

3. Gregory E. Smoak, *Ghost Dances and Identity* (Berkeley: University of California Press, 2006). Smoak argues that the tenets of the Ghost Dance predated Mormonism in the West (125). See also Ronald Niezen, *Spirit Wars* (Berkeley: University of California Press, 2000), 133.

4. Amanda Porterfield, *Healing in the History of Christianity* (New York: Oxford University Press, 2009), 129–33.

5. Emerson Hough, *The Story of the Cowboy* (New York: Grosset and Dunlap, 1897), 341.

6. The populist movement is well studied. For a contemporary analysis of populism, see Frederick J. Turner, "Dominant Forces in Western Life," *The Atlantic Monthly* 79, no. 474 (April 1897): 433–43. For the role of labor in populism, see James Peterson, "The Trade Unions and the Populist Party," *Science and Society* 8, no. 2 (Spring 1944): 143–60. See also Ronald P. Formisano, *For the People* (Chapel Hill: University of North Carolina Press, 2012); Charles Postel, *The Populist Vision* (New York: Oxford University Press, 2009); Michael Kazin, *The Populist Persuasion* (Ithaca, N.Y.: Cornell University Press, 1998); Robert C. McMath, *American Populism* (New York: Hill and Wang, 1993).

7. John S. Goff, *Arizona Territorial Officials Volume II* (Cave Creek, Ariz.: Black Mountain Press, 1978), 89.

8. Notes from Bertha Tewksbury Acton, 22 March 1989, Dedera Papers, box 42, file 28.

9. Newton was presumed to have drowned in the Salt River on 11 April 1892. See *Arizona Silver Belt*, 14 May 1892, 3.

10. "Local News," *Arizona Silver Belt*, 23 April 1892, 3. Ephraim Fuller returned with Newton's horse; Harry lived in New Hampshire. The obituary of J. D. McCabe also confirms the common belief that Newton drowned in the Salt River, in "Sudden Summons," *Arizona Silver Belt*, 16 April 1892, 3.

11. "Tragic Death of Wm. Middleton," *Arizona Silver Belt*, 21 February 1891, 3.

12. *Arizona Silver Belt* refers to a belief among some residents, in the aftermath of Graham's death, that Newton's death was not accidental; see "Tom Graham Killed," 6 August 1892, 3.

13. See, for example, "District Court," *Arizona Silver Belt*, 30 November 1892, 1, and "District Court," ibid., 1 December 1892, 1.

14. There are different reports about when Rhodes was arrested. The *Arizona Republican* gave no time but indicated that it was soon after Rhodes returned to Tempe, around noon. The *Phoenix Gazette*, however, reported that Rhodes was arrested by Constable Gallardo later that night, at 10:00 P.M. (4 August 1892).

15. "Murdered," *Arizona Republican*, 3 August 1892, 1. See also *Arizona Silver Belt*, 6 August 1892, 3.

16. *Arizona Silver Belt*, 10 December 1892, 3, and "Tewksbury Did Not Plead," *Arizona Republican*, 4 August 1892, 1.

17. See Joe Gaimer, "One Father, One Family," Gaimer.com, http://www.gahimer.com/FamilyHistory/HistoryStories/files/Huson-Edward-Wing.html (accessed 17 Dec. 2017). Huson was a native of Iowa, and his father was a doctor who relocated the family to Wyoming. Young Billy first took up the jeweler's trade before studying law.

18. Representing John Rhodes was Albert C. Baker, a former district attorney and assistant United States attorney, and Joseph Campbell, a former district attorney and probate judge. See *Portrait and Biographical Record of Arizona* (database online), Ancestry.com (accessed 17 Jan. 2018), 41–42, 982–83; original data from *Portrait and Biographical Record of Arizona: Commemorating the Achievements of Citizens Who Have Contributed to the Progress of Arizona and the Development of Its Resources* (Chicago: Chapman Publishing, 1901). Representing the territory was District Attorney Crenshaw, who would later be joined by District Attorney Frank Cox. Until Cox could return from California, Crenshaw asked Judge Webster Street to assist him.

19. "The Beginning," *Arizona Republican*, 9 August 1892, 1.

20. Ibid.

21. Ibid.

22. Tom Graham's pistol was believed to have been taken off the body of John Tewksbury. See Hazelton, "Hazelton Manuscript," 146.

23. "The Third Day," *Arizona Republican*, 11 August 1892, 1, and "A Dramatic Scene," *Arizona Weekly Journal-Miner*, 17 August 1892, 4.

24. "A Dramatic Scene," *Arizona Weekly Journal-Miner*, 17 August 1892, 4.

25. *Arizona Republican*, 10 August 1892, 1. The *Arizona Weekly Citizen*, 13 August 1892, 3, identified the man as Porter Moffet and describes him as holding the chair between Graham and Rhodes. Both actions may have occurred.

26. This account relies on "The Avenger" in the *Arizona Republican*, 10 August 1892, 1, and "John Rhodes' Hearing," *Arizona Silver Belt*, 13 August 1892, 3. The *Arizona Sentinel*'s "Tried to Shoot Him" and the *Arizona Weekly Citizen*'s "To Square Accounts," both from 13 August 1892, 3, gave a different account: that Reverend Melton stopped the shooting by grabbing Annie's arm. Since the Phoenix reporter was on site, and possibly the Globe reporter, I take their accounts to be the more reliable.

27. The *Phoenix Gazette* reported a different outcome, that Sheriff Montgomery pushed Annie Graham into the arms of her father, as quoted in Hanchett, *They Shot Billy Today*, 101–102, although both outcomes were possible.

28. "The Third Day," *Arizona Republican*, 11 August 1892, 1.

29. Dr. Helm, who had testified for the territory on the nature of Graham's wound, was also recalled as a witness and testified that it was Duchet who had told him that Graham said he had been shot by Tewksbury.

30. "Rhodes' Story. No Sir, I Did Not Shoot Tom Graham," *Arizona Republican*, 16 August 1892, 1.

31. Testimony of Samuel Finley, *Territory of Arizona vs. Ed. Tewksbury* (1892), 522–23. *Arizona Silver Belt*, 19 March 1896, 2, reported that Tewksbury rode twelve miles to turn himself in.

32. "The Other Side," *Arizona Republican*, 13 August 1892, 1, and "The Tewksbury Case," *Arizona Silver Belt*, 12 January 1895, 3.

33. "Phoenix Excited," *Morning Call*, 12 August 1892, 1.

34. "Another Day," *Arizona Republican*, 17 August 1892, 1.

35. "Tewksbury Interviewed," *Arizona Silver Belt*, 20 August 1892, 1.

36. *Phoenix Gazette*, 17 August 1892, 1, reported Huson's statement differently, that he "was at first inclined to believe the defendant guilty of the murder, [but] the defense has so conclusively proved their alibi that I must release the prisoner."

37. "Local Notes," *Tombstone Epitaph*, 21 August 1892, 8.

38. *Arizona Weekly Citizen*, 27 August 1892, 1.

CHAPTER 10. THE TRIALS OF ED TEWKSBURY

1. "A Remarkable Case," *Arizona Silver Belt*, 19 March 1896, 2. See also "A Third Trial," ibid., 26 January 1895, 2.

2. See *Tombstone Epitaph*, 21 August 1892, 8.

3. "Tempe Meets: In the Matter of the Graham Murder," *Arizona Republican*, 28 August 1892, 1.

4. C. O. Austin testified to tracking the hoof prints from the scene of the murder (see *Arizona Republican*, 16 March 1893, 2; 30 May 1893, 2; and 9 May 1893, 2). C. N. Taylor appears to have been Charles N. Taylor, part owner of the Mormon Girl Mine on Cave Creek (*Arizona Republican*, 23 April 1893, 2).

5. Reverend Hitchcock was also actively engaged at the time in holding revival meetings at the Tempe Baptist church. See "Our Tempe News," *Arizona Republican*, 5 April 1892, 4.

6. "Armed Riders," ibid., 28 August 1892, 1.

7. The transcript of the preliminary hearing lists Wharton's name simultaneously as H. L. Wharton and H. O. Wharton. *Territory of Arizona vs. Ed. Tewksbury* (1892), 1–2 (including title page).

8. "Thinking of It," *Arizona Republican*, 6 September 1892, 1.

9. *Commonwealth of Massachusetts vs. John W. Webster*, 5 Cush. 295, 59 Mass. 295, 320 (March 1850), http://masscases.com/cases/sjc/59/59mass295.html.

10. *Territory of Arizona vs. Ed. Tewksbury* (1892), 640–44.

11. "Without Bail," *Arizona Republican*, 9 September 1982, 1.

12. See "Oiled and Adjusted," ibid., 15 November 1892, 5, and "The District Court," ibid., 16 November 1892, 5.

13. *Arizona Republican*, 1 December 1892, 1; *Arizona Silver Belt*, 3 December 1892, 3. The *Arizona Republican* reported in "District Court" on 30 November 1892, 1, that seven jurors were dismissed.

14. *Arizona Silver Belt*, 3 December 1892, 3.

15. Ibid., 10 December 1892, 3.

16. "Tewksbury Did Not Plead," *Arizona Republican*, 16 December 1892, 5.

17. "For a Change of Venue," ibid., 18 April 1893, 5. Hanchett reports that the motion was filed a month later (*They Shot Billy Today*, 41).

18. "The Tewksbury Case," *Arizona Republican*, 17 May 1893, 5. See also Goff, *Arizona Territorial Officials*, 140.

19. *Arizona Republican*, 20 April 1893, 5, and 30 April 1893, 1.

20. Ibid., 4 July 1893, 5.

21. *Arizona Silver Belt*, 27 August 1892, 2.

22. Judge Edwards of Globe City and his new law partner Tom Fitch, recently from California, composed the defense team. Pima County District Attorney Hereford and Maricopa County District Attorneys Cox and Street constituted the prosecution. See "Territorial Items," *Arizona Silver Belt*, 11 November 1893, 1.

23. *Arizona Silver Belt*, 4 November 1893, 3. The *Coconino Weekly Sun*, 9 November 1893, 1, however, reported the trial date starting on 2 December.

24. *Arizona Daily Star*, 17 December 1893, 2, and 21 December 1893, 4.

25. Ibid., 17 December 1893, 2.

26. Ibid., 4 January 1895, 3.

27. Ibid., 21 December 1893, 4. Hanchett (*They Shot Billy Today*, 35), citing the *Daily Star*, incorrectly reported that the prosecution rested its case on 18 December 1893, and that the defense began and ended its case the following day.

28. *Arizona Daily Star*, 23 December 1893, 4.

29. "Telegraphic Notes," *New York Tribune*, 24 December 1893, 5. See also "Will Get a New Trial," *The Morning Call*, 24 December 1893, 2. Hanchett's description of events and dates places the jury decision and time on the previous date, reported in the New York City paper as 22 December. See *They Shot Billy Today*, 38–39.

30. *Arizona Daily Star*, 24 December 1893, 1.

31. Paul Thomas Hietter, "Lawyers, Guns, and Money" (Ph.D. diss., Arizona State University, 1999), 174.

32. *Arizona Daily Star*, Thursday, 3 January 1895, 1.

33. Ibid., 4 January 1895, 3, and 6 January 1895, 4. Frank Cox and Webster Street appeared for the prosecution, joined by the newly elected District Attorney Lovell. Judge Joseph Campbell again represented Ed Tewksbury, with two new attorneys, Judge William H. Barnes, and J. H. Martin.

34. Ibid., 5 January 1895, 4.

35. Ibid., 6 January 1895, 4.

36. Ibid., 9 January 1895, 4.

37. Ibid., 11 January 1895, 4.

38. "From Friday's Daily," *Tombstone Epitaph*, 10 February 1895, 3.

39. This story was originally published in the *Phoenix Gazette* and then reprinted in the *Arizona Daily Star*, 12 March 1895, 4.

CHAPTER 11. "WHAT DREAMS MAY COME"

Author's note: The title of this chapter is from Shakespeare's *Hamlet*, act III, scene 1.

1. Gerald Horne, *The White Pacific* (Honolulu: University of Hawaii Press, 2007), 92–128.

2. *Arizona Daily Star*, 12 March 1895, 1; Thomas D. Schoonover, *Uncle Sam's War of 1898 and the Origins of Globalization* (Lexington: University Press of Kentucky, 2003), 66–87.

3. John H. Lienhard, *How Invention Begins* (New York: Oxford University Press, 2008), 28–32.

4. George S. May, "Putting the Nation on Wheels," in *Michigan: Visions of Our Past*, edited by Richard J. Hathaway (East Lansing: Michigan State University Press, 2012), 170–74.

5. Lienhard, *How Invention Begins*, 19.

6. Christopher Herbert, *Victorian Relativity* (Chicago: University of Chicago Press, 2001), 172–76; John S. Rigden, *Einstein 1905* (Cambridge, Mass.: Harvard University Press, 2006), 85–99.

7. Troy Rondinone, *Great Industrial War* (New Brunswick, N.J.: Rutgers University Press, 2010), 78–89; Postel, *Populist Vision*, 263–265.

8. Stephen Cresswell, *Mormons and Cowboys, Moonshiners and Klansmen* (Tuscaloosa: University of Alabama Press, 2002), 238–39; Thomas E. Sheridan, *Arizona* (Tucson: University of Arizona Press, 1995), 180–85.

9. See Melissa Stinson journal, quoted in Hanchett, *They Shot Billy Today*, 192–204.

10. McGuire, citing an earlier study of the Santa Fe Railway land grants, actually attributes cattle rustling as one of the key reasons why the Aztec Land and Cattle Company filed for bankruptcy in 1900. See *Mixed-Bloods, Apaches, and Cattle Barons*, 47.

11. Abruzzi, *Dam That River!*, 34–35. Citing records from the LDS colonies along the Little Colorado River, Abruzzi estimates that by 1893 "as fully as one-half of the cattle in Apache County perished."

12. After Graham's murder, there was a report in the *Arizona Weekly Citizen*, 6 August 1892, 2, that Hiram Yost, who had been tending Graham's herds in Pleasant Valley, was missing. Some believed that Yost had been murdered by the Apache Kid, who was still on the run, but others could not help but wonder if Yost was a casualty of the Pleasant Valley War. The actual fate of Hiram Yost is another historical mystery of Pleasant Valley. The documentary trail disappears after that solitary report in the *Arizona Weekly Citizen* speculating that he had been killed. There is no further mention in any other territorial journal about Yost or his remains being found, nor is there record of a coroner's inquest or any court action resulting from his supposed death. At the same time, other herders were reported murdered in the Rim country: Alfred Hand was murdered the following year near Cave Creek, reported in "Military Misrule," *Arizona Silver Belt*, 16 April 1896, 2, and Bud Campbell was killed on Cibecue Creek near Pleasant Valley on 5 December 1895, reported in "The People Demand Redress," *Arizona Silver Belt*, 15 July 1896, 2, and "Military Protection to Settlers," ibid., 27 August 1896, 2. See also McClintock, *Arizona, Prehistoric, Aboriginal, Pioneer, Modern*, 486. For suspicions of Yost's murder, see "Interview with Mrs. John McTaggart, 8 December 1961," 2, Dedera Papers, box 42, file 40, and Ellison, *Back Trackin*, 8–10.

13. "The Cibicue Affair," *Arizona Republican*, 25 December 1895, 8.

14. "Lieutenant Fenton informed Frank Ketcherside that he saw cattle there of the 'flying V' brand," meaning that Apaches had driven cattle from the Vosburg ranch, in ibid.

15. To be sure, Voris and the other posse members, as well as the territorial press, insisted that their mission was peaceful and that the Apaches were to blame as the aggressors. See "A Race for Life," *Arizona Silver Belt*, 14 December 1895, 3. The story was also carried in the "An Indian Killed," *Graham Guardian*, 20 December 1895, 1; "The Apache Trouble," *The Argus*, 26 December 1895, 1; and "Plea for Protection," *Arizona Silver Belt*, 8 February 1896, 1.

16. "Another Indian Killing," *Arizona Republican*, 24 December 1895, 1.

17. "The Ellison Sensation," ibid., 27 December 1895, 1. The editors still seemed a bit defensive about running the story (if not trying to avert responsibility) by inserting the subtitle that "two Tonto Basin men believe the report without foundation."

18. Hunt went on to become the first governor of the state of Arizona, and after serving several terms, was appointed U.S. Minister to Siam by President Woodruff.

19. *Arizona Daily Star*, 17 December 1893, 2.

20. Tewksbury served with Constable Dave Gibson, *Arizona Silver Belt*, 22 February 1900, 5.

21. Western States Marriage Record Index, Marriage ID#32935, lists the marriage of Edwin Tewksbey [*sic*] and B. R. Lopez on 12 March 1897 in Dudley, Arizona, in volume 1A, 127, http://abish.byui.edu/specialCollections/westernStates/westernStatesRecordDetail.cfm?recordID=32935 (accessed 7 Sept. 2017), BYU (Provo) L. Tom Perry Special Collections.

22. "Local Notes," *Arizona Weekly Journal-Miner*, 3 October 1888, 3; "Territorial Items," *Mohave County Miner*, 10 November 1888, 3.

23. From the *Argus*, see "Local and Personal," 12 November 1898, 5; "Local and Personal," 31 December 1898, 5; "The Fourth," 8 July 1899, 4; and "The Local Field," 21 July 1900, 3. (The *Argus* became the *Holbrook Argus* in 1900.) From the *Holbrook Argus*, see "Washington's Birthday," 23 February 1901, 1, and "Attempted Murder," 19 October 1901, 1. See also Pyle, *Women of the Pleasant Valley War*, 145.

24. "Local News," *Arizona Silver Belt*, 28 November 1901, 8, identifies the mine as the O.D. Mine, whereas the "Local News," ibid., 12 December 1901, 8, article names the mine as the United Globe Mine.

25. Ed Tewksbury appears to have suffered from atherosclerosis, a thickening of artery walls that is greatly exacerbated by heavy smoking.

26. Twitchell, *Leading Facts of New Mexican History*, 373.

27. U.S. Bureau of the Census, *Twelfth Census of the United States, 1900*, Schedule No. 1: Precinct 12—Population, State: New Mexico, County: Sierra, Precinct: 12, Engle, Sheet 7B, Ancestry.com (accessed 1 Jan. 2018); original data from *Twelfth Census of the United States, 1900* (T623, 1854 rolls), Bureau of the Census, National Archives and Records Administration, Washington, D.C.. See also Hanchett, *They Shot Billy Today*, 141.

28. Transcribed news report "James D. Houck, local '——' 3/31/21," in Dedera Papers, box 44, file 12.

29. Shakespeare, *Hamlet*, act 3, scene 1.

30. The *California Death Index, 1930–1939*, 6052, indicates that Rose died in Riverside, California, whereas Pyle places her death in Banning, Riverside County, California, in *Women of the Pleasant Valley War*, 90–91.

31. Pyle, *Women of the Pleasant Valley War*, 136.

32. Eva Blevins eventually remarried John, and they moved to Phoenix. Ibid., 146.

33. U.S. Bureau of the Census, *Twelfth Census of the United States, 1900* (T623, 1854 rolls). Washington, D.C.: National Archives and Records Administration, 1900.; *Los Angeles Ward 4, Los Angeles, California*; Roll: 89; Page: 3A; Enumeration District: 0044; FHL microfilm: 1240089.

34. U.S. Bureau of the Census, *Fourteenth Census of the United States, 1920*—Population, Precinct 6, Pasadena Sanatorium [South Pasadena City], sheet 14A. Annie Hagan is listed as an inmate at the Pasadena Sanatorium. Tellingly, beyond her personal information as a widow, the rest of her background information is listed as "unknown," suggesting that she was unable or unwilling to communicate this information.

35. "Interview with Mrs. Estella Converse Hill," 2, Dedera Papers, box 44, file 8.

36. "Estella Graham Converse Hill Dictation," 22 January 1962, 8, Dedera Papers, box 44, file 8.

37. Hanchett states that Hagan remarried, and indeed genealogical records linked to Hagan seem to suggest this. However, the Hagans' record ends some time before with the 1920 census, when Annie Hagan is listed as a widow. A Thomas Hogan was indeed living in Los Angeles in 1920, married to Emma Hogan, and researchers have assumed that this was Thomas J. Hagan. However, the Thomas Hogan listed in the 1920 census was not Thomas J. Hagan. Hogan was born in Ireland and married to Emma Hogan as early as 1910, while records clearly indicate that Thomas J. Hagan was married to Annie Melton Graham at that time.

38. Hanchett, *They Shot Billy Today*, 140.

39. Ibid., 295.

40. The Maricopa County Cemetery was renamed Twin Buttes Cemetery, and closed in 1994.

41. Geronimo, *Geronimo's Story of His Life*, 54.

42. Ibid., 45.

43. I encountered two different spellings of Coloradas's name. Geronimo's memoir uses "Mangas Colorado," whereas Sweeney uses "Mangas Coloradas," which is the correct Spanish spelling for "red sleeves," in *Mangas Coloradas: Chief of the Chiricahua Apaches* (Norman: University of Oklahoma Press, 2011).

44. Geronimo, as quoted in Lee Miller, *From the Heart* (New York: Knopf, 1995), 260. This quotation is slightly different in Geronimo, *Geronimo's Story of His Life*, 43–54.

45. Goyaałé was born in 1829.

46. As quoted in Peter Aleshire, *Reaping the Whirlwind* (New York: Facts on File, 1998), 143, quoting from David D. Roberts, *Once They Moved Like the Wind* (New York: Touchstone 1993), 313.

47. As quoted in Hanchett, *They Shot Billy Today*, 45–47.

48. Rhodes served as one of the jurors in the coroner's inquest of the killing of Henry Midleton at Al Rose's ranch on 23 September 1887, but Tom Graham was not implicated in this affair. See Hanchett, *They Shot Billy Today*, 278–79.

49. "Roster of the Arizona Rangers," *Arizona Trails*, http://genealogytrails.com/ariz/

rangers-list.htm (accessed 18 Dec. 2012), shows the enlistment year for McKinney and Rhodes as 1906.

50. McKinney, "Reminiscences," *Arizona Historical Review* 5, no. 1 (April 1932): 33–54; "Reminiscences (Continued)," ibid. 5, no. 2 (July 1932): 141–45; "Reminiscences (Concluded)," ibid. 5, no. 3 (October 1932): 198–204.

51. Reports of Graham's boast came from several quarters. Drusilla Hazelton stated that Tom admitted to Annie Graham that he killed John Tewksbury. Members of the Tewksbury family certainly believe that Graham made such a boast. He reportedly "bragged in a bar in Globe that he had killed John Tewksbury," and in a 1924 letter, Mary Ann Rhodes wrote: "Tom Graham said that he killed John Tewksbury and thought he did something great." It is unclear, however, whether Graham's confession meant that he actually pulled the trigger of the weapon that killed John Tewksbury, or that he was complicit in the events that resulted in Tewksbury's murder. Either way, the pistol owned by Tom Graham, which Annie possessed after his death, is said to have been taken from the deceased body of John Tewksbury. See Hazelton, "Hazelton Manuscript," 148–51; William D. Brown notarized statement, 10/14/92, in Dedera Papers, box 42, file 28; and Mary Ann Rhodes transcribed letter reprinted in Hanchett, *They Shot Billy Today*, 45–47. See also Hanchett, *Arizona's Graham-Tewksbury Feud*, 75.

52. John Rhodes testified that he saw Graham in Tempe almost on a daily basis, although they did not speak to one another.

53. Joseph Boyer testified that Ed Tewksbury picked up grapes and peaches at Boquet's ranch, three miles east of Tonto Creek, between 1:00 and 2:00 P.M. in Testimony of Joseph Boyer, *Territory of Arizona vs. Ed. Tewksbury* (1892), 583–84. Jacob Lauffer testified that Tewksbury returned to George Wilson's ranch in ibid., 611. George Wilson testified that he sent Ed out to a horse ranch they called the Tanks, about ten miles south of Newton ranch, in ibid., 627.

54. In studying the psychological and physiological responses to combat among U.S. veterans of the Revolutionary War, the Civil War, and the Second World War, Christopher H. Hamner observed: "Anxiety often peaked during periods of inactivity, when the individual soldier had ample time to reflect on his circumstances," and that the stress of face-to-face combat often left them with "fewer psychological reserves to hold their fears in check." See *Enduring Battle* (Lawrence: University Press of Kansas, 2011), 70–71, 73–74.

55. Combat veterans experiencing PTSD report a persistent reexperiencing of the traumatic event. See Dave Grossman, "Human Factors in War," in *The Human Face of Warfare*, edited by Michael Evans and Alan Ryan (Sydney, Australia: Allen Unwin, 2000), 22.

56. See Dave Grossman, *On Killing* (Boston: Little, Brown 1995), 74–75, 87, 95–96, 243–45. See also Karl Marlantes, *What It Is Like to Go to War* (New York: Atlantic Monthly Press, 2011), 29–40.

57. Shakespeare, *Hamlet*, Act 4, scene IV.

58. Nicholas Blomley, "Law, Property, and the Geography of Violence," *Annals of the Association of American Geographers* 93, no. 1 (2003), 121.

59. Benton-Cohen, *Borderline Americans*, 9.

60. Limerick, *Legacy of Conquest*, 19.

61. Ivan Lee Kuykendall published *Ghost Riders of the Mogollon* (Naylor) in 1954, only to have it suppressed by the threat of a lawsuit by some of the descendants of the conflict. As a consequence, only a few hundred copies were released. Western American author Amelia Bean encountered no such resistance in publishing *The Feud* (New York: Doubleday) in 1960. This version of events is perhaps so romanticized that its resemblance to historical families is minimal. In January 1992, CBS aired the made-for-TV movie *Gunsmoke: To the Last Man.* Although the movie is based on the events of the Pleasant Valley War, Academy Award winner Earl W. Wallace, who also wrote *How the West Was Won*, created a number of fictional characters to drive the story of Matt Dillon, who retired from his post as marshal of Dodge City and became a rancher in the Arizona Territory. The stealing of his cattle by the Tommy Graham gang leads Dillon to the middle of a blood feud that had been raging for years in Pleasant Valley. By the time the movie ends, the former marshal, as a knight errant, gives a weakened lawman new strength, stops the feud, breaks up the cattle rustlers, and shoots all of the vigilantes dead.

BIBLIOGRAPHY

MANUSCRIPT COLLECTIONS

Arizona Historical Society Library and Archives, Tucson. ahsref@azhs.gov.
  Barnes, William Croft. Papers, 1878–1945. MS 0017.
  Barnes, William Croft. Photographs, ca. 1890–1936. PC 010.
  Clara T. Woody Collection, 1876–1977. MS 0887.
  Ellison, Glenn R., 1891–1983. Papers, 1964. MS 245.
  Ellison, Glenn "Slim." Correspondence and Drawings, 1965–1974. MS 1463.
  Ellison, Jesse Washington Photograph Collection, 1841–1934. PC 040.
  George Hochderffer Collection, 1863–1964. AHS-ND.3.
  Hazelton, Drusilla. "Hazelton Manuscript, 1977." MS 344.
  Hochderffer, George. Papers, 1950. MS 356.
  Pearce, Joseph Harrison. Papers, ca. 1903–1957. MS 651.
  Portraits—Graham, John (photo file). Barcode 41258.
  Portraits—Graham, Mr. & Mrs. Thomas H. (Anne Melton) (photo file).
    Barcode 41259.
  Portraits—Rhodes, John (Record no. 44885).
  Portraits—Tewksbury, Edwin (photo file). Barcode 45902.
  Portraits—Tewksbury, John (photo file). Barcode 45904.
  Voris, Robert, and Dale Stuart King. "The Pleasant Valley War."
    Oral history interview by Clara T. Woody, 23 March 1976. Transcript and
    three sound cassettes.
  Woody, Clara T. Gila County Photographs, ca. 1885–1935. PC 158.
  Woody, Clara T. Papers, 1876–1879. MS 0887.

Arizona State Library, Archives, and Public Records (formerly the Arizona History
and Archives Division), Phoenix. https://www.azlibrary.gov/.
  Great Register of Gila County, Arizona.
  Great Register of Maricopa County, Arizona.
  Great Register of Yavapai County, Arizona.
  Record Group 6—Secretary of the Territory.
    Subgroup 5: Crime, series 9.
  Record Group 100—Apache County.
    Subgroup 04: Justice Court. 1882–1947.
      Territory of Arizona vs. John and Thos. H. Graham
        (court transcript, 13 June 1885).

Subgroup 05: Recorder. 1874–1954.

Subgroup 06: Sheriff. 1887–1888.

Subgroup 08: Superior Court. 1876–1964.

Record Group 103—Gila County.

Subgroup 8: Superior Court. 1881–1981.

Series 01. Shared Court Records, 1881–1976. Microfilm Reel 69.9.1. Marriage Licenses and Index, Volume 1, 1881–1888.

Record Group 110—Pima County.

Subgroup 08: Pima County Superior Court. 1864–1995.

Record Group 113—Yavapai County.

Subgroup 04: Justice Court. 1864–1975.

Subgroup 8: Criminal Division, 1865–1965. The following records of the District Court of the Third Judicial District, County of Yavapai, Territory of Arizona, are found here:

Territory of Arizona vs. Francis Tewksbury (1883).

Territory of Arizona vs. Gilleland and Tewksbury (1883).

Territory of Arizona vs. Edwin Tewksbury and James Tewksbury (1884).

Territory of Arizona vs. Edwin Tewksbury, John Tewksbury, James Tewksbury, George Blaine, William Richards, and H. H. Bishop (1884).

Territory of Arizona vs. F. M. McCann (1884).

Territory of Arizona vs. James Tewksbury and William Richards (1884).

Territory of Arizona vs. Thomas Graham and John Graham (1884).

Territory of Arizona vs. Al Rose, Miguel Apodaca, Louis Parker, William Bonner, Richard Roe, and John Doe (1887).

Territory of Arizona vs. Ed. Tewksbury, James Tewksbury, Joseph Boyer, James Roberts, George Newton, Jacob Lauffer, and George Wagner (1888).

Territory of Arizona vs. James Tewksbury, Edwin Tewksbury, Joseph Boyer, James Roberts, George Newton, Jacob Lauffer, and George Wagner (1888).

Territory of Arizona vs. Louis Parker, Thomas Graham, Miguel Apodaca, Thomas Carrington, William Bonner, Joseph Ellenwood, and William Gould (1887–1888).

Territory of Arizona vs. Thomas Graham, Louis Parker, Miguel Apodaca, Thomas Carrington, William Bonner, Joseph Ellenwood, and William Gould (1888).

Arizona State University Hayden Library, Arizona Collection, Tempe. https://www.asu.edu/lib/archives/arizona.htm.

Bushman, John. Papers, 1867–1926. Film 9379.

Don Dedera Papers 1955–2008. MSS-280.

Ellison, Glenn R. "Slim." Collection, 1965–1981. MSS-35.

Flake, Osmer D. "Some Reminiscences of the Pleasant Valley War and Causes That Led Up to It." Unpublished ms., in Levi S. Udall Papers, Film 9355.

Shute, G. W. "The Pleasant Valley War." Unpublished ms., Phoenix, 1954.

Udall, Levi S. Papers. Film 9355.

Watts, Joshua. "The Organization and Evolution of the Hohokam Economy Agent-Based Modeling of Exchange in the Phoenix Basin, Arizona, AD 200–1450." Ph.D. diss., Arizona State University, 2013.

Young, Arch Bryant, Jr. "A Social History of Globe, Gila County, Arizona." B.S. in Ed. thesis, University of Missouri, 1933.

Boone County Historical Society
    1860 United States Federal Census, Des Moines Township, Boone County.
    1880 United States Federal Census, Des Moines Township, Boone County.
    Iowa State Census Collection, 1856, Boone Township, Boone County.

Brigham Young University, Harold B. Lee Library, L. Tom Perry Special Collections. https://lib.byu.edu/special-collections/.
    Joseph Fish Typescripts of Histories and Diaries, 1902-1970. MSS 2010.
    Standifird, John Henry. Papers, 1857. MSS 44.

The Church of Jesus Christ of Latter-day Saints. Church History Library. https://history.lds.org/section/library?lang=eng.
    James Pearce Interview, 9 January 1921. MS 18476.

The Huntington Library, Art Collections, and Botanical Gardens, San Marino, California. www.huntington.org/.
    John Addison Hunt Biography, ca. 1951. mssFAC 1435.

Library of Congress Prints and Photographs
    Photograph: "Armed Apaches on Hillside, 1886." LC-USZ62–55389.

Northern Arizona University, Cline Library Special Collections and Archives Department. http://library.nau.edu/speccoll/.
    George Babbitt Oral History Collection, NAU.OH.57, Series Four, 1949–1960.
    George S. Tanner Collection, 1876–1977, NAU.MS.176.
    Roscoe G. Willson Collection, 1868–1976, MG 124.
    Tonto Basin Research Collection, 1910–1976, NAU.MS.454.

Sharlot Hall Museum Library and Archives. http://oldhtmlarchive.sharlot.org/.
    Blevins, Martin P., 20 February 1887, letter to "Delila and Gim." Doc. box 199, folder 7.
    Doesha, Charles "Charley." Surname Vertical File.
    Graham, Thomas H. Surname Vertical File.
    Horton, L. J. "Pleasant Valley War," unpublished manuscript. The Pleasant Valley War. Doc. box 18, folder 5.
    Tewksbury Family. Surname Vertical File.

Texas State Library and Archives Commission. https://www.tsl.texas.gov/.
A[ttorney] G[eneral] Report 1900, Index Card Collections.

University of Arizona Main Library, Special Collections.
  Forrest, Earle Robert. Papers, 1895–1960. MS 274.
  Hereford, Francis Henry. Papers, 1877–1929. AZ 311.
  McKinney, Joseph Thomas. Papers, 1841–1927. AZ 087.
  Territory of Arizona vs. Ed. Tewksbury (1892). "Recorder's Transcript of
    Preliminary Examination." AZ 142.
  Udall, Levi Stewart. Papers, 1842–1974. MS 293.

NON-PUBLISHED PRIMARY WORKS

Allison, Robert. "The Blevins Family: An Episode in the Pleasant Valley War." Arizona
  Pioneer's Historical Society, 1936. Don Dedera Papers, box 42/OV1, file 2.
National Archives and Records Administration. *U.S., Civil War Pension Index: General
  Index to Pension Files, 1861–1934.* Online publication—Provo, Utah: Ancestry.com
  Operations Inc, 2000. https://search.ancestry.com/search/db.aspx?dbid=4654.
Pearce, Joseph Harrison. "Pearce Reminiscences, 1903–1957." Arizona Historical Society,
  Arizona History Museum (Tucson), 28.
Record of Enlistments in the United States Army, Volumes 150–151 (1866–77) Indian Scouts.
  Washington D.C.: National Archives. Microcopy 233.
Seiber, Al. 1889 Deposition Regarding Garret "Bob" Sixby's Claim against the Government
  for the 1882 Apache Raid. PDF in possession of the author.

MEMOIRS AND PUBLISHED PRIMARY WORKS

Allison, Hattie Middleton. "An Indian Raid: As Told by Hattie Middleton Allison, to
  Her Children." *Arizona Cattlelog.* November 1953, 12–21.
Ancestry.com. *Arizona, Death Records, 1887–1960.* Lehi, Utah: Ancestry.com Operations,
  Inc., 2016.
———. *U.S. Army, Register of Enlistments, 1798–1914.* Provo, Utah: Ancestry.com Opera-
  tions, Inc., 2007.
———. *U.S. Civil War Draft Registrations Records, 1863–1865.* Provo, Utah: Ancestry.
  com Operations, Inc., 2010.
———. *U.S. Civil War Pension Index: General Index to Pension Files, 1861–1934.* Provo,
  Utah: Ancestry.com Operations, Inc., 2000.
Barnes, Will C. *Apaches and Longhorns: The Reminiscences of Will C. Barnes.* Tucson:
  University of Arizona Press, 1982.
Beard, George Miller. *American Nervousness: Its Causes and Consequences; A Supplement
  to Nervous Exhaustion (Neurasthenia).* New York: Putnam, 1881.
*The Bensel Directory Co.'s Tempe Directory 1892: Containing a General Directory of the
  Citizens, Street Directory, Etc.* Tempe, Ariz.: McNeil Company, 1892.
Burns, Mike. *The Journey of a Yavapai Indian: A 19th Century Odyssey.* Edited by Susan
  L. Rockwell. Princeton, N.J.: Elizabeth House, 2002.

———. *The Only Living One to Tell: The Autobiography of a Yavapai Indian*. Edited by Gregory McNamee. Tucson: University of Arizona Press, 2012.

Cook, Sherburne Friend. *The Conflict between the California Indian and White Civilization*. Berkeley: University of California Press, 1943.

Coolidge, Dane. *Arizona Cowboys*. Tucson: University of Arizona Press, 1938.

Cremony, John C. *Life among the Apaches, 1849–1864*. San Francisco: A. Roman and Company, 1868.

Cruse, Thomas. *Apache Days and After*. Caldwell, Idaho: Caxton Printers, 1941.

Dunn, Jacob Piatt. *Massacres of the Mountains: A History of the Indian Wars of the Far West*. Vol. 1. New York: Harper and Bros., 1886.

Ellison, Glenn R. *Back Trackin*. Globe, Ariz.: Tyree Printing, 1975.

Endicott, William C. "Report of the Secretary of War," 30 November 1888. *Annual Report of the Secretary of War, Being Part of the Message and Documents Communicated to the Two Houses of Congress at the Beginning of the Second Session of the Fiftieth Congress, in Four Volumes*. Vol. 1. Washington, D.C., Government Printing Office, 1888.

Fish, Joseph. *The Life and Times of Joseph Fish, Mormon Pioneer*. Edited by John H. Krenkel. Danville, Ill., Interstate Printers and Publishers, 1970.

Flake, Lucy Hannah White. *Autobiography and Diary of Lucy Hannah White Flake*. Provo, Utah: Brigham Young University, 1953. Reprinted as *To the Last Frontier: Autobiography of Lucy Hannah White Flake*. N.p., 1976.

Gatewood, Charles B. *Lt. Charles Gatewood and His Apache Wars Memoir*. Edited and with additional text by Louis Kraft. Lincoln: University of Nebraska Press, 2005.

Geronimo. *Geronimo's Story of His Life*. Taken down and edited by Stephen Melvil Barrett. New York: Duffield, 1906.

Goff, John S. *Arizona Territorial Officials Volume II: The Governors 1863–1912*. Cave Creek, Ariz.: Black Mountain Press, 1978.

Horn, Tom. *Life of Tom Horn, Government Scout and Interpreter, Written by Himself*. Santa Barbara, Calif.: Narrative Press: 2001. Originally published in 1904 for J.C. Coble by the Louthan Book Co. in in Denver, Colo.

Jones, Daniel Webster. *Forty Years among the Indians: A True Yet Thrilling Narrative of the Author's Experiences among the Natives*. Salt Lake City, Utah: Juvenile Instructor Office, 1890. https://archive.org/stream/fortyyearsamongioobjone#page/n5/mode/2up (accessed 15 Dec. 2017).

Kearney, Richard. "Writing Trauma: Narrative Catharsis in Homer, Shakespeare, and Joyce." In *Making Sense: Beauty, Creativity, and Healing*, edited by Bandy Lee, Nancy Olson, and Thomas P. Duffy, 131–43. New York: Peter Lang, 2015.

Kinman, Seth. *The Seth Kinman Story*. Edited by George Richmond, H. Niebuhr, and Edith Butler. N.p., 1876. Republished as *Seth Kinman's Manuscript and Scrapbook*, transcribed by Richard H. Roberts, Ferndale, Calif.: Ferndale Museum, 2010.

McKinney, Joe T. "Reminiscences." *Arizona Historical Review* 5, no. 1 (April 1932): 33–54.

———. "Reminiscences (Continued)." *Arizona Historical Review* 5, no. 2 (July 1932): 141–45.

———. "Reminiscences (Concluded)." *Arizona Historical Review* 5, no. 3 (October 1932): 198–204.

Miles, Nelson A. "The Future of the Indian Question." *North American Review* 152, no. 410 (January 1891): 1–10.

———. "Report of Brigadier-General Miles, Headquarters Department of Arizona, 8 September 1888." In *Annual Report of the Secretary of War for the Year 1888*, 124–32. Washington, D.C.: Government Printing Office, 1888.

Niels and Lars Petersen Family Organization. *The Petersen Family of Gannebro Huse: Niels Petersen Descendants*. Pinedale, Ariz.: Petersen Publishing, 2001.

Northern Gila County Historical Society. *Rim Country History Illustrated*. Payson, AZ: Rim Country Printery, 1984.

Report Booklet Published for the State in 1876. Carson City, Nev.: State Publishing Office, 1876.

Revised Statutes of Arizona Territory, 1901. Columbia, Mo.: E. W. Stephens, 1901.

Summerhayes, Martha. *Vanished Arizona: Recollections of the Army Life of a New England Woman*. Glorieta, N.Mex., Rio Grande Press, 1970.

Treaty of Guadalupe Hidalgo, February 2, 1848. http://avalon.law.yale.edu/19th_century/guadhida.asp.

U.S. Department of Agriculture. *Grasses of the Arid Districts: Report of an Investigation of the Grasses of the Arid Districts of Texas, New Mexico, Arizona, Nevada, and Utah in 1887*. Washington, D.C.: Government Printing Office, 1888.

U.S. Department of the Interior, Census Office. "Table 5—Population of States and Territories by Minor Civil Divisions, 1880 and 1890." In *Report on Population of the United States at the 11th Census: 1890*, 60. Washington, D.C.: U.S. Government Printing Office, 1895.

U.S. Office of Indian Affairs. *Annual Report of the Commissioner of Indian Affairs to the Secretary of the Interior for the Year 1887*. Washington, D.C.: Government Printing Office, 1887.

U.S. President. *Executive Orders Relating to Indian Reserves, from May 14, 1855, to July 1, 1902*. Compiled by the Indian Office under Authority of Act of Congress, Approved May 17th, 1882 (22 Stats., p. 88). Washington, D.C.: Government Printing Office, 1902.

SECONDARY WORKS

Abruzzi, William S. *Dam That River! Ecology and Mormon Settlement in the Little Colorado River Basin*. Lanham, Md.: University Press of America, 1993.

———. "The Social and Ecological Consequences of Early Cattle Ranching in the Little Colorado River Basin." *Human Ecology* 23, no. 1 (March 1995): 75–98.

Aleshire, Peter. *The Fox and the Whirlwind: General George Crook and Geronimo: A Paired Biography*. New York: Wiley, 2000.

———. *Reaping the Whirlwind: The Apache Wars*. New York: Facts on File, 1998.

Ambrose, Stephen E. *Nothing Like It in the World: The Men Who Built the Transcontinental Railroad, 1863–1869*. New York: Simon and Schuster, 2000.

American Psychiatric Association. *Diagnostic and Statistical Manual of Mental Disorders: DSM-5*. 5th ed. Arlington, Va.: American Psychiatric Association, 2013.

Anderson, H. Allen. "Continental Land and Cattle Company." *Handbook of Texas Online*. Texas State Historical Association. http://www.tshaonline.org/handbook/online/articles/aqc03.

———. "Hashknife Ranch." *Handbook of Texas Online.* Texas State Historical Association. http://www.tshaonline.org/handbook/online/articles/apho1.

Apache County Centennial Book: 1879–1979. St. Johns, Ariz.: Apache County, 1979.

Arizona Pioneer and Cemetery Research Project. "Middleton Ranch Cemetery." http://apcrp.org/MIDDLETON%20RANCH/Middleton_Ranch_082807.htm (accessed 29 May 2013).

Arrington, Leonard J. *Great Basin Kingdom: An Economic History of the Latter-Day Saints, 1830–1900.* Cambridge, Mass.: Harvard University Press, 1958.

Arrington, Leonard J., and Davis Bitton. *The Mormon Experience: A History of the Latter-Day Saints.* 2nd ed. Urbana: University of Illinois Press, 1992.

Aschmann, Homer. *Environment and Ecology in the "Northern Tonto" Claim Area.* New York: Garland, 1974.

Ash, George Rickard, Jr. "Frontier Authority: Authority in the New Mexico–Arizona Territories, 1848–90." Ph.D. diss., University of Arizona, 1973. http://arizona.openrepository.com/arizona/bitstream/10150/565296/1/AZU_TD_BOX313_E9791_1973_237.pdf.

Atwater, Elizabeth V. *The Jicarilla Apaches, 1601–1849.* New York: Garland, 1974.

Baars, Donald L. *The Colorado Plateau: A Geologic History.* Albuquerque: University of New Mexico Press, 1983. Originally published as *Red Rock Country* (Natural History Press, 1972).

Bain, David Haward. *Empire Express: Building the First Transcontinental Railroad.* New York: Viking Penguin, 1999.

Ball, Larry D. "Commodore Perry Owens: The Man Behind the Legend." *The Journal of Arizona History* 33, no. 1 (Spring 1992): 27–56.

Bancroft, Hubert Howe, and Henry Lebbeus Oak. *History of Arizona and New Mexico, 1530–1888.* Albuquerque, N.Mex.: Horn and Wallace, 1962.

Barnes, Will C. *Arizona Place Names.* Revised and enlarged by Byrd H. Granger. Tucson: University of Arizona Press, 1960.

———. "The Pleasant Valley War of 1887: Genesis, History, and Necrology." *Arizona Historical Review* 4, no. 3 (October 1931): 5–34.

Barrett, Carol, and Harvey Markowitz, eds. *American Indian Biographies.* Pasadena, Calif.: Salem Press, 2005.

Basso, Keith H, ed. *The Cibicue Apache.* Longrove, Ill.: Waveland Press, 1986.

———. *Western Apache Raiding and Warfare: From the Notes of Grenville Goodwin.* Tucson: University of Arizona Press, 1971.

Bell, Bob Boze. "The Battle of Big Dry Wash: Al Sieber and U.S. Troops vs. Na-ti-o-tish's Apaches." *True West* (1 August 2007). https://truewestmagazine.com/al-sieber-a-us-troops-vs-na-ti-o-tishs-apaches/ (accessed 30 May 2013).

Bender, Averam Burton. *A Study of Western Apache Indians, 1846–1886.* New York: Garland, 1974.

Benton-Cohen, Katherine. *Borderline Americans: Racial Division and Labor War in the Arizona Borderlands.* Cambridge, Mass.: Harvard University Press, 2009.

Binder, Marc D., Nobutaka Hirokawa, and Uwe Windhorst, eds. *Encyclopedia of Neuroscience.* Springer Berlin Heidelberg, 2009.

Bishop, William Henry. *Old Mexico and Her Lost Provinces; A Journey in Mexico, Southern California, and Arizona, by way of Cuba.* New York: Harper and Brothers, 1887.

Blackhawk, Ned. *Violence over the Land: Indians and Empires in the Early American West.* Cambridge, Mass.: Harvard University Press, 2006.

Blomley, Nicholas. "Law, Property, and the Geography of Violence: The Frontier, the Survey, and the Grid." *Annals of the Association of American Geographers* 93, no. 1 (2003): 121–41.

Blumenthal, Terry D. and Joseph C. Franklin. "The Startle Eyeblink Response." In *Methods in Social Neuroscience*, edited by Eddie Harmon-Jones and Jennifer S. Beer, 92–117. New York: Guilford Press, 2009.

Boddington, Craig, ed. *America: The Men and Their Guns That Made Her Great.* Los Angeles: Peterson, 1981.

Bourke, John Gregory. *The Diaries of John Gregory Bourke Volume 1: November 20, 1872–July 28 1876.* Edited by Charles M. Robinson III. Denton, Tex.: University of North Texas Press, 2003.

———. *On the Border with Crook.* New York: Charles Scribner's Sons, 1892.

Braatz, Timothy. *Surviving Conquest: A History of the Yavapai Peoples.* Lincoln: University of Nebraska Press, 2003.

Breslow, Lester, ed. *Encyclopedia of Public Health.* New York: Macmillan Reference USA, 2002.

Brisbin, James S. *The Beef Bonanza; or, How to Get Rich on the Plains.* Philadelphia, Pa.: J. B. Lippincott, 1881.

Brooks, James F. *Captives and Cousins: Slavery, Kinship, and Community in the Southwest Borderlands.* Chapel Hill: University of North Carolina Press, 2002.

Brown, Robert. *The Races of Mankind: Being a Popular Description of the Characteristics, Manners, and Customs of the Principal Varieties of the Human Family.* Vol. 1. London: Cassell, Peter, and Galpin, 1873–76.

Burrus, Ernest J. *Misiones norteñas mexicanas de la Compañía de Jesús, 1751–1757.* Mexico City: Antigua Librería Robredo de José Porrúa e Hijos, 1963.

Caplan, Eric. *Mind Games: American Culture and the Birth of Psychotherapy.* Berkeley: University of California Press, 2011.

Carlson, Frances C. *Cave Creek and Carefree, Arizona: A History of the Desert Foothills.* Scottsdale, Ariz.: Encanto Press, 1988.

———. "James D. Houck: The Sheep King of Cave Creek." *The Journal of Arizona History* 21, no. 1 (Spring 1980): 43–62.

Carmony, Neil B., ed. *Apache Days and Tombstone Nights: John Clum's Autobiography, 1877–1887.* Silver City, N.Mex.: High-Lonesome Books, 1997.

Carranco, Lynwood, and Estle Beard. *Genocide and Vendetta: The Round Valley Wars of Northern California.* Norman: University of Oklahoma Press, 1981.

Chapman Brothers. *Portrait and Biographical Record of Arizona: Commemorating the Achievements of Citizens Who Have Contributed to the Progress of Arizona and the Development of Its Resources.* Chicago: Chapman Publishing, 1901.

Christy, Howard A. "Open Hand and Mailed Fist: Mormon-Indian Relations in Utah, 1847–52." *Utah Historical Quarterly* 46, no. 3 (Summer 1978): 216–35.

Church History in the Fulness of Times. Salt Lake City, Utah: The Church of Jesus Christ of Latter-day Saints, 1989.

Clay, Darin M. "Understanding the Human Physiological and Mental Response to Critical Incidents." School of Law Enforcement Supervision Session 18, 2001. Criminal Justice Institute, University of Arkansas Systems. http://www.cji.edu/site/assets/files/1921/darin_clay.pdf (accessed 1 Aug. 2017).

Coates, Lawrence G. "The Mormons and the Ghost Dance." *Dialogue: A Journal of Mormon Thought* 18, no. 4 (Winter 1985): 89–111.

Compton, Todd M. *A Frontier Life: Jacob Hamblin, Explorer and Indian Missionary.* Salt Lake City: University of Utah Press, 2013.

Cook, Sherburne Friend. *The Conflict between the California Indian and White Civilization.* Berkeley: University of California Press, 1976.

Cozzens, Peter, ed. *Eyewitnesses to the Indian Wars: 1865–1890.* Volume 1: *The Struggle for Apacheria.* Mechanicsburg, Pa.: Stackpole Books, 2001.

Cresswell, Stephen. *Mormons and Cowboys, Moonshiners and Klansmen: Federal Law Enforcement in the South and West, 1870–1893.* Tuscaloosa: University of Alabama Press, 2002.

Croxen, Fred W. "History of Grazing on Tonto." Paper presented at the Tonto Grazing Conference, Phoenix, Arizona, November 4–5, 1926. www.rangebiome.org/genesis/GrazingOnTonto-1926.html (accessed 30 May 2013).

Davis, Wayne, ed. *St. Johns, Arizona Stake Centennial: 1887–July 23, 1987.* St. Johns, Ariz.: Church of Jesus Christ of Latter-day Saints, St. Johns Arizona Stake, 1987.

Davisson, Lori, and Edgar Perry. *Dispatches from the Fort Apache Scout: White Mountain and Cibicue Apache History through 1881.* Tucson: University of Arizona Press, 2016.

Dean, Eric T. *Shook Over Hell: Post-Traumatic Stress, Vietnam, and the Civil War.* Cambridge, Mass.: Harvard University Press, 1997.

Dedera, Don. *A Little War of Our Own: The Pleasant Valley Feud Revisited.* Flagstaff, Ariz.: Northland Press, 1988.

Devine, David. *Slavery, Scandal, and Steel Rails.* New York: IUniverse, 2004.

Donegan, Kathleen. *Seasons of Misery: Catastrophe and Colonial Settlement in Early America.* Philadelphia: University of Pennsylvania Press, 2014.

DuBois, Susan M., and Ann W. Smith. *The 1887 Earthquake in San Bernardino Valley, Sonora: Historic Accounts and Intensity Patterns in Arizona.* Tucson: University of Arizona Press, 1980.

Eagle, Gillian, and Debra Kaminer. "Continuous Traumatic Stress: Expanding the Lexicon of Traumatic Stress." *Peace and Conflict: Journal of Peace Psychology* 19, no. 2 (May 2013): 85–99.

Eargle Jr., Dolan H. *Native California: An Introductory Guide to the Original Peoples from Earliest to Modern Times.* San Francisco, Calif.: Trees Company Press, 2000.

Eaton, Robert C. *Neural Mechanisms of Startle Behavior.* New York: Plenum Press, 1984.

Eghigian, Greg, ed., and Gail Hornstein, contrib. *From Madness to Mental Health: Psychiatric Disorder and Its Treatment in Western Civilization.* Piscataway, N.J.: Rutgers University Press, 2009.

Ellinghausen, Laurie. "'Shame and Eternal Shame': The Dynamics of Historical Trauma in Shakespeare's First Tetralogy." *Exemplaria* 20, no. 3 (2008): 264–82.

Farish, Thomas Edwin. *History of Arizona*, Vol. 2. Phoenix, Ariz.: Filmer Brothers Electrotype Company, 1915.

Farnsworth, Janet. "The Hashknife Cowboys and the Snowflake Saints." *True West* 42, no. 5 (May 1995): 40–43.

Faulk, Odie B. *The Geronimo Campaign*. New York: Oxford University Press, 1993.

Fazio, Steven Adolph. "Marcus A. Smith, Arizona Politician." Master's thesis, University of Arizona, 1968. http://arizona.openrepository.com/arizona/bitstream/10150/551996/1/AZU_TD_BOX263_E9791_1968_201.pdf.

Ferguson, Charles A., Steven J. Skotnicki, and Wyatt G. Gilbert. "Geologic Map of the Tonto Basin, 7.5′ Quadrangle, Gila and Maricopa Counties, Arizona." *Arizona Geological Survey Open-File Report 98-16* (August 1998), 1–15. Tucson: Arizona Geological Survey.

Flake, Lester. *Tales from Oz*. N.p.: Les Flake, 19–?

Flake, Osmer (Oz) Dennis. *William J. Flake: Pioneer, Colonizer*. N.p., 195–?

Flake, S. Eugene, ed. *James Madison Flake, Nov. 8, 1859–Feb. 4, 1946: Pioneer, Leader, Missionary*. Bountiful, Utah: Wasatch Press, 1970.

Flammer, Gordon H. *Stories of a Mormon Pioneering Community: Linden, Arizona, of the Little Colorado Arizona Mission, 1878–1945*. Sandy, Utah: Excel Graphics, 1995.

Formisano, Ronald P. *For the People: American Populist Movements from the Revolution to the 1850s*. Chapel Hill: University of North Carolina Press, 2012.

Forrest, Earle R. *Arizona's Dark and Bloody Ground*. Tucson: University of Arizona Press, 1979. Originally published in 1936 by Caldwell Printers of Caldwell, Idaho.

Galassi, Francesco M., Thomas Böni, Frank J. Rühli, and Michael E. Habicht. "Fight-or-Flight Response in the Ancient Egyptian Novel 'Sinuhe' (c. 1800 BCE)." *Autonomic Neuroscience: Basic and Clinical* 195 (2016): 27–28.

Geary, David C. "Fight-or-Flight Response." In *Encyclopedia of Social Psychology*, edited by Roy F. Baumeister and Kathleen D. Vohs, 351–52. Thousand Oaks, Calif.: Sage Publications, 2007.

Geertz, Clifford. *The Interpretation of Cultures: Selected Essays*. 1973. Reprint, New York: Basic Books, 2000.

Glasrud, Bruce A., and Michael N. Searles. *Buffalo Soldiers in the West: A Black Soldiers Anthology*. College Station: Texas A&M University Press, 2007.

Goff, John S. *Arizona Territorial Officials Volume I: The Supreme Court Justices 1863–1912*. Cave Creek, Ariz.: Black Mountain Press, 1975.

Goodwin, Grenville. *The Social Organization of the Western Apache*. Tucson: University of Arizona Press, 1969.

———. *Western Apache Raiding and Warfare*. Edited by Keith H. Basso. Tucson: University of Arizona Press, 1971.

Gorby, Richard. "Arizona's Governor Zulick Fell into Political Disfavor." Sharlot Hall Museum Library and Archives, Days Past Archives, September 14, 1997. https://sharlot.org/library-archives/index.php/blog/arizonas-governor-zulick.

Greene, Jerome. *Indian War Veterans: Memories of Army Life and Campaigns in the West, 1864–1898.* New York: Savas Beatie, 2007.

Gregory, Brad S. *Salvation at Stake: Christian Martyrdom in Early Modern Europe.* Cambridge, Mass.: Harvard University Press, 1999.

Grey, Zane. *To the Last Man.* New York: Walter J. Black, 1921.

Grossman, Dave. "Human Factors in War: The Psychology and Physiology of Close Combat." In *The Human Face of Warfare: Killing, Fear and Chaos in Battle,* edited by Michael Evans and Alan Ryan, 5–24. Sydney, Australia: Allen Unwin, 2000.

———. *On Killing: The Psychological Cost of Learning to Kill in War and Society.* Boston, Mass.: Little, Brown, 1995.

Haley, James L. *Apaches: A History and Culture Portrait.* Norman: University of Oklahoma Press, 1981.

Håmålåinen, Pekka. *The Comanche Empire.* New Haven, Conn.: Yale University Press, 2009.

Hamner, Christopher H. *Enduring Battle: American Soldiers in Three Wars, 1776–1945.* Lawrence: University Press of Kansas, 2011.

Hanchett, Leland J., Jr. *Arizona's Graham-Tewksbury Feud.* Cloverdale, Calif.: Hanchett, 1994.

———. *They Shot Billy Today: The Families of Arizona's Pleasant Valley War.* Cave Creek, Ariz.: Pine Rim, 2006.

Hansen, Klaus J. *Quest for Empire: The Political Kingdom of God and the Council of Fifty in Mormon History.* East Lansing: Michigan State University Press, 1974.

Haury, Emil Walter. *Canyon Creek Ruin and the Cliff Dwellings of the Sierra Ancha.* Tucson: Arizona State Museum, University of Arizona, 1934.

Hayes, Jess G. *"And then there were none . . ."; A Long-Buried Chapter in Apache History.* Globe, Ariz.: Tyree Printing Service, 1965.

———. *Boots and Bullets: The Life and Times of John W. Wentworth.* Tucson: University of Arizona Press, 1967.

Herbert, Christopher. *Victorian Relativity: Radical Thought and Scientific Discovery.* Chicago: University of Chicago Press, 2001.

Herman, Daniel Justin. *Hell on the Range: A Story of Honor, Conscience, and the American West.* New Haven, Conn.: Yale University Press, 2010.

Herman, James P. "Central Nervous System Regulation of the Hypothalamic-Pituitary-Adrenal Axis Stress Response." In *The Handbook of Stress: Neuropsychological Effects on the Brain,* edited by Cheryl D. Conrad, 117–53. Hoboken, N.J.: John Wiley and Sons, 2011.

Herrera, Carlos R. *Juan Bautista de Anza: The King's Governor in New Mexico.* Norman: University of Oklahoma Press, 2015.

Hietter, Paul Thomas. "Lawyers, Guns, and Money: The Evolution of Crime and Criminal Justice in Arizona Territory." Ph.D. diss., Arizona State University, 1999.

Hine, Robert V., and John Mack Faragher, *The American West: A New Interpretative History.* New Haven, Conn.: Yale University Press, 2000.

Horne, Gerald. *The White Pacific: U.S. Imperialism and Black Slavery in the South Seas after the Civil War.* Honolulu: University of Hawaii Press, 2007.

Horr, David Agee, ed. *American Indian Ethnohistory: Indians of the Southwest.* New York: Garland, 1974.

Hough, Emerson. *The Story of the Cowboy.* New York: Grosset and Dunlap, 1897.

Hunt, Bobbie Stephens. *Those Days Are Gone Forever: History and Stories of Heber-Overgaard.* Mesa, Ariz.: Mead Publishers, 2002.

Hyde, Anne F. *Empires, Nations, and Families: A New History of the North American West, 1800–1860.* Lincoln: University of Nebraska Press, 2011.

Ingstad, Helge. *The Apache Indians: In Search of the Missing Tribe.* Lincoln: University of Nebraska Press, 2004.

Jacoby, Karl. *Shadows at Dawn: An Apache Massacre and the Violence of History.* New York: Penguin Random House, 2009.

Jenkerson, Harold D. *Arizona's Bloody Gold: The Pleasant Valley Feud and The Lost Dutchman's Mine.* Book Two. Datil, N.Mex.: Alegres Enterprises, 1998.

———. *The Bloody Pleasant Valley Feud: Arizona Territory, 1882–1892.* Vols. 1, 2, 3. Datil, N.Mex.: Alegres Enterprises, 1998.

Jentzen, Jeffrey M. *Death Investigation in America: Coroners, Medical Examiners, and the Pursuit of Medical Certainty.* Cambridge, Mass.: Harvard University Press, 2009.

Johnson, Annie Richardson, and Elva Richardson Shumway. *Charles Edmund Richardson: Man of Destiny.* Tempe: Ariz. Publication Services, 1982.

Johnson, Dave. "G. W. Gladden—Hard Luck Warrior." *National Association and Center for Outlaw and Lawman History Quarterly* 15, no. 3 (1991): 1, 3–6.

Johnson, David. *The Mason County "Hoo Doo" War, 1874–1902.* Denton: University of North Texas Press, 2006.

Kavanagh, Jennifer. *Stress and Performance: A Review of the Literature and Its Applicability to the Military.* Santa Monica, Calif.: Rand Corporation, 2005.

Kazin, Michael. *The Populist Persuasion: An American History.* Ithaca, N.Y.: Cornell University Press, 1998.

Kessell, John L. *Mission of Sorrows; Jesuit Guevavi and the Pimas, 1691–1767.* Tucson, University of Arizona Press, 1970.

Kohlke, Marie-Luise, and Christian Gutleben. *Neo-Victorian Tropes of Trauma: The Politics of Bearing After-Witness to Nineteenth-Century Suffering.* Amsterdam: Editions Rodopi, 2010.

Krenkel, John H., ed. *The Life and Times of Joseph Fish, Mormon Pioneer.* Danville, Ill.: Interstate Printers and Publishers, 1970.

Kurtz, Lester R., and Jennifer Turpin, eds. *Encyclopedia of Violence, Peace, and Conflict.* San Diego, Calif.: Academic Press, 1999.

Lienhard, John H. *How Invention Begins: Echoes of Old Voices in the Rise of New Machines.* New York: Oxford University Press, 2008.

Limerick, Patricia Nelson. *The Legacy of Conquest: The Unbroken Past of the American West.* New York: W. W. Norton, 1987.

Lockwood, Frank C. *The Apache Indians.* Lincoln: University of Nebraska Press, 1987.

MacKell, Jan. *Red Light Women of the Rocky Mountains.* Albuquerque: University of New Mexico Press, 2011.

Marlantes, Karl. *What It Is Like to Go to War.* New York: Atlantic Monthly Press, 2011.

Martín-Baró, Ignacio. "Political Violence in War as Causes of Psychological Trauma in El Salvador." *International Journal of Mental Health* 18, no. 1 (Spring 1989): 3–20.

Maxwell, Margaret F. "Cordelia Adams Crawford of the Tonto Basin." *The Journal of Arizona History* 26, no. 4 (Winter 1985): 415–28.

May, George S. "Putting the Nation on Wheels: The Michigan Automobile Industry to 1945." In *Michigan: Visions of Our Past,* edited by Richard J. Hathaway, 169–272. East Lansing: Michigan State University Press, 2012.

McClintock, James H. *Arizona, Prehistoric, Aboriginal, Pioneer, Modern: The Nation's Youngest Commonwealth within a Land of Ancient Culture.* Vol. 2. Chicago: S. J. Clarke, 1916.

———. *Mormon Settlement in Arizona: A Record of Peaceful Conquest of the Desert.* Phoenix, Ariz.: Manufacturing Stationers, 1921.

McCoy, Joseph Geiting. *Historic Sketches of the Cattle Trade of the West and Southwest.* Edited by Ralph P. Bieber. Lincoln: University of Nebraska Press, 1985.

McGuire, Thomas R. *Mixed-Bloods, Apaches, and Cattle Barons: Documents for a History of the Livestock Economy on the White Mountain Reservation, Arizona.* Archeological Series 142, Arizona State Museum. Tucson: University of Arizona, 1980.

McLoughlin, Denis. *Wild and Woolly: An Encyclopedia of the Old West.* New York: Doubleday, 1975.

McMath, Robert C., Jr. *American Populism: A Social History, 1877–1898.* New York: Hill and Wang, 1993.

Meissner, Christian A., and John C. Brigham. "A Meta-Analysis of the Verbal Overshadowing Effect in Face Identification." *Applied Cognitive Psychology* 15, no. 6 (2001): 603–16.

Meissner, Christian A., Siegfried L. Sporer, and Jonathan W. Schooler. "Person Descriptions as Eyewitness Evidence." In *Handbook of Eyewitness Psychology: Memory for People,* edited by R. Lindsay et al., 3–34. Mahwah, N.J.: Lawrence Erlbaum, 2007.

Michno, Gregory. *Settlers' War: The Struggle for the Texas Frontier in the 1860s.* Caldwell, Idaho: Caxton Press, 2011.

Miller, Lee. *From the Heart: Voices of the American Indian.* New York: Knopf, 1995.

Moore. R. Laurence. *Religious Outsiders and the Making of Americans.* New York: Oxford University Press, 1987.

Neal, Tess M. S., and Carl B. Clements. "Prison Rape and Psychological Sequelae: A Call for Research." *Psychology, Public Policy, and Law* 16, no. 3 (2010): 284–99.

Neumann, Frank. *Earthquake Investigation in the United States.* Special Publication No. 282 of U.S. Department of Commerce. Rev. ed.. Washington, D.C.: U.S. Government Printing Office, 1953.

Nickerson, Raymond S. "Confirmation Bias: A Ubiquitous Phenomenon in Many Guises." *Review of General Psychology* 2, no. 2 (June 1998): 175–220.

Niezen, Ronald. *Spirit Wars: Native North American Religions in the Age of Nation Building.* Berkeley: University of California Press, 2000.

Northern Arizona University Ecological Restoration Institute. "Apache-Sitgreaves Forest." http://www.eri.nau.edu/en/arizona/apache-sitgreaves-national-forest (accessed 30 May 2013).

O'Neal, Bill. *Cattlemen vs. Sheepherders: Five Decades of Violence in the West, 1880–1920.* Austin, Tex.: Eakin Press, 1989.

Painter, Nell. *Sojourner Truth, A Life, a Symbol.* New York: W. W. Norton, 1997.

Peterson, Charles S. *Take Up Your Mission: Mormon Colonizing along the Little Colorado River, 1870–1900.* Tucson: University of Arizona Press, 1973.

Peterson, James. "The Trade Unions and the Populist Party." *Science and Society* 8, no. 2 (Spring 1944): 143–60.

Pflaum, Christopher C., Steven S. Duncan, and Eric C. Frye. "Historical Averages and the 'Real Rate' of Interest." Kansas City, Mo.: Spectrum Economics, March 12, 1997. www.spectrumeconomics.com/wp-content/uploads/pdf/Historical-Averages-and-The-Real-Rate-of-Interest.pdf (accessed 31 Aug. 2017).

Plous, Scott. *The Psychology of Judgment and Decision Making.* New York: McGraw-Hill, 1993.

Porterfield, Amanda. *Healing in the History of Christianity.* New York: Oxford University Press, 2009.

Portrait and Biographical Record of Arizona. Chicago, Ill.: Chapman Publishing, 1901.

Postel, Charles. *The Populist Vision.* New York: Oxford University Press, 2009.

Powell, Allan Kent, ed. *Utah History Encyclopedia.* Salt Lake City: University of Utah Press, 1994.

Pyle, Jayne Peace. *Women of the Pleasant Valley War.* Payson, Ariz.: Git a Rope! Publishing, 2014.

Pyle, Jinx. *Pleasant Valley War.* Payson, Ariz.: Git a Rope! Publishing, 2009.

Raines, Rebecca Robbins. *Getting the Message Through: A Branch History of the U.S. Army Signal Corps.* Washington, D.C.: Center of Military History, United States Army, 1996.

Reedstrom, Ernest Lisle. *Apache Wars: An Illustrated Battle History.* New York: Barnes and Noble Books, 1995.

Rees, Ellen Greer. *Greer Men and Ellen C. Greer.* N.p., 1953.

Repasch, Marisa, Karl Karlstrom, Matt Heizler, and Mark Pecha. "Birth and Evolution of the Rio Grande Fluvial System in the Past 8 Ma: Progressive Downward Integration and the Influence of Tectonics, Volcanism, and Climate." *Earth-Science Reviews* 168 (May 2017): 113–64.

Rigden, John S. *Einstein 1905: The Standard of Greatness.* Cambridge, Mass.: Harvard University Press, 2006.

Robbins, William G. *Colony and Empire: The Capitalist Transformation of the American West.* Lawrence: University Press of Kansas, 1994.

Roberts, Brian. *American Alchemy: The California Gold Rush and Middle-Class Culture.* Chapel Hill: University of North Carolina Press, 2000.

Roberts, Brigham Henry, ed. *History of the Church of Jesus Christ of Latter-day Saints.* Vols. 1–8. 2nd ed., revised. Salt Lake City, Utah: Deseret Book, 1948–1952.

Roberts, David D. *Once They Moved Like the Wind: Cochise, Geronimo, and the Apache Wars.* New York: Touchstone, 1993.

Robinson, Charles M., III. *General Crook and the Western Frontier.* Norman: University of Oklahoma Press, 2001.

Rogers, John J. W., and M. Santosh. *Continents and Supercontinents*. New York: Oxford University Press, 2004.

Rondinone, Troy. *The Great Industrial War: Framing Class Conflict in the Media, 1865–1950*. New Brunswick, N.J.: Rutgers University Press, 2010.

Roth, Mitchel P. *Historical Dictionary of Law Enforcement*. Westport, Conn.: Greenwood Press, 2000.

Ruland-Thorne, Kate. *Gold, Greed and Glory: The Territorial History of Prescott and the Verde Valley 1864–1912*. Baltimore, Md.: PublishAmerica, 2007.

Russell, John A., and Michael J. Shipston, eds. *Neuroendocrinology of Stress*. Hoboken, N.J.: John Wiley and Sons, 2015.

Salmón, Roberto Mario. *Indian Revolts in Northern New Spain: A Synthesis of Resistance*. Lanham, Md.: University Press of America, 1991.

Samayoa, Joaquín. "Guerra y deshumanización: Una perspectiva psicosocial." *Estudios Centroamericanos* 42, no. 461 (1987): 213–25.

Scharnhorst, Gary. *Bret Harte: Opening the American Literary West*. Norman: University of Oklahoma Press, 2000.

Schmitt, Martin F. *General George Crook, His Autobiography*. Norman: University of Oklahoma Press, 1986.

Schoonover, Thomas D. *Uncle Sam's War of 1898 and the Origins of Globalization*. Lexington: University Press of Kentucky, 2003.

Schroeder-Lein, Glenna R. *The Encyclopedia of Civil War Medicine*. Armonk, N.Y.: M. E. Sharpe, 2008.

Schuster, David G. *Neurasthenic Nation: America's Search for Health, Happiness, and Comfort, 1869–1920*. Piscataway, N.J.: Rutgers University Press, 2011.

Secrest, William B. *When the Great Spirit Died: The Destruction of the California Indians, 1850–1860*. Fresno, Calif.: Quill Driver Books, 2002.

Sheffer, H. Henry, III, and Sharyn R. Alger. *The Pleasant Valley War: Cattle and Sheep Don't Mix*. Apache Junction, Ariz.: Norseman Publications, 1994.

Shelton, Laura M. *For Tranquility and Order: Family and Community on Mexico's Northern Frontier, 1800–1850*. Tucson: University of Arizona Press, 2011.

Sheridan, Thomas E. *Arizona: A History*. Tucson: University of Arizona Press, 1995.

Shute, George Walter. *The Pleasant Valley War*. Phoenix, Ariz.: N.p., 1954.

———. "Pleasant Valley War—Revisited." *Arizona Cattlelog* 2 (April 1956): 38–59.

Smoak, Gregory E. *Ghost Dances and Identity: Prophetic Religion and American Indian Ethnogenesis in the Nineteenth Century*. Berkeley: University of California Press, 2006.

Southworth, Dave. *Feuds on the Western Frontier*. Round Rock, Tex.: Wild Horse Publishing, 1999.

Sporer, Siegfried L. "Describing Others: Psychological Issues." In *Psychological Issues in Eyewitness Identification*, edited by Siegfried L. Sporer, Roy S. Malpass, and Guenter Koehnken, 53–86. Hillsdale, N.J.: Lawrence Erlbaum, 1996.

Staal, Mark. "Stress, Cognition, and Human Performance: A Literature Review and Conceptual Framework." *NASA Scientific and Technical Aerospace Reports (STAR)* 44, no. 13 (July 5, 2006): 1–168.

Steinberg, Ted. *Down to Earth: Nature's Role in American History*. New York: Oxford University Press, 2002.

Stevens, Garth, Gillian Eagle, Debra Kaminer, and Craig Higson-Smith. "Continuous Traumatic Stress: Conceptual Conversations in Contexts of Global Conflict, Violence and Trauma." *Peace and Conflict: Journal of Peace Psychology* 19, no. 2 (2013): 75–84.

Stockel, H. Henrietta. *Salvation through Slavery: Chiricahua Apaches and Priests on the Spanish Colonial Frontier*. Albuquerque: University of New Mexico Press, 2008.

Stone, Charles P. *Notes on the State of Sonora*. Washington, D.C.: Henry Polkinhorn, printer, 1861.

Stratton, Emerson Oliver. *Pioneering in Arizona: The Reminiscences of Emerson Oliver Stratton & Edith Stratton Kitt*. Tucson: Arizona Pioneers' Historical Society, 1964.

Strobridge, William F. *Regulars in the Redwoods: The U.S. Army in Northern California, 1852–1861*. Spokane, Wash: Arthur H. Clarke, 1994.

Susa, Kyle J., and Christian A. Meissner. "Accuracy of Eyewitness Descriptions." In *Encyclopedia of Psychology and Law*, edited by Bryan L. Cutler, 285–87. Thousand Oaks, Calif.: Sage Publications, 2008.

Sweeney, Edwin R. *From Cochise to Geronimo: The Chiricahua Apaches, 1874–1886*. Norman: University of Oklahoma Press, 2010.

———. *Mangas Coloradas: Chief of the Chiricahua Apaches*. Norman: University of Oklahoma Press, 2011.

Taylor, Tobi Lopez. "Trinidad Lopez and the Naco Cemetery." *Archaeology Southwest* 20, no. 4 (Fall 2006): 13.

Taysom, Stephen C. *Shakers, Mormons, and Religious Worlds: Conflicting Visions, Contested Boundaries*. Bloomington: Indiana University Press, 2010.

Thiel, Kenneth J., and Michael J. Dretsch. "The Basics of the Stress Response: A Historical Context and Introduction." In *The Handbook of Stress: Neuropsychological Effects on the Brain*, edited by Cheryl D. Conrad, 67–116. West Sussex, UK: Wiley-Blackwell, 2011.

Thomas, Alfred Barnaby. *The Jicarilla Apache Indians: A History, 1598–1888*. American Indian Ethnohistory: Indians of the Southwest 8. New York: Garland, 1974.

Thrapp, Dan L. *Al Sieber: Chief of Scouts*. Norman: University of Oklahoma Press, 1995.

———. *The Conquest of Apacheria*. Norman: University of Oklahoma Press, 1979.

———. *Encyclopedia of Frontier Biography*. Vol. 1. Lincoln: University of Nebraska Press, 1991.

Tone, Andrea. *Age of Anxiety: A History of America's Turbulent Affair with Tranquilizers*. New York: Basic Books, 2008.

Tourney, I. W. "The Gradual Disappearance of the Range Grasses of the West." *Science* 23 (January 5, 1894): 9.

Trimble, Marshall. *Arizona Outlaws and Lawmen: Gunslingers, Bandits, Heroes, and Peacekeepers*. Charleston, S.C.: The History Press, 2015.

Tuchman, Barbara W. *The March of Folly: From Troy to Vietnam*. 1st ed. New York: Knopf, distributed by Random House, 1984.

Turner, Frederick J. "Dominant Forces in Western Life." *The Atlantic Monthly* 79, no. 474 (April 1897): 433–43.

Twitchell, Ralph E. *The Leading Facts of New Mexican History*. Cedar Rapids, Iowa: Torch Press, 1912.

U.S. Geological Survey. "Geologic Provinces of the United States: Colorado Plateau Province." http://geomaps.wr.usgs.gov/parks/province/coloplat.html (accessed 29 Dec. 2012).

Utley, Robert M. *Frontier Regulars: The United States Army and the Indians*. New York: Macmillan, 1973.

VanderMeer, Philip. *Desert Visions and the Making of Phoenix, 1860–2009*. Albuquerque: University of New Mexico Press, 2011.

von Richthofen, Baron Walter. *Cattle-Raising on the Plains of North America*. Norman, University of Oklahoma Press, 1964. Originally published New York: D. Appleton, 1885.

Wampler, Vance. *Arizona: Years of Courage, 1832–1910: Based on the Life and Times of William H. Kirkland*. Phoenix, Ariz.: Quail Run Publications, 1984.

Weber, David J. *The Mexican Frontier, 1821–1846: The American Southwest under Mexico*. Albuquerque: University of New Mexico Press, 1982.

———. *The Spanish Frontier in North America*. New Haven, Conn.: Yale University Press, 1992.

Wenegrat, Brant. *Theater of Disorder: Patients, Doctors, and the Construction of Illness*. New York: Oxford University Press, 2001.

Wentworth, Edward N. *America's Sheep Trails: History, Personalities*. Ames: Iowa State College Press, 1948.

Westover, Adele B., and J. Morris Richards. *Unflinching Courage*. Joseph City, Ariz.: John H. Miller, 1963.

Whiteley, Meredith Haley. *Miracle on the Salt River: Water, Family, and Farming in the Arizona Desert*. Charleston, S.C.: The History Press, 2014.

Whiteman, C. David. *Mountain Meteorology: Fundamentals and Applications*. New York: Oxford University Press, 2000.

Wiltbank Esther, and Zola Whiting, eds. *Lest Ye Forget*. St. Johns, Ariz.: Apache County Centennial Committee, 1980.

Wohl, Ellen. *Islands of Grass*. Denver: University Press of Colorado, 2009.

Woody, Clara T., and Milton L. Schwartz. *Globe, Arizona: Early Times in a Little World of Copper and Cattle*. Tucson: University of Arizona Press, 1970.

———. "War in Pleasant Valley: The Outbreak of the Graham-Tewksbury Feud." *Journal of Arizona History* 18, no. 1 (Spring 1977): 43–68.

Wooster, Robert. *The American Military Frontiers: The United States Army in the West, 1783–1900*. Albuquerque: University of New Mexico Press, 2001.

Works Project Administration. *Arizona: A State Guide*. The Arizona WPA Writer's Project, sponsored by the Arizona State Highway Commission. New York: Hastings House, 1940.

Yebing Yang, JingJing Tang, Yuan Jiang, Xufeng Liu, Yunfeng Sun, Xia Zhu, and Danmin Miao. "Development of the Acute Stress Response Scale." *Social Behavior and Personality: An International Journal* 39, no. 5 (2011): 713–21.

Zachariae, Barbara. *Pleasant Valley Days, Young Arizona: A History of the People.* Rev. ed. Apache Junction, Ariz.: John Denmark, 2001.

Zappia, Natale A. *Traders and Raiders: The Indigenous World of the Colorado Basin, 1540–1859.* Chapel Hill: University of North Carolina Press. 2014.

INDEX